Praise for
Of Stones and Spirits

I recommend world traveler Lisa Paulson's perspectives on historic moments—China's cultural revolution, Castro's Cuba, stalemate in the Middle East, Tito's Yugoslavia—on Brazil's mysterious spirit world, on a "Futures-Creating" seminar in Japan, and while floating down the Rhone River in France.

Stones have stories to tell. Spirits link us to important dimensions in understanding a changing world. Traveling with her extensive family, Lisa Paulson looks and listens. Her reports draw you in.

— Henry M. Halsted III, Vice President Emeritus, the Johnson Foundation, Racine, Wisconsin

For Lisa Paulson, travel is more than ticking off a list of traditional sights. Her travels, like her marriage, family, and spiritual sensitivity, have never been scripted or perceived separately from one another. Her latest book, *Of Stones and Spirits,* is a poetic narrative spanning over half a century and four continents of travels by herself and with her husband Bel, and eventually includes their children and grandchildren. They arrived in countries to serve, to understand critical moments in history, to seek new ideas for living, or to search for family roots. We learn how different concepts about education, healing, meditation, and living consciously and sustainably became deep and permanent for herself, her marriage, and her role as co-founder of the High Wind community experiment. Lisa's "You-are-there" style places the reader directly into each journey.

— Robert A. Pavlik, Coordinator, Project for Community Transformation, College of Professional Studies, Marquette University, Milwaukee, Wisconsin

Lisa Paulson's *Of Stones and Spirits* will give you fascinating insights into the interesting places and people of the countries where she and her husband Belden lived and worked. You'll see Italy (Rome, Naples, and Sardinia) and Brazil through the eyes of a woman engaged in the culture, not merely observing it. Then, in her later travels, she piques your interest and stirs your curiosity with vivid descriptions of popular destinations such as Tuscany and the Mediterranean coast, along with other, more mysterious, locations, such as the prehistoric caves of southern France. She'll inspire you to research diverse cultures and perhaps be more adventurous in your own travels, as the Paulsons and their lucky cohorts have been with theirs.

— Don Murray, Academy Award-nominated, Hollywood Walk of Fame-honored actor; author of the biography *Marilyn and Me*, cofounder of the Homeless European Land Program

Traveling widely is easy; traveling wisely is hard. Lisa Paulson has managed both feats in *Of Stones and Spirits*. She has given us lively snapshots of places as little known as the remote Isle of Erraid in Scotland (complete with an essential glossary) or as familiar as the never-tiring hills of Tuscany—always with her own twist, interwoven with an engaging account of her life with Bel, her husband of six decades. Bravo! We who benefit from your travels salute you.

— Karl E. Meyer, author of fourteen books spanning much of the world, which he has covered as a foreign correspondent (*Washington Post*) or commented on as an editorial writer (*The New York Times*)

Bob — your passion and curiosity as a fellow adventurer have taken you on journeys we share —
Affectionately,
Lisa

OF STONES AND SPIRITS

Sixty Years of Travel

Lisa Paulson

Thistlefield Books

All photos, unless otherwise noted, are from the personal collection of the author.
Cover photo by Anne Strainchamps. The Greek ruin of Priene in Turkey: human presences (Steve and Nick) are tiny alongside the majesty of the Temple of Athena and Mt. Mykale.

First Printing 2014
Printed in the United States of America

ISBN-13: 978-0-9816906-3-6
Library of Congress Control Number: 2013947442

Editor: Carolyn Kott Washburne
Design and Production: Kate Hawley, Kate Hawley by Design
Proof reader: Paula Haubrich

Thistlefield Books

Published by Thistlefield Books
W7122 County Road U
Plymouth, Wisconsin 53073
(920) 528-8488
www.thistlefieldbooks.com

Of Stones and Spirits is available through Amazon.

Other books by Lisa Paulson available through Thistlefield Books:

Voices from a Sacred Land: Images and Evocations

An Unconventional Journey: The Story of High Wind, From Vision to Community to Eco-Neighborhood

For Bel, my partner
in all of these adventures.

There comes a time when you realize that everything is a dream, and only those things preserved in writing have any possibility of being real.

James Salter

Acknowledgments

Bel, it was your unerring drive and courage to go places and to undertake tasks that few others had thought about, which was the impetus behind most of the trips described in the first part of my book. I will be forever grateful that you then caught the same exhilaration of the almost off-the-radar vision that had enticed me to Scotland in our middle years. Armed with these future-oriented ideas, it was the combination of our complementary strengths that enabled us to create and nurture the ecological community, High Wind. Finally, in more recent decades it was your unquenchable curiosity that gathered up family members to explore—over and over—some of the unusual, exotic areas of the world.

To these family members: our sons Eric and Steve, with their wives, Angelynn and Anne, and the grandchildren, Lark, Niko, Katie, and Nicky—not to mention extended family, Doug, Marge, Susie and Ed—I feel so blessed that in varying configurations you were part of these many treks. Your myriad interests, talents, sensitivity, and enthusiasm have enriched the trips immensely. Our compatibility as a "mob" traveling in close proximity has been astonishing.

Bel and I are indebted also to the wonderful people we encountered across the world and to our colleagues in the various projects. Without their cooperation and empathy, these remarkable experiences would not have happened.

I am deeply grateful to my superb editor, Carolyn Kott Washburne, who read my travel journals, was intrigued, and convinced me to turn them into a book. With her uncanny talent for sensing the larger picture, she saw how everything fit together and masterfully organized and polished the very disparate episodes.

It was Kate Hawley, my genius designer/producer guru who, with her creative artist's eye, saw how to perfectly mesh text and photos.

And to my discerning, supportive readers, Bob Pavlik, Don Murray, Henry Halsted, and Karl Meyer, many, many thanks.

Table of Contents

Introduction

Early on I was bitten by something of an obsessive compulsion to write about whatever I happened to be seeing, doing, feeling, or thinking about. This affliction extended, as well, to keeping a pen handy whenever I went on trips—and there have been a lot of these, especially since encountering my future husband over fifty years ago.

In November 1952, at age twenty-four, I was backpacking around Europe and paused to check out an unusual social assistance project in war-destroyed Naples, Italy. Casa Mia had been created and run by a young American, one Belden Paulson, whose reputation as a quirky risk-taker had preceded him, and I was looking for a way to plug into just such a humanitarian effort. I showed up, unannounced, late one night in the waterfront slums of Naples where Casa Mia (My Home) was located. Bel was startled, but on the strength of our having been college classmates (though we'd never met), he hired me on the spot to work at his center.

Three months after arriving in Naples, I mailed home to my parents in western Massachusetts a report that depicted a slice of my new life. This became the first "travel essay" included here, and ever since, I've been recording adventures across the globe—first with Bel, and then eventually with one or another of our two sons, their kids, and extended family members (identified at the end of this book). Fifty-nine years later, I pulled these trip reports (over fifty of them) out of my memorabilia closet to see how they've held up after all this time.

Looked at in aggregate, I saw that the essays and their stories fell roughly into three categories: travels having to do with a specific, felt mission, often with political overtones; travels inspired by a vision that triggered what might be called a quest for spiritual meaning; and travels that were purely for fun and relaxation—fueled by curiosity and a thirst for adventure.

Because most of these travels have involved our family as it evolved and grew—"family affairs"—I've introduced most essays with background that connects the snapshots, the selected episodes, and provides continuity as our focuses and agendas unfolded over the course of roughly the last half of the twentieth century. Some pieces are purely atmospheric, while others, especially in our earlier years, reflect our maverick tendency to jump into situations that tilted against mainstream attitudes and values.

Readers will be drawn into the global political situations we landed in, often at critical crisis points. They may pick up the fervor of an era when people worldwide were hungry for new ways to think and act and believe. And they will come along with us to explore destinations that include distant, exotic cultures and ambiences. Besides Italy, some of the places I write about are Brazil, China, Japan, the USSR, Cuba, the Middle East, and countries in Europe—as well as some choice spots in the US.

I notice that as time goes on, we've tended to favor destinations that both intrigue and restore our souls, that are respites from lives overcrowded with people and projects. These might be rural environments where green hills or rugged peaks preside over isolated villages, with their pastures of wildflowers and sheep, or where restless seas crash against rocky shores or lie becalmed in turquoise perfection. They are spots where all of us can place our "other" lives in perspective, process what we've done and where we've been. It's where we can soak up periodic doses of wild nature and where life is experienced at a considerably slower pace.

Looking back at that long-ago time, maybe we were foolhardy and naïve. Maybe it was a different time, but in the '50s, '60s, '70s, and '80s, we had ideas that we thought could change the world. Happily, recklessly, we plunged into situations that seriously challenged the status quo, the establishment. We stirred things up with iconoclastic zeal. I don't see this happening so much now. It is somewhat out of vogue to have big dreams and the chutzpah to hop in, feet on the ground, to effect fundamental societal shifts. "Our" kind of globally humanitarian, eminently philosophically and environmentally correct and "sensible" initiatives are attributed to out-of-touch idealists. And now, as the twenty-first century gets underway, with its cynicism, speed, slickness, and sinister muddling and meddling with financial, political, and religious institutions—we find ourselves personally more cautious about joining the fray. Our ideas and experiences are still out there, though, described or alluded to innocently in this benignly labeled collection of "travel essays."

You'll notice that in more recent years, we've tended to seek out and bask in the purely natural outposts, still magnificent and undamaged by the likes of a myopic, selfish humanity. It is here that we are drawn to regain equilibrium, to brace for whatever is to come. The family trips (escapes) invariably morph into opportunities for all of us to "get down to it"—to discuss animatedly over late-night bottles of good Chianti what has *really* been important in our lives, in our relationships to each other, and in our views about the direction of civilization. It's the periodic, ritual reflective bonding of the tribe—a nourishment we crave.

On one hand, we may be trying to block out the noise of the present overload of sheer information. On the other, our pre-twenty-first-century brains may be seeking the necessary distance, hidey-holes in which to truly think the big thoughts again, to share them and watch them grow in fertile ground with the people who matter most to us.

Part I

Traveling with a Mission
Socio/Political Projects and Explorations

Teachers and students spill out of Casa Mia's big iron gate.

Arrival in Naples
Inklings of My Future

October 1952–August 1953

Backstory

My friend Annie (Anne Louise Coffin) and I had been traversing Europe for two months, scaring up one wild adventure after another, but then, as our money started running low, we realized we had to find a way to support ourselves. Our initial, vague plan had been to sail from Italy to Israel to work on a kibbutz. But by the time we got to Rome and had checked the cost of a boat, we realized our funds were too depleted for the $75 needed for the trip from Bari to Haifa. Down to one twenty-five-cent meal a day, we stopped in our tracks and began looking for jobs in Italy. Almost immediately Annie landed a translating position at FAO (the Food and Agriculture Organization of the UN).

Because I was primarily interested in finding some way to be of service in the wake of the terrible devastation of World War II, I dropped by the office of the World Council of Churches, headed—improbably—by an elegant White Russian prince. Puzzled and intrigued by the fact that I said I didn't care at all about making money, but would only ask for board and room in return for volunteering, the prince scratched his head. Eventually he came up with a project he was familiar with in Naples, the Italian Service Mission. Part of the work of this Protestant group was supplying relief to Iron Curtain refugees sequestered in five camps ringing Naples. Another arm of the Mission that he was a little hazy about was a social assistance center in the heart of the worst waterfront slums of the city. Called Casa Mia, it was run by a young American, Belden Paulson.

At this point, my ears pricked up. A Bel Paulson had been a college classmate of mine; we'd never met, but he was a well-known leader on campus. I decided that this was too much of a coincidence to ignore and made plans to leave almost immediately to see what this project was about. Here is the story of my arrival at Casa Mia.

It Looks Like Dante's Inferno

It's already dark when Annie and I step off the Rome-Naples train on October 29. Armed only with our knapsacks and Bel Paulson's name, we start off on foot to find Casa Mia. The so-called streets in the Granili area, where supposedly the center is located, have no names. We'd heard that Naples was the roughest spot in Europe, but one has to see it to realize what this means. Because

Granili stretches right along the waterfront docks, it was just about flattened by both German and American bombers in the war. Some twenty thousand homeless people are living (and dying) here in caves, grottos, and crevices in the crumbling walls. We pass two children ages four or five kneeling on the ground, nursing a tiny fire built from a few scraps of paper, a pathetic effort to keep warm for a brief moment. Old people crouch among the stones, watching us curiously, or staring at nothing—people with no place to go. The luckier ones have found "homes" in the ghostly ruins of buildings standing jagged against the sky.

Walking along through wide fields of rubble, we retrace our steps several times but have no luck locating the center. The proprietors of the miserable shops where we ask the way can only give urgent warnings to hang onto our luggage for dear life and to speak to no one—at least this is what we think they're saying, mainly through sign language. All around us is a feeling of eerie hostility. We're nearly ready to give up the search.

Then, suddenly, after asking repeatedly about a "Signor Americano," one little boy jumps up and shouts "Beeel!" From nowhere, a whole gang of barefooted kids materializes and multiplies, and we're literally propelled past a brilliant forge with sparks flying and deposited in front of a high, iron gate. A sign reading Casa Mia shows that we've arrived at our destination. The youngsters (who all come for programs at the assistance center) yell and pound the gate until it opens. We squeeze into a muddy courtyard. Bel appears at the top of a narrow stairway, squinting into the darkness, astonished to see two American females in the middle of the night.

"Remember me, Louise Hill, from Oberlin?" I ask brightly (I've recognized him immediately). He doesn't, but graciously invites us to come in. We explain the situation, and he calls Casa Materna, an orphanage on the outskirts of Naples (another project of the Italian Service Mission), to ask if we can spend the night there. Then he offers us supper from great pails of food left over from the American Navy's kitchens—the Sixth Fleet is anchored in the bay—which is donated every day for the center's feeding program.

The next morning, after we've bedded down at Casa Materna, Bel confers with Dr. Teofilo Santi, the dedicated medical doctor who heads the Mission. When Santi hears that Annie has landed a job in Rome, he asks, "What will we do with the other one?" Bel says, "Hire her."

So I am accepted as a semi-volunteer at Casa Mia, where I will work with Bel for the next nine months. As I learn Italian (quickly, because no one on the staff of twelve speaks English except Bel), I move from organizing the office correspondence to assessing the needs of families in the dismal caves and ruins filled with desperate squatters. I also help generally at the busy center that welcomes some five hundred Granili homeless to a multifaceted program.

Casa Mia (sponsored by the Congregational Christian Service Committee in New York) is the first social settlement center in Italy—a concept pioneered in the United States and adapted in Naples by Bel in spring 1952. The idea of a settlement center is for the staff not only to work in the epicenter of dire need, but also to live there among the people they are helping. Bel and a couple of other staff live on site, but as there is no space for me, arrangements are made for me to sleep at the Casa Materna orphanage, founded in the early part of the century by Dr. Santi's Methodist parents.

Casa Mia runs a medical clinic, kindergartens, literacy classes for all ages (during the war no one could go to school, so now many young adults can't read), carpentry/woodworking training, and women's groups for health education and sewing. We believe that simply giving relief in the form of food and clothing will not enable these people to support themselves, although we do offer what is often the only meal of the day for each participant, as well as periodic clothing packages for his or her entire family.

As a Protestant minority, we are careful never to push religion, and we certainly never proselytize. We don't want to usurp the territory of the Catholic priests in our area, who, nevertheless, insist we are "buying souls with American dollars" and threaten to excommunicate their constituents who come to our center. This doesn't deter many in Granili, however. They recognize that we are there to encourage a general spiritual rejuvenation, restore a forgotten dignity, and, above all, demonstrate a fresh way of life where hope can grow from trust and love.

Over the following months, the experience I acquired was profound and searing—and deeply satisfying. And along the way, Bel and I managed to fall in love (proximity is a wonderful stimulus), and I realized I had met the person with whom I wanted to spend the rest of my life.

Life, Work, and Politics at Casa Mia

Here are excerpts from an article I sent back to the United States for *Advance*, a publication of the Congregational Church.

It's a Sunday in January 1953, my day off, and I've decided on a chilly winter's morning walk from Casa Materna to Casa Mia instead of riding my usual tram. The sharp blue sky and brilliant sun

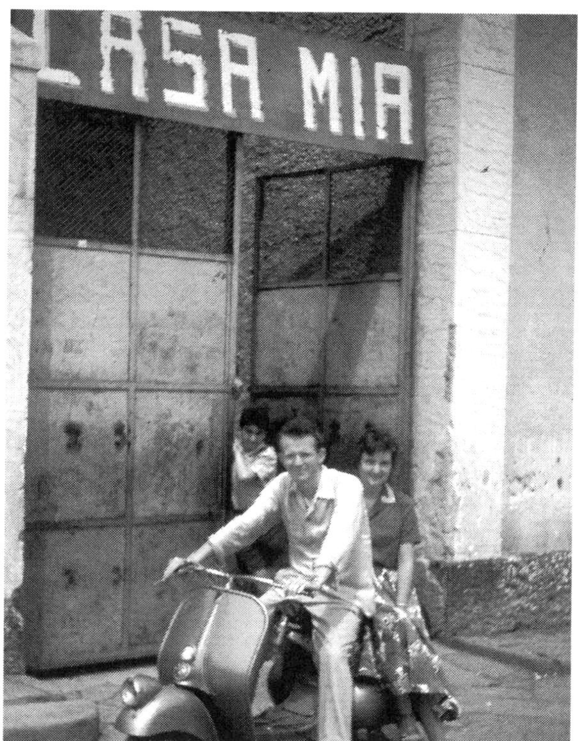

How we got around Naples

camouflage the dingy stucco buildings and filthy streets. Mt. Vesuvius, in its new, white vestments, presides proudly over the city.

I weave through knots of laughing, darting hoodlums, then around the potato-filled donkey cart whose owner is shouting to the housewife in a third-story window. Before she lets down her basket on a string for the produce, she bargains for the best price. Here's a rotund old lady struggling to keep her broken shoes on her feet while balancing a great tray of fresh eels on her head; she's nearly upset by a herd of bleating Nubian goats trotting urgently by. Forests of laundry flap over the sidewalk. A young swain, slicked up with satin tie and well-oiled hair, surveys the crowd from atop the shoeshine tower. The blind beggar blinks happily into the sun as he crouches against a pile of rubbish. "American cigarettes, cheap, black market," he croaks.

The gaunt mother in the shadow of the splendid cathedral—"Please, Signorina, six children, husband with no work, nothing to eat, please, for the love of the Holy Mother." A little, one-legged boy swings along on his crutch after his more agile playmates and calls, "Hey, Miss, you Americana?" Four old men are bent intently over a card table set in the middle of the sidewalk. A giant sea of balloons bobs gently past. The seedy gentleman leaning on his black-hooded monster: "Take your picture, Signorina?" There's a sudden roar as a tram thunders by, lurching over the sidewalk. I note "Viva the Immaculate Conception" plastered along the walls at regular intervals. The district priest lifts his skirts daintily as he weaves in and out of the mammoth cheeses, pigs' heads, and goat kids hanging from hooks in the doorways. The cacophony swells as the chanting of vegetable vendors drowns out the steady pulse of a hurdy-gurdy from the little amusement park I'm passing.

Then a cold shadow drops over me, and I notice that the street is suddenly deserted. Looking up, I see a huge building whose gloomy walls stretch for nearly half a mile and blot out the sun.

This is the Granili barracks. Twenty thousand people—bombed out of their homes during the war and crowded into this and another neighboring "public refuge"—thought the wretched shelter was to be only a temporary step before quickly finding a place in a new life: a new home, a job. However, they discovered little by little that the long-sought peace was turning ironically into a bitter warrant to join the permanent poor. The planes may have stopped screaming overhead in 1945, but the end of the war stopped everything else, too. In some sections, mile after mile of what had once been streets and houses is now flat fields with crumbled heaps of debris scattered about. Every so often one lonely skeleton of a building thrusts crazily into the sky. The city fathers allow the dust to settle around these silent reminders with little thought of resurrecting them. Almost every factory in Naples has been destroyed, and jobs are simply not available, especially to the thousands of "refugees" in Granili who had already lost their balance and have been pushed off the crowded treadmill of survival.

A wall poster for a communist mayoral candidate reads: "Vote for Vesuvio. He promises new homes, new schools, new life for the homeless."

Then, after an initial shout of recognition, a wave of little kids suddenly envelops me, kids who come every day to Casa Mia. There's a particularly exuberant quality about these youngsters—a new, can-do spirit seems to be taking hold. Despite their bleak home lives, they show a fierce talent for winning, whether it's kicking a soccer ball, or rolling discarded butts into cigarettes, or adroitly picking the pockets of the unwary on crowded trams.

This was my Sunday morning on the streets of Naples.

Now I'll take you deeper into the local scene. We needn't just speculate on what has been happening to these people of Granili when it's easy for Bel and me to find out by visiting one of their miserable little "homes." For now, they must be called homes, since eight years have gone by and still there seems to be no prospect of a solution.

It takes a few minutes for our eyes to see again after entering the cavernous black hall of the Granili barrack. We step carefully along the narrow planks thrown over a puddle of filthy water and knock on one of the doors. In a few seconds, we're in the midst of a family. At first it's hard to make out by the almost-worthless swinging electric bulb just how many people are jammed into the tiny compartment, which is marked off by newspaper and cardboard partitions. They don't even have a whole room to call their own but must share the same damp and perpetually sunless cellar with three other families.

Despite the cold, the air is stifling and almost impossible to breathe. The five influenza-wracked children gazing out from one bed and the old man crouched on a box in the corner with his tubercular cough feel it, too. The unemployed father, lying across a dirty mattress, stares up at the moist ceiling. Only the mother is occupied: kneeling in the center of the stone floor, she is nursing the few wood coals that are heating a tiny pot of beans, the one meal of the day.

We catch at once the curious atmosphere of tense desperation and complete apathy. These people all seem to be waiting mutely for something, but even they don't know what anymore. It has been so long since any positive goal came within reach that their initiative is dulled almost to paralysis. They no longer have the physical strength or spiritual hope to pull themselves up again. It is among such wrecked masses that Italy's Red or Black "menaces" are constituted—not that these people know or care about extremist ideologies, but simply because they hear the empty promises of the politician who shouts loudest about a nirvana with jobs, houses, and schools.

After we chat a few minutes with this Granili family, they begin to realize we're genuinely concerned about their basic right to be human beings. The initial suspicion melts away in astonishment when they see we haven't come to grind the political or clerical axe, to milk them even drier, to squeeze out the last shred of individual dignity. They creep up from the dark corners and begin to talk. Other heads multiply in the doorway, and before long, the room is packed with people opening their dammed-up souls. For many, it is the first time in years. People become primitively self-centered when they are preoccupied with their own daily fight to survive, and they don't listen to each other's cries.

Happiness, security, beauty—these are values we Americans throw around easily, but for thousands of children living in Granili, they have no meaning at all. Ever since these children were born, they've known only lives of ugliness and suffering. They are never sure of eating even a chunk of bread each day. Lack of sanitary facilities (one toilet per thousand people), water, and soap makes keeping clean a futile task. During the cold, rainy winters, they often don't have shoes or warm coats to venture outside the terrible walls of Granili, to learn to read in school or even to share the wonder of world travelers who come to see the fabled, palm-studded arc of shoreline stretching from Naples around to Sorrento. Even the natural happiness of parents loving children is sometimes missing, since the mothers and fathers are continually so tortured by the fear of not having work to feed their big families that they can be distracted by little else.

This is the same picture discovered a year ago by Bel and Dr. Santi. The real tragedy is not so much these day-to-day hardships but the fact that there seemed no hope they would ever be alleviated. Granili dwellers had truly been abandoned by the world when the little miracle happened—Casa Mia.

Each morning at 8:30, several hundred youngsters swarm in through the big gate to participate in the center's varied activities: a daily medical clinic; a kindergarten for the very little ones; first grade for six to eight-year-olds; literacy classes for children who never learned to read and write but who are too old to enter public school; singing groups; after-school recreation; embroidery, weaving, and woodwork clubs; and league soccer teams of homeless boys who compete with other Naples squads. To further the aim of working with each family as

Literacy class at Casa Mia

a whole unit, the mothers come in the morning to help sew for the periodic clothing distributions, to receive health instruction and personal counsel, and to talk over their children's work with the teachers. The gate doesn't close again until 9:30 at night when the evening classes for tailoring, adult literacy, radio telegraphy, and English are finished. Each person has eaten one hot meal, often his or her only one for the day.

In a letter I wrote home to my parents after the holidays, I described some of my own activities and discoveries:

> Over Christmas, when Bel was tied up, I took over his English class of young men from the University of Naples. We had a good time, and I tried it again the following week. Then later I got a call from two women studying Japanese at the Oriental Institute who'd gotten my name from the US Information Service; they wanted to arrange an exchange: I would teach them English while they would help me with Italian. I met with them, along with a young medical student from Iraq. Through him, I picked up an Italian, about forty, who heads the military information in Naples. The first few times we met in a café in town, and now I've succeeded in luring them out to the center.
>
> As with Bel's class, the primary objective is not really teaching English, but developing social consciousness among the upper crust in Naples, acquainting them with the needs and what we are doing. This class of mine is proving particularly interesting, since the chief job of the Italian gentleman is smoking out communism. The Arab is probably communist, and the girls have many communist friends, though they call themselves socialists. We always get off on politics, although each one has taken me aside and said we daren't discuss anything around the others. I feel I'm in the middle of a spy ring! Both men are continually trying to get me to go out with them to dinner "so that we can *really* talk frankly."

The whole political situation in Italy is both sad and exciting. We in the States don't know what it is to have no decent alternative to vote for at all. The national elections come up next spring and may decide many drastic changes for Italy. Currently the communist-led left (allied with the socialists) is about 40 percent, while the remaining Catholic Christian Democrat Party, along with the two smaller monarchist and fascist parties, hold the balance. Should this communist coalition win the national election, it would be the first communist foothold in the West won in free elections.

The choice of "thinking" people is the Liberal Party—that of revered philosopher Benedetto Croce. The liberals have the best minds and idealists in the country, but unfortunately they never took the trouble to drum up a mass following as did the others. Consequently they are practically powerless. They are joining with the Catholics, so we have an ironic situation: after fighting tooth and nail with the Church at every turn, they must turn around and get votes for them, not only to support the liberals but to prevent a split and so keep the communists out.

Dr. Santi was asked to run for the Liberal Party, but doesn't know yet if he will. It would mean giving up his medical practice and the Mission (the Mission because he'd be fighting Achille Lauro, the monarchist mayor of Naples who helps us now). Santi is dubious, but we're trying to convince him that a much bigger issue is at stake, and that his first duty should be to the whole of Italy. If he were elected, he'd be the first Protestant in Parliament.

Yesterday Bel and I, with Ken (from the US Navy Sixth Fleet anchored in the bay, who comes to help at Casa Mia) went out to our soccer game. The Bel Boys won 6-2. They've all decreed that I have to attend every game now, as they only seem to win when I come.

These were a few snapshots from my introduction to life and work in Naples. There were also heady moments of tearing around the lovely curved bay on the back of Bel's Vespa, or sipping cheap champagne (twenty-five cents a bottle) after a movie (where we'd go to warm up after days in our unheated building when my fingers got too stiff to type), or a glorious splurge dancing at a night club on New Year's Eve . . .

The Refugee Camps

One activity of our three-pronged Italian Service Mission was delivering services in the five refugee camps circling the city. These camps were filled with Iron Curtain fugitives who had fled from their now-communist homelands in Eastern Europe, landing in Italy as "country of first asylum." Most of these folks were labeled "hard core"—i.e., they had been rejected by every country they had applied to for immigration—and were doomed to live into the foreseeable future in these barbed-wire prisons. We worked under the World Council of Churches, based in Geneva, Switzerland, ministering to Protestant, Greek Orthodox, and Muslim refugees. Jewish and Roman Catholic organizations took care of their own constituencies. The Italian government and the United Nations High Commission for Refugees shared jurisdiction over the camps.

On a Tuesday in November, I drive out to the San Antonio camp with Elisa Florio, chief liaison between our Mission and the refugees. We stop first at our warehouse in downtown Naples to pick up clothing packages. Most of the clothes come from CARE, and all of us put in time sorting and making up bundles, both for the homeless Neapolitans who come to Casa Mia and for the refugees in our caseload.

All but one of the camps consist of crude cement blockhouses where each family lives in one cold, damp room. In the other camp, they live in the Allied Army barracks, thrown up on the Salerno beachhead. Each one is heavily guarded and surrounded by high walls topped with barbed wire. I have a chance to talk with many of the refugees, visiting in their rooms and trying out my French, Italian, and German. Most come from behind the Iron Curtain, though some are German. Unlike the poor Neapolitans, all are delighted that Eisenhower was elected: "Now America, the greatest lover of freedom, will start a war and rid the world of communism so we can go home again!"

These people live and dream every minute of getting to America. Many write to friends and relatives there for sponsorship but get no replies. No one cares about them; they are truly forgotten. Some have been in since the end of the war, most for at least five years. So they go on existing, hoping, and giving up hope. Some do a little to keep busy in the camps; they teach, paint, make lace, play cards, and organize prostitution, but this is hardly a remedy for broken spirits. Even though many are trained technicians, they can't get jobs; they're not allowed to compete with Italians when unemployment in the country already approaches 50 percent. So they must be on relief, getting their food from the camp kitchen and their clothes from charity. This is bitterly degrading and demoralizing to all, especially to those who formerly occupied much the same social position as we.

One very cultured Belgian woman is married to a Russian, and so was thrown into prison at the beginning of the war. The couple had been shifted from one camp to another ever since, and now are considered too old to emigrate.

A fine Romanian family invites us for lunch in their room—for a bowl of spaghetti and bread (we pass around the utensils, as there aren't enough). She had previously been married to an Italian, and after they had three children, she discovered that he was already married. Then she met her present husband, and, finally, after much red tape, they are to be married next Sunday by the Orthodox priests. We're invited to the wedding and a baptism; the couple has one little child of their own now, named Hope. All four kids will be baptized at the same time and given the name of the father. He, too, has been through much; six other members of his family were condemned to death, either for resisting the Nazis during the war or perhaps later, when they objected to the occupying Russians—they don't clarify.

I talk at length to a lovely young Arab girl with two babies. She is nearly wild with anxiety because her husband, a Spaniard, was taken away suddenly last week and put in prison. She has no idea why and has no way to reach him. And so it goes—every case a tragedy. I find sickness everywhere: syphilis, epilepsy, TB. Many people have gone insane from treatment in concentration camps.

We are told of a case in one of the camps where a tubercular mother threw herself under a train as the only solution. She'd been trying for several years to emigrate. Her husband was cleared to go, but she, having TB, could not, and, by law, the children have to remain with the mother. So by killing herself, she freed the rest of the family to leave.

In the afternoon, we drive up a steep mountain to visit one poor Muslim in a TB sanatorium. The Mission has known him for some time and is helping him get his papers and find lawyers for his trials. Just last week when everything was set, he found out that he had tuberculosis. At that point, he lost all hope; he didn't want to live. When he spots our car winding up the road from the village, he rushes out to meet us, nearly breaking down at the thought that anyone would remember and come to see him.

Bel and Dr. Santi are trying to work out a plan to create a whole village of refugees in southern Italy so they can live as human beings again, even if they can't get out of the country.

It's the following Sunday, and Dr. Santi, Florio, Bel, and I are invited to the San Antonio camp for the wedding and baptism ceremonies of the Romanian family I'd met the week before. We arrive at 10 a.m. and find that the Mass has already begun. It's being held in the "church," a tiny, dark, cement room not more than twenty feet square. The rain (it rains every day now) has leaked through in several spots. In a Greek Orthodox service, there are no seats, so the congregation stands for four hours; the spirit, though, is lovely. The two bearded, long-haired priests solemnly go through the service, pausing occasionally in the dignified ritual to repair to a corner to change robes they unpack from suitcases. There are about ten ragged people in the congregation who sing the Russian chants beautifully.

After about two hours, the bride and groom enter, a very moving moment. At one point, a priest places gold cardboard crowns on their heads and leads them in a procession three times around the tiny cell, swinging a pot of incense. Two official witnesses march behind with long tapers. Then the couple drinks from a cup of wine that is passed back and forth between them until it is drained. It's a strange mixture of the very formal, old-world ritual and the complete informality and intimacy of the stark surroundings. Everyone chats together continually, often with the priests and the wedding party.

Next we all adjourn to an even smaller room in the dormitory where the family lives. This is for the baptism of the children, which by custom must always be performed in the home. Everybody crowds around a little clearing in the center where a tin tub of water is placed. This ceremony lasts at least an hour, with the children being brought in nude and dunked in the tub (the oldest is nine). There are little rituals, such as taking three snips of hair from each. Because it's the day of the family's patron saint (Saint George), this calls for another ceremony, considered as important as Christmas. A huge cake, over a foot high, is brought in, over which the priest pours wine. Then he calls four people (including Dr. Santi) to hold the cake on their fingertips, making it revolve slowly while many prayers are said—the four kissing the cake at intervals. All most remarkable and strange to us; we never know from one minute to the next whether we might be asked to stand on our heads! At one point, the priest goes around the room asking for our names so we can be included in a prayer.

Finally we sit down for a feast that lasts another four hours. First we drink cherry brandy, then wine is served throughout. They never allow our glasses to be empty, even when we hide them. After a while we're a little fearful as to whether we'll be able to walk out. There's spaghetti, tripe fried in breadcrumbs (it tastes to me like a barnyard), fried potatoes, beans, bean soup with whole red peppers, and many cakes and cookies. Finally we are served fruits, a chocolate peppermint pie with whipped cream, and an interesting cake of grain, sugar, and nuts that somehow held together when baked. Thick, Turkish coffee tops it all off. The bride and groom never sit down during the entire, long meal, the bride laboring in the kitchen the whole time and the groom serving us.

I chat with the priests in French. They have been refugees twice, first from Russia, now from Yugoslavia. They've just gotten permission to emigrate to Florida, so will leave soon and we must find new priests for the camp. We arrive home after 10 p.m., after listening to a refugee playing sad Russian tunes on her viola.

Celebrations

Despite the misery we witnessed and worked with daily, Bel made sure there was periodic relief from these horrific realities. He introduced me to the "other" Naples that I'd not had a chance to see, since I had plunged into the Mission work immediately on arriving.

In the midst of our most hectic period of holiday preparations at Casa Mia, in December, Bel comes home with two tickets for the San Carlo opera. It's *Othello,* and magnificent. Roberto Rossellini is directing, his first opera. Unlike some operas I've seen, where the actors seem to stand around a lot making stiff gestures in between singing, this is real drama. It's a four-hour performance, and we celebrate afterwards with good pizza and beer.

I have not yet seen the famous downtown waterfront area of Naples, so one evening Bel suggests a walk along Santa Lucia, the great, beautiful curve of bay around which the city lies. It's incredible to think I'm living in such a spectacular spot—that is, in terms of natural beauty. The sidewalk runs right alongside the water. Thousands of lights blink along the shore and are banked up the hills that rise behind. Off to the south, the great shadow of Vesuvius is just visible, leaning protectively over us. By day, the heavy industries belch their orange fires, yet late at night, strolling on Santa Lucia, there is almost perfect silence, just the gentle slapping of water on the rocks and an occasional splash as a fisherman in a rowboat adjusts his lines. Dozens of these boats rock quietly at anchor, some with little, one-man shacks built in, glimmering faintly.

Homeless kids come to Casa Mia for progams that include what is often their only meal of the day

On this hazy, warm night, the world seems to drop off after the breakwater, some fifty feet out. The soft darkness of the water blends without horizon into sky, illuminated only vaguely by a misty moon. A little boy runs out, urgently pushing a drooping flower into our faces, hoping for a cigarette in return. There's a muffled laugh from two drivers of horse-drawn carriages as they huddle under their blanket. The clacking of a tram grows to a roar, and then fades off again into the lonely night. Yet even in this main square, it seems an empty peace, suffering Naples having crawled into its miserable huts and holes, out of sight.

Periodically the Mission organized memorable events for the homeless who came to Casa Mia and for the orphans at Casa Materna. Bel had built up a strong connection with the American presence in Naples—both the Navy's Sixth Fleet and the US diplomatic personnel, particularly the US Information Service (USIS) that loaned us films to show in our outdoor courtyard. Every evening Bel pushed a cart over the cobbles to pick up leftover food in big pails from the military kitchen. And several sailors, hungry for "meaningful activity," came faithfully to help out with the kids.

Monday is our party at USIS for all the Casa Mia kids and their families. We discover that the auditorium loaned to us will hold only 250; however, we manage somehow to squeeze in four hundred children and at least that many others with the addition of an adjoining room. It's quite a sight to see these great mobs of ragged Graniliites swarming into the plush US Information Center headquarters, many mothers carrying and nursing babies. The manager is a little bewildered, but also very impressed.

A few of us go down early to set up chairs and haul packages we've wrapped. It's total bedlam, but the program goes well, with Dr. Santi giving an inspired talk and everybody cheering and shouting. Afterward the masses parade back through the streets to Granili, about forty-five minutes away, all proudly carrying their presents aloft. Our staff stays to clean up afterwards, and then we return to the center to prepare for a major open house the next day. This involves setting up elaborate exhibits, including a display showing the history of Casa Mia and the entire Mission in photos. I work all night with four of the other staff before going home to Casa Materna to take a bath and change clothes.

We have a marvelous time preparing, clowning around, making tea at intervals. This is the third night running without sleep for three of the guys. I can take one night without any trouble, but don't see how the others keep going. Bel falls into bed around 1:00 and never hears a thing, despite the fact that we have the lights on in his room (where we're working), are singing at the top of our lungs, and perform a wild Mexican Hat Dance.

In one corner, we put up a big map of the world, with a relief of the Palestine area and a crèche scene sitting on top, with lovely effects of stars and angels above blue lighting. Bruno, our manual arts instructor, has constructed a large-scale model of the center showing all the details in every room—little scenes of each activity and class with wooden figures of the staff and participants.

I ride with Bel on his Vespa out to the Casa Materna orphanage for Christmas Eve dinner. Following tradition, we eat eel, boiled first, then fried. We finish with a dessert a little like our sticky popcorn balls. Then there's Bingo with all the children (I'm drafted to call the numbers), and at midnight, sparklers are stuck on the Christmas tree and all around the room, and lighted. The whole city of Naples is like our July 4th, with firecrackers, rockets, bombs exploding in the streets—that keeps up all night. Not especially Christmassy!

Christmas day: after an 8:00 a.m. soccer game, we return to the center to escort fifty of our hungriest kids up the road to the Hotel Grilli, the Navy kitchen, for a turkey dinner. The tiniest children can barely carry the great trays full of food. They're completely bewildered by the amount, and can't begin to eat it all; there are two kinds of meat, two vegetables, several desserts. A lot of it they don't like because it's so sweet (sweet potatoes, corn, peas). Their first thought is to wrap up what they can't eat to take home to their families; every child hikes back to Granili with a package.

Intense Sadness and Intense Beauty: A Death in Granili

There were many times when the horror of what we saw and experienced threatened to overwhelm us. This was one of them. But at the same time, there was a poignancy and eventual terrible beauty about the event that validated our dream and all our efforts.

It is February 1953. One of the young girls who had been coming to Casa Mia since its beginning a year ago has died. Maria was a laughing, happy child of fourteen until a few weeks ago. An "old timer" at the center, just recently she'd been having a great time with the beach colony, going every day to swim at Casa Materna. Then about a month ago, she came down with some sort of illness that centered in her throat. When she got sicker and sicker, the family reluctantly took her to the hospital. In the public hospital, as is so often the case with poor people, the doctors tried a new, experimental cure. From that point, Maria went immediately downhill. The parents came to take their daughter home to Granili where, within a few days, she died.

The family has collapsed, completely paralyzed by grief. Two of our social workers go over to try to cook a little and to make funeral arrangements. Casa Mia covers the cost because the family has no money and can't raise any through friends. The night after the death, Bel and I go to visit, winding through the dreadful dark, dank corridors of the half-mile-long Granili barrack (that was once where Napoleon kept his horses in the military). We climb the battered, crumbled stairs, feeling our way along the walls, trying not to breathe the cold yet stifling air.

Entering the "home" (one small room), we find some fifty people jammed in, some weeping violently, most just sitting and staring. The mother, in bed, has gone totally berserk. She throws herself on Bel and me, kissing us wildly. Her hair is deliberately disordered, and she has scratched her face in huge gashes—a Neapolitan custom, we learn. Alternately she screams for her lovely daughter to return, and then sinks back moaning. For four days, she has eaten nothing and has made no effort to take care of the rest of the family.

Maria herself is lying on an elevated platform, beautifully arrayed like a bride in her white communion dress and veil. A bowl of white-coated almonds rests near her white slippers. Her older brother keeps throwing himself on the body with crazed sobs; we find out later that he tried to buy drugs to commit suicide, then came down with a fever of 105. The tragic thing is that a six-year-old brother has the same disease as his sister, yet no one is paying any attention to him in the corner. The mother cares only that she has lost her only daughter.

Apparently all of Granili has been waiting for Bel to come—a task he hasn't relished but knows it is very important to the family. They even want him to bring his camera to take pictures of Maria, but he draws the line there. Through all of this, the local priest has never once come near, out of spite because of the connection to Protestants. Casa Mia was the center of this family's life, and it was here that they turned naturally in time of trouble. Here was the one element of kindness and love and strength that they had.

The next morning the funeral procession starts out from Granili. It is headed by the hearse, a horse-drawn, white-and-glass carriage, moving slowly toward the cemetery. Hundreds of people walk behind. When they reach Casa Mia, six of Maria's close friends lift the coffin down from the carriage and carry it to our door so that she may pay a last farewell to the place she loved most, the place that had really been "My Home." It is a very deep tribute to us, showing maybe more vividly than anything else what a profound influence the center is having. Then they all return to the hearse and the cortege disappears down the street.

At the Mouth of Cristallini Cave

In May, shortly after Bel and I returned from our month in the Middle East (described in the following chapter), fresh opportunities for programs opened up at Casa Mia, and I graduated to a new phase of the work.

My own work has suddenly become more clearly defined. A while back, I had begun to enter the individual casework field, visiting families all over Naples. About three weeks ago, when we were in the Cristallini Cave (Bel is trying to find homes for several of the families still living inside it), I saw that that entire zone was uniformly desperately needy. Conditions were even worse than at Granili. I hit on the idea of making a family-by-family study of one little street just outside the Cave, finding out the precise problems and situations of every family, then trying to develop some activities that would help these "permanent poor" as a whole. The idea was applauded by the rest of the Mission.

So every day I go to Vico Tronari to talk informally with each family, working my way systematically from one miserable little "home" to the next. Because it's a zone really forgotten by everyone, our sudden attention is a great event. Since almost the first day the word has spread, and now flocks of people, many of whom I haven't yet visited, crowd around, pouring out their pent-up troubles and almost dragging me into their houses. There's a pathetic sameness to the overall situation. Several families live together in one squalid room. Everyone is unemployed. Neither the Church nor city government nor political parties have any interest in helping them. They're lucky if they can pick up 200 or 300 lire every few days from odd manual labor jobs, and this must support maybe ten people.

The domestic chores aren't overly taxing. It's usual to eat one meal every other day, and this would be beans or pasta. In almost every family, it's common to find tuberculosis, diphtheria, meningitis, or bronchitis, plus a collection of the common diseases such as measles and chicken pox. Every child shows the marks of cruel malnutrition, and many simply die from this. I am given a photograph of a small corpse, a child who died after having nothing to eat (frequently babies expire as soon as they can no longer nurse). This one is laid out in a white dress with huge open eyes, staring. It is the child of one of my favorite families, and they have three others who, though living, look almost as terrible.

The sad thing is that we can do very little. When working in a concentrated area where all cases are equally urgent, it's impossible to start handing out material aid. There are two reasons: first, our firm principle is that material assistance alone doesn't accomplish anything; the other is that once you start helping one family in this way, you'll be forced to do exactly the same for all the others, and we simply don't have the means. One of the saddest discoveries is the older people, those over forty who can no longer find even the little odd jobs to help from day to day. Although they may have living children, these adult children generally have huge families themselves who are also starving (sex being the only readily available recreation), so they can give no support.

According to law, it's the right of every person without a job to have a *libretto di povertà*, a card that entitles them to state aid, giving either a small monthly allowance ($2), a little pasta, or free hospitalization. However, the number of poor is so overwhelming that the officials long ago gave up even pretending to honor the cards. Sometimes it's possible to get help if a person pays $20 or so under the table to one of the municipal clerks, but who has a sum this size?

Another ugly reality is that people who receive such aid are "friends" of the government who have to be catered to but have no actual need at all. Nothing is possible without very strong "contacts." When applying for public assistance, an official is sent to look over the house. If he sees any furniture, even if the people are actually sleeping on the ground, he instantly refuses, saying there is no need. No consideration is taken of the fact that these are vestiges of many previous decades, and you can't eat chairs. Even so, little by little, the people are selling whatever they possess, even needed pots and pans and clothes.

One thing I'm doing is collecting all data on cases where assistance was applied for and refused. Then I go to the sectional municipality and present the facts and find out just why. There are many cases where some aid was given previously and then stopped—for example, pensions from war dead and those mutilated. Everywhere I get different stories about this assistance. The people themselves know very little, and I'm sure the officials are purposely being confusing and evasive. Most discouraging, of course, is the fact that the people have lost faith in the government and don't even bother to apply any more for anything. They just die. So I get them on the ball to put in an application. If they get a positive response, good; if not, I can go with the family history and plead the case.

A tangible way to help would be to place some of the young people in state trade schools where they could learn to do something during a six-month course while earning 600 lire a day. As yet, we are still in the stage of taking applications, and then Bel will take them to the Department of Labor.

Another project of Bel's is making contact with new factories, most not yet built but that will be backed by American funds. These factories are on the lookout for reliable personnel, so Bel's idea is to help find the workers for them, using the inexhaustible supply of unemployed we know. People are streaming in so steadily now that you'd think we were an employment bureau. The factory managers (like the one at Remington Rand opening next year) are grateful for the interest and help of an American. None of them trusts Italians, and generally they end up by offering Bel a job.

A third immediate assistance we can offer the people at Cristallini is the use of our new medical clinic just opened in that precinct. There they receive free examinations and counsel as well as medicine. For those too old and feeble or too ill to move, I can get the municipal doctors to make visits. These are notoriously worthless, but better than nothing. One sad old man has had terrible pain in his legs for two years and cannot even move out of his chair. No doctor has ever come to see him, so he has no idea what the ailment is. He is completely alone in the world, and has no one outside to help.

After talking with a large number of the families, ideas for broader programs are beginning to take shape. For example, an astounding number of adults are illiterate. Then there are the hundreds of weak, hungry children. We're thinking of helping fill these two needs in one shot: an evening literacy school for adults and a morning distribution of milk, bread, and jam for the children of these adults. In this way, we would not just be giving material aid but asking people to give something of themselves.

Finding a location for these new activities proved challenging, because the pastors of the several Italian Protestant churches we approached to donate space saw this as an ideal opportunity to evangelize. They had little interest in just helping from a social viewpoint. To try to feed such people or teach them anything, they felt, would be a total waste. "They are animals, have always been so, and cannot be changed," the pastors said. When we carefully explained our experience at Granili and our philosophy and aim, one Baptist minister ended up offering a room for literacy and a hot plate to heat up milk for the children.

A Critical Election and a Communist Rally

In the beginning of June 1953, crowds came to vote in what could have turned out to be the first free election to usher in a communist government in Italy. Bel and I were excited to witness some of the frenzied, historic campaigning.

The critical elections loom nearer—one week from today. Actually, there is no doubt anywhere I've been that any but the Christian Democrats will win, even if by a small margin of 51 or 52 percent. But the numerous other parties are frantically propagandizing. One of my favorite sports is reading all the new posters plastered every day on the buildings as I ride to work. In the evening, it's impossible to go anywhere without running into huge rallies.

Kindergarten at Casa Mia

The most frequent of these are the communist. Organizers march through the streets waving flags, gathering hundreds of people and momentum. Then, by the time they arrive at the piazza designated for the rally, the numbers are impressive and everybody is sufficiently whipped up. There is generally a huge red backdrop adorned with the hammer and sickle and a large stage where the shirt-sleeved speakers hold forth. Loudspeakers blare out from every corner. The crowds are so dense in the square that no vehicle can pass. Maybe fifty police will be hovering on the outskirts to be handy in case of riots. It's interesting that in my visits at Cristallini, most people think I represent some party, usually monarchist, and try to impress me as being good party members so as to receive more aid.

It's the final week before elections, and all the big guns have come to speak in Naples. Bel and I make our way to Piazza Plebiscita to hear Togliatti, the communist candidate (and national leader of the party). The great square, packed with maybe two hundred thousand people, is accented brilliantly by red banners everywhere. Crowds have been imported by truck and rail from all over southern Italy to participate. Togliatti holds forth from a vast, elevated stage against a backdrop of impressive pillars—the spot where the big orations have been given for centuries. He's an impressive speaker. Fortunate for him is that he can justly call out all the faults of the reigning parties—the Christian Democrats and monarchists—while still expounding in the realm of idealism about what the communists believe and can offer. He's safe, because there's little chance (for the moment anyway) of his party winning. People believe that if he wins, there would be a civil war.

After the main speech, the mobs are worked up to an even higher pitch and march en masse down Via Roma. Almost everybody is wearing a red neckerchief, sweater, or hat. They chant like a college cheering section, scream the party hymns, and nearly go wild passing the office of *L'Unità*, the communist newspaper. They whistle when passing the headquarters of one of the opposition parties (a sign of disapproval). There's an enthusiasm unmatched by any of the subsequent rallies, yet no violence. The following night during the fascist rally, three people are shot and fifty injured. During the entire week, anti-riot squads are poised all around for immediate action. We

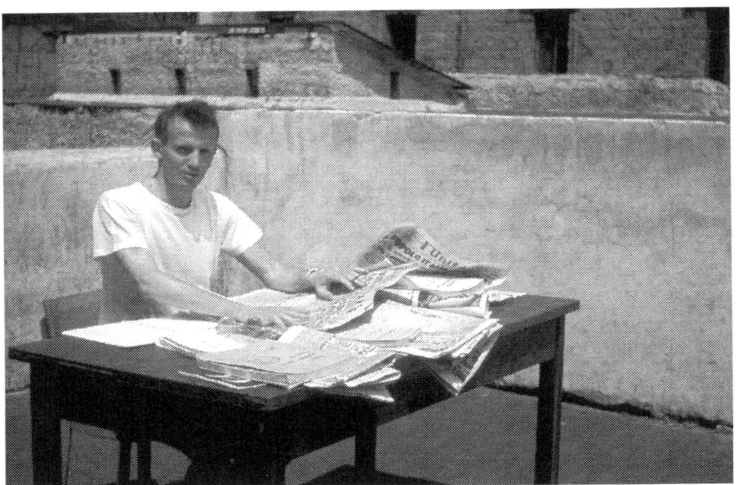

Bel's desk at Casa Mia

also hear Lauro, the monarchist mayor of Naples, but because of a Casa Mia staff event, we miss De Gaspari, the Christian Democrat candidate and party head.

The elections took place, the Christian Democrats won, and Naples settled back into its old lethargy. The crowds had been stirred up emotionally, never really thinking what it was all about, and so as soon as the rallies stopped, they lost interest. They never even cared enough to find out who had won.

A Saint's Day and a Bomb Scare

As Bel and I neared the end of our tenure in Naples, there were a couple of events in our neighborhood to recount.

Today is Saint Peter's day. These saints' days seem to come along about once a week and, of course, everything shuts down for the festivities. A life-sized statue approaches our center from the nearby church. It's carried on high through all the neighboring streets by parishioners, followed by a loud, martial band. For honoring any holy personage, the highest tribute is manifested by the most possible noise: dance and marching bands, and always deafening fireworks. The festivities accelerate, always centered around the wooden saint who watches over his flocks proudly, surrounded by flowers and candles.

Workmen set up a rickety bandstand near Casa Mia, and then start collecting 5 and 10 lire from all nearby residents and passersby. Then the band assembles: violin, guitar, accordion, and traps, plus a singer—and the noise begins. As the wine is poured down, the musicians get louder and drunker, as does the audience. I'm sure all the priests are also well lubricated. Everybody in the area brings out chairs, and hordes of mothers nursing babies appear, lining the street and enjoying the fun. The standbys take turns improvising as singers, and a few jump out to dance, especially the tiniest kids.

The bomb scare: Suddenly one morning we notice people in the palazzo next to ours tearing outside in all states of undress, women with their hair down, clutching children and a few belongings. There's a lot of shrieking and rushing in circles. It seems there's an oil tanker sitting in the harbor that's on fire and about to blow up. Actually, there is some reason for the hysteria, since in 1943, a similar ship exploded and, though a mile or two away, leveled all the buildings in this area and killed hundreds in the center of the city. Huge flaming pieces even flew as far as the Portici suburb and to the top of the Posillipo.

Police are careening all around in their jeeps, and the warning appears to be valid, so we hand over the kids to their parents on the spot and march all the rest who've come to the center for activities down the back street away from the harbor. Not that it's any safer there, but it gives them the feeling we're doing something. Mothers are weeping, genuinely frightened, and most of the girls are sobbing violently. Our staff thinks it's pretty exciting and somewhat amusing. Then, not long after, the all-clear sounds, but not before all the buses and trams have been halted and the people herded into underground shelters. Afterward there is even some doubt as to the verity of the alarm. Our clinic doctor believes it's either a trick of the communists or of bandits wanting to loot the stores when their owners run away. Nobody ever finds out.

Two months later Bel and I said goodbye to our close colleagues at Casa Mia and sailed home to America where we married and where Bel began graduate study at the University of Chicago.

Reflections

Naples was a remarkable, on-the-ground experience for both of us, three years for Bel and nearly a year for me. Best of all was that Naples brought us together around some shared dreams and set the scene for decades more of incredible explorations together. Both of us were very green, in our early twenties, not long out of the ivory tower of college idealism and innocence.

For Bel, there was the initial lure of pure adventure when he had boarded a student ship and then hopped on a bicycle to cross the Swiss Alps. But beyond simple wanderlust, I'm sure he was being drawn by the same serious concerns that had inspired his mother to become a social worker through Hull House in Chicago and then to head the Red Cross effort in Poland after World War I. It was his mother's connection to the settlement house movement that suggested to Bel the idea of creating the first social settlement center in Italy—to carry aid work beyond simple relief to work more deeply on human rehabilitation at all levels.

During two post-college years with the Experiment in International Living, I had become closely attuned to the importance of a global perspective. My job was to help send young Americans abroad for experiences of total immersion in foreign families. After leading a group of college students to Europe, I was ready to go back on my own. It was a kind of pre-Peace Corps zeal that led me to Italy and to want to help alleviate the poverty and pain I saw in that war-destroyed country.

Bel's vision of assistance on an individual scale soon grew to devising strategies that could nurture whole segments of a stressed populace. Beyond providing for immediate physical needs (food, clothing, medical care, skills training), he also reached into various strata of the local society to waken consciousness. He brought some of the closed-minded clergy, the oblivious upper classes, government officials, and business leaders—as well as the American military stationed in Naples—into Casa Mia's orbit. He showed them how they might begin to lift the area into a state of greater equilibrium and well-being. I came along to plug into programs already underway, and to help implement new ones. In dealing with the complexities of Italy's political world, including the threat of communist electoral success, Bel was stimulated to take on more study, which brought us to graduate school in Chicago.

Both of us were grateful and excited to have been present in Naples at this unique moment in history, with opportunity to make a small dent in a huge problem.

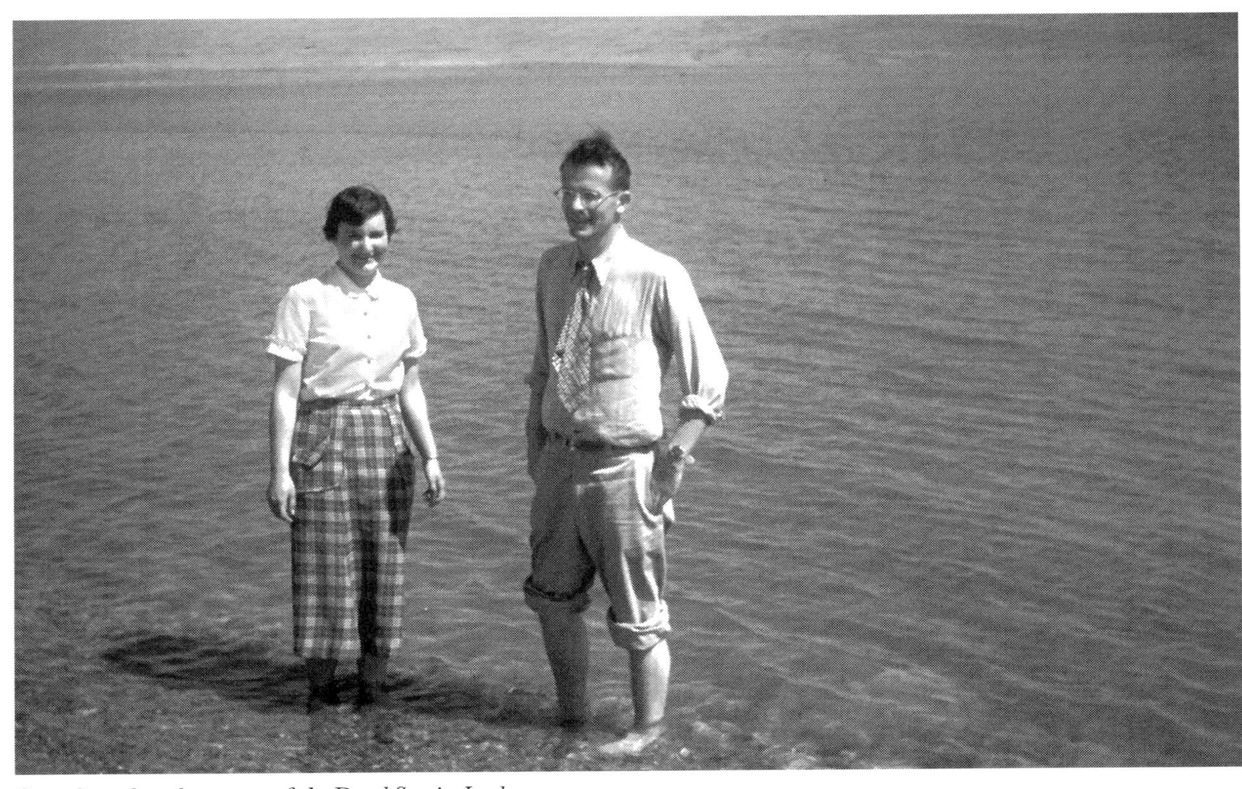

Sampling the salty water of the Dead Sea in Jordan

Time Out—
A Middle East Adventure
Old Jerusalem: Arab Hospitality and Christian Pilgrims

April 1953

Backstory

Spring was approaching, and Bel and I felt we badly needed a break from the intensity of life at Casa Mia. Bel had a strong curiosity about the heated situation across much of the Middle East, and I was remembering my original plan to volunteer at an Israeli kibbutz. We put our heads together and began scheming for a getaway trip to points East. Armed with names of friends or contacts involved in creative refugee rehabilitation projects or innovative technical assistance programs, we mapped out our route. In Jordan and Israel, we were particularly interested in seeing personally how the Arab/Israeli tensions were playing out. We also enticed a couple of our pals from the American Sixth Fleet to go along for some of the journey—partly because they'd be fun company, and partly to satisfy the concern of Bel's parents about appearances (two young, unmarried people traveling unchaperoned was not done in those days!)

The plan was to catch a ship from Bari on the east coast of Italy and sail up the Mediterranean after a quick stop in Alexandria, Egypt. We'd land in Lebanon, work our way down through Syria to Jordan, spend Easter in Old Jerusalem (at that time the city was partitioned into Jordanian Arab and Israeli sections), and then cross over into Israel. We'd sail back via Greece to check on agricultural projects and then travel overland through Yugoslavia to learn about its political climate.

It was tough making sure that all the systems were securely in place at Casa Mia that would allow us to be gone for a month, but it was even harder to drag Bel to the train for Bari. We made it with just three minutes to spare.

Every step of the trip proved provocative and enlightening, but because I'm focusing primarily on our Naples work, I'll include here only a few of the highlights.

Setting Sail

We're out to sea from Bari early Sunday evening under a full moon and bushels of stars. Most of the next day we follow down the Greek coast, where grey rocks rise sharply, almost fjord-like, out of the water on either side. We imagine this as the spot where Scylla lured the unfortunate sailors ashore with her fatal songs. The old feeling I always get at sea creeps up again: that I'm suspended between two worlds, that time itself as a human expediency is a meaningless device here.

We hurry off the gangplank of the *Enotria* to spend a few hours in the dusky, tented bazaar in Alexandria. Here we're suddenly inundated with everything exotic: Arab men in striped pajamas hunched cross-legged in the dust around crooked urns of water, inhaling smoke through long hookahs; Muslim women gliding by, almost invisible under black veils; heavy incense, dark coffee in little cups, stray bits of sunlight sneaking in and glinting off copper utensils and brocades.

When we land in Beirut four days later, there is no sign of our friends Ken and Dick (who were hitching a ride on a Navy plane). So after spending the night in this jewel of a city with an administrator at the American University, we decide to head south alone. It's the morning of Good Friday.

Midnight Arrival in Old Jerusalem

We barrel down the Damascus road to Jerusalem in a huge, shiny DeSoto taxi (costing only $12 to traverse three countries). Our hooded Arab driver switches radio stations nervously between suggestive belly dance music and Beethoven's Eighth Symphony. The other passengers—sleek city men in red fezzes and bony, gowned Bedouins—guffaw periodically at our exasperation at long waits at Lebanese, Syrian, and Jordanian customs. The officials are always polite at these stops, ushering us into private sitting rooms for Turkish coffee and cigarettes.

At one border, a group of disheveled Arabs glowers behind prison bars. When we reach the Old City of Damascus, we head for the souk (market) and are swept up in the melée of crowds shopping frantically. (Spoiler alert: I buy a length of white brocade in case I might need it for a future wedding dress—a wedding to "whomever.") We also accidentally bump into our two Navy comrades, and they join us in our taxi.

Past snow-covered Mr. Hermon, we ride through layers and hours of wilderness. Bare mountains of rock and stubble, grey and majestic, dwarf sparse Arab villages of tents or beehive huts. Occasional herds of sheep, goats, or cattle are the only movement. Then it's night in the desert, stars touching every horizon and glinting off the silver points on the helmets of Arab soldiers guarding razor-wired army camps.

Finally, around midnight, we arrive in Old Jerusalem. There are no glaring lights, just a great shadow of wall as we pull up to the Damascus Gate. At this point, we're prepared to roll out our sleeping bags in the nearest alley, but a little one-eyed chap hurries up to us. He says, "It is my business to make sure that no one enters my city without a place to stay." We follow him through mazes of streets (or narrow alleyways where no cars could fit), black tunnels, and steep stairways. One after another of his sleepy friends, responding to his knocks on their shutters, indicate that "the inn is full." On and on through shadowy, empty bazaars, our own hollow clacking on the cobblestones is the only sound.

We Are Pilgrims Too

Then suddenly we're brought to the front of a church. A crowd, including many soldiers, mills silently around the courtyard. "You may stay here," says our friend. What is this place? We're dazed and tired, and then gradually understand that this is actually the Church of the Holy Sepulchre, the spot thousands of Christian pilgrims cherish most, the place where they believe Jesus was crucified. We have been led here blindly by the little (nearly blind) Arab man without knowing how or why. It just happened through an odd series of accidents: our deciding to push on to Jerusalem this day instead of waiting until Easter; our chance meeting with the "Good Samaritan" with no apparent axe to grind; one after another of the homes he tried being closed to us so that this church is our only remaining possibility for refuge.

We enter the building and find a jumble of bodies, mostly black-hooded women squatting on the wooden scaffolds that support the ancient building. Lumps of humanity wrapped in blankets line the walls. Our Arab guide leads us up a broken staircase to a large, dusky room. More folks in black shawls are sleeping or murmuring quietly, stretched on the stone floor or propped against the altar rail.

Wrapped in sleeping bags and blankets in a corner on the stone floor, the four of us are immediately an intrinsic part of this phenomenon—no longer gaping tourists who look and move on. Locked into the church to keep out the thousands of other pilgrims who would swarm in at too early an hour in the morning, we too become expectant worshipers who have come to see God give to the world the Holy Fire at the tomb of the Christ. This is apparently a genuine miracle that occurs every year at dawn on Easter morning: a blue light begins to pour out of the rock where Jesus was laid. This turns into a column of white light and then becomes fire from which candles all over the church light spontaneously.

All night long our senses are flooded with new experiences. Periodic bursts of incense float down, Greek Orthodox choirboys sing hour after hour an oriental plainchant that rings in my ears for days. Staring up into the dark, vaulted recesses of the ceiling from the floor, inhaling the damp must clinging to the stones next to our noses, offers a humbling perspective. False prides, dignities, pretenses melt away in this literal leveling process. Through the night, Bel and I scribble our impressions and feelings in our journals. By now we are too excited to sleep.

For once, different sects that bicker all the rest of the year become just Christians together, standing collectively in hushed wonder at the "greatest sacrifice." The ugly, dirty hodgepodge of the architecture of the Holy Sepulchre becomes almost beautiful in symbolizing this odd unity. Armenian Orthodox in our room pray before a Russian icon. Roman Catholics chant in another. Abyssinian Catholics pound their great scepters in yet another. These people have tramped hundreds—perhaps thousands—of miles on foot to be together now. All of us are seeing and living this miracle in the house of God.

Loaves and Fishes

When we leave the church early on Easter morning—actually before the appearance of the Holy Fire in order to escape the crush of humanity—we climb Palm Sunday Road. This is a dusty lane leading past the Garden of Gethsemane. It is quiet and lovely, with flowers and the same gnarled olive trees that supposedly shaded Jesus. We continue on up to the top of the Mount of Olives, where we've decided to hold our own little Easter ritual. We celebrate with "loaves and fishes"—Arab flatbread and tins of sardines. Looking out across the valley to the city of Jerusalem clumped on another hill, each of us sinks into our own private reverie and imagining.

Dheishen refugee camp outside Bethlehem

Forced to flee from Israel when the Jews took over in 1947, they thought it would be for only a few days so they left behind everything in their houses. Now there is no chance to return. The Israelis have taken their land and houses, and their money is frozen in Israeli banks. These are the real destitute, living in tents that are wet and freezing cold in winter with water running through, and unmercifully scorched in summer with not a tree in sight. There is no chance to cultivate on land that is solid, bare rock.

In Jericho, we are invited into one family's tent. We see the destruction of these people's spirit and their material suffering. They receive almost-starvation doles of food from the United Nations Relief and Works Agency (UNRWA). We too catch the bitter spirit of the injustice. As so many pointed out, "Two wrongs don't make a right." The Jews may have been persecuted for centuries, but were they justified in turning around and stealing property that wasn't theirs? Our sense is that the United States and Britain are continuing blindly to sponsor this wrong, refusing to recognize the Arab view, pouring money into Israel for military protection as well as economic aid.

So it is with heavy hearts that we prepare to enter Israel.

Political Pawns

Bethlehem, the River Jordan, the salt-encrusted Dead Sea—we soak up the ambience of these desert landmarks. But then we want to see first-hand some of the appalling Arab refugee camps we've heard about. Unlike the refugees we work with in Italy (who seek resettlement), these people present a different, hopeless problem. They refuse to find new homes. Their one fixed thought is to return to Israel (or Palestine, as they call it). They are the ideal pawns in the hands of the Arab governments that stir up hatred of Israel among the refugees and foster the refusal to be resettled in Arab lands. More or less a million of them sit encamped in the barren wilderness and hills from which they can look down into the lush green valleys and orange groves that were once theirs.

Israel: Millennial Dream Realized—Or Chimera?

Spring 1953

Backstory

After being overwhelmed by the grief and anger of the Arab refugees in the camps in Jericho, it was indeed with heavy—and somewhat guilty—hearts that after our Navy friends returned to duty in Naples, Bel and I moved to the next stop on our itinerary. We needed to keep reminding ourselves that the tremendous weight of centuries of persecution of the Jewish people had culminated in what had to be considered a miracle: finally, a safe haven for Jews from every corner of the globe, a land where every settler could unpack dreams of "the good life" and could set about creating this from scratch. With their bare hands, they dug into the unyielding soil with almost superhuman energy and fervor that had been stifled for millennia. We arrived to witness this flowering.

Lush Fields and Exuberant Spirits

Fresh on the heels of visiting the refugee camps, we are so fired up with indignation that we're prepared to dislike and distrust everything we see in Israel. We only want to get through this country as fast as possible, feeling ourselves traitors to be coming here. Even entering the country feels harrowing and ominous: we have to cross a no-man's land between Arab and Jewish Jerusalem, a space we walk while guns from both sides are trained on us.

Gradually, though, in our journeying about and in spite of our initial discomfort, the spirit that is the fine Israel begins to seep in on us. To begin with, there's the taxi driver who takes us all over Tel Aviv to find a place to stay, excitedly talking ideals and refusing to accept any payment. Then we start to notice the great desire in everyone we meet to work hard and to sacrifice for this precious dream.

We feel caught in the middle of a very sad situation, seeing right and wrong on both sides. Back during the 1947 war, the Jews had begged the Arabs not to go, but, incited by neighboring Arab governments that thought they would win the war, they fled anyway. Then the Jews won the war, and Jews began pouring in from all over the world, taking over the vacated homes and land. Now, of course, the Arabs can't return. They talk of being raped and murdered by the Jews, and vice versa—probably both true. At one early point, the Jews asked for a coalition government with the Arabs, offering them the fertile Galilee. But the Arabs wanted all or nothing—so they lost all. They are left with their wilderness where, oddly enough, with its poverty, we can much better imagine Jesus wandering than in the lush, well-kept fields of Israel.

Israel seems very American to us, with its fast pace and progressive technologies, modern buildings, and English-speaking populace. The kibbutzim are as we had expected: there is a beautiful, exuberant spirit of loving each other, the determination to struggle through any hardship for the country that is at last their own, and terrific pride in their projects. These settlements dot the rolling land with neat clusters of bungalows, luxuriant orange and banana orchards, well-ordered fields tilled with the most modern equipment, and extensive collections of prime livestock.

Even at the edge of the Jordanian wilderness on the east shore of the Sea of Galilee, a little fertile paradise has been made of the Ein Gev settlement—truly a miracle. The kibbutzim we visit are the completely collective variety. No money passes hands; the residents receive clothes, food, and personal articles for the asking. The children are reared separately in baby houses, seeing their parents only after work.

Several glorious days are spent basking in the Galilee, where it is hot summer. We hike in the Galilean hills, thick with golden cosmos and scarlet poppies, then rest from the blistering sun in the shade of fanning palms. At night we watch men fishing just as Peter did two thousand years ago, luring their catch into nets with lights. The Sea, not so big, is as smooth and quiet as a mirror. Yet on the ridge just above, Syrian guns are always pointed down on the Israeli border settlements—and Syrian soldiers swoop down periodically to raid them.

After working our way across Israel, we admire the work of friends who run a Quaker assistance center in the port city of Acre for both Arabs and Jews, and are ready to head out again.

Reflections

We pondered the two major thorns in Israel's side that we felt could have a severe impact on its future prospects. The unsettling reality (or maybe it was the unreality) of the state of Israel kept niggling: the false economy, where much of the country's money comes from the United States. It seemed clear that if we were to pull out this support, Israel would probably collapse. We also found disturbing the growing military atmosphere—necessary because of hostile lands on all sides—that was causing bitter disillusionment in the original Zionists, the real idealists who had settled in the beginning. Now, sixty years later, the situation has hardly changed. At this retrospective writing, it is certainly no nearer a solution acceptable to both sides.

Greece: What Tourists Never Saw, and What No Longer Exists

Spring 1953

Backstory

Although the Mediterranean Sea was unusually calm, for some inexplicable reason, I was horribly seasick, lying miserably on deck the whole time we sailed westward from Haifa. Hugging the coasts of Turkey and Rhodes, we were finally liberated in Piraeus, Greece, and ready for our next exploration.

Athens and the Acropolis

In Athens, we immediately look up Congregational Christian Service Committee workers and then the World Council folks we'd met in Geneva. They put us up, feed us, and drive us around in their jeep. Generally we find the city uninteresting, and after traveling through the rest of Greece, are able to appreciate the many service workers in outlying projects who scorn those cooped up in Athens offices with no real contact with *people.*

The one great joy is the Acropolis, which, though we see it in drizzling rain, is still dazzling. Perched on a hilltop high above the city, the Parthenon stands quietly aloof from the modern development below, proudly oblivious of the passage of over two thousand years. We stand among its brilliant marble pillars, staring off beyond the hill into space; it's surrealistic—a perfect structure hanging in nothing. Then, looking a little harder, we spy the knoll nearby where Socrates drank the hemlock.

Traveling Like the Greeks

Soon we leave Athens, dragging ourselves up before dawn to board a bus for Ioannina, for what will be a rugged, thirteen-hour trip going north. It's gorgeous, though, and the hours melt away as we follow along the Adriatic coast on white cliffs that drop straight into the sea.

There's a young boy on the bus whose sole occupation seems to be passing out paper bags to people afflicted with motion sickness, and there are plenty of these. About three-quarters of the passengers are soldiers who sing lustily the whole way. Singing is of great importance to the Greeks; almost all military companies march in song. It's a strange kind of music, surprisingly oriental, with a definite Arabic influence. Unlike the restrained dignity we find among strangers on American buses, anyone in Greece is apt to burst into a long, penetrating solo, from the broken-shoed peasant to the dapper businessman. Even the tall, robed patriarch of the Orthodox church, with his high, black crown, joins the fun, appreciating the jokes, puffing on his cigarette, and combing out his long beard and hair that hangs half-way down his back.

Everywhere we see soldiers and military encampments—sometimes large barracks, sometimes flocks of tents—but, more often, lonely soldiers huddled over a mess kit and fire in front of a crude hut or cave in the mountains. Many tramp beside pack mules, heavy with supplies. Every bridge is guarded at either end by a sentinel with rifle and bayonet. We realize that Greece is one terrific armed camp. It's easy to see why, since she is surrounded by three communist countries.

Many villages consist entirely of thatched houses. In one, we see a procession of all the villagers on mules or horses, doing a sort of follow-the-leader across fields and through streams. Toward the end of the line is a girl in ornate costume. This, we're told, is a marriage ritual; the husband is leading his bride to their new home.

Rest stops are interesting. The driver simply stops the bus every three or four hours, and everybody piles out onto the surrounding, totally exposed rocky plains. Here the Orthodox priests have a distinct advantage; with their long skirts, they can squat discretely in the open fields, while the rest of us cannot be so modest.

Modern Agriculture for Poor Albanian Refugees

Ioannina at last—this is our target, our chief reason for coming to Greece. Located here is the Brethren (peace church) project we'd heard about in Geneva. Since it's agricultural, we're anxious to study it as a possible model for our South Italy project to resettle refugees from our camps. Ioannina is a wonderful little town of fifteen thousand, surrounded on all sides by jagged, snow-covered peaks.

We're taken in immediately by the team and fed peanut butter and apple butter sandwiches—luxuries we haven't seen since leaving the United States, making us aware of the sharp difference between their standard of living and ours in Naples. They seem unable to exist without importing the American standard, while we've gotten quite used to a *low* Italian one.

The next morning we skip out to the dedication ceremony for a new refugee kindergarten. As we arrive, three robed priests are busy chanting, swinging the incense bucket around and throwing holy water on everybody. Then on into the refugee camp proper, where former Albanians are jammed into cubbyholes in endless rows of quonset huts.

Edson Sower and his team of four are bringing modern agricultural methods, seeds, and equipment to outlying, poverty-ridden villages near the Albanian border. It's no fancy mass production directed from an office as are, unfortunately, too many government projects. These young men and women go out every day to one of the eight little villages, usually staying five or six days alone. They plow right along with the farmers, show them how to plant, how to take care of chickens, how to can vegetables. They help set up committees of villagers to decide how to divide up village-held land, and how and when each man will work his share, using equipment lent to them by the World Council. Many of the towns were destroyed during the civil war and weren't able to rally afterwards. The smallest and most neglected of these have been picked out for help. And, of course, the scope of the work always goes beyond

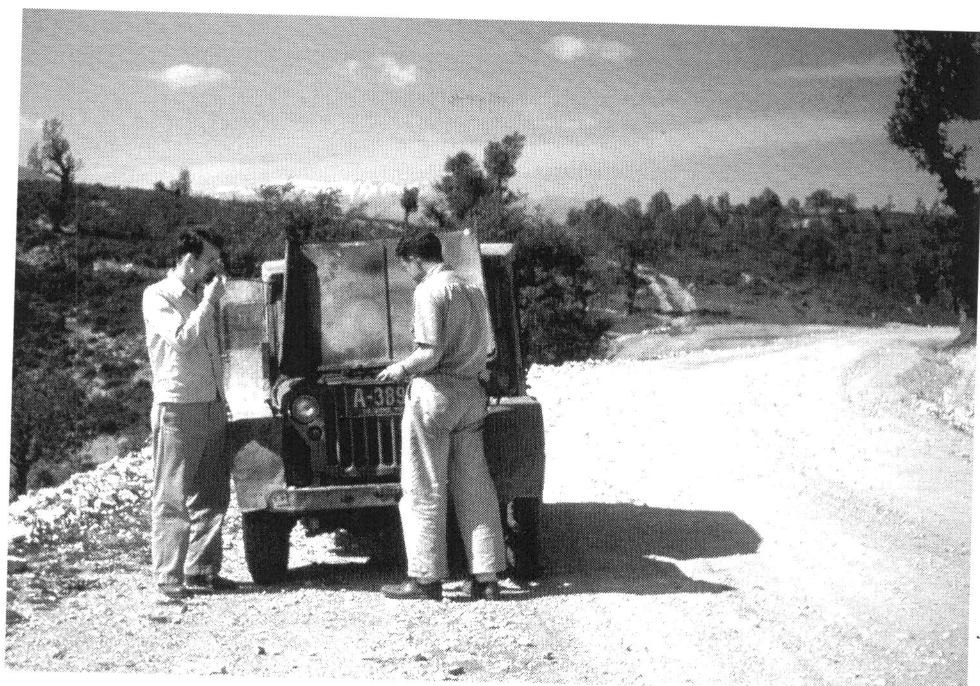

Cooling the jeep en route to Rizany refugee village

this specialized aid, with social work and health education.

Experiments in the Villages

The first day we drive to a village built six months ago for Albanian refugees. Forty families have been selected from the camp and brought out to start from scratch. The people sleep on the floors of tiny stone bungalows, but their spirits run high, and all are anxious to learn and produce, to become independent once again. It takes us five hours to get there in a rickety old jeep that boils over and stalls continually as it chugs over the high mountain passes. Returning that night, we have even more trouble with the car, stopping every few miles to hunt for water and to push the vehicle into starting—often perilous, because there is no guardrail between the narrow road and drops of several thousand feet. Being so close to the Albanian border, we're stopped frequently by soldiers and have to show special passes.

The next day we travel north to where the team has been working for several years to drain a huge swamp, building an expensive drainage tunnel. There's no road here, so to reach this valley, we cut through the wilds like a tank, following boulder-strewn creek beds, climbing 45-degree sand banks. Finally, it's like entering Shangri-la to come upon a lush valley, now almost free of water and ready for cultivation. We pull out our sandwiches and fruit to eat in the warm, beautiful grass. On all sides, shepherds wander quietly with their herds of tinkling goats and sheep. A little knoll rises about five hundred feet from us, and on top is the Albanian border. Although it feels absolutely peaceful, we're told that Albanian machine guns are trained on us all the time, with hidden soldiers watching our every move.

The villages here are perched high above the fields, the houses clinging to the steep rocks. Most are inaccessible except on foot or by mule, which

Rizany: Albanian refugee village

the team members sometimes use. The biggest challenge is getting these people to think about the future, to plan the planting to get as many crops as possible—three are possible in this climate.

We climb up to visit one village, looking into the one-room schoolhouse where children give flowers to each of us. Back down into the valley to see sheep cheese being made—milk being the main product from sheep. There are also lots of goats, the herds always on the move, tended either by children or by women who are either knitting or spinning yarn from wool on a small frame as they walk. We note that in general, only the women seem to be working, carrying the heavy loads, plowing the fields, looking after the family and house. The husbands sit all day in the coffee houses, laughing and joking.

We finish our Greek odyssey with a thirteen-hour bus ride to Salonika, across very high mountains with deep snowdrifts, part of the way above the clouds. We pass numerous "monasteries," usually lonely little caves stuck on the sides of cliffs where solitary ascetics live and pray.

Our destination is Anatolia College (whose president was a year behind us at Oberlin College), located in the hills outside Salonika. At tea here we meet Charles Lindsay, a charismatic British Quaker who takes us to visit his nearby project. He has a primitive wooden barrack (built by the Nazi occupation), a little piece of land, and a few chickens. He brings forty girls a year from isolated, backward villages to train them in homemaking, a two-year course. The emphasis is on the greatest possible simplicity, on creating the feeling that, rather than a school, they are all one family, living and working together. The girls are taught to feel free to criticize the directors and make suggestions. He has four Greek teachers.

Lindsay has no desire to expand or to accumulate more buildings. "Those material things destroy the ideal behind the work," he says. The courses are practical: health, sewing, cooking, child care. Each year the school adopts a tiny baby from an orphanage and each girl takes a turn being its "mother," looking after it twenty-four hours a day. Then, after a year, the baby is placed in a home.

Our last stop in Greece is a quick visit to the American Farm School, and then friends drive us to the train station in Salonika, where we catch the Orient Express to Belgrade, Yugoslavia.

Tito's Yugoslavia: Shadowy Bastion of Communism

Spring 1953

Backstory

We had one more country to explore before returning to "reality" in Naples. In Greece, we were slowly working our way northward, and from Salonika, it was a short hop over the border into Yugoslavia.

No Murders on the Orient Express

We're primed by the lurid films featuring this fabled train and find that it almost lives up to its shadowy image. It's a twenty-hour ride. We're lucky to find one of the tiny half-compartments for only four passengers. Fortunately, we can sleep a little, making pillows of our sleeping bags. It's somewhat eerie, because there are no electric lights, just one dripping kerosene lantern that swings around crazily and that we have to hold for each other in order to write out all the customs declarations. We sit endlessly at the border, the officials busy at I'm not sure what; they vanish, and we see nothing of them for four hours.

In late evening, we blast into Belgrade, the capitol city, and step out into the main square to hunt a place to stay. The first thing we notice is the silence. Cars are practically nonexistent; there are even very few taxis. People are hurrying about, but they, too, seem to be speaking in whispers. We have no sense anywhere of being followed or spied on as some do in Yugoslavia, but we certainly feel an odd constraint and lack of gaiety.

Faces in a Communist State

No one in Yugoslavia seems to know English, while many speak German. I find myself resurrecting what little I can from my sophomore year in college. It works, after a fashion. Here and there we discover a few key people who speak Italian—better yet. We spend a day wandering around, mostly to absorb the general ethos. Women in overalls work on the street crews and on construction jobs just like the men. Interesting to us: some of the best restaurants (which cost plenty—nearly a dollar for a meal) are frequented chiefly by men who are obviously laborers. Very few wear ties. Finding out later that they make, in general, $50 a month, we can't figure out how they afford such eateries. But, of course, they don't have expenses such as cars, which all our US factory workers own. Even a bicycle is out of the question for most.

We look up friends in the US Embassy and pick up literature on the political ideology of the state. Since pulling away from Russia, Yugoslavia has completely changed its approach to communism. Now they point to Russia as the bad example of what happens with a state capitalism. They say quite openly that Yugoslavia is going back to free enterprise before it's too late. Consequently, each person can own his/her own land, although the size of the piece is limited. A certain portion of the proceeds must go to the state, but what remains above this, which depends on the person's own initiative, is theirs.

In a huge public park (that reminds me of the Tuilleries in Paris) we find good symphonic music. Strauss waltzes and national folk tunes blare everywhere on loudspeakers. We relax on a bench under the shade trees and talk, checking out the crowds and watching the red sun sink over the factory buildings on the other side of the Danube. All Belgrade must be out here with their families. Groups of school kids are strolling in their fur hats and soft Serbian shoes with the pointed toes turned up. Yugoslavia is the one country we've visited where the old peasant embroidered costumes are still worn every day. It's a lovely spot, and we remark that it's a wise dictator who realizes the need for places of peace and beauty. On the other hand, all that night in our hotel (we are sure the sheets weren't washed), we can hear the communist tanks rumbling by under our window.

A Whiff of Cloak and Dagger

Next, traveling north all night, we land in Zagreb. We meet a young man who speaks Italian, finds us a cheap hotel, and takes us to a delightful Franz Lehar operetta, performed by local talent. They are surprisingly good.

The next day our new friend suggests a tram ride out to a nearby farm village that's especially famous for its native costumes. On the way, he makes it clear that he's going to share information and ideas that could imperil him if authorities overheard—so he's taking us to the countryside where there's no surveillance. Because it's Sunday, everybody is out on a public terrace drinking beer, being hilarious, and dancing to accordions and violins.

We're introduced to people in several homes; they're anxious for our news and (very pro-American) are eager to show us whatever we want. They're especially astonished to hear we've just been to the Holy Land. Most are very devout in this northern Roman Catholic area, while farther south it's all Greek Orthodox. Churches are open, although the situation is somewhat like Italy, where freedom of belief is in the statutes, yet anyone who doesn't go along with the position of the state is automatically barred from any important job. Therefore, it's bad for any communist to be seen attending church. Most of these folks detested the communist guerillas, and one old man grinds his teeth as he shows us the spot in his front yard where they slaughtered a big group of Germans. In every house we're offered the little cakes they all bake for Sunday callers.

As in Russia, probably not more than five percent are communist. Conditions are certainly not as harrowing in Yugoslavia as behind the Iron Curtain, but there's a lot of dissatisfaction. A communist dictator (Tito) is a communist dictator. Professional people such as doctors and lawyers, although essential, are considered "nonessential" non-producers, and are paid accordingly. Even the most capable earn less than laborers. For us, seeing the rough workmen enjoying the best entertainment and restaurants is a refreshing sight after the terrible discrimination in Italy.

Everyone here seems to cling to Americanisms; I've never seen a USIS so jammed with people reading magazines and papers as in Zagreb. There's no sympathy for Russia. These people came too close to be fooled. Even during the alliance with Russia, they didn't believe a word of the propaganda, as likewise they couldn't believe all the evil deeds attributed to the United States. I should think it would terribly undermine the people's faith in a leader who one minute swears to one set of facts and the next minute tosses them all off as lies. But the people aren't fooled very much, and they say no one in Russia is fooled either. A revolution here, however, they feel is out of the question, since the police are just too vigilant.

"Home" to Italy: Trieste and Venice

We reenter Italy by way of Trieste, stopping there to visit several refugee camps. The World Council, working here, is dealing with the big mess of Iron Curtain escapees and also with the Yugoslavs who are involved in border disputes with Italy. They predict that all these thousands of refugees may be moved down to the Naples area in June after the national elections. We hope not!

On our last evening we stop off in Venice for five hours between trains. This is surely *the* magical city: high arching bridges over the canals, no automobiles, just boats sidling up to the quays. Big streams and tiny ones everywhere, glimmering in the shadows between the dark palazzi. We make our way to Piazza San Marco, the huge, central square lined with long, Italian Renaissance buildings with precise, delicate decoration, thousands of lights and endless columns. We plop down at a table to nibble ice cream and listen to two orchestras playing chamber music, one at either end of the piazza. A full moon is shining, and gondolas are sliding by on all sides. And (perhaps parenthetically), I should add that this seems the perfect spot for Bel and me to finally voice what we've both been feeling, and that has become more obvious on this trip: over the past months we've gradually fallen in love and now can begin to talk about marrying and building a life together.

The final lap from the Naples train station to Casa Mia is necessarily by horse carriage to transport all the stuff we've accumulated, much to our own amusement and to all who see us arrive.

Reflection

Our month away gave us a fresh perspective on our own work as we weighed our efforts and methods against those of the projects we visited. We learned a lot, including about ourselves, and also gained new respect for what we've been able to accomplish in Naples. We came home refreshed and ready to dig in again to the myriad challenges of Granili and the refugee camps.

(clockwise) Actors Hope Lange and Don Murray check out a refugee's artichoke field; a rare picnic in the hills above the rocky Mediterranean coast; Lisa and Eric try on the typical local Sard apparel.

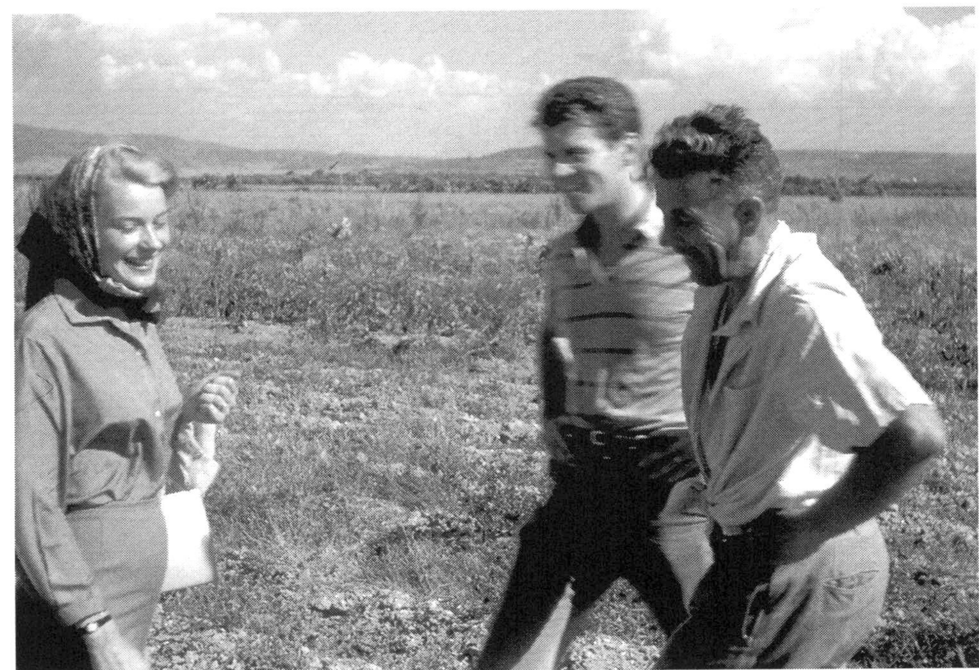

Sardinia
Echoes from the Bronze Age

September 1957 – August 1958

Backstory

In fall 1957, our family (now three of us) sailed for ten days from New York to Naples, and from there caught the overnight ferry to the rugged, mysterious island of Sardinia.

To back up: In October 1956, toward the end of Bel's coursework for a doctorate at the University of Chicago, we were surprised by a visit from Don Murray, our conscientious objector-actor friend who in 1953 had succeeded Bel at the Casa Mia social settlement center in Naples.

After three years, Don was back in the States. He stopped at our little student prefab to reminisce half the night with us about Italy, and also reported that he had just finished making a film, *Bus Stop*, opposite Marilyn Monroe. As a result, he said he had a bit of money in his pocket and was thinking again about pursuing his dream of helping the refugees in the camps where we had all worked. Along with humanitarian assistance for bombed-out Neapolitans at Casa Mia, Don had concentrated most of his energy and passion on the plight of those "hard core" escapees from behind the Iron Curtain. This group had no apparent hope of leaving their barbed-wire confinement because no country would accept them for immigration.

Don was anxious to get going on his dream and asked Bel to fly to Italy with him to mount a project that might get even a few of the refugees out of the camps. Bel's reluctant response: "A great idea, Don, but I'm still in the middle of my PhD. We also have a two-week-old baby in the back room. I don't see how I could possibly get away now." Don begged him to at least consider going along to Italy to study the situation. Bel agreed to this minimal exploration, and the following spring they flew over.

After conferring with officials in the camps, with the United Nations, and finally with the Italian government, Don and Bel presented a proposition. Because unemployment in mainland Italy was so high at that time, it was difficult for the refugees to get permission to move out to compete with the local workers. Also, there was little prospect of their ever becoming self-sufficient. This was not the case, however, on the island of Sardinia off Italy's west coast, and the officials were open to risking a project there. For years, the population of Sardinia had been severely decimated by deaths from malaria, but since the disease had been eradicated after World War II, the island was overdue for development. We were told that if we were to buy land there, the government would offer substantial subsidies as well as all kinds of agricultural assistance.

Don and Bel were immediately excited about the creative possibilities this conjured up. It could be a way to actually begin to clear the camps after the refugees' many years of suffering and would lift the burden from the groups that had to support them.

Bel returned and we talked it over, agreeing that this could be a significant opportunity. Of course, we decided we had to go (against the judgment of both sets of parents). We put the doctorate on hold and packed up for another stint in Italy, this time with eleven-month-old Eric.

Our family spent the next two years in the town of Oristano on the west coast of Sardinia, finding that we were almost the only Americans on the entire island. With the help of several volunteers from peace groups, we brought fifteen refugees from the camps who, with us, were willing to stick out their necks to begin a new life—which the camp psychologists had predicted would be impossible because "these people are simply too destroyed by their experiences to start over."

Bel and Don—always intrepid risk takers who were spurred on by the possibility of proving the experts wrong—were only more determined to make this new refugee community work. Located near a small town not far from Oristano, they called the project HELP (Homeless European Land Program). With material assistance and advice from the Sardinian agronomists, the 135 acres we bought were leveled, irrigated, and planted, and small poultry and concrete block industries were established. Some of the refugees ended up marrying local women.

The following is a "color piece" I wrote at the time that gives a sense of what this curious, somewhat primitive, lovely island was like over fifty years ago. Along with the very demanding work with the refugees, we also took every opportunity to get to know and understand Sardinia, from top to bottom—the richness of its culture, the people, and the unusual crafts that were unique in each village.

An Island Still Backward and Isolated

Sardinia is strange and beautiful, almost unchanged for centuries, and about as developed as was the United States around 1800. Until fairly recently, there were some 76,000 cases of malaria a year, which effectively isolated the island from mainland Italy. In 1946, the Rockefeller Foundation DDT team found tribe-like villagers dwelling in the heights of the mountainous interior. Afraid to venture down into the swampy plains areas, the people wore protective masks, a habit still seen in the streets, where women often wrap the lower half of their faces in black shawls, even though the team had completely eliminated the disease by spraying nearly every inch of the island.

The lonely distances between communities make looting and highway robbery a temptation to bandits. One night not so long ago, the most notorious of these stole into Orgòsolo, a village in the mountainous interior, to post a list on the cathedral door of the thirty-seven people he had killed. Once in a while, a solitary shepherd goes berserk in the hills, but the carabinieri (police), along with sickness brought on by the hardships of fugitive mountain existence, have almost erased banditry. Nevertheless, the police advise us to notify them whenever we plan prolonged trips into the mountains; if we don't report back in three days, they will go in with jeeps and dogs to hunt for us. Occasionally, even now, we hear of incidents where motorists in remote regions come upon a road blocked, and while they are stopped, robbers gallop down from the hills to relieve them of valuables—or to kidnap them for ransom.

Though there are numerous motor scooters and some cars, the chief means of transport outside the cities is by donkey and horse cart (to Eric's delight). Flocks of sheep and pigs wander nomadically everywhere, accompanied twenty-four hours a day by their shepherd, with a sleeping blanket folded over one shoulder and a staff or large umbrella in hand. At night, our headlights often pick up a sea of green lights that turn out to be sheep's eyes, and donkeys will be ambling alone near the roadside or drinking from rock springs.

During our first year in Sardinia, our only transportation is a motor scooter; Bel rides his Lambretta the few kilometers out to our project on the land. On Sundays, we often take it on family outings to the beach a half hour away—I perch behind with Eric on my lap taking a nap. The second year we graduate to a Cinquecento ("500"), a minuscule Fiat that Italians have nicknamed "Topolino" (Mickey Mouse). Its back seat is a glorified board, and the bicycle-like tires blow out every time we drive any distance. Generally it doesn't start without a push.

Remnants of a Culture at Least Five Thousand Years Old—and Other Antecedents

Nuraghi (prehistoric towers of unmortared stones up to forty feet high) punctuate the plains, as well as remains of pre-Christian Roman, Carthaginian, and Phoenician towns. In some spots, rows of tiny caves line the hillsides, their four-foot ceilings indicating the curious race of pygmies that occupied them several thousand years ago. Along with its neighboring Roman civilization, strong cultural influences on this country came from the Saracens, Spaniards, and Greeks. These are perhaps observed most readily in the Sard dialects and folk music. And in Alghero, the ancient walled city on the idyllic west coast, pure Catalan Spanish is spoken. Our own relic, a two-thousand-year-old millstone turned up by a bulldozer on our land, waits to be enshrined in a future museum.

The Present-Day Culture

Sheep are raised for meat and for milk to make cheeses. However, because sheep are plentiful, their wool is a major byproduct, and weaving is the principal Sard handcraft. Each village has preserved its own ancient intricate designs and geometric symbolisms, working them into rugs, tapestries, and saddlebag-type purses. In some remote towns, such as Tonara, one sees the women in nearly every home either at their looms or spinning the wool onto crude sticks they carry around, twirling them against their thighs.

Most of the women outside the cities still wear the full, ground-length skirts (often several at a time), and on special occasions they don stiff,

Weaver in the hill town, Tonara

heavily embroidered blouses, brocade vests, and tight black velvet jackets—as does our lovely helper Angela, who lives with us. One of the late afternoon sights in Oristano and Simaxis (the latter village is next to our refugee resettlement project) is the procession of barefoot women, their garments sweeping the dust and their bodies erect under tall, stone water jugs balanced on little pillows on their heads. Homeward bound, too, file farmers on bicycles, each with a hoe on his shoulder. A red sun, just before dropping over the distant peaks, blazes through acres of lacy white almond blossoms, making them appear even whiter. The sun catches the patches of bright green grass that seem to grow only under the terraced olive trees and glances off the freshly shaved henna trunks of cork oaks.

Our Amenities

We have snagged one of the new "modern" apartments in Oristano, the fourth largest city (population twenty thousand). Elegant on the outside, our third-floor walkup is cavernous and bare, and we hurry to pick up the few necessary items of shoddy furniture sold locally. Amenities such as running water are rare indeed, and we're lucky to have water available spasmodically. This means that plumbing, generally, is practically unknown. A recent survey by the European Productivity Agency disclosed that in the western section of the island, the village with the best sanitary facilities boasted only 25 percent of its houses with any such arrangement, including outhouses. (In the villages, each house has its *cortile*, a section of the yard designated for relieving oneself.) There is no central heating anywhere, despite near-freezing temperatures during the winter rainy season. The rest of the year it's mostly cloudless, dusty, dry, and blisteringly hot.

Television sets are found in most homes (with programs transmitted from Rome) and seem almost an anachronism; this innovation has probably done more to modernize Sardinia than any other single factor. Housekeeping, as in days of old, is a full-time affair for both Angela and me. Shopping takes a couple of hours a day, because our minuscule and unreliable refrigerator holds very little—necessitating frequent hikes to the open market to bargain for every item. Laundry, all by hand, takes another two or three hours. Before coming, I had joked about washing Eric's diapers in the river as they do in most of the villages. We wash diapers in the bathtub and then hold them up one at a time to dry in front of the one tiny, electric plug-in heater, the only heat source in our frigid, damp building. Because it rains almost every day in winter, a daily chore is cleaning mold out of leather shoes and suitcases and trying to air them on our balcony in the infrequent appearances of sun; our pristine plastered walls have become green with mold.

Preparing a simple soup lunch takes another hour. There are no cans, or the few I find in the puny grocery store are too expensive—it's not the accustomed approach to food here, and there is little call for packaged goods. Thinking up ways to disguise the meat takes time and ingenuity. There are no beef cattle; when a cow gets too old to give milk, it is slaughtered, and is even tougher than you'd imagine. Hot water must be hauled from the bathroom for washing dishes. It's thought, even in our brand-new building, that maids don't merit the luxury of hot water in the kitchen, they are expected to heat it on the stove. Angela sweeps the marble floors daily and throws pails of water over them (mops are unknown); they dry when she skates over them with rags under her slippers.

We don't have a telephone; a private phone would be astronomically expensive. If a call comes in for us, somebody in the bar up the street runs to our apartment to fetch us and we run back to talk. There is no transatlantic communication by telephone at all. When Don Murray, in California, needs to discuss a complicated situation about the refugee project, he will wire us and Bel flies or takes the ferry to mainland Italy to take a call there. We write a lot of letters.

The Face of Poverty

Footnote for economics students: the average daily earnings of a manual laborer are about $1.25. A skilled head mason may get a maximum of $4.00. Angela works fifteen hours a day, never takes even five minutes out (at great protest from us), won't take off more than half a day a week, if that. She makes $16.00 a month, which is considered extravagant. Our neighbors are on our backs for making their own girls discontented; we should have at least four kids to merit that kind of pay. We have a few other revolutionary ideas too: Angela eats with us, calls us by our first names, and uses our bathroom to bathe instead of the usual rusty tin pan. To give an idea of one cause for the poverty: nearly all merchandise costs more than similar items in America. Meat—almost any kind—is at least $1.00 a pound (more than double what we pay in the United States), and consequently finds its way only rarely to the table of even the well-to-do.

Despite the fact that Sardinia is on the brink of tremendous development of its literally untapped and potentially rich plains (one reason we chose to settle the refugees here), the individual farmer still has not been able to scrape up enough from his skimpy plot to afford irrigation or power equipment. He still guides his hand plow behind a team of oxen, his wife or child following to sprinkle in the seeds. Because the small plow can't dig a deep enough furrow, daily cultivation with the hoe is necessary to keep the weeds down.

This unceasing struggle to stay alive and eating—first battling malaria and then battling the dry, unyielding soil—has left a mark the newcomer notices immediately. In Naples, for example, one remembers laughing voices breaking into song and quick, jaunty steps—in short, the spirit of a people who may not have much but who have learned to live from one day to the next without worry, often by their agile minds rather than by real work.

When the Farmers Come into Oristano

Glancing around Piazza Roma in the center of town at noon, one is reminded somehow of flies on a wall. Dozens and dozens of men of all ages lean silently against the buildings lining the square. They are not chatting but are simply watching, their ruddy faces unsmiling, black eyes solemn. A good number of them have come in from neighboring villages; they wear the traditional bronze velour suits, pants tucked into knee-high boots, and wide, golf-type caps mashed flat on their heads. Fed up by the bleakness of solitary farming, these men may feel compelled to seek the warmth of the city, the hubbub of market stalls and horse carts creaking past. They absorb it for a few hours and then return to their hoes and shovels. The farm women also come into Oristano, but they are busy peddling their produce. Because there are no toilets of any kind, it's not uncommon to see them step daintily off the curb into the street and stand, feet astride, their ankle-length skirts handily hiding the urgent business at hand.

Sard men in mountainous Orune

in the house, worrying about the safe return of her man. No doubt this is a carryover from the days when travel was really perilous. Likewise, if the wife is sick, the husband will not leave her bedside for even a minute but hovers over her, lamenting and sympathizing loudly.

It seems that many girls rely on the special vision of *il mago* (the fortune teller) to guide their precarious love lives. Angela, in a desperate moment, went to consult him and returned with—among other rather astounding examples of psychic powers—a direct quotation of some of my remarks she couldn't possibly have known.

Courtship Is a Tricky Business

A great earnestness about life carries over into local social customs. For instance, a girl who has been engaged and then jilted usually will never again be touched by another man. She is permanently soiled. Being seen just once promenading on the street with a man constitutes being engaged. So courting is a deadly affair, and it is considered quite justified for a girl to do away with the man who leaves her for another. Around Christmas, there was such a case in a village near us. Immediately after the ceremony, the couple stepped out of the church where the former fiancée was waiting in the square. She raised a gun and shot him dead. There was no prosecution.

Once married, the seriousness of the bond is intensified. If the husband goes off for a short business trip, even for a day, the wife cannot go out socially. She must not be seen gossiping in the street or otherwise enjoying herself. Instead, she remains

Of Spirits and Faith

The supernatural plays a large part in these peoples' lives. It seems that everyone has had contact with the dead and feels there is nothing strange about it. Repeated visitations from someone recently deceased means he is doing penance for an earthly sin; finally, in embarrassment, his relatives have a Mass said to release his soul and send him away. Apparently this always works. Angela's father appears to have a special power; he can foretell, through contact with departed spirits, the exact time and manner of death of the people in his village, even when the death is to be sudden or accidental.

Oristano has its own holy man, Padre Pietro, an old priest from the order of San Ignazio. A favorite confessor, he knows and understands the sins brought to him even before they are spoken.

His "apartness" was first recognized years back when he knelt to pray one afternoon in the street. A torrential downpour began, and when he rose, those around him were soaked, while he alone was untouched by the rain. Most Sardinians, by the way, have never heard of Protestants; a non-Catholic is simply an atheist, a nonbeliever.

Certainly it's important for development experts to help raise economic standards in remote spots like Sardinia. But equally important must be the realization that it is not only the "enlightened" who can teach. One finds a small element on the island that has escaped the age of cutthroat competition and overemphasis on specialization, and expresses its faith in the goodness of the "whole person." The following incident, though amusing, shows that in such areas perhaps lies an antidote to the frenzy and sometimes distorted values of our own culture. Word had gotten out that the newly established EPA headquarters in Oristano needed a couple of stenographers. Into the bustling office came a brown-robed, bearded Franciscan with two middle-aged ladies in tow. "Can they type?" asked the personnel man. The friar looked up in childlike surprise. "No," he replied, "but they have good characters."

Reflections

Our two years in Sardinia were crammed with obstacles that stretched Bel and me to our limits, especially Bel, who constantly and creatively had to cope with the unpredictable refugee psychology and sometimes mercurial volunteers, as well as all the bureaucratic red tape in securing the promised assistance. Together the American volunteers and the refugees constructed the little village that ultimately was deemed a success when the land, the crops, the small businesses, and the houses built were all turned over to the refugees when we left.

One of the scariest challenges was generating funds to keep the project functioning. Bel wheedled assistance from every organization he could think of, traveling frequently to Rome and Naples. At times, he had to hide from local bill collectors when there simply was no money. In March 1958, the money Don and his wife, Hope Lange, had been supplying was running dangerously low, so Don came up with a scheme to bring Bel and me (and others) to Hollywood to appear on the then-popular TV show, This Is Your Life, in which the host surprises the guest by reviewing his or her life, in front of an audience that includes friends and family. Bel was to be the unwitting victim. Telling the story of HELP, and making a plea for donations, the program brought in $90,000 to keep the work afloat. Bel returned to Sardinia immediately afterward (we had left Eric there with Angela), but I came down with hepatitis, contracted from the rusty needles my doctor brought wrapped in newspapers to treat an outbreak of boils. I recuperated with my parents and wasn't permitted to go back to Italy for seven months.

Toward the end of our stint, the United Nations High Commissioner for Refugees (one of the critical players in maintaining the refugee camps) was so impressed with our pilot project for resettling hard-core escapees that the UN asked Bel to join their staff in Rome. His job would be to design a model for a larger Sardinia program and to coordinate efforts to clear the camps in Italy.

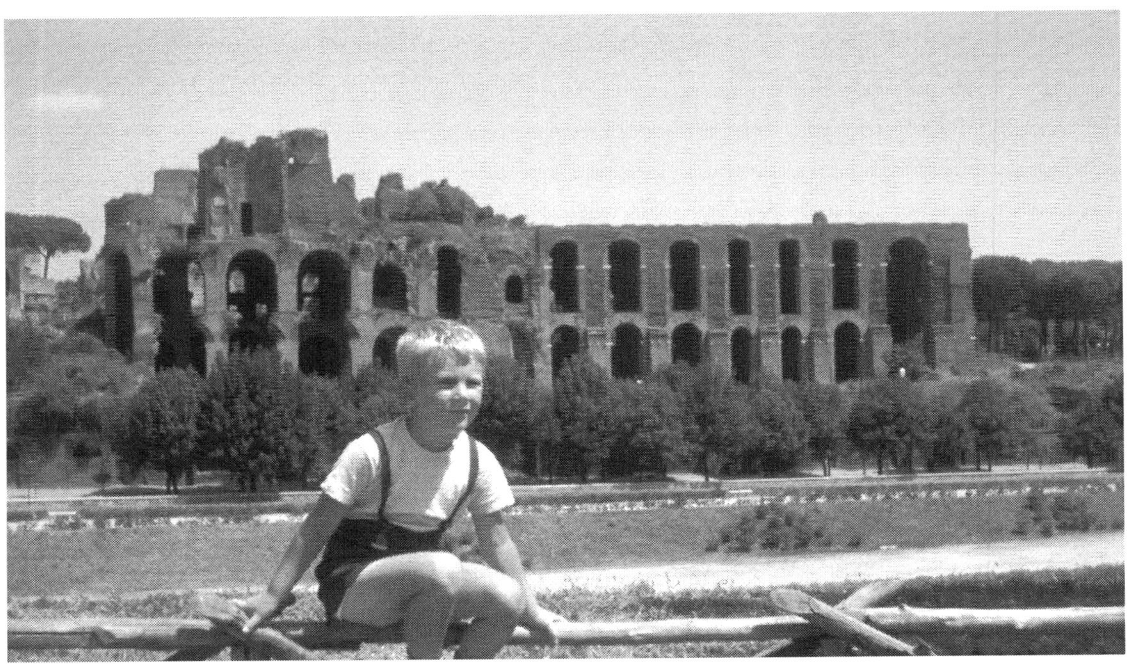

Eric ponders the ancient contests that took place in the Circus Maximus.

The family at home in the garden, Rome

Rome
A Venerable Civilization Meets La Dolce Vita

January 1960 – September 1961

Backstory

It wasn't as if we suddenly leaped from our primitive two years in Sardinia to some decadent dolce vita (sweet life) when we moved to Rome. But it certainly was a radical shift.

We left the Sardinia project in fall 1959 for a short, needed rest in the States. Then Bel went on to Rome to begin his assignment with the UN High Commissioner for Refugees. He was to devise a plan to empty the camps and resettle Iron Curtain escapees elsewhere.

Eric and I, now eight months pregnant, flew over after Christmas and settled into the comfortable apartment Bel had found for us in a woodsy section of the city.

So commenced a couple of years that were totally different from our time on the "frontier" in Sardinia. Our Roman neighbors and friends were expat writers, actors, and journalists, as well as the international diplomatic community. Intellectual Sunday lunches on the sea, idyllic afternoons climbing over crumbling ruins, and forays to some of the lovely, historic, Italian hill towns made for a heady, cosmopolitan experience. This was very different from my first arrival in Rome in 1952 when, weak from hunger, I was reduced to sitting on curbs!

If I were to sum up the dominant themes of our life in Rome, it would have to be celebrities and sickness, plus, of course, Bel's hard work, both with the UN and his continuing relationship with the Sardinia project. He was attending meetings throughout Europe, running back and forth to the refugee camps, visiting institutions across Italy to find sites for refugee placements, and trying to break through the lethargy of public bureaucracies.

We had the good fortune to participate in a rarified, sophisticated circle of the international intelligentsia. A chance meeting with another young mother with her kids on a nearby playground, as well as when I enrolled three-year-old Eric in the Montessori preschool up the street, led to close friendships with Americans making films, writing novels, or reporting for newspapers and magazines.

An evening out on the Via Veneto might find us at a sidewalk café where *Today Show* host Dave Garroway was being filmed. Peter Ustinov sat in front of us one night at the Baths of Caracalla outdoor opera. We enjoyed a Sunday lunch at actor Martin Balsam's beach house with Gerald Green, who had recently won prizes for his novel *The Last Angry Man*; currently he was scripting a movie for the Italian film producer Dino di Laurentiis, along with Alex Nicol, who starred in spaghetti westerns. Alex and Gerry and their families lived next door to us, and we shouted back and forth from our windows.

At an embassy personnel picnic, Winie Vagliani, a stunning young African American woman, entertained us with singing and guitar playing from her acting stint in the recent Fellini film *La Dolce Vita.* Another time we heard Earnest Borgnine noodling on the piano for movie guests at a reception following the Italian premiere of Don Murray's film *The Hoodlum Priest*. That same visit, I took Don's *Hoodlum Priest* co-star Cindi Wood to the Colosseum, where we happened to bump into Ted Kennedy. And everybody knew Audrey Hepburn was in town house hunting. Enough name-dropping—but it was rather surreal!

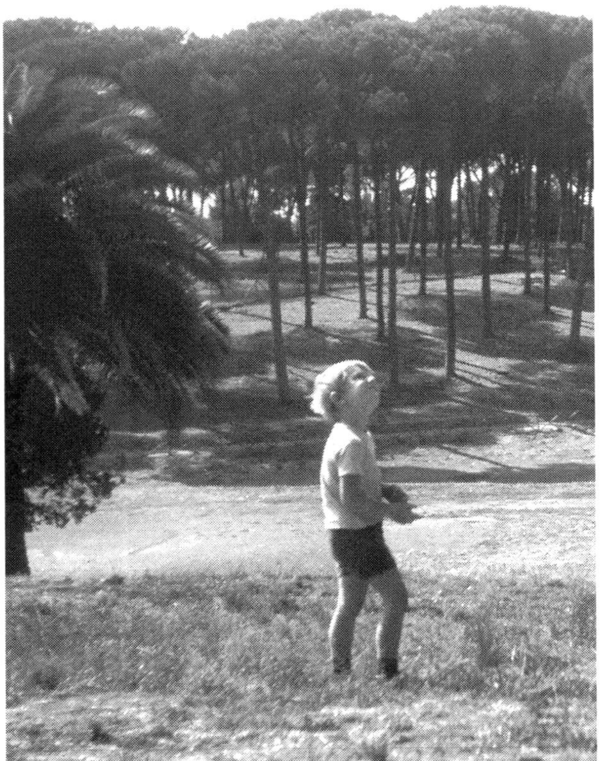

Eric in Villa Savoia

On quite the opposite side of all this glamour was the almost constant struggle with illness. It started with Steve's birth. I'll shift to the account of his arrival. Although Rome didn't offer quite the bizarre flavors and practices that marked our life in Sardinia, there were also a few other notable episodes that catch bits of the culture we experienced at that time.

A Valentine's Day Delivery

In the small hours of February 14, 1960, I suddenly wake up, realizing that one Steven Paulson—son number two—is on his way. Now comes the test: Bel and I speeding as fast as possible across the seven hills of Rome from the far northwest corner of the city where we live to a hospital in the far southwest. Fully aware of the torturous traffic and obstructions we'd probably encounter, we had made several dry runs. Using our best route, it took us nearly an hour, bumping into construction barricades, dead ends, and one-way streets that looped in circles. Not good when we'll need to get to the hospital fast for the delivery of a second baby!

The ancient gods are with us, though, because it's happening at 3:00 a.m. and not during midday gridlock. Bel phones the doctor, I grab my bag and leap (lumber) to the car. The streets are completely empty, and in fifteen minutes flat, we're zooming up the Gianicolo hill to arrive at Salvator Mundi International Hospital. It's an eerie sensation to be careening through all the great piazzas, past the fountains and well-known monuments of the Eternal City, feeling that we're the sole inhabitants. At that hour we *own* Rome. We make no stops, since all the red lights are switched off after midnight.

Quickly I'm rushed to the delivery room, but there's no sign of Professor Mittiga, my obstetrician. The midwife and assisting Swiss nun assure me they're very well qualified, but nevertheless they instruct me to "go easy and not push" until the doctor arrives. Finally he sails in, strips to his undershirt, and whips on a white butcher's apron. The midwife has been offering occasional whiffs of gas, but I'm convinced that this does nothing but give the patient something to do. Italian births are definitely natural. With no restrictions, Bel hovers just outside the delivery room to hear all the commotion and Stevie's first yell when he clocks in at 5:12 a.m. Very different from Eric's birth in Chicago three years earlier, when fathers were relegated to a remote lounge and could only view their new offspring through glass—for a week after the birth. He's enormously relieved not to have had to officiate at a back-seat delivery.

We're thrilled to inspect immediately our small, spiky-haired valentine, and I proudly note that I beat the queen: Elizabeth's Prince Andrew was due a day earlier, an event anticipated in all the Italian papers, and he has yet to make an appearance. Stevie's arrival gets a squib in the Rome *Daily American.*

Six days later, when we're to bring him home, Eric rushes out to the driveway to see if we're arriving. When we carry Stevie in, bundled in blankets and cap against the winter cold, Eric beams with excitement and demands that we "open it up" to see the prize therein. He pats the soft hair and exclaims, "Feel his soft fur, just like a little puppy!" It's the beginning of a lifelong relationship of (mostly) remarkable mutual affection and compatibility.

We find that Italian doctors have rather different ideas about feeding babies. Instead of pushing solid foods as soon as possible, our pediatrician prefers that Stevie have only milk for the first three months, and preferably six. He also doesn't advise giving vitamins—big in the States.

The Jinx Is Upon Us

Now the fun begins. For openers, within a month of Stevie's arrival, he develops an innocuous-looking bump on his tummy. It turns out to be a virulent staph infection, apparently—we learn later—contracted from the head baby nurse. I promptly catch the bacterium through nursing and begin to have a full-blown recurrence of the nasty boils that had plagued me in Sardinia.

For the next year, I struggle with deep, painful abscesses that have to be drained and excised. There seems to be no end in sight, and at one point, I'm hauled off to the hospital with a high fever, excruciating pain, and delirium. Stevie must stop nursing abruptly, and Bel scrambles to learn about bottle feeding. I reject the formula the pediatrician advises—mostly water and sugar—to insist on half milk and half water. But then Bel has to go off urgently to Germany for a week on his UN job. In desperation, he throws our dilemma out to our church congregation. Immediately two separate families step forward and take the kids for a week. Then my mother jumps to the rescue and flies over on three days notice to join Bel and our daytime helper in handling the household.

Things gradually look up, although I'm a regular customer at the hospital off and on for the next year as doctors operate and try one experimental medication or vaccine after another. At this time, there is no known remedy for staph infections, and nothing works for me.

Exotic Ailments

We become very well acquainted with our pediatrician, who makes house calls. While Eric suffers with chronic bronchitis and agonizing earaches, Dr. Bachetta also diagnoses him with rickets and says he may need leg braces. For two years, he does wear specially made shoes with lifts. We then begin to wonder about Stevie's bulging abdomen; apparently he has an enlarged liver, resulting in splayed ribs and the fat tummy. The verdict is a calcium deficiency and inability to assimilate vitamin D, which has led to a softening of the bones—so he, too, may have rickets. Our ever-zealous doctor finally announces that both kids suffer from functional heart murmurs.

Upon leaving Italy, both Eric and Stevie bloom immediately with good health. I'm not sure whether all this (and my staph) says something about an esoteric Italian medical profession in a certain era, or just that Italy is an inhospitable ambience for some foreigners.

Where We Live

Gigantic umbrella pines tower around our quiet neighborhood, singing with the soft sirocco, the hot wind blowing up from the Libyan desert. The ping of tennis balls starts around 6:00 a.m. in the courts next door, giving a year-round holiday atmosphere. Our four-bedroom, ground-floor apartment opens onto a garden, with a riot of acacia and oleander, marguerites, jasmine, roses, hydrangeas, and dahlias (and weeds). It's a great place for soaking up the sun if we don't mind passers-by peering curiously at us through the iron grating.

After Sardinia, we feel highly civilized. True, we can't eliminate the daily treks to the market, laundry is all by hand, the oven holds just one cake tin, there's no hot water in the kitchen, and there's no drinking water except in the kitchen. We don't expect American amenities, though, and even after six months, I still get goose bumps careening through the mad traffic on some homely errand, catching on the way the lush gardens of the Villa Borghese with its pools and kids crowded around the Punch and Judy show or riding the donkey carts; young, black-robed priests hurrying past the shooting fountains in the piazza at Saint Peter's; the Colosseum, where Eric always insists the lions are still caged. All this on my way to the UN commissary or the camera store.

Every day I wheel Stevie's carriage to the nearby Villa Savoia, the vast estate of former kings; Eric kicks his soccer ball there with his friends or Bel. We're a block from the Priscilla Catacombs, with its stacked skulls and maze of blackened passageways deep underground, where persecuted Christians hid from the Romans. At every turn, there's the rich juxtaposition of the new and trendy with clear remnants of the very old.

Displaying One's Vehicle Confers the Ultimate Prestige

A momentous occasion: our *portiere* (building concierge) has just acquired a car, and it's hard to imagine anyone prouder. It's a tiny, antique Fiat that he probably bought for $100, with the steering wheel on the "wrong" side (it's on the right in this left side country), and other anomalies. But each day he's out there with all the other privileged car owners, carefully going over his treasure—first with a feather duster, and then lovingly sponging it down and polishing every inch of the battered body, even though the shine has long since gone. This seems to be the great

Roman pastime because acquiring a car is still such a prestige thing. Cars are not the necessity they are in America, and our second-hand Hillman never gets washed except when it goes to the garage for a grease job.

One day I see the ultimate in this ritual. Many vehicles have plastic covers that are put on for protection whenever the car is not in use. One fellow was spending an hour painstakingly washing his cover, not just his car.

It's not just cars, though. I go to the park and see a young mother teetering on high heels and dressed to the teeth pushing her baby who is outfitted in pristine white, as they all are, in a super-deluxe carriage. Buried under the luxurious blankets covering the little white bundle is a transistor radio blaring the latest rock and roll. Even the poorest Romans (like our helper, Letizia), must make a *bella figura* (an elegant impression) by splurging on a baby carriage for $160. We found our well-worn hand-me-down through the commissary exchange.

The same mentality is evident when we invite some of Eric's Italian schoolmates over to play. They all rush to the garden and Eric immediately shimmies up our tall acacia tree. The little boys stare in bewilderment and envy. Because they never appear outside except in their spotless, Sunday-best clothes, they've never been allowed to touch dirt or climb trees and haven't the faintest notion how to begin.

Another cultural difference is the apathy and cunning found everywhere in Italy. People tend to move slowly and take forever to complete jobs—for instance, in construction. Outmaneuvering is possible every time there is a fluid money transaction, as in bargaining. Vendors try to fleece us, taking advantage of dumb foreigners. We have to be alert to stay ahead of clever ploys, and we've gotten pretty good at this—at least we believe we're good at it. The calculating, dickering, challenging give-and-take happens seamlessly, automatically, with pleasant surface demeanors. Each player knows the game, the part he or she plays, and the conclusion is usually a satisfying draw for both. At least we Americans feel that's what has happened, although maybe we've really been bested in the end by practitioners of the bargaining game who have been at it far longer than we.

This is the kind of dance performed every time we try to agree on the cost of renting an apartment and how much of the utilities bill we'll be responsible for. When we call them on obvious extortion, they grudgingly admire our savvy just as we can admire their cleverness. It's all part of the charming, exhilarating interaction we've learned to enjoy. We can appreciate all sides of the Italians we come in contact with.

My Roman Romeo

Amidst all the trauma of the various ailments that have plagued us during our first year in Rome, there's one light and amusing note. Before he became my doctor to deal with the staph abscesses, I'd heard fabulous tales about Dr. DeStefano, the most brilliant surgeon in Italy. He's just been made "professor" at age forty and is also the most eligible bachelor in town. He has the effect of causing every woman who sees him to swoon. He looks the part, too; he's tall and dark, with sooty bedroom eyes, and, of course, he waves around a monstrous cigarette holder with flip arrogance.

Our relationship has always been strictly professional. One day, though, I show up at the hospital with a new Bridget Bardot-like hairdo—trying to cheer myself up after months of grueling pain and surgeries. Dr. DeStefano notices immediately and uncharacteristically starts asking a number of personal questions. I should begin to smell a rat, but since he's always rather glib and kidding, I imagine it's just more of the same.

After examining my wounds, he asks me to wait, and at that point, I notice that, mysteriously, all the sisters have disappeared from this wing of the hospital. He steps back into the room, swiftly turns the key in the lock with one hand, and yanks down the window shade with the other. Before I have an inkling of what's happening, he sweeps me into his arms in a deft Latin embrace. My first reaction is to haul off and slug him. Then I realize it's a tricky situation: if he gets mad, he could send an outrageous bill and we'd be completely helpless.

Gradually I get disentangled and laugh off his "You weren't disappointed were you?" with a little spiel about the difference between American and Italian women. We do a lot of "playing" before marriage, I explain, but generally calm down afterward. Here, however, a man hesitates to touch a virgin. Except in dolce vita circles, girls are protected and inviolable, but once married, no holds are barred. They're fair game, and more often than not, they respond. I'm sure that this little clinch, if allowed to continue, in another five minutes would have ended us up on the examining table.

Driving home, my astonishment and indignation give way to amusement and even gratitude. For so long, I've felt myself totally unattractive with all my boils and bandages—and then suddenly I'm viewed as a desirable female. Bel sees the humor in the episode, too, and looks forward to hearing about my latest adventures after every visit. And there are indeed repetitions or attempts. We keep hearing of other similar incidents, some even involving the nuns. Where but in Italy!

Royalty up Close, If Not Personal

"Pussy Cat, Pussy Cat, where have you been?" might be our theme for the week, what with the royal visitors from Great Britain. Queen Elizabeth and her husband, Prince Philip, are in town for a state visit, and Rome is completely disrupted by the event. A tremendous cortege accompanies every move of the queen and prince. Each street I set out to take turns out to be blocked by cordons of police, creatures in plumed centurion helmets flashing in the sun, or by officious motorcycle brigades. The cavalry, foot soldiers, and costumed, trumpeting heralds complete the escort.

The day of their arrival, Eric and I are also bitten by royal fever and go down to the piazza at the Colosseum, where the couple is to pass and supposedly stop for brief ceremonies on a draped velvet stand. Long streams of Cadillacs, Mercedes Benzes, and the official, dark-blue Italian Fiats roll up, and diplomats jump out (including sandaled Africans in bright togas) and rush to the stand. It turns out, though, that the royals will not stop, and at the change of plan, the diplomats leap back into their cars and zoom off, ladies clutching their new hats. Motorcycles roar up and down the front lines of the crowds to keep them back, trying to run over the toes of anyone two inches out in front (to the terror of the children). Actually, when the open car finally heaves into view (preceded by a helicopter and squadrons of jets almost clipping the Colosseum), I'm so nervously occupied with trying to find the car in my camera viewfinder that I never do see anything but the backs of the royal heads.

As the crowd breaks up, we go to watch the many military regiments, each with its own band playing. Eric is fascinated by the drumbeats and everyone marching in step, displaying an armory of pistols and rifles with fixed bayonets. He's especially thrilled when a couple of colorful soldiers reach down to pat him on the head.

Frustrated at not getting a really good look at the queen, I decide to try again next day. Eric and I buzz off to the Campidoglio (the town hall), where the mayor is to receive the visitors and present them with a wolf statuette (Romulus and Remus). We arrive an hour early and jockey for a prime spot about ten feet from where Elizabeth and Philip are to descend from the car. We actually have to stand for two hours, but Eric is game and stays interested in everything.

One of the most interesting things is watching some two hundred large cars drive up and let out the cream of Roman high society—nearly all chauffeured—who are invited to the ceremony. It's a real fashion show, with most of the ladies in mink stoles and elegant costumes of brocade, chiffon, and silk. This time we get a fine view of the queen, at a distance of just a few feet. She's very lovely, which I had never realized from her pictures. Her porcelain skin is immaculately made up, and she's wearing a light blue brocade *redingote* (a thin, open coat) with matching high, net hat. They climb out, the duke towering over a foot above her. The speeches are conveyed by loudspeaker—hers and the mayor's—in their respective languages. Elizabeth smiles, waves, and accepts flower bouquets before the couple circles the piazza, standing up in the car for all to see.

The Italians, still frustrated monarchists at heart (the monarchy was officially abolished after World War II when Italy became a republic), have played it all up prominently in the papers. For example, they've devoted long articles to the controversy among the noble ladies who complained at being told they couldn't wear their tiaras to the opera when the queen was attending—probably because they would be seen as competing with her.

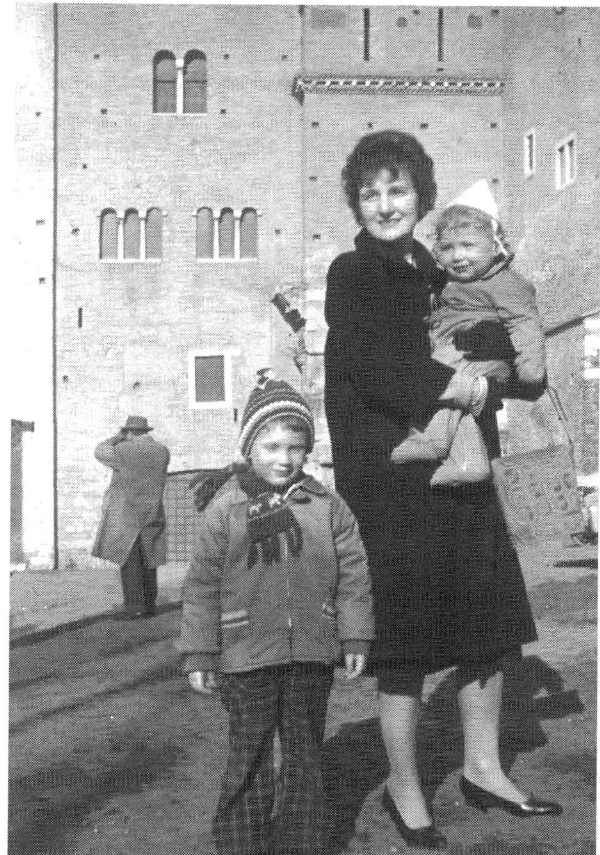

Lisa and the boys in Rome

The next day I waste an entire morning driving to the FAO (Food and Agriculture Organization under the UN) commissary to shop, only to find that the police have shut the gates because Philip is about to appear for an inspection. Then I'm off to collect some publications from the British Consulate and discover they're closed for the day because all British subjects are invited to a royal reception. Then I nearly burn up the car gunning it endlessly on the hill at Via Quattro Fontane while trapped in traffic that is heading for the Palazzo Barbarini for yet another shindig for the queen.

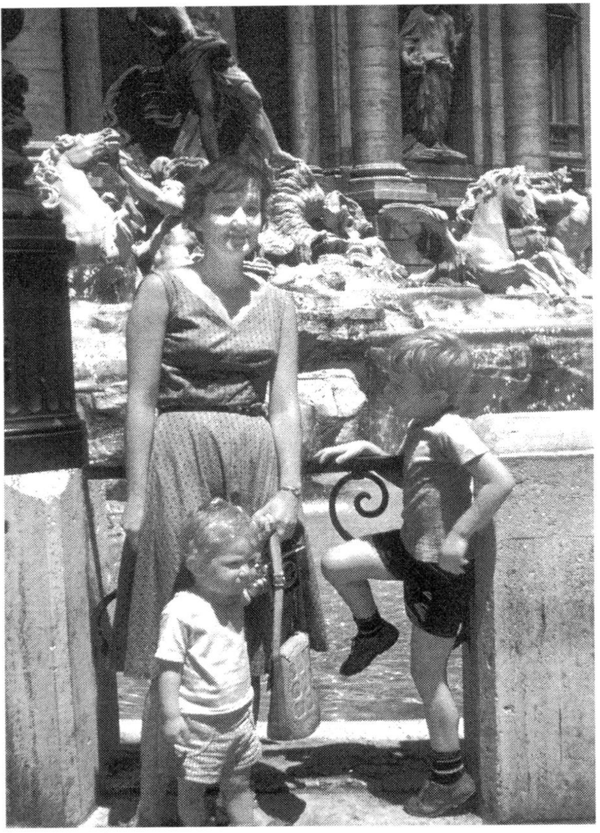

We toss coins in the Trevi Fountain to assure our return to Rome.

Our AP correspondent friend, Gene Levine, has had to follow the queen wherever she goes but mostly only gets to talk to her press representatives. He says it's the kind of assignment they all hate. There's very little to write up, especially when so much else of greater importance is going on in the world, yet such a visit can't be ignored. And Rome really laps it up.

The day after, feeling a bit breathless and weary after all the confusion, I escape to the acres of rose gardens on the Aventine Hill. Through ancient trellises and arbors heavy with perfumed blossoms loom the distant Palatine ruins. As I wander up the narrow streets, high, vine-covered walls blot out all the nearby traffic, and the only sound is an old man scything roadside poppies and grasses. Scuffing quietly along in the dust, I come upon a tiny park whose tall, thick pines and cool, splashing fountains shut away the burning sun. As Eric would say, "God makes some very lovely things, doesn't he!"

Then faint sounds of music draw me next door to the loveliest Roman church yet, Santa Sabina. Light shafts in through the leaded windows onto a white-clad Dominican father who, alone in the nave, is thundering joyously to the heavens on his organ. I may come back this evening for a special Eucharist Mass with a procession and singing by the monks.

Bel's Job Challenges

This is a book primarily about the impressions and idiosyncracies of the places we've traveled to or lived in around the world, so I'm not including many details about Bel's work. But the reason we are here in Rome, of course, is that the UN officials were so impressed by the project Bel and Don Murray created in Sardinia—the almost miraculous turnaround of the refugees' attitudes and capabilities—that they hired Bel to attempt this kind of solution on a broader scale on the Italian mainland.

Much was accomplished in the camp clearance operation with the UN and Italian government. However, it has been something of a shock for Bel to leave a project that he crafted and directed with a free hand for two years and then find the project's innovation reined in. There are some petty jealousies, and colleagues of the successor organization find it difficult to grasp the thinking patterns of the refugees who have been stagnating for years in the camps.

The new directors of The Homeless European Land Program (HELP) in Sardinia are rightly trying to push the refugees into a cooperative model where they will have a chance to train and work up to positions of responsibility and eventually share in the profits of the various businesses. But a model is required that understands that there are different categories of refugees. Some feel capable of going out on their own and handling their own decisions, while others find it's safer to work for someone else, to be told what to do and earn a secure daily wage. To be successful, the project has to accommodate both types. Although Bel has come to feel close to them and knows them very well, he no longer is running the operation and needs to stay out of the way. In any event, HELP has provided a new, self-sufficient life for a number of refugees, and has provided a model welcomed by policymakers.

Reflections

The Rome chapter is finished now, and the nostalgia is a sweet, sad ache. The color, vitality, apathy, crudeness, elegance, beauty, dirt, and historic majesty are uniquely irresistible, and even the trickery and inefficiency we could overlook with a smile once we learned how to match wits with the Italians in their own games. Forests of superb pines within a great city, fountains that are thundering geysers or delicate sprays in every piazza—only in Rome!

In fall 1961, I flew back to the United States with the two boys while Bel stayed on in Italy for several more months. With his UN job finished, he knew it was time to complete the PhD, and he'd decided to write it on the volatile political situation in Italy. He holed up in an Irish Augustinian monastery in Genazzano, a hill town southeast of Rome where he'd made friends with the former secretary of the local Communist Party. Genazzano was Italy's most communist-voting village. Together, Bel and Athos Ricci, the former secretary now turned poet-philosopher roamed the village and countryside with a tape recorder. They talked with the full spectrum of citizens, from the communist mayor and his functionaries to Christian democrats, the priest, wine growers in their fields, school teachers, old fascists long out of favor, and some of the original, proud aristocracy.

There followed nearly a year of transcribing and translating tapes back in America, which led to the PhD dissertation and a book on Italian communism, *The Searchers.* Bel then joined the University of Wisconsin at Milwaukee, teaching political science and helping to shape the first Peace Corps groups. A joint assignment to represent the university in a major field research project took him to Brazil for short stints, and five years later Brazil would become our family's next big overseas adventure.

Fishermen drag their jangada *out of the surf; they sail for up to a week at sea on this raft.*

Brazil
Of Spies and Spirits

October 1967-August 1968

Backstory

In fall 1962, our family of four moved to the American Midwest. Having balanced the offer of a job with the US government's Latin American aid program against a chance to combine fieldwork abroad with teaching at a prestigious university, Bel chose the University of Wisconsin.

While we were still in Italy, Senator Hubert Humphrey had followed our Sardinia project and had become very interested in this solution for the larger problem of refugees still in the camps. He kept in touch, and when Bel was finishing his stint with the UN in Rome and looking for his next move, Humphrey told him he should think about getting involved with the new Alliance For Progress. Its first big project was to be in Northeast Brazil because this was the hot spot in South America. It was where revolutionary ferment was beginning to boil up, with the Peasant Leagues and worker-priests leading the charge. President Kennedy was worried about Brazil going communist and, of course, this was one of the largest and most influential countries in Latin America.

Humphrey thought Bel's connection with communism—having done the research in the communist village of Genazzano after leaving the UN—would translate well in applying this kind of inside knowledge to the situation developing in Brazil.

It is reported that Humphrey's keen interest in our example of sending American volunteers to a need in Sardinia led to his helping create the Peace Corps.

When Bel returned to the United States in 1961, Humphrey arranged for him to talk with the new director of the Alliance in Washington who was overseeing a program in Northeast Brazil. Bel weighed this job against the last-minute offer to teach at the University of Wisconsin. One reason he chose the latter, but not the most important, was that because he had always worked as a semi-volunteer, the government had to place him at the lowest end of the pay scale.

He secured an assignment to teach in the political science department of the university's Milwaukee campus, but he was especially enticed by a joint appointment with statewide University Extension. There he could bring his Italy experience to Brazil.

Soon after he was hired, Bel was off to Rio de Janeiro for an international conference. Then he was awarded a grant to assemble a research team for the following summer in Northeast Brazil. The Northeast is a sprawling, drought-ridden region, a kind of raw frontier, that, at the time, was restless with revolutionary fervor. Most of its daunting problems stemmed from the vast chasm between the very rich and the very poor.

Plans for a more extensive research project in Brazil were not to materialize for another five years, during which time Bel concentrated on consolidating his position as a professor—teaching, publishing his book on Italian communism, *The Searchers*, and organizing an array of projects dealing with poverty and racism in inner city Milwaukee.

Meanwhile, I was going through major culture shock. For most of the past decade, I had lived abroad on the front lines of unbelievably exciting, cosmopolitan adventures. I had been a day-to-day partner with Bel in much of his hands-on work with bombed-out Neapolitans and Iron Curtain escapees. Our life in Rome during his two years with the United Nations was definitely exhilarating. Then, suddenly, I was a suburban American housewife with two little kids while Bel was out struggling with the university bureaucracy and securing a toehold on the academic ladder.

I was not part of his work life except when I hosted some of the gargantuan and often out-of-control cocktail parties that were de rigueur in the uninhibited 1960s. I was involved with Steve's nursery school and jumped into the Milwaukee arts scene: I played cello in the Civic Orchestra, studied painting, and organized a modern dance class for faculty women. But even though we bought a house after a couple of years and I spent time helping polish Bel's book, I was restless. Where was that heart-pounding, life-on-the-edge existence that had fed both Bel and me as a team, which had brought us together? Where was the fundamental meaning in my life? I was going through an acute identity crisis.

Then, in 1967, came a social science research grant for a year in Brazil. This is what we'd been waiting for; all four of us welcomed this chance to leap once again into the unknown, the exotic. We rented our Milwaukee house and happily flew off south of the equator. Eric had just turned eleven, and Steve was seven.

Marathon Flights

Getting to Northeast Brazil is a grueling trip—via Trinidad, Caracas, and then Belém at the mouth of the Amazon River in northern Brazil. All of our takeoffs and arrivals have been between 11:00 p.m. and 5:00 a.m. With a mountain of hand luggage (tape recorder, typewriter, briefcases, innumerable small satchels), all four of us have to be ready to jump to "battle stations" whenever we move, each to his/her assigned three or four pieces. It's a chore when Steve has to be dragged from a deep sleep at 3:00 a.m. to shoulder his share and march for twenty minutes across a jungle landing strip in Belém and then stand in line for an hour at customs while all the bags are opened. At one point, Eric staggers into a dark street, sits down on the suitcase he's carrying, and falls sound asleep, barely to be rescued from a bus careening around the corner.

We circle Fortaleza in the state of Ceará. It's on top of the bulge, some five hundred miles east of Belém. As we dip down, we're struck by the wide, empty, white beaches fronting the Atlantic Ocean, which stretch as far as we can see. They dwarf the little knots of buildings that comprise what is considered a major city in Northeast Brazil, our home for the next year.

Then reality sets in. No one meets us, so we proceed on our own to Rua Silva Paulet. A phone call summons the landlady, who comes to hand us the key to our house, wishes us luck, and retreats hastily. It seems the place has been empty for several months, which here is an open invitation for vandals to climb in and carry off anything of interest. Our large, airy, "furnished" house is nearly bare of furniture.

Camping Out

Thus commences our "camping" adventure. For nearly a week, and then sporadically for the next three months, there is no water except for one faucet in the garden; the plumbing doesn't function, so we haul buckets upstairs. There's no electricity, and with every gust of wind, the sockets shoot flames and the ceiling fixtures crackle and spit fire. It takes three crews five days to get the refrigerator going. It's a bit disconcerting to discover that when the water finally does arrive, the contents of the toilet, when flushed, whoosh by under the shower and sit there two inches below the gaping tiles. The whole side of the shower was knocked open to the outdoors to repair a pipe and never filled in. We have trustingly assumed that sewage is eventually carried off to sea or wherever, but alas, we find that each house has a pit dug beneath, and when this overflows, you just dig another.

Another interesting aspect, which especially delights the boys, is the wildlife. The pleasantest visitors are the small lizards that zip over the walls and ceilings like lightning. There are magnificent, four-inch flying cockroaches found everywhere, but they have a special affinity for the kitchen and bathroom—the breadbox, the shower, and on our toothbrushes. Ants appear in troops when the signal goes out that a feast is in the offing; I even found a swarm of tiny ones in our bed. Then there are the bats. Every time we leave a window open at night, we hear them chattering, and one will swoop in and dart all over the house.

One night, as we're busy herding some aggressive cockroaches out the front door, Steve shrieks, "Quick, shut it before the bat gets in!" One day a seven-inch tarantula appears on the kitchen ceiling, sitting harmlessly enough, but Bel dispatches it with a broom. All such visitors diminish temporarily after a heavy spraying by the public pest agency, even the nightly mosquitoes. When this happens, we must move all furniture, food, clothing, and pots outside and stay away for most of the day.

We're trying not to show too much culture shock by the household inconveniences we think must be normal. But both Brazilians and Americans we meet are horrified at our trials and say we must leave immediately. A suggestion to our landlady that we're about to move proves to be the magic word, and next day we're besieged by an army of plumbers who pull out the ancient, rusty pipes, and the ailing toilet is tossed out a window. In its place is a sleek cement number, its innards neatly and forever sealed from view within the wall. All that is visible is a pristine white button, and we tremble to think how things would be repaired now; there's no way even to reach into the fetid tank to wiggle the float by hand.

The entire interior is now being painted, the electricity has been ingeniously patched up by a Peace Corps handyman, lamps have been made of large wine jugs, and a makeshift couch has been constructed with an excelsior-filled mattress. Things are much calmer, and we're able to start "living" and enjoying some of the really delightful aspects of Brazil. Precautions—boiling and then filtering drinking water, washing all vegetables and fruits in bleach, never walking around the house or yard barefoot—soon become second nature.

The "Early Symphony" and Driving Etiquette

One loses track of such regulatory devices as calendars and clocks. I have yet to see a clock anywhere in the city, but there must be some primitive mystique that enables certain rituals, like garbage collections, to occur with frightening punctuality. Before 5:00 a.m., the "Early Symphony" is well into the development section with simple motifs overlapping now in contrapuntal crescendo. Certain neighborhood canines have been vocal most of the night, but an abundance of roosters are poised to announce the rising sun at 4:30. The dogs begin conversing in earnest. The people next door have just acquired a black lamb that complains continually and adds to the chorus.

Across the street, wandering among ornate fountains and shining tropical foliage, is a princely billy goat that responds hoarsely to the plebeian bleats of his kin. Next, a procession of squeaking, creaking, two-wheeled carts jounces over the cobblestones, drivers whipping their donkeys into vocal protest as they jockey for first crack at the customers with a bit of produce from the country. Barefoot boys lope past hawking giant red snappers carried on sticks across their shoulders where only the remembrance of a shirt flaps in faded strips.

Driving in Brazil requires a special note. Almost none of the regulations we know seem to exist here; even signaling is rare. Climbing into your car is rather like taking off in one of those little bumper cars in amusement parks: you just go, anywhere, at any speed, seldom stopping, regardless of other traffic around you. The roads have no divider lines; some are as wide as a six-lane highway, others are narrow. Most roads outside the downtown area are so badly cobbled that it's like bouncing over a dry creek bed; heavy treads, like snow tires, are necessary.

If an approaching vehicle suddenly veers over into your lane, you calmly adapt to its British penchant and switch to your left also, and nobody panics. When you want to pull up in front of a house on the left side, you simply duck over and stop, pointing in the opposite direction; to stop across the street (in front of someone else's house) might be quite suspicious.

We've discovered that there is a definite pecking order in the vehicular realm; size has a good deal to do with right-of-way. (We bought a 1963 *rural*, like a safari truck, meaning a vehicle meant for rough roads.) Little Volkswagens defer to the larger sedans (of which there are few), which in turn respect the jeeps and *rurais.* It's not that the smaller car owners have any humanitarian feeling in letting the larger ones pass, but they know if they don't, they will shortly be squashed. So we lordly ones just lean on the horn at each intersection and step on the gas.

The Rest of Our Household

An assortment of vendors, beggars, and would-be maids pass by the house continually. Instead of doorbells, here they use the Chinese custom of clapping outside your gate. We spent a couple of weeks interviewing household helper prospects (some obviously with active TB—one pretty girl with a bad cough got down on her knees weeping that if I couldn't hire her, she'd just go back to the interior and die; I arranged for her to go to the city lung specialist, but heard nothing further). I settle on Maria, a fine young Indian woman from the *sertão*, the dry interior region (see the Glossary for the definition of Portuguese words used in this chapter). She is totally illiterate. We pay her $12 a month, generous by local standards.

The sixth member of the household is Mishki, a three-month-old mutt who pads around like a young lion cub. It's good to have a watchdog, they say, though we're safer than most because the general/governor for the entire region lives next door. The moon glances off two helmets and bayonet rifles as the general's guards saunter up and down all night. Eight more guards are parked inside the house with two submachine guns. Down the road, leaning their kitchen chairs against the governor's pink wall, are three soldiers. Despite such military displays and talk of ferment (mostly in American magazines), revolution seems a long way from Fortaleza. Life continues as it has for decades, as far as we can tell, with the very rich living it up with extravagant parties, luxury purchases, and multiple servants, while they take advantage of the poor who are too used to subservience to object.

The only unrest since we came was in the first week when some medical students got angry at the conservative statements of their professor and next day boycotted his class. He gave a test and gave all the absentees zero, and they started a small riot, demonstrating and shouting "Down with all reactionaries!" (Brazilians, Yankees, and AID, the US assistance program). The cops arrived and started hosing the insurgents, at which point some of the students leaped onto a roof and threw down some tiles. One hit the policeman wielding the hose; he dropped the hose and it twisted, knocking down all his fellow lawmen. Everybody went home and felt better.

Getting in the Swing of It

The boys have adapted well. They walk to an English-speaking school run by Baptist missionaries. We might have preferred a Brazilian one, but their school year begins in March, which proves too confusing. At the Baptist school, the teaching is excellent, and six to a class would be hard to beat.

The climate is fantastic. Though plenty hot at noon, the temperature rarely climbs above 85 degrees. By 3:00 p.m., the sun is already dropping and it's too chilly for the beach. A sheet is sufficient for sleeping; it may fall to 72. It's most pleasant to step out onto one of the upper balconies outside our bedroom and lie in the hammock, watching the full moon glint off the shiny palm fronds rattling gently. Or to lean over the back balcony while drying off from a shower and feel I'm in an isolated tree house. A giant cashew tree cuts off sight of everything below, and massive tangles of bougainvillea and other assorted flowering trees create a veritable jungle.

The ocean is omnipresent, magnificent beaches abound, and it's only a question of finding time to go. At low tide, the waves are perfect for jumping; at high tide, they can be overwhelming. One Sunday, we go for an outing to a remote village with a group of Brazilians and Americans. There's fine swimming in a warm green sea, climbing over the *jangadas*—fishing rafts with sails—parked along the shore, and then we explore the towering dunes that stretch off and out of sight.

One evening we're invited by Bel's university professors, all Brazilian, to a party in the country, a *luarada*, or celebration of the full moon. Everyone goes a little mad in the balmy air, the great white globe sailing in and out of cloud wisps. Whiskey and coconut "water" flow, exotic dishes are produced, the red ants bite, and by 4:00 a.m., most of the guests have ended up in the swimming pool.

Bel has developed a good relationship with the Institute of Anthropology of the University of Ceará through its director, Professor Luis Fontenelle, whom we had met in Wisconsin the year before. Bel has recruited six student research assistants to help

A broken arm doesn't impede Steve's sporting life: soccer, jumping the waves at the beach, or catching bugs.

conduct interviews throughout the state and to compile the resulting political and economic data. Some are upper class and have special access to political machinations on this level (they move in the same social circles as some of the power brokers), while others are more interested in and adept at penetrating the poorer strata. With their work, Bel hopes to obtain a good overview and then will concentrate on getting to know key people in depth himself.

More and more Bel sees that Fortaleza is the real center of power for the entire state; the big plantation owners tend to live here, and the lesser potentates in the villages usually don't have final say. Suspicion, scorn, and hostility are felt toward Americans in varying degrees. Brazilians, generally, tend to have conflicting feelings of national pride and frustrated inferiority vis à vis their influential northern neighbor; they often believe they're being manipulated and exploited by the United States. Some people who have been here for a long time see this hostility increasing, though so far, beyond a faint mockery, animosity is seldom shown openly toward individuals.

Bel's aim is to align himself primarily with Brazilians, especially those at the Institute, who have no contact with the American community (this latter consists mainly of professors hired in the USAID government program for agricultural assistance). He has started a weekly graduate seminar, trying to stimulate interest in creating a political science department here where none now exists.

Bel Is Admired as a Real "Revolutionary"

After three months of listening to a new language, a subtle miracle occurs and we find that, all of a sudden, we can understand most of what is directed at us. Our own fluency is improving considerably, if not our grammar. The boys are picking up some vocabulary and enjoy testing it on the Brazilian kids across the street.

Now, in late December, three degrees below the equator, it should be summer, (i.e., the rainy, hot season, versus winter, which starts in May when it's dry, windy, and slightly cooler). As yet, however, the rains haven't begun and people are worried that maybe this will be the year of the great *seca*. Every eight to ten years there is a total drought when it doesn't rain at all in the *sertão*, the desolate interior lands, and crops can't be planted. That's when the inhabitants pile into trucks by the thousands and migrate south to seek jobs and swell the slums of Rio and Sao Paulo. Thousands more stay in the Northeast and may starve to death. It's during the *seca* that politics operate wildly, with promises and manipulation of government relief funds and supplies.

Bel's research is set up and about ready to go. He meets daily with his six assistants at the Anthropology Institute, and together they've hammered out and pretested a forty-page questionnaire. Field trips to the interior to interview the important leadership in the state are next. The object of the research project will be to find out why the political system in Northeast Brazil doesn't do more to alleviate the starvation and poverty in this drought-prone area. One wonders why the local mayors don't allow the constructed reservoirs to be used for irrigation and food production. They tend to keep tight control of their fiefdoms, exercising power by perpetuating the plight of the poor.

By talking directly to all the social strata in the villages, Bel's team will attempt to identify facts—how the system really works—as a solid basis for encouraging economic development in the state.

Such field research is a new concept, at least in the field of political science. To illustrate the concept of "action" and applied research in his political science seminar at the Institute, Bel talks about his work in Italy and inner city Milwaukee. The students are incredulous; no one here gets into action of this type—research and academic respectability come with digging out material from libraries. Actually going out to talk to real people is suspect and often met with hostility. The students can't believe that Bel and Don Murray would set up a project as they did in Sardinia, and, craziest of all, would give away all the assets to fifteen refugees. And they really can't believe that Americans would want to help the black ghettos. As time goes on, though, these protégés (some of whom are Maoists—to the left of the communists) have come to believe that there are some North Americans who are even more "revolutionary" than they.

The Accidental Cellist

I happen to meet Orlando Leite, the gifted head of the local Conservatory of Music, and he says they need cellists badly; there is only one in the city. So one morning, on my way to market, I drop by to tell him I'll play there if they can scare up an instrument. The receptionist leaps up and exclaims that "everyone" has been waiting for me. She propels me into Orlando's office, and he immediately cancels the piano lesson he's giving and rushes me to the cellist, Hiram, who, in turn, dismisses his pupil. By this time, I'm definitely leery. They drag me to another room, thrust Hiram's cello into my hands, and say, "Play!" Actually, it's not that bad; they call in the first violinist and pianist and we launch into a Haydn trio that, fortunately, I know well. A few days later they scrounge up a battered cello—no easy feat in the Northeast—and it's delivered late one night.

So I'm deep in rehearsals once more: chamber music with the Conservatory staff, who are fine musicians, and with the local symphony. The latter has a way to go; mainly it's a collection of older men with few teeth. One is a giant Swiss, another an Italian from Rome. There's a fierce Armenian who stamps out after delivering an apoplectic tirade on how he'd be damned if he'll give up his precious Sunday for an extra performance. The atmosphere is casual. Players wander in up to a half hour after starting time, the concertmaster ambles around giving an "A" to each player, and if he thinks we're a hair off, he reaches down and twists our tuners.

Saga of the White Dress

My biggest challenge in the launch of my Brazilian musical career is managing to come up with the proper costume. I have four days to procure the required white dress for a hastily scheduled concert. So commences a wild marathon of racing back and forth between two dressmakers, pleading with one of them, Isolda, to make my outfit. She tries to brush me off because she's swamped with eighteen dresses to make for numerous *festas* before the weekend. If I buy the material, though, she says she'll at least cut it out. Next there's a merry-go-round chase fighting Christmas mobs in some twenty fabric shops before I find the right sateen. To more stores for the lining, and still more to locate a zipper. Back to Isolda, who grumps loudly, but eventually slashes out the dress—just by looking at me, no pattern needed. I'll have to find another dressmaker to actually make the dress, and end up with a friend of Maria. Chaguinha seems not to understand a word of my poor technical vocabulary as I explain what I want, and I leave with misgivings.

The next day, though, we go back to view the wreckage and find it's come out beautifully. We crowd into a tiny back room with half dozen curious neighbor women who've come, perhaps, to stare at my American undergarments. A number of chickens hop in from the courtyard, and several hundred flies hover lazily as Chaguinha pedals her machine, making adjustments. I rush back to Isolda's where she's to cut out a special collar. She chops it out, but refuses to sew it on, and hands it back. Panting, I hurry home to pick up Maria and we're off again to Chaguinha's in rush hour traffic, half an hour away.

The last straw is on the homeward lap when the car coughs to a halt. I get out and hike in the dark to the nearest gas station some five blocks away, collect a small boy to bring a container of gas, and commandeer a customer to drive us to the car. So ends the saga of the white dress, duly completed in time, at the cost of $1.75. Oh, yes, a slight anticlimax: when I go to the last rehearsal, Orlando announces that the concert is postponed until the following week. But it finally comes off, and the elegantly lacquered and coiffed high society files into the ancient, ornate José Alencar Theater. The orchestra manages, the singers are superb, and the bats swoop back and forth.

A Very Different Christmas "Service"

Our Christmas comes and goes with barely a flutter. Somehow it's hard to generate the proper spirit when little cheeks are flushed red, not from an afternoon of firing snowballs or snuggling around the Yule log but from the heat and sweat of the tennis court. Palm trees in the neighborhood are bravely festooned with colored lights, and a few Portuguese carols waft across the mimosas from the nearby Baptist church. Our own tree is a jaggy little dead branch in the front yard wrapped in foil and hung with dozens of glittery paper ornaments. A fine swim in the ocean and a starlit supper of lobster and barbecued filet at a waterfront café complete our agenda.

Perhaps the closest approximation of a Christmas church service is experienced when Bel and I attend a Macumba ceremony, the Northeast Brazil version of voodoo. We're invited by Raimunda, the Macumba leader, who, by day, is the maid of the former Peace Corps doctor.

We drive to Raimunda's *favela*, or slum settlement, not far from the beach, and park in deep, soft sand. It's an odd sensation to be in the midst of at least a hundred little huts, and yet there is no sound or light; electricity doesn't extend to this area. A sky full of stars illuminates white figures flitting in and out of doorways. It's totally silent except for the muffled thud of our footsteps.

We're ushered through a barricade where more white robes are assembling. Raimunda, a petite grandmother, appears. Suddenly here is no maid but a high priestess in sparkling silver crown, white harem pants, white sneakers, and a white satin, Batman-type cape embroidered with a shiny blue fish. As matriarch of the *favela*, she makes all major decisions and finds jobs for her "family." She commands complete allegiance.

Raimunda beckons us into the Macumba hut, and the door is locked behind us; it's forbidden for minors to watch. The room is less than twenty by thirty feet. Close rows of green and white pennants festoon the ceiling. A great, white standard stands in one corner, and pictures of the Madonna, Jesus, and the saints are pinned over the walls. The tiered altar is covered with blue satin and jammed with more statues of saints, from St. Francis to St. George on his horse. A number of fish are included. Whether this has to do with the early Christian symbol or the marine influence on these people, we can't figure. Macumba is a curious mix of Christianity and African beliefs and rituals; it reflects a blending of the Catholicism of Brazil's Portuguese settlers and the worship of multiple African deities brought by the slaves they imported.

"Spirits" at Work: Primal Instincts and Trances

Raimunda chalks a white star in the center of the dirt floor, then lights some twenty candles on the altar and sticks some into the corners and around the large "leaning pole" in the middle of the room. The participants begin to line up, three deep on one side, all in long, white satin or embroidered cotton skirts. Many are young women. Seven men take part, also in white, lining the opposite wall. The ceremony commences, curiously similar to parts of the Roman Catholic and Greek Orthodox Masses, with kneeling, crossing, clapping.

Raimunda, presiding at the altar, leads the chanting and singing, which begins simultaneously with the boys playing the bongo drums, shakers, and triangle stationed at the front. The voices sometimes pulsate with responsive Hail Marys, sometimes burst into wild hymns, and at times slide into the primitive West African Yoruba chants to which the Macumba is linked.

As each woman moves out, she lies flat on the floor and kisses the star. As soon as the music starts, the white figures start to jiggle and twitch in jerky, samba-like rhythms. The women roll and stagger around, falling against others who catch them or keep them from stumbling into lighted candles. Their heads are down, faces covered by mops of wild stringy hair that sweeps the dirt. An assistant priestess produces a pot of burning incense and goes around swinging it in everyone's face until the air is so thick we can barely see. Each participant rushes to inhale the smoke to get even dizzier.

Raimunda is waving and shouting her ritual at the altar, then invites the congregation, one by one, to come up to be blessed. They kneel before her, are embraced on each cheek, and then are twirled three times, moaning, jerking, and careening off, clutching and clinging to the center pole to regain equilibrium. When one woman goes into a deep, shuddering trance, Raimunda throws a bottle of perfume on her. From time to time, Raimunda sails out the door (for liquid fortification?), and finally brings the *cachaca* (rum) bottle back and plunks it down on the altar.

We leave after two hours, before the participants get really worked up, fall into trances, and pass out completely. They "work" almost through the entire night.

Bel—the New James Bond?

What has been settling into a somewhat calm, predictable, daily routine suddenly explodes into something entirely unexpected. Bel describes it in a letter back to the States:

> On January 6, I was denounced publicly in a major Brazilian leftist newspaper. The interview hit several other papers, including *Jornal do Brasil* (*The New York Times* of Brazil) when their editors smelled a possible scandal. I was attacked as an academic Goldfinger, weaving a sinister plot to deprive this country of some of its most precious natural resources—akin to "Camelot," the ill-fated CIA plan, several years earlier, to extract information or assert influence in Chile. It was starting in Ceará, they said, and would spread throughout Brazil, then probably through all of Latin America.
>
> What are these "natural" resources?? Information. What information? Data on how people live and behave politically. Why is this sinister? Because I am a North American, and at the moment, hysteria is sweeping Brazil about all things tainted with "Yankees." Why am I "stealing" Brazilian natural resources? Because, to date, no one here has been interested in doing a political study (there being extremely few political scientists), and now, suddenly, I seem to be grasping the jugular of certain social scientists who "have not had the opportunity" to study their own scenery.
>
> It started out as a simple assault on this threatening "American team." I should have had my "team" of wife and two children pose for sensational photos, but instead it was decided to photograph the six Brazilian students and one Brazilian professor who are associated with me. Larger ramifications soon developed. I found myself becoming a tool of university politics, the "outs" using me as fodder (attacking Americans is fashionable) for removing the director of the Institute of Anthropology where I am based.
>
> We soon discovered what's really going on behind the scenes. A disgruntled local communist was forced out of the Party two years ago and now is staking everything on becoming a true national hero. If he could attack and push me out, stop the research, attack the university and state government, and discredit them all, he could become the "man of the moment" for the Party. This was especially so because recently the annual Brazilian communist congress decreed that they'd had enough of the "go-slow", pro-Russian line and now it was time to try the Castro-Mao model.
>
> Now, almost two weeks have swept by. We are still here, and the house hasn't yet been blown up. Undoubtedly our next-door neighbor, the commanding general of the region, knows some of these details. The military stays in the shadows but swings a heavy stick at critical moments. One of these days we might also expect a call from some CIA agent or Department of State emissary from Rio checking out the nature of this

new "operation" in the Northeast they hadn't learned about through channels.

Meanwhile, as the revolutionary forces rattle their sabers outside, our peaceful research continues. My six students haven't quit yet, although for several days they were looking at me out of the corners of their eyes. The Institute people have urged me to "march ahead," so I ordered 25,000 sheets of paper for the questionnaire. It remains to be seen, of course, whether the deputies and other influential figures will talk. We don't know yet, either, how visible I can be in working directly—interviewing people—or whether I must restrict myself to working through others so that the faces are always Brazilian.

Every day brings new developments. The fellow who summoned the reporters to report the "CIA plot" is depicted in the papers as the head of the Institute of Anthropology when he was actually a minor research technician without a bachelor's degree. His brother, who was a guest at our house in Milwaukee two years earlier, was dismissed as acting director of the Institute when Fontenelle came in to assume the position. This chain of events accounts for the jealousy underlying an outwardly political issue.

It's interesting that the whistle-blower has well-publicized psychiatric problems; he's a loose cannon who has attacked the Peace Corps, the United States generally, and the military Brazilian government. When the Communist Party thought him a risk, they kicked him out, but now he's gotten the ear of the far-left militant students, and there is fear everywhere of some uncontrollable surge of violence.

Our Household Helpers

None of this has really had any bearing on our life on Rua Silva Paulet. Our neighbors and local tradespeople are friendly, our employees loyal.

I'll say a word about the three people working for us. Maria lives in and has turned out to be a remarkably able, intelligent, and enjoyable person to have around. I have to push her to take off even an occasional Sunday. Like thousands of others, her beginnings were rough. She grew up in the interior *sertão* with fifteen brothers and sisters. Her mother died when she was nine, and she then had to start working full time in the blistering fields picking rice, beans, and cotton. The almost-nonexistent wage she earned was turned over to her father, and she had to forage for her own clothes. None of the children was allowed to go to school. In 1958, the year of the great drought, she took her chances and traveled alone and terrified to Fortaleza (she was fifteen), and hired out as a maid. Her ambition all along has been to buy a sewing machine and begin to earn as a seamstress. Finally she's worked out a deal to buy a second-hand pedal type; she'll pay half now from what she's saved and the rest from future salary. We'll all go to get it in the jeep, a momentous occasion.

Didiza, a woman of about thirty, comes once a week to wash and iron, on a scrub board with bars of soap. She has two small daughters and no husband. As often happens among slum dwellers, young wives are abandoned as soon as the first child is weaned—i.e., when they become a burden. She lives in one of the many *favelas* ringing the city, in a tiny mud shack the size of a bathroom. Overjoyed when Maria rescues some large palm fronds pruned from the general's garden, she comes to get them with a donkey cart, and will use them to build a roof over the tin charcoal stove that is her kitchen.

The third member of the team is Pedro, a young man in his mid-twenties who comes every other afternoon. A near genius, he fixes everything

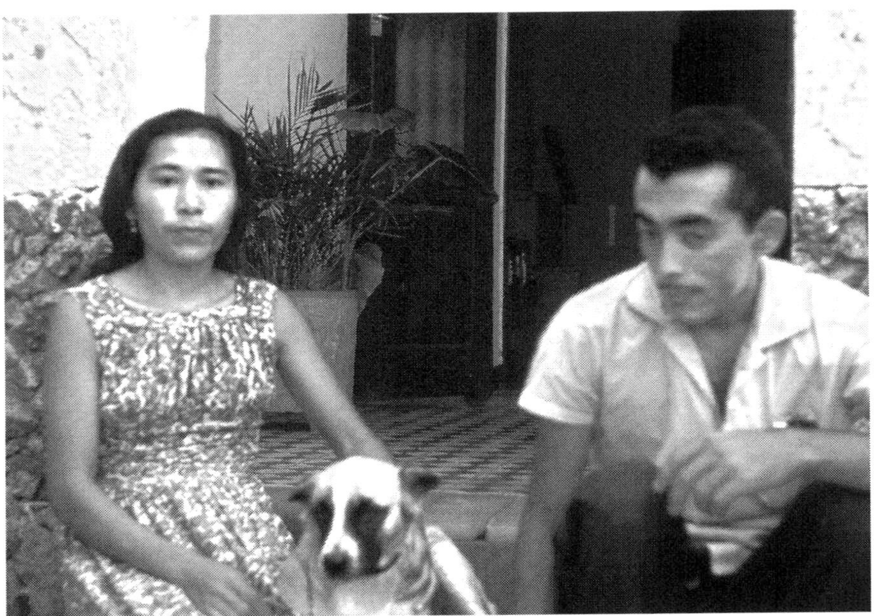

Maria and Pedro, indispensable household helpers, with our beloved Mishki

from electrical connections to serious plumbing defects. He builds tables and gates, constructs screens (for two bedrooms), washes the car and dog, waxes the floors, and paints the walls. He's dreamed up a weird sprinkler system to water the hibiscus and rubber plants, tends the coconut palm, papayas, and mimosas, and cuts the sparse grass with a pen knife on his hands and knees, blade by blade. He is badly strapped with six kids, one just born. Another died of malnutrition last year, and they all have the bulging stomachs and huge, hollow eyes of hunger. With his talents, he could earn handsomely in a trade but lets all these possibilities slide out of sight; it's just too hard to think beyond today, to summon the drive and initiative to show up for work regularly as one would have to do, for instance, with a plumbing company.

A Taste of the *Sertão*

We get our first glimpse of the *sertão*, the arid area in the interior. Rather than finding it grim and desolate, reminding us of the thousands who live there at sub-subsistence level, I find it strangely lovely. I feel more strongly positive about Brazil than previously, probably because for the first time I'm away from the clatter and demands of the city. There's a dreamlike tranquility that stretches off, seemingly forever.

We've been invited to a family *fazenda* (plantation) near Quixadá, a four-hour drive southwest of Fortaleza. Five families, about thirty of us, leave in caravan at dawn. I pack a quantity of boiled water, our four hammocks, and a cake. About halfway, we go off the paved road onto the "washboards." The dirt is red clay; clouds of red dust rise behind us and settle slowly over the surrounding scrub. Vegetation consists mainly of clumped bushes that are almost bare of foliage. From time to time, we come upon a small, dammed-up reservoir, always a sparkling royal blue against the red sand. At one point, a couple of *vaqueros* (cowboys) in heavy cowhide, over-the-hip coats, leather hats, and tall boots gallop furiously past, chasing recalcitrant cattle through the stiff brush. Halfway we fill up with gas, and everybody drinks beer or Coke, the last available refreshment before we're dependent on what we've brought.

We turn into the Martins' lands at last and follow a dusty road where all the low, bare bushes lining it shine silver. The constant rattling of these twigs contributes to the eerie feeling of being on a stage set for another planet. It's odd to be looking at a wintery scene of bare, brown branches, and yet to feel summer heat. We ford a couple of streams, bounce over hummocks and gulches more suitable for tanks, open and close numerous cattle gates, and finally roll up to the farmhouse. Each family is assigned a room in the spacious, whitewashed, tile-roofed structure, and we string up our hammocks on hooks.

The next two days are devoted to sheer relaxation, lying around chatting or sleeping in hammocks on the vast veranda. The numerous children are more energetic; they explore the sizable reservoir, poling out on a makeshift *jangada.* Eric and Steve fish and hunt birds with the older Brazilian boys, and ride bareback on horses and donkeys. We go out to watch the farm operation; two hundred tenants (forty families) take care of eleven thousand acres. One group is feeding sugar cane into a machine that strips and chops it. Then, endlessly, they stir milk and sugar boiling over a wood fire in a copper cauldron; the result will be a smooth, sweet spread called *doce de leite.* We tramp through cotton fields, plantings of oranges, pineapple, and beans, and admire an innovative irrigation system. In between, we stuff ourselves with sumptuous meals—always with at least three kinds of meat at a time.

The night is cold, and we all sleep hard in our hammocks. Then there are more expeditions to inspect five hundred head of magnificent cattle with long, droopy ears, a kind of Brahma. Tenant farmers work three days a week for the Martinses on their land and three days on their own land (that the Martinses have given to them, along with seeds and houses), and they split half the crop of the latter with him. They tell us that just a few good rains turn the entire *sertão* into a green paradise overnight.

We start home when it's almost dark. There is added excitement when the spark plug connections on our car start falling off every few kilometers and Bel has to keep leaping out to stick them back on. Then he roars ahead to catch the taillights of the cars disappearing ahead. To be lost or stranded with a disabled vehicle out here could maroon us for several days. People and animals are on the roads in force at dusk: goats, sheep, and cows are all walking home. We note solitary graves with white stones and wreaths of dead flowers at the road's edge; there are no cemeteries out here, and very few houses. People are gathered around bonfires to socialize and warm themselves against the cool winds that come with night. A few wax palms glitter and sway in the brilliance of a three-quarter moon.

The Beggars

On a recent saint's day, we're downtown and pushing through a sidewalk crowd to see what the entertainment is. There's a man with his small boy, two small monkeys dressed in skirts and frilly bonnets—and one large boa constrictor. The boy is standing off in a corner, bored, with the snake around his neck. The snake is also tired of the whole business and sways listlessly. The monkeys pass the hat. Then, on a signal, the boa drops to the ground, and the monkeys drag it to a suitcase with a small hole cut in the top. They jam the snake's head in it and hoist and tug at the rest of the great length, the reptile assisting slightly by crawling in very slowly. The monkeys leap up and stamp on the last bit of tail to push it in.

Every gimmick is used by the hoards of beggars lining every downtown street. Some pursue us, tugging at our clothes and mumbling about a sick husband. Tiny children accompany their ragged mothers or go it alone. Others stand at our elbow in even the more elegant stores, and, as I open my purse to pay for a purchase, hold out their hands.

There are more deformed and crippled cases

here than I've seen before: hunchbacks, bowlegs, shrunken limbs, stumps of legs or no legs, the enormous feet of elephantiasis, the crumbled extremities of leprosy. I've seen one man for the past two weeks with a great, open, raw sore swarming with flies; I wonder if he keeps scraping it or pouring salt into it so it won't heal. Huge numbers of the blind abound. A sudden blast on a trumpet, triangle, or accordion accompaniment signals a parade of blind men, guided by several small boys. There's one street lined exclusively with blind men and women crouched on their haunches in the shade of the buildings, selling lottery tickets.

Beggars come frequently by our gate, too, clapping for attention. If they seem in real need, Maria gives them bananas or bread. Some scoff at this and want only cash; Maria sends these packing, saying they'll only drink it up at the nearest bar. One old man stops by, explaining that his wife is desperately sick; he wants to go to a shrine some fifty miles away to pray to a certain saint there, promising to lead a good life if only the saint will help. He is asking for bus fare to the village and a bit more for the shrine's coffers. By the time Maria relays all this and I've dug up 100 cruzeiros (four cents), the old man has shuffled off.

Life on the Back Roads

The raucous Carnival Week has passed and we're into March. The rains of approaching winter have held off until now. They are very late. Though the showers are not continual or overly oppressive, we find that everything is damp, and a new ritual is our daily airing of clothes, shoes, and suitcases to keep down the mold.

Bel is winding up a series of journeys to the major economic centers in the interior of the state. Accompanying him have been the assistant director of the Institute and several of his research team. Contacts are made with the mayor and other key personages in a town, and then the students stay on for a week or two to conduct the interviews. It's interesting that despite the indignation of detractors about extracting secrets "endangering the national security," no one of the over two hundred already interviewed has objected to the questionnaire. In fact, more often they've clamored for the distinction of being considered a "community leader."

In Iguatu, the team sits up nearly all night with the director of the local radio station discussing everything from Brazilian politics to the Vietnam war. The tremendous power of radio and television is noted; just as Brazil is skipping the railroad age and moving from donkey cart to airplanes, so, too, to a surprising degree, it is skipping the written word and moving from complete ignorance to the sphere of mass communication via the airwaves.

Most of the researchers' nearer trips are by jeep; a memorable one includes a fishing village reached only by a three-kilometer hike over towering sand dunes. The exodus proves especially exciting when they agree to take a pregnant girl in labor with complications to the nearest hospital; it takes four men to hoist her over the dunes in a rocking chair.

The team visits distant towns by bus. After one foray, Bel and his co-director, Paolo, board a bus at Crato at 4:00 a.m. for the ride back to Fortaleza. Several times they doubt whether they'll make it; part of the road is washed out, and the bus skids and swerves in deep mud. The driver carries no shovels or equipment. Several times they get stuck, but somehow twist out of the sinkholes of this forgotten hinterland where people still live in mud shanties, have no doctors, and can't read. It takes them eighteen hours to cover four hundred miles.

Face-offs between Brazil and the United States—Rumor and Innuendo

Violence, or the show of violence, is taken for granted here a bit more than at home. A few months ago, an American teenager was out with friends. Realizing it was getting late, he started running up the street when he was a block from his house. One of the night cops (who prowl up and down, signaling back and forth to each other with bird-call whistles) thought he was an escaping robber, and with no warning or waiting to get close enough to identify the boy, shot him in the leg. Approaching, the policeman saw his mistake, apologized, and walked off, leaving the victim in a pool of blood on the sidewalk. There are no facilities to care for such cases in the hospital; with no nurses, a patient's family brings hammocks to sleep in the hospital and provide care and food themselves. So this boy's leg wound had to be cured at home, a long, painful business. There was no recourse possible through the police department.

On the other hand, Brazilians see the United States as a far greater embodiment of violence, animosity, and power display. Rumors circulate around the country, all having to do with American speculation and "takeover" in Brazil. Somebody claimed he was traveling into some isolated estuary of the Amazon region and suddenly came face to face with an American military platoon pointing machine guns in his face. A Peace Corps group recently had a serious time exonerating itself from charges of rushing to plant an American flag on a mountaintop; they'd gone for a quiet picnic in the hills and certainly planted no flag, but the gossipmongers can't resist such juicy possibilities. Brazilians see the Peace Corps volunteers as inexperienced kids trying to change people who don't want to be changed, and who feel uncomfortable when these young Americans try to empathize with them and live on their level.

And, of course, they object to all American businessmen, technicians, and speculators who are making money off Brazil and taking away the profits. "There are just too damn many American faces around, and it's making us nervous," they say. Brazil has not yet had its great moment in history, and her people are fiercely nationalistic, sensitive, and defensive. They can't bear to think that anyone else could do better.

One form of unrest has been getting publicity worldwide. The Peasant Leagues of Brazil have been on the move. This is a confederation of the landless in the poverty-ridden Northeast—mainly in the state of Pernambuco, just south of Ceará—agitating against the rich plantation owners. Joining this movement are the "worker-priests," a radical arm of the Catholic Church that has broken with the more traditional clergy. Though they haven't been able to accomplish much in the way of tangible change because the military government keeps the lid on, they still reflect the unrest that bubbles just beneath the surface in Brazil. Bel's project has not come into contact with the group, nor has it been affected directly by its struggle against the vastly wealthy landowners.

The Violence Spreads

While papers in the United States are full of the assassinations of Martin Luther King Jr. and Robert Kennedy, this May there are also rumbles in Brazil. A month ago police killed a student in Rio who was demonstrating for better cafeteria facilities. It was a freak incident but sufficient to touch off mass movements, marches, and battles with the cops in many cities.

One day while Bel is working on the tenth floor of the archives building in the center of town, a flood of umbrellas swarms by. It's a contingent of students, two blocks long, chanting in a pouring rain. Their major objective is USIS, the US information office, which they break into, wrecking the floors and walls, as well as all loose furniture, movie projector, films, and typewriters. Later in the afternoon, when I drive to the US-Brazilian cultural center to return books to the library, there is a helmeted contingent of soldiers hovering in the lobby and idling in military trucks across the street. The army is on twenty-four-hour alert, troops leaning on their bayonets and submachine guns at every downtown street corner.

Bel sounds out his students on the USIS assault. Their feeling, generally, is approval; the United States can do with one more lesson. They're surprised and chagrined when the US consular officer extracts a promise from the Brazilian government to cover the loss. Why shouldn't the United States pay? Four thousand dollars is nothing to us, they say, and, besides, American entrepreneurs (exploiters) have stolen so much wealth from Brazil that this is small potatoes in retaliation. The fact that a major reason for the march was to protest the niggardly amount of money allocated by the Brazilian government for new professors, and that the sum the government must now pay USIS would have covered one professor's salary for a year, is immaterial. This protest is a matter of "principle." Attacking American property is a natural adjunct to attacking the Brazilian government, which they believe gets directives from Washington.

A number of large cities have been taken over by the military, including Rio. Thousands of troops are massed to keep students from gathering. Officials acknowledge that they must get at the causes of unrest. They must recognize the cry for more and better schools. But even with liberal legislation, they can't suddenly wipe out the deficiencies of several generations' standing, and so the bitterness is bound to continue, at least for a while.

We aren't allowed to forget the hate, even in remote Fortaleza. On several tense mornings, the mayor calls the Agronomy School where the American USAID group is based and tells them, for their own safety, not to come to work. For the past month, US-manufactured cars have been ordered off the streets. We're grateful for the anonymity of our rusty Brazilian jeep. The Peace Corps headquarters has been threatened, but is too hard to reach (on a ninth floor), at least by a student mob.

Despite all of this, Bel's research continues uninterrupted. The questionnaires are nearly completed, and the coding is in progress. His six students and the social sciences faculty have been remarkably loyal. We recognize that this is turning out to be a singular adventure in participant observation dealing with university and state and local politics in a developing country.

How the System Works

Along with the blood-and-thunder situations, there are comic aspects, too. A possibly exaggerated story of favoritism is presently going around. Some years back, a good friend of the governor was without work and asked if there weren't something that could be done to help. Why, of course, said the governor. Next day he called the man and told him there was a job all arranged. Fine, what kind? Teaching at the university. But I never taught before; what subject? Greek. Greek! But I don't know any Greek. That's all right, no problem; just show up tomorrow in the classroom and there won't be any students. So the man went and was horrified to find that four students had signed up. Somehow he managed to stumble and bluff through the hour, and then rushed to the governor. Never mind, soothed the governor, I'll fix everything; just go back tomorrow and you'll see. Fearfully, the "professor" marched back to his class—and, lo, no students. They were all in jail.

Try Not to Break an Arm

We get our own glimpse, firsthand, into a local institutional procedure, namely the hospital system.

It happens when Steve is brought home from the school playground with a fractured elbow (a much heavier student landed on him during a playground game). We try to reach the highly recommended pediatrician who runs a children's hospital to get his advice, but he is out for siesta. So we drive to the hospital and find that everybody is out for siesta. After an hour, they finally round up the radiologist, and he consumes another hour taking four x-rays, all excruciating because they have to stretch Steve's arm in different directions. The last straw is when the technician comes up from the darkroom to say the photos haven't come out and they'll have to take them all again.

Eventually the chief arrives and recommends a bone specialist who runs another hospital. It takes two more hours for him to show up, Steve wailing all the time that he can't stand the pain another minute. The orthopedist holds off for still another hour, saying he can't set it right away because we must wait for the swelling to stop. At last, they bring Steve into one of the waiting rooms and plop him on the table while other patients look on curiously. Though I protest, they insist that it's necessary to put him to sleep. This entails collecting an anesthetist who sets up his little portable ether apparatus. Steve breathes dutifully into the mask, reporting afterwards that he went off into "another dimension." Bel is instructed to hold down his legs, though his own are none too stable at this point. So the cast goes on, and two weeks later is off. Despite a good deal of pain, Steve is never severely handicapped; we even wrap the cast in plastic so he can wade part way into the ocean.

While on the subject of the boys' school, I'll mention the home visit of one of their teachers. The school is Baptist-run, created primarily to board the children of evangelical Baptist missionaries who are off converting the heathens in the Amazon area. The nonbelievers include not only the indigenous Indian population there but also Catholics—who don't count as Christians. One day Sister Helen (an excellent teacher) stops by our house. She notices the bottles of wine and rum on our sideboard, and her face drops. She launches into the somber pronouncement that, unfortunately, Bel and I will never be with Eric and Steve in heaven. The boys are "saved," she assures us, but clearly we are headed in the other direction. Alcohol constitutes a grave impediment. When we ask the boys about their acceptance of Jesus, they're somewhat vague and nonchalant. Bible classes, with graphic picture books displaying the fires of Gehenna (hell, the place of eternal misery), are an interesting part of the everyday curriculum, but they're not sure what they've signed onto.

Magical Evenings

Despite the political unrest and a few personal challenges, there are splendid compensations. A full moon is coming up, and we're invited to celebrate with another *luarada*. Some twenty of us—Americans and Brazilians—haul our supper to cook on one of the remote beaches. It's a marvelous night; the temperature is in the high seventies, the water more than lukewarm. An incredibly huge, orange moon pushes up rapidly over the horizon and sails higher through patches of scudding clouds. The sea glints like beaten metal.

We dig pits, pile on logs, and roast our filet steaks. The dozen or so kids play tap-tap-the-icebox, running and diving behind the dunes, kicking up spray along the shore, or falling deliciously into the water to retrieve a soccer ball. Somebody unpacks a guitar and we sing around the fire. Eric and Steve stretch out on the sand, staring at the stars, and try not to fall asleep.

Other evenings—every one equally balmy—find us exploring the innumerable little cobbled streets around our house. We peek into lavish gardens to watch Brazilian nightlife on the wide terraces and verandas; some very wealthy families may have modest furnishings inside because all entertaining takes place in the gardens. Orchids climb the trunks of coconut palms, colored lights wink from tall branches into tiny reflecting pools. On the sidewalks, scores of hula hoops twirl on gyrating youngsters; apparently it has taken ten years for this fad to reach Northeast Brazil. Wild West hoofbeats ring out down the block, and a lone horseman gallops past, forcing us to dive into the gutter. A majestic Brahma bull swaggers by, three small boys squeezed behind his hump. Four unattended donkeys reach a busy intersection and amble nonchalantly across, the stream of cars swerving expertly but not slowing.

The maids from nearly every house are leaning over the gates gossiping or are wrapped in the arms of their *namorados* against a wall. A Ford Galaxy pulls up behind a line of Impalas and other Galaxies (they are produced in São Paulo) and discharges four immense ladies with monumental hairdos, brocade gowns, and gold slippers. They disappear up an elegant walk flanked by rich, dark, mango trees—but not before an appalling creature has materialized from the pavement, crawling, crab-like, on all fours, except belly-upward. The harsh streetlight catches his sucked-in brown cheeks, grimy rags, and worn bare feet—or are they hands? They look the same. He tells the matrons he will guard their car.

The Racial Issue

We often hear that Brazil has solved its racial problem, that there is complete integration and tolerance. It's apparent to us, however, that whoever is making these pronouncements is badly deluded. Maybe there are no actual Jim Crow signs, and rioters don't scream "Black Power!" but, clearly there are two worlds here. Perhaps because of a longer history of racial mixing, those who are visibly white cling even more fiercely to their identity than our American white racists.

You have only to glance at a person to have a pretty good idea of his or her "station" and general job category. The darkest skins nearly always connote the menial laboring tasks. Soldiers (enlisted men) are fairly dusky. Shop clerks are a bit fairer. Bank clerks are lighter yet, as are other white-collar workers, though they are still not Nordic. The elite or aristocracy are dead white, and this seems to be an ideal. The professors, doctors, lawyers, army officers, top businessmen, and their wives fall into this pallid category. Some enjoy the sun and are well tanned, but most seem proud of the "preserved-under-a-rock" look. It's as if to be at all swarthy means they've had to live and work in the outdoors.

Of course, this is a huge generalization with many exceptions, but it is borne out surprisingly often. A big weekly magazine recently pointed out how shocked people are to see a Negro-type man and a light girl walking together in the street. Many examples were shown of housing discrimination, with prejudice as blatant as in the States:

of a black being refused an apartment, told it was taken, and an hour later it is rented to a white client. This happened, in fact, to a Peace Corps couple, he white and she Puerto Rican. He arranged for a house and the next day came to sign the lease with his wife. Excuses were quickly made and the door slammed. Mistakenly, perhaps, Brazil is considered a happy choice for Peace Corps volunteers of color. One young black woman we know—vivacious, attractive, and capable—has had an uphill struggle here. There are stories of blacks going into high-class bars and being served once, but if they come back, they find the price has tripled.

People say it's primarily an economic discrimination, but for all but a few exceptions, it comes down to the same thing. The darker ones are the poor who can't climb out of their class either by intermarriage or a better job. In a way, they're ghettoized more effectively than those in our more fluid "land of opportunity." Even a year or two of school is far beyond the wildest dreams of the poor in the barracks and shacks. We talk of the culture gap in our society that makes it hard for the black child to be accepted and to learn at the same rate as the white kids with whom he wants to integrate. The difference is so great here that virtually no one even attempts to lessen it. Young children sit around listlessly, mostly naked, with their malnourished stomachs bulging.

Northeast Brazil could become so much. It has endless land, untapped resources, and human power to train. Literally hundreds of thousands of our products would find a market if manufactured here. A few examples: a wall pencil sharpener (everybody at the Anthropology Institute goes around with bleeding fingers from sharpening with razor blades); toilets that flush paper (a basket is always placed next to the bowl for this purpose); envelopes and stamps that actually stick (a large glue pot is provided in the post office)—ad infinitum. Brazil is crying for the big economic surge, yet, oddly, seems centuries away from it, too. What is it: the climate that traditionally saps ambition and slows the pace? Lack of precedent and example? So fierce a pride that outsiders (even from the more sophisticated south of the country) are savagely rejected if they try to innovate? Lack of a development class? Lack of progressive political leadership? Inadequate schools?

An Affinity for the Macabre

Because cemeteries are important architectural and cultural elements in the Brazilian scene, the four of us decide on a field trip to the São João Batista cemetery at the edge of the city. A more lugubrious atmosphere could not be manufactured for a film set. Crowded tightly up to the entrance gate are the myriad tiny burial vaults of each family. Tall and thin, their peaked roofs are crowned with ponderous crosses or statues. Their once-white exteriors are weathered, moldy, and blackened. Climbing down among them, we peep through their barred windows. There is just room for an altar about four feet across, covered with embroidered linen, silver candlesticks and dusty artificial flowers. Most prominent, both inside and hung on the façade, are huge, garishly tinted photos of the deceased resting beneath. Inscriptions give detailed accounts of the manner of death and degree of grief suffered by the survivors.

Faceless crones trudge up and down the narrow lanes, bent under shoulder yolks supporting the two buckets of water they ceaselessly carry for the grave plantings. But these are sickly and dry; no green trees relieve the mile-long forest of spiky, black sepulchers, jammed back-to-back. Several bare branches thrust up along a far wall, in which (I'm not joking) two large vultures are standing sentinel. Our Dracula-oriented children relish it all, of course, and leap over the soft mounds to inspect carved skulls and to watch the gravediggers at work.

Not long after our cemetery trip, I go with Maria to the wake of her elderly, jaundiced friend whom we had visited several times. We are ushered into the house by neighbors. Dona Carmina's coffin is set up on a crude black box in the tiny living room, candles burning at the head and foot. A net covers her face to keep off swarms of flies buzzing angrily. Her blind old husband laments forlornly that he has not seen her since the illness started six months before. I guess a priest had been called, but the crucial thing is that she was holding a candle at the moment of death, to speed (or light?) the journey to heaven.

Because of a law that all burials must take place within twenty-four hours (there is no embalming), the internment is scheduled for this afternoon, with no church service. This law, incidentally, has proved ticklish for Americans in tropical countries, and I understand that sometimes bodies have been smuggled out in disguised boxes. Maria declines to go to the burial because of a small cut on her hand; a strong superstition forbids anyone with illness, bleeding, or an opening in the skin from entering a cemetery. The condition, she says, will immediately be aggravated, swell up, and become infected due to bacteria in the putrid ground.

The Spy Saga Continues

Suddenly the *reitor*, the university chancellor, suspends Fontenelle on suspicion that he is harboring an American spy at the Anthropology Institute. A federal deputy demands an investigation and appoints a committee of inquiry. Fontenelle moves his entire staff to the philosophy building across the street, and only Bel and his six students remain at the Institute.

A month later there are rumors that the Institute itself will be closed and all papers therein confiscated. Though such edicts usually take days, if not weeks, to enact, Bel and the students quietly begin to move their mountains of questionnaires out in briefcases, a few at a time. Any large bundles would be noticed by the various informers, always loitering across the street. Two days later, the axe falls; the Institute is locked, and armed guards are posted at the door. A proclamation from the *reitor* suspends the research, along with Bel and Paolo, his Brazilian counterpart, meaning that "officially" they are not to continue the project. Police detectives swarm all over, photographing each room, pawing through the burned toilet paper in the back yard after a hot tip that incriminating documents have been hastily destroyed.

Slapstick elements increase. While Fontenelle is meeting with his staff in the philosophy building, one of the initial agitators barges in and says he has a right to hear all they are saying. One of the faculty refutes this and is punched in the face by the agitator—whom Fontenelle calmly lifts by the collar and deposits outside the door.

Meanwhile, Bel moves his operations to our house, where the team continues to work. The questionnaires are coded and the final results are written up. The investigating committee calls in everybody concerned: Fontenelle, the students, Bel—even janitors. What's becoming clear is that the whole rumpus has little to do with Bel's "spying," but he provides a handy excuse for a larger intra-university political intrigue. Some of the strongest opposition to Fontenelle is coming from people close to the *reitor*, with daily tidbits fed to the press from the university's PR man. Bel's name appears over and over in three-inch headlines. When will he again be favored with so much attention!

With no evidence, the whole campaign fizzles, and by the time the committee gets to around to questioning Bel, it is actually apologizing. Under some duress, the *reitor* presides over a ceremony exonerating everyone. The agitator can't stand not having the last word, though, and gives notice that he intends to kill Fontenelle anyway, so the latter and his two assistants start packing loaded revolvers in their glove compartments. We find it a pretty amusing circus.

Now students break into the Agronomy School that houses the twelve-man USAID team. Papers are destroyed and the Americans are forced to sit home. If the University of Ceará fails to support them, they'll probably cancel the contract and return to the States. Today the wife of the USIS head comes to pick me up, and on the way, a rock narrowly misses her windshield. So the Paulsons aren't the only targets. Clearly to us, Americans must go from such troubled spots all over the world. Only then might the people simmer down to the point where they'll look at their own ills for a change rather than pointing hysterically at the unwitting gringo scapegoats.

The Only American Hero

Oddly, or perhaps not, the only remaining magic symbol of America is the Kennedy name. Bobby's death has produced an astounding impact here; Brazilians feel the same catastrophic loss as with John. Rich, poor, conservative, radical—they all feel as though they've lost a close relative. There are extras in all the papers giving hour-by-hour reports after the shooting. Headlines run half a page high. Bel is interviewed and long articles are published with his comments about the assassinations of both King and Kennedy. The unanimous feeling is that with Bobby has gone America's last hope for decency. He was the only idealist, the only honest person in the country, the only one who could resolve the Vietnam War, the only one who understood the world's problems. His fiercest defenders are the communists and Trotskyites. Everything shuts down for three days, and special Masses are sung in all the churches.

Stark Poverty at Our Gate

The latest twist in door-to-door begging is trying to give away children. There is a hullabaloo out at our gate. A ragged six-year-old child is screaming and trying to run away. Her gaunt, barefoot mother is yelling at her. Our Maria gets the story: the woman's husband died and left her with six small kids in the interior without support. So she undertook the long trek—days—on foot with the whole brood, carrying two little paralytic boys. She explains how they all slept in the street the night before and got soaked in a downpour. None of them has eaten since yesterday. She has left all but this one pretty girl sitting on a curb across the city some five miles away. Now, in desperation, she's scrounging the better neighborhoods for a bit of food, and is literally attempting to give her children away.

She offers this one to Maria to bring up. "She won't get in the way or make trouble. If you could just give her a little milk and bread in the morning, and, once in a while, a little dress. Please, please!" If her livelihood didn't depend on working for other families, Maria might well say yes. The woman is frantic: "Rosinha, wouldn't you like to stay with this nice lady? She'll take care of you, and you'll have plenty to eat." Rosinha bursts into tears and rushes, panic-stricken, down the street. The mother promises to come back and begs an empty can to collect leftover rice and bread. She doesn't return.

We find that, in the Northeast, anyway, there's literally no existing structure through which someone with progressive ideas about economic and social ills can work. It's practically impossible to generate funds or even interest. Granted that the welfare system at home is often clumsy, yet if somebody is starving, there is unemployment compensation, aid for unwed mothers, Social Security, a soup kitchen, and other charities. Here you may watch your kids die of hunger, and so you must beg. Even with training (literacy), there are few jobs for the lower levels and no use fooling poor people into thinking there are. The upper class knows this and expends little time on stop-gap efforts. It looks the other way and holds the masses in place.

The Paranormal Is Pretty Normal Here

The next narrative jumps to quite another field, yet maybe it's not entirely unrelated: both deal with aspects of a still-developing culture.

Maria sits down next to me to sort beans. She chats about her last Sunday off, and I learn that she spent it at the morgue section of the medical clinic. She had gone there to find out about her sister who had died here in childbirth in 1954. What prompted this after so many years?

"Do you remember," she asks, "when I came home Sunday night and went straight to my room while I was cooking supper?" Apparently her head was splitting, she had a terrible stomachache, and she could only lie, shivering, in her hammock with an uncontrollable chill. "When I opened my eyes, there was this tall woman standing next to me, looking at me. I jumped up, scared to death, and the person faded back." Thinking she might have been dreaming or feverish, Maria wrapped the hammock tightly around herself. But then she felt a tugging, someone urgently plucking at the hammock. Quickly, she sat up and saw the woman leaning over her, long black hair streaming down, covering her face.

Terrified, Maria ran out to the kitchen and began peeling carrots, but the crippling pains and cold soon sent her to lie down again. Once more she dozed until the apparition again appeared, this time throwing itself on top of Maria, the long hair spreading and tangling. Escaping to the kitchen, Maria sat shaking and silent. There were no more visitations, but for several nights, the same chill and violent headache would return.

Three days later, her friend, Santa, stopped by with a young man. He watched Maria for a while as the girls chattered, then said, "You didn't sleep well last Sunday, did you?" No. "You had a bad chill and headache?" Why, yes, startled. "There was a woman with very long, dark hair who appeared in your room, who pulled at your hammock, who threw herself on you?" "Yes, yes! But I never told anyone, not Dona Lisa, not Santa. What does it mean? "

It turns out that this man—José—belongs to the local Spiritist group that focuses on contacts with the dead via spiritual mediums. He seems to be aware of everything happening in both this realm and the next; he tells her that the apparition is that of her long-dead sister. That he knows they had been very close, and when Josefa died, she wanted to stay always near, especially in times of sickness, in the hope of taking Maria away for good. Awed, Maria weeps. She tells of Josefa's marriage at seventeen out in the *sertão*. Maria was thirteen, and Josefa had been like a parent since their mother died years before. The sister's first baby died at birth, and the next one arrived the following year.

Soon she was awaiting a third but eventually realized that things weren't right. An ambulance was arranged to drive her to Fortaleza. Doctors delivered a dead baby and gave Josefa transfusions and injections. Fifteen days later she suddenly died. Because no one was there to claim the body, the hospital arranged for the burial. The husband arrived and was told that she had been taken to the cemetery, dressed in her nightgown; wrapped only in a sheet, she was placed in the big common pit used to bury the poor who have no family to care for them. Maria explains this to me with tears falling into the beans.

José tells Maria to come to his meeting, where they will perform a ritual to send the spirit away. She can't go the night of the séance, but José reports the next day that the sister's ghost was present. He had urged it not to bother Maria, saying that she was in the world of the living while Josefa was dead. Josefa refused. José explains that Maria herself must attend for the exorcism to work properly. Later she does go, watching all the mediums sitting around a big table while the spirits enter one or another of them to speak. But Josefa is not there; she has gone away after all.

Now It's My Turn

For no apparent reason, except maybe a little too much sun, I develop a searing headache and burning eyes. When I become partially paralyzed, unable to move my hands or feet properly, I'm suddenly very frightened and tense. I think I may be losing my mind, and even begin to wonder whether I'll make it out of Brazil alive. Bel calls in a US-trained doctor we know, and he can't find anything physically wrong. He says this kind of puzzling situation is fairly common in the region, but there are no obvious answers, at least in the medical profession. He suggests that I breathe into a paper bag.

On a Saturday night, José visits again, and, apropos of nothing, he says, "There's someone sick here with a bad headache, isn't there? Especially bad around the eyes?" Yes. Maria hasn't mentioned this to anyone. He concentrates for a while. "She once visited a Macumba session, didn't she?" Yes. "And there was some dispute with the high priestess over money?" Maria recalls the business of my borrowing Raimunda's sewing machine in January, and then giving her money the next time I attended a Macumba session. Afterward, Raimunda claimed to have understood the money was for Macumba, and that I should give her more for the sewing. I had felt it ample for both.

Anyway, the verdict was that Raimunda—or, unconsciously, through her spirit guide—had put an evil eye spell on me in that moment of anger. So now there is a departed soul attached to me, someone who died from a head trauma who is inflicting a similar punishment on me, intending to disable me, though not necessarily to do me in.

José explains that Maria is on the way to becoming a medium herself. His theory is that because she lives with me, she's sensitive to my illness, and this spirit has been jumping back and forth between us. When I have the headache, she doesn't, and vice versa. We check this out the next day and find it is true. The best way to exorcise the spirit, José says, is for me to go to the next Macumba session, be friendly to Raimunda, drop a modest contribution in the plate, and then make an excuse to leave after just ten minutes. Under no circumstance must I cross my arms or legs (my usual stance when leaning against the wall watching), because this would prevent the spirit from leaving. Another option would be to attend a Spiritist meeting where José officiates. Since for some time I've been curious about Spiritism (imported in the nineteenth century from France), and we learn that they will be "working" the following evening, we all decide to go there.

A Spiritist Exorcism

We pile the boys, Maria, Santa, and a couple of their friends into the jeep and drive out to a *favela* near the dunes. We find the small mud-and-plaster house, jammed with sweating, tattered humanity sitting on benches in the rear. Up in front, a bar separates the congregation from the *mesa branca*, a large table covered with an embroidered, white cloth. Seated around the table are a dozen or so psychic mediums. Their elbows are on the table. Their hands cover their eyes. We crowd into the little building, and people make room on the benches. José spots us and hurries back to get my exact name. Then he beckons for me to come down to sit next to the table, "to observe more carefully."

Meanwhile, the first of three short sermons is in progress by a leader of the Spiritist center. There are few of the gaudy trappings of the Macumba in the room. It is bare except for six or eight standard pictures of Jesus, a few of the Virgin, and a large one of St. Joan of Arc. The sermons are like those of many evangelical churches: exhortations to love your enemies, be kind to your neighbors, live with dignity and honesty even though you are poor and hungry all the time—your reward will come in the next world. The congregation is urged to consult with the doctors who are daily effecting cures for many afflictions (the Spiritists also have their own herbal pharmacies). Next to where I am sitting is a curtained door, and a steady stream of patients is ducking through. Sharp groans and wails issue from time to time.

Next commences the real business of the evening: communicating with departed spirits. José and Santa are the chief mediums, intoning alternate or overlapping, ritual prayers. They move around the table, touching the head of each medium. This immediately causes those seated to tremble violently, their breath coming in rasping pants. They moan, shriek, and weep, writhing, leaping up, clutching their heads. José or Santa calm them down with a steadying arm, pulling the messages from them. Apparently the spirits "come down" and enter one of the mediums. They speak through the mediums, whose voices turn gravelly and alien. José, on catching a message, calls out, "Who is there here called Marina? There is a spirit who wishes to talk to Marina."

A final bell sounds, and the entire congregation, eyes closed, heads raised, breaks into a long, earnest hymn. Someone turns up the wick on the kerosene lantern that swings overhead from the tiled roof. The mediums are instructed, at last, to lay their hands down on the table, palms up. A few have to be assisted back to reality. I'm not sure whether my "case" has been pleaded, but I catch José's eye a few times, and afterward he has me write down my name, presumably to keep working on the exorcism.

We climb back into the jeep, and I ask Maria what happened. She explains, "Your spirit came down during the session, in that curtained, back room. This is where the 'bad spirits' come, and the doctors deal with them there." Astonishingly, as we're riding home, my head clears, I'm completely relaxed, and the paralysis is rapidly disappearing. Apparently my spirit has departed from our side for the upper regions.

I don't know what to believe. Is this coincidence? Power of suggestion? Or did an exorcism actually take place? At this point, I don't really care which it might be. The important thing is that something worked, and I am cured. Bel calls a medical doctor friend to report on what has happened. He shrugs and says that one must simply accept the fact that there is no medical explanation.

Reflections

We left Fortaleza in mid-July for a sparkling windup in Rio and climbed into the Incan ruins of Machu Picchu, high in the Peruvian Andes. The boys and I flew on to the States while Bel returned to Ceará to complete the final stage of research, settle Maria in a new dwelling and job, and close up the house.

Bel sent me a series of clippings from the Fortaleza press. He reported that the last two boxes he shipped had been confiscated by the customs officials. Fresh suspicions that the "American spy" was stealing national secrets caused the university to form yet another investigating commission to examine the contents of the boxes. A few questionnaires had been included, though the majority of items consisted of Bel's own books, five tennis balls (which were cut open and checked), two boxes of Brazilian cigars, and tourist maps. All the items were painstakingly listed in the articles.

The results themselves were, of course, carried by Bel personally. He planned to publish them first in Brazil, for the mutual benefit of both countries. We imagined that it might be some time, however, before another North American professor ventured into academic collaboration in this part of the world.

Bel ended up with pioneering research, learning about the political system that could advance the region's economic and social development. Throughout the turmoil, the students stayed engaged, and at the critical moment, Wanda, his most radical student, publicly stood up to defend the research. He realized that Americans need to learn how to function in areas like this—there are many in the world—restless, sometimes fervently anti-American, but also realizing the need for international collaboration. It was a frustrating but profound learning experience for him, shared by his Brazilian team.

Besides the obviously colorful descriptions of our life and challenges in Fortaleza, it should be pointed out that there were some very positive results. Bel's counterpart at the local university, Paolo, learned a great deal through their research project together, and he later became the *reitor* (head) of the University of Ceará. Following our return to the United States after the Brazil year, Bel arranged for two bright Brazilians to come to Milwaukee, and shepherded them through their MAs and PhDs. Bezerra went back to teach at the University of Ceará, and Hélio became a high-level official with the Brazilian government in the new capitol of Brasilia.

As to the rest of the family, for each of us, the year was an intense, over-the-top adventure that lived up to all our expectations—and also threw us a lot more curves that we never anticipated. The inherent drama and grandeur of the landscape, the excitement of watching a culture still forming and

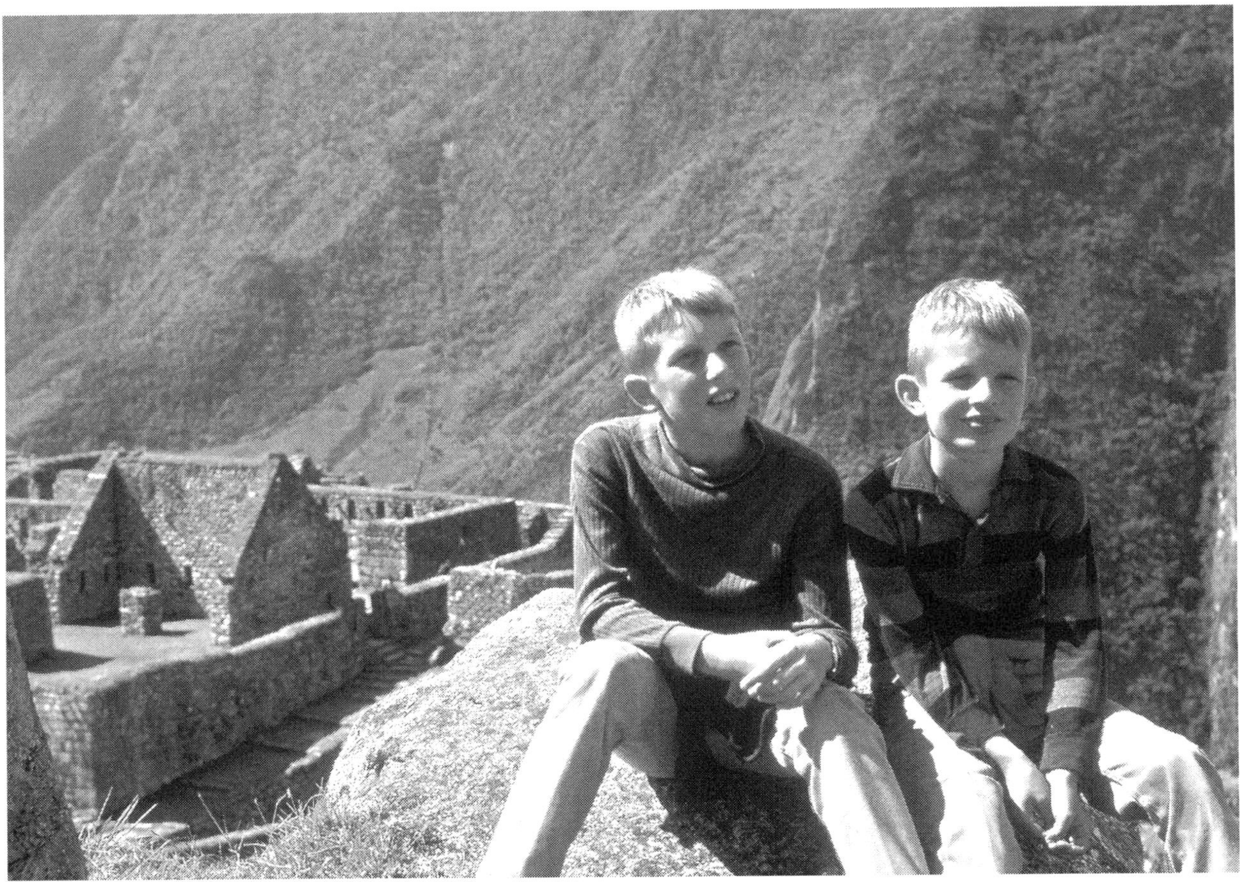

On our way home from Brazil, there's a stop at magical Machu Picchu

unfolding, the stark, unexpected contrasts with life in America—would take a while to digest.

One aspect of the culture that especially fascinated me was the whole range of supernatural phenomena, which to Brazilians seemed entirely normal. I sensed strongly that in Brazil the veil separating this world from the next is very thin. Because the connection to the spirit world is so prevalent—taken for granted in everyday life—I believe that this realm is, indeed, a lot closer there than it is at home. We noticed that most people, even the more educated, performed little superstitious rituals (like lighting candles on the sidewalk), "just in case." When I returned to America, it was curiosity about these beliefs and practices that led me to the paranormal research and explorations of levels of consciousness that were to fill my life for the next several years.

Recently a writer, who had just returned from Brazil, reported that the country has finally—suddenly—come to realize its longtime dreams of future prominence. He had first visited in the mid-1990s when it was what he called an archaic world. Astonished now at the almost miraculous shift, he hardly recognized it—fully confident of its place in the global scene, a sophisticated leader in many fields.

We haven't been back, but we know that Fortaleza is bristling with high rises and upscale hotels. This signifies progress, of course, but I think we'd miss our miles of totally deserted white sand beaches, the empty "haunted" castle up the street where our boys crunched over broken glass to summon up nineteenth century ghosts, and the goats and cows ambling freely through the downtown business district.

There is also something very salutary—really a magical blessing or gift—that seems to happen when a family goes off together to live in a foreign land. In the United States, it's normal for family members to dash off in different directions for disparate activities all day (or bury themselves in their electronic gadgets); they may not even connect for meals. On the other hand, an experience like ours bonds the family as nothing else could. In Fortaleza, there was no radio or television, so we had to create our own collective entertainment. Every night there was the ritual, ferocious canasta battle fueled by roasted cashews, or a sleuthing safari around the neighborhood. We all played tennis at a local club, and most days we managed to get to the beach to jump the waves or race the dog in the sand. Family excursions farther afield were adventures we all relished. Just being strange fish, isolated from our own kind, pulled us together powerfully—an effect that still holds strong after more than forty years, and keeps propelling us into big family trips.

Lunch time in Hangzhou

(below) 1992 conference kicks off with a spectacular ceremony engineered by the International Technology and Economics Institute in Shanghai

Enchantment and Repression:
Jarring Juxtapositions in China

April 1989 and April 1992

Backstory, 1989

Twenty-one years have elapsed since my last recounting of an adventure that falls in the category of this section that I've termed "socio/political." There have been a number of other trips in between that come under the other headings of "visionary" or "just for fun."

I won't attempt to bring the peregrinations of our family up to date through that long period, but will jump directly into this particular journey on the other side of the globe.

Roger Collis, a close friend from Seattle and an adventurous colleague in previous enterprises, had taken his family around the world in the early 1980s. Roger was particularly fascinated with China, where he made solid local contacts. When he returned, he immediately proposed to Bel that the two of them take a study group to China to assess the state of a culture in intense flux, and where they might delve into the current mindset of some of the billion citizens of this country so "foreign" to us. He also needed sponsorship of an academic institution to provide intellectual legitimacy and logistic help. Bel could provide the backing of the University of Wisconsin, and together they could offer an opportunity for an up-close experience of China.

Since Bel had begun teaching university seminars on a range of issues dealing with where the world and our own culture were going—the beginning of a "futures studies" curriculum—he conceptualized this series of trips that would fit in very well. With help from their knowledgeable Chinese national guide, Ling Zhang (who anglicizes her name to be Frances for us), he and Roger made excellent contacts with forward-minded thinkers. Meetings with research organizations were arranged. In their subsequent trips, they worked with these prestigious institutes to organize an annual global conference in Shanghai on themes such as global interdependence and the interrelationship of environmental and economic themes within a framework of science and technology. They brought in some top leaders from around the world to speak to several hundred attendees. These conferences were an integral part of our study trips.

The plan came together for the first three-week excursion in April 1989. It proved to be so successful that Roger and Bel repeated the program over the next three years. I went along twice, for the first and fourth trips. My notes covered 1989 and 1992. Because a few of the places visited were the same for both of these expeditions, I've meshed some of the descriptions. Other experiences were unique to particular trips. Rather than lapse into a travelogue—"we went here, and then here . . ." —I've picked out some of the memorable impressions, incidents, and communications for snapshots that were burned into the minds and hearts of all of us who participated. For the record, though, and for those who need to visualize our stops as we traversed this very large country, here is our China itinerary in 1989: Hangzhou, Shanghai, Beijing, Xian, Tsaodan, Chengdu, and Guilin.

There were eleven of us, from age seven to sixty-eight (including several friends) who signed up out of curiosity and anticipation of a strong collective experience. Gathering the group in Seattle, we flew for thirteen hours to Hong Kong, tried to dispel the jetlag from our foggy brains, and continued on via Dragon Air to the romantic Chinese city of Hangzhou. There we were met by Frances, who accompanied us across the country and smoothly facilitated our transportation, lodging, and meetings.

Hangzhou: Buddhists, Bicycles, and Traditional Healing

After the density, bustle, and sophistication of Hong Kong, setting down in Hangzhou seems truly another civilization. There are almost no cars—just buses, trucks, and a constant stream of bicycles, many of the latter pulling carts weighed down with cargo. Every inch of land appears to be cultivated, and there are miles of tunnel (plastic hoop) greenhouses.

At dusk, West Lake is magical. The air is dreamy and soft. Long, low boats cut silently and serenely through water that holds the last light. Friends or lovers hold hands as they stroll slowly along the esplanade and through lovely gardens of spring peach blossoms and gnarled sycamores. In the far distance loom misty mountain peaks.

All the inhabitants of one nearby village work their entire lives on a huge tea plantation. We see workers in the fields and visit the factory where the sixteen grades of tea are processed and packaged; tea has been produced here for a thousand years. Other villages are raising rice and cotton. Together, many villages—several thousand people in each—comprise the West Lake Commune. The rule of one child per family is strictly enforced, but in the countryside, agricultural workers are allowed two if the first is a girl. The more well-to-do can pay a $3,000 fine to have an extra child.

Silk, from abundant mulberry trees and silkworms, is another major industry. We visit the sprawling factory where six thousand workers are involved in processes from sorting cocoons to dyeing and spinning the thread to printing the resulting silk.

At the imposing Center for Traditional Medicine in Hangzhou, centuries-old healing methods are trusted and are in great demand. Conventional doctors may not agree with these beliefs and techniques, but often they share the same buildings with traditional practitioners. We watch a Qigong doctor work on a paralyzed woman who has been lifted onto the table by two companions. The doctor makes quick movements above the woman's body, which seem to pull her arms and legs invisibly; he is working on her aura—the energy field believed to surround living things. She thrashes wildly, then smiles, and, remarkably, climbs off the table on her own. In another room, doctors are busy with four people lying on beds, either with acupuncture needles sticking out of their faces, necks, and backs, or with electrodes attached to their bodies.

Our group meets with a Dr. Chen for a lesson in Qigong "meditation." We're told to respond spontaneously to our thoughts with movement—meant to show how the mind can create problems, emotional imbalance, and physical illness. There's much singing, shouting, puffing, jumping, and writhing—something like expressive dancing. With Qigong, one learns to ignore distracting thoughts so that the electrical energy balance is maintained. Basically, this practice—first noted around 700 BCE in China—is used to promote healing and general well-being through motion and breath. It is only recently that Qigong has been "discovered" by the West. Later I arrange for a private session with Dr. Chen. He digs into the back of my aching neck, presses three points on my forehead, and smooths and flutters his hand over my abdomen, then controls my breathing by raising and lowering his hand until I feel I'm floating off the bed—bliss!

We rent bikes to pedal (flow) with the throngs of other bicycles up the main thoroughfare of Hangzhou. Dodging the buses and huge trucks is scary enough, but it takes real grit to follow Frances's signal to make a quick left turn; this involves cutting authoritatively across a phalanx of twenty speeding bicycles abreast to duck into a side street. Miraculously we don't lose anyone and soon are approaching a small mountain to visit a Taoist temple/monastery at the top. There we find pictures of deities, candles, incense pots, and ancient instruments being fiddled in shadowy corners. A venerable, grey-bearded monk approaches to take our pulse in order to pinpoint physical ailments.

Another expedition takes us to the Mountain of the Buddha. We climb past 470 statues of the Buddha carved from limestone where pilgrims are sidling up to touch the Laughing Buddha's belly for luck. Candles burn in caves and in enormous temples with gaudy altars. Monks in dusty, brown robes and shaved heads shuffle around in the temples selling candles and incense. The crowds are on their knees or bowing vigorously to the statues.

On a trip out to the countryside, we traverse fields of rice and yellow rape for making canola oil. At tiny Fuyang, we take a small boat to an island, where we're greeted by firecrackers and a parade of small boys banging cymbals and percussion instruments. A bullock-drawn cart trundles us to the little village. Here the product is rice paper. It's spread out everywhere to dry—trampled, washed, separated, dried—all by hand, a process handed down from the nine-hundred-year-old Han Dynasty. We watch men pull water from ponds by foot treadle and pulley.

Shanghai: We Meet the Academic Power Structure and Devour Pigeon Eggs

Here, in this city of twelve million, our first contact with the Chinese power structure is solidified. We meet with Professor Fang Kai Bing and his colleagues at the Institute of Science of Sciences, a prestigious group that connects the general society with the government to promote economic progress. Later, at the International Technology and Economy Institute, Dr. Zhu Rong-Lin greets us with formal speeches of welcome.

We launch immediately into philosophical topics that surely would be considered nonacademic or "fringe" in America. These professors say they are fearful of the Newtonian particle science of fragmentation that is "ruining Western industrial countries" and will spread to China. They declare there is more wisdom in the ancient Asian and Mayan cultures. Further, they suggest, "We may all have come from another planet and, at some point, we may move off this earth to another." Holism and environmental consciousness are central to their thinking and work. We are surprised and delighted; these concepts are also the focus of own work at this point in the 1980s, but in the United States, they are definitely considered to be far out and often suspect (more on this in a subsequent section).

"We must go back two hundred years to a time before specialization," says Dr. Zhu. "Remember that at the end of his life, Einstein—a deeply spiritual person as well as a scientist—adopted the inclusive Universe perspective; he went off into quantum physics and chaos theory. He eschewed the classical view of physical laws and posited that humans cannot understand the true nature of reality. This was an eminent scientist who sensed we were going down a dangerous path."

As a result of these meetings, it is decided that next year the Chinese research groups will join with the University of Wisconsin to sponsor a large, international conference in Shanghai. Those gathering will explore the difficult relationship between sustainability and economics, with the goal of creating a global think tank to come up with solutions and steps toward implementation.

The Institute throws a stunning banquet for our group: pigeon eggs carved into rabbits, rice with sweet pastes, lotus root and bird's nest soups, the gelatinous webbed feet of ducks, five-inch shrimp, carp, sesame cakes, "thousand-year-old" eggs, dumplings on leaves in wooden *bentos* (little wooden lunch boxes), and potato bits candied with pink sugar. With our chopsticks, we pluck exotic samples from maybe twenty platters arrayed on a huge, central lazy Susan. There is lively conversation (in English and sometimes through translators), many toasts, and gifts of cork sculptures. Everybody exchanges business cards—a formal ritual whenever we meet a new group (we learned for the next trip to bring hundreds!).

We're whisked off for a blur of sightseeing: the famous Yu Gardens, with their brick carvings and dragon wall built in the Ming Dynasty, a river boat trip to open ocean, and a spectacular acrobatic exhibition. At a carpet factory, we watch workers weaving and clipping to sculpt bas-relief rugs; in another room, women are sewing a tapestry with human hair.

Beijing: The Government and Military Flex Their Muscles Up Close

On arrival in Beijing, one of our group (somewhat facetiously) requests "a riot." We've heard of student unrest in Tiananmen Square following the death two weeks before of daring reformer Hu Yaobang, and we're curious as to exactly what may be happening. Our guides say it's too dangerous to go there, but after a couple of days, we persuade Frances to take us.

Tiananmen is vast. A huge picture of Mao and communist flags adorn one building, and enormous revolutionary sculptures abound. On a central, raised obelisk is a blown-up photo of the dead Hu Yaobang with funeral wreaths. Thousands of excited, hopeful students have jammed the square. A long line snakes around the obelisk; students reverently climb the steps to read a wall of handwritten notes and to leave their own. It's prudent and necessary to express feelings anonymously because, clearly, surveillance is heavy. Someone has scrawled a big sign that says in English PRESS FREEDOM. The students are optimistic, even sure, that this massive, peaceful demonstration asking for basic civil rights—a free press and free speech—will be perceived as logical and nonthreatening by the government, and will finally be met with humanity and understanding.

Bel is fascinated and sits down on a wall to scribble impressions of this awesome, historic scene, and attracts a couple of students who are anxious to interpret the scene for him. Then a man in a business suit sits down beside him and pleasantly asks questions. Does he think the students' action is good? Does he approve of the recent, violent rioting in Xian? Is he a reporter? Bel replies that he's an American professor, that he feels the students are right to protest peacefully, and that the cause of democracy can be helped.

Zhe, our local Beijing guide, is standing nearby and is terrified that Bel—an obvious foreigner—is actually writing notes and talking to the students. She warns him that plainclothes police are everywhere. "The man who spoke to you is probably secret service or a policeman," she says. "A wrong word or move could bring your instant arrest." On top of each tall lamppost looms a closed-circuit television camera, watching all that's going on in the square, identifying any suspicious-looking person. When students move in eagerly to surround our group and ask questions, Zhe hustles us away.

After three days, the students are still refusing to go back to classes until reforms are made by the government.

The day after our visit to Tiananmen, we meet with half a dozen members of the Foreign Policy Institute. They are surprisingly open to discussing the protest. When they ask our opinion, Bel explains that the civil rights demonstrations and Vietnam War protests in the United States were widely covered by the media—which played an important role in changing peoples' minds, and effectively brought results. We go around the room so that each of us, Americans and Chinese, can speak to the issue. Our group is divided: some are strongly anti-communist and critical of the repressive government; others commend the authorities for remaining peaceful.

The academics we speak to at this time are more than eager to share their outrage with us, urging us to carry news of their desperate cause to the outside. Our group feels honored to be present at such a momentous time.

Two weeks later, the tanks moved in with soldiers in open trucks, imported from distant provinces—so as not to be contaminated by the students' viewpoint and, therefore, possibly sympathetic. The whole world knows how it turned out. Hundreds of the students encamped in Tiananmen Square and on the streets of Beijing were killed and their brave bid for democracy brutally crushed. The Chinese government was not ready to loosen control. It was only behind the secretive walls of intellectual strongholds that radical ideas could be aired.

Tsaodan: To Meet Another Revolutionary—An American

A few days after our adventure in Tiananmen Square, we followed up a lead I'd explored before leaving for China. I'd known about Joan Hinton for many years. Her mother, Carmelita Hinton, had founded the famed progressive Putney School in Vermont, and in the early 1950s I had close contact with the faculty when I worked down the road at The Experiment in International Living. Joan had been an outstanding young physicist and landed a plum job during the war; she worked on nuclear fission for the Manhattan Project with Enrico Fermi. After we dropped the atom bomb on Japan in 1941, she found to her horror that her work building nuclear reactors had contributed to creating the bomb. There was so much secrecy about the Los Alamos project that she had no idea whatsoever of the real purpose. She thought they were creating a demonstration nuclear explosion that would force the Japanese to surrender.

She immediately quit her job, became a peace activist, and went to D.C. to protest the US role. When her outrage was ignored, she flew to China in 1948. She wanted to get as far as possible from what she'd been doing as a nuclear scientist, and also to be close to the people of Asia. She was in Shanghai when it was bombed by the Japanese, and fled to Beijing, always running to liberated areas and staying in safe houses with communist revolutionaries until authorities discovered them. Nearly caught, she finally reached Mongolia and hid there. Meanwhile, the United States was calling her a spy and accused her of helping China develop its own atom bomb—a ridiculous fabrication. She wasn't allowed back to visit until the Cold War thaw.

Joan and her husband, Erwin (Sid) Engst, were committed Maoists (she had married shortly after moving to China, and made it her home until her death in 2010). They thought the 1949 revolution exciting and important for the poor and oppressed of the huge country. They were part of the ferment and lived on a commune where their daughter, Karen, was born. Joan had previously worked on a social work project with the left-wing Mme. Sun Yat-Sen, and had met Chairman Mao, Chou En Lai, and others of the First Revolution. Joan thought the Cultural Revolution of 1966 was an instructive initiative because it showed what would *not* work—it was mainly a move by students to remove the greedy, corrupt individuals at the top who were grabbing power and money as they tried to bring back capitalism. The students were backed by Mao, who was again rising to power after his Great Leap Forward had faded. The job of the students, dubbed "Red Guards," was to stamp out traditional historical and intellectual elements and to punish the bourgeoisie by taking their property and sending them to farms in rural regions. Joan and her husband remained loyal to Mao but had no sympathy for the brutal tactics.

When we visited Joan's husband, Erwin, recuperating from heart surgery in a Beijing hospital, he told us that he and his wife couldn't agree with the present tactics of the student demonstration in Tiananmen. They felt it would only end in violence and would probably lead to another real revolution because "everyone" was now against the government. Sid emphasized that the present government of Deng Xiaoping was totally corrupt—stashing bank accounts abroad and not caring about the needs of the people. This was shortly before the government crackdown. We doubt he and Joan would have condoned the kind of mayhem that erupted in the square.

Erwin arranges for our group to visit Joan's rural dairy project. They have lived there since 1953, and their life's work is to design and build up Chinese dairy businesses.

Frances helps to facilitate our visit to the dairy farm. There is much hassle to get permissions not normally allowed for tourists. Our bus driver is not at all happy as we slip and splash around on muddy back roads. Finally we arrive at remote Tsaodan, which has become a premier model experimental government milking station. The head of the farm greets us with tea, and then Joan enters, wearing baggy pants and a Mao jacket and hat. Obviously, at age sixty-six, she is now a legendary figure throughout China. Frances is in such awe that she doesn't know how to approach her. This is clearly a remarkable woman whose idealism has taken her to the most basic grassroots involvement.

Joan tells us that when they first arrived in the area, it was all grass. It was only after liberation was underway ("liberation" is the term used to describe the communist takeover in 1949) that they could finally bring in equipment to break up the hard soil. Five thousand people currently live on the farm. Joan is obviously passionate about her projects, which she explains as we hike around in the mud. All the equipment was built from scratch. Eventually Joan could take her technicians to visit dairies in the United States, where they watched closely, noting meticulously what they'd seen. When they came home, they set about designing and making their own machines from stainless steel to create all the parts needed for sophisticated milking equipment. Just recently the farm's dairy head had toured America; he had never seen a motor vehicle until he was seventeen. Now their milking parlor is a proud model for all China.

Our discussion moves to the disdained Chinese government, which, Joan says, cares nothing about the needs of the people. All the new construction we've been seeing (we see thirty cranes at a time in Beijing) is unproductive; it is for apartments no one can afford. There is no consciousness about the environment and pollution. People envy the West but are also resentful of Westerners who come to live and travel in opulence. She urges us to push our own obviously ideological stance with everyone we meet, as this offers a very different image of America. "The Chinese tend to stereotype the United States, just as you often fit China into a monolithic mold," she says. "In many ways, China and America have an affinity, and Chinese and American people tend to like each other as individuals."

I get a chance to share a cherished moment with this unusual icon. When I ask about a restroom, Joan leads me out to the back of the meeting building to a lean-to. She indicates two sets of cement footprints. Both of us position ourselves over adjoining holes and companionably answer nature's call.

The Forbidden City and Then Points West: Xi'an and Chengdu

We're given a day to wander on our own through the Forbidden City, called "Center of the Universe" by the emperors who lived there. We enter through the Gate of Supreme Harmony, guarded by stone lions to ward off evil spirits. Trudging through enormous courtyards, we explore an endless string of buildings that housed all the needs of the emperor's vast household, including quarters for his concubines and posts for their eunuch guardians. A treasure house displays musical instruments of jade, tapestries, and a gold box to hold the hair combed from the empress. Wherever we go, seven-year-old Thaddeus in our group attracts crowds; the Chinese marvel at his red hair, pick him up, carry him around, and take his picture.

After a day at The Great Wall, we're off on a jammed Russian plane to Xi'an in the middle of China. A Reuters reporter warns us that students are roughing up tourists in restaurants there, though we have no trouble. A farmer in Xi'an unearthed the first terra cotta warrior in 1974 when digging a well. More of these life-sized figures of soldiers, which go back two thousand years, are gradually being uncovered. Under a huge stadium roof, we see a thousand of them, along with their horses and chariots, lined up in battle array—with distinctive facial expressions, meticulously wrought uniforms according to ranking, and a full complement of weaponry. This is considered the most important excavation of the twentieth century. The tomb of the Emperor Qin Shi Huang, who established the first feudal empire, the Qin Dynasty, has not yet been opened. The emperor ordered the figures to be created and placed with him in his tomb to defend him in the afterlife.

All seven hundred thousand workers and childless concubines were sacrificed and buried as well, to safeguard the secrets of the project.

We fly on to Chengdu, our farthest point west, the capitol of Sichuan Province. Chengdu is close to Tibet, one topic we dare not bring up in China, including with our otherwise wonderful, affable Frances. There is no question in the minds of the Chinese that Tibet is a legitimate part of China and must be subdued. Any suggestion that it has a valid right to freedom or independence is met with frosty glares or anger.

Our Minshan Hotel is huge, new, gaudy. Nude nymphs dance across the lobby walls, all black marble and glass. A cellist is playing unaccompanied Bach in a bar, a disco flashes with strobe lights, and elegantly dressed patrons are hopping around. From our windows, the ubiquitous forest of construction cranes we see in every city interrupts our views. Even in this distant outpost, construction and modernization are feverishly underway.

We're taken to visit a Chengdu middle school. The children delightedly sing and perform for us, and then their teachers crowd around and plead with us to send Americans to teach them English. Years later this was the seed that suggested to Bel the value of creating his innovative Global Learning Center within the Milwaukee school system. (The idea was to open the eyes of children—in this case, central city middle schoolers—to the opportunities for travel, and perhaps work, abroad, mingling with cultures around the world.)

We go on to inspect the Dujiangyan Irrigation System, one of the amazing feats of China. Begun in 250 BCE, it divides the Minyan River with a diversion embankment shaped like the mouth of a fish; an inner river flows into irrigation canals. Bends in the river deposit silt strategically and send it into another sluiceway—all dug and shaped by hand. We stop at a Sunday market, surrounded by Mongol shoppers, and thread our way around baskets of squawking geese, babies, dead pigs strapped on the back of bikes, and old men in Tibetan-type hats smoking twelve-inch pipes or cigarettes upright in holders bent vertically.

From there we go to the sacred Taoist Mountain of Peace, thinking that at last we've discovered a spot where we can momentarily escape from the ever-present, noisy mobs. But we can barely climb the path; we're overwhelmed with crowds of Chinese tourists or pilgrims, continuous tchotchke stands, and pesky bearers who want to carry us up in canopied chairs that they balance on bamboo canes. There's absolutely no place to find privacy, we conclude, except in our hotel rooms.

Before reentering Chengdu, we must drive through the compulsory carwash, to keep the dirt and dust out of the city. There are eight washes abreast—something like the tollbooths on our interstates—with officials in snappy uniforms supervising. Even horse-drawn hay carts have to go through.

Our three weeks end with a boat trip on the magical Li River; we travel there also in 1992, and I describe it in the next section, which details high points from that trip. I've also saved wrap-up observations for Reflections at the end of this chapter.

Backstory, 1992

After their first study trip to China in 1989, Bel and his co-leader, Roger Collis, organized three more in consecutive years. As before, they attracted participants from across the United States as well as friends from Europe. I joined the group again for the fourth and last trip, and it didn't take much to persuade our younger son, Steve, a radio journalist/producer interested in broad social issues, to sign on. Roger's wife, Katherine, came along as well. Our itinerary this time included Hangzhou, Shanghai, Beijing, Kunming, and Guilin. As before, I'm not repeating accounts of some of the places we visited twice, but have combined descriptions, either in the 1989 chapter or in this one, 1992.

As part of two earlier trips, Bel and Roger had rallied political and academic leaders in Shanghai to sponsor major conferences to address some of the pressing challenges facing the world. They also lighted fires under China to begin initiating some important reforms in its own backyard.

After retracing some of the same steps of previous visits, the group flew to Hong Kong and then to Hangzhou, where we were met by Frances (Ling Zhang), the very competent national guide who had accompanied us on the other trips. After the usual acclimatization to the different rhythms of China—the slow agrarian pace in the tea fields and in the mountaintop monasteries—we were off to Shanghai for the culminating conference. Again it was organized by Bel's counterpart, Professor Zhu Rong-Lin at the International Technology and Economy Institute, and cosponsored with the University of Wisconsin. The title: "Global Conference on the Interrelationship Between the Environment and Economic Development." This was a topic fast becoming China's most urgent issue.

As we rolled up to our ultra-chic hotel in Shanghai, we were greeted by an enormous green-and-white banner that boldly proclaimed to the entire city our intention of "Turning the Whole World Green." As at the two previous gatherings, scientists, economists, entrepreneurs, and government officials came to present papers to the several hundred conference-goers. The previous January, Bel, as part of a "citizen diplomacy delegation" in Moscow, had cochaired a workshop urging the creation of a global think tank to look at some of these problems that were beginning to affect the entire world, and to brainstorm solutions (more about this in the following chapter about a 1990 delegation to the USSR). Now he was pushing the Chinese and others who had come to Shanghai from a number of countries to join together to make this a reality. With its strong environmental component, the conference organizers saw this meeting as the forerunner of the upcoming Earth Summit to be held in Rio de Janeiro.

A Conference in Shanghai: "Turning the Whole World Green"

We're barely settled in when we're hustled out to the huge plaza in front of the hotel. A truckload of little girls in white dresses arrives, then the army, then a band, and then a truck filled with crates of a thousand pigeons. They all line up under our flagship banner. After being duly impressed, our group is whisked away to an upstairs room in the hotel to meet privately with the mayor of Shanghai and other dignitaries. We sit in soft chairs, and the ubiquitous green tea is served in lidded cups on plates with hot, wet towels.

Then we're hustled down for the ceremony, jostling for space amid hundreds of spectators ringing the front steps, where Bel and Roger stand with the top civic brass. There are speeches, the girls perform a cheerleading routine, and martial music blares. Beautiful young women in long dresses cut a green ribbon, a large globe is unveiled, and Bel hands a green branch to a parrot (a little boy in a parrot costume). A hot air balloon hovers. The pigeons are released and fly to nearby trees; just as I'm snapping a picture of them, I get a splat on my head, which Steve tries to wipe off—gobs of green slime. I retreat to wash it off. A special luncheon is next (dubious food but elegant service), and then a yawn-inducing afternoon of perfunctory speeches. Bel and Roger wrap it up with their own talks and are interviewed for television. Afterward we all mingle with the conference-goers. Steve chats with a journalist, one of the simultaneous translators.

As part of the conference program, a field trip is scheduled. A motorcade of vans takes us to Pudong on the edge of the city; this is supposed to be the locale for a new model of an environmentally conscious area. We're surprised that nothing about it suggests "green." They tell us that everything there is to be bulldozed to make way for high-rise apartments and an industrial complex. Next we're ferried to the brand new Shanghai Stock Exchange (Mao must be turning over in his grave!). They usher us to a window overlooking the exchange floor, with thirty-six new brokers in smart orange vests. There is one international stock available (to foreigners).

That night is the culmination of the three-day conference—a pop concert/spectacle in our honor in a huge stadium with eighteen thousand spectators. Having no idea what to expect, we're escorted to "ringside" soft armchairs next to the Communist Party's Central Committee. There's a wild, deafening dance performed by kids and adults with an "end-of-the-world" motif, with flashing strobes and rolling smoke. Acts by top Chinese, Taiwanese, and Hong Kong rock stars follow—imitative of Michael Jackson and Elvis and John Denver—to screaming applause. Mimed comedy acts push environmental themes; with dramatic scenery, colored lights and exaggerated movements, the meanings are clear. Tea is served in our seats, and we're given bells to ring.

At one point during the conference, Steve and Katherine make contact with a Chinese video crew. They begin talking in the hotel lounge, but when someone mentions Tiananmen, the crew instantly stops the conversation and gestures for silence. They are afraid the room is bugged. One of them had made a documentary of the June 4 massacre of 1989 (never shown in China, of course). He is still on a hit list and must be very careful. Steve and Katherine aren't sure if the Chinese are feeling them out to smuggle the tape out of the country.

The next morning, at the Institute of Contemporary Foreign Relations (a think tank group), we ask what is next after Deng. The reply: "Socialism, but with 'special Chinese characteristics.'" Clearly a very different China, of seismic proportions, is unfolding.

Ominous Portents for The Great Wall Excursion

We fly to Beijing and land in a full-bore dust storm, probably gusting down from Mongolia. It's eerie to go to Coal Hill expecting the panoramic view we've seen before, but we find that visibility is almost nil. Instead, we decide to check out Tiananmen Square. But there, too, we find people covering their heads, walking against strong winds blowing grit into their mouths and eyes. Our hair becomes stiff with dust, and we begin to cough and choke. In the gloom, crowds have gathered to watch the soldiers with fixed bayonets take down the red flag in the square; we can barely see them. Sweepers in the streets are all wearing masks, and children riding on the backs of bicycles have nets over their heads.

This should be a premonition. When we ride the bus for the hour-and-a-half trip to The Great Wall—past steep cliffs and large boulders—we find that road also ominously murky with dust. The surrounding peaks are mysterious in the haze, and then we spot a ring of flames near the top. It's a fire going out of control in very dry brush, punctuated incongruously with the lovely pink-and-white fruit trees in bloom around us.

Steve is part of our study group—here climbing The Great Wall

Our group starts to climb the historic wall that was constructed between 475 and 221 BCE in order to protect the southern part of China against warlike Mongolian nomads. The steep steps are precipitous enough that some of us need to cling to the wall for support as we climb. The wall is six thousand kilometers long and went up in sections or stages, connecting periodic beacon towers. It took a million people (a fifth of the population of China) to build; many of these died while working and were buried in the wall. Such is the magnitude of the wall that the earliest astronauts reported that it was one of the only objects on Earth they could see from space.

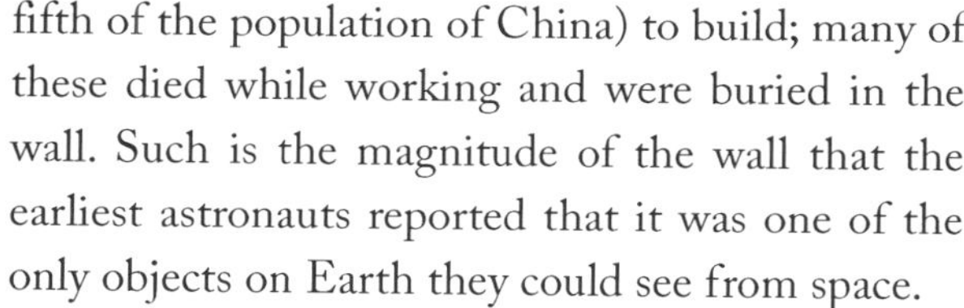

Elaborately costumed Mandarin warriors with swords pass us on the steps. They march in cadence, their faces appropriately menacing, perhaps to entertain (or intimidate) the crowds. Steve and Roger revel in scrambling down from the point where the wall ends officially to explore the rougher, "no trespassing" terrain.

Our group straggles down after a couple of hours, and while we're perusing the souvenir shops, Roger rushes up to report that Kitty, one of the group, has fallen and injured her leg badly. She's stranded high on the wall. At that point, we have to collect everybody fast and get to our bus, parked on the other side of town. As we approach the bus, streams of trucks and police cars and fire vehicles are roaring by, filled with soldiers—everyone is recruited to fight the fire in the hills. Roger, Bel, and Steve race up to carry Kitty down from the wall. Slowly the bus is able to maneuver into the traffic lanes, but the problem is to reach a point nearest the wall.

Meanwhile, an apoplectic policeman is ordering our bus to move on. The driver explains that we have an injured person coming, but this has no effect. With all the fire vehicles claiming priority, we're clearly out of line in blocking traffic. Our driver inches the bus a few feet while the policeman continues to scream, and then, in fury, grabs the driver's license and takes it away.

Finally Kitty arrives and is hoisted aboard. Her husband had hunted for a medic, but they're all away at the fire. We start off for a Beijing hospital. Clearly the driver is in serious trouble—he's lost his license and is faced with a heavy fine that could mean a month's salary. Maybe he'll even lose his job—all for being a Good Samaritan. All the way back, he weeps in despair, while Kitty lies in shock and pain. We see graphically how China works: usually the letter of the law prevails, and compassion is unknown, or not dared, in official territory. Eventually, however, the driver does get his license back, and the group collects money for his fine.

The group all signs Kitty's cast and we say goodbye. She's too frightened to have the hospital operate on her broken leg and just wants to get back to the United States as fast as possible. She'll be flown out immediately.

An Enchanted World

We fly southwest to Kunming in Yunnan Province, not far from the Vietnamese and Burmese borders—invited by Frances' family who live here. We drop down over fields patterned with green crops and startling red soil. Kunming is a city of half a million, mostly of the Yi Nation, one of fifty-five ethnic minority groups in China, in addition to the predominant Han Chinese. It's situated six thousand feet up on a plateau ringed by mountains. Our hotel is across from a lovely lake, and soon we're off to explore gardens and pagodas, and to take a boat ride poled gondola-fashion by two women. After dinner, we're caught in a mob of women selling gorgeous embroidery; the style is cruder, and, to me, more attractive than the refined work on satin we usually see. Several blind men in white are lined up with chairs offering massages. Women are getting haircuts in other chairs, also along the roadside. Noted: a lady on a bike in fancy dress, lace gloves, and a brimmed party hat; a girl with a very tight leather skirt just over her rump, black stockings, and four-inch heels. These are juxtaposed with ancient women and men in Mao shirts slouched in dusty doorways eating out of bowls.

Frances' brother takes us to the Institute for the Preservation of Endangered Species that he directs; we wander through fields and a greenhouse with plants so rare they are found nowhere else on Earth. They also have a butterfly propagation program. At lunch with the staff, we hear that they badly need funding for their work, and dream of creating a village where visitors may come for short stays to learn about living more ecologically.

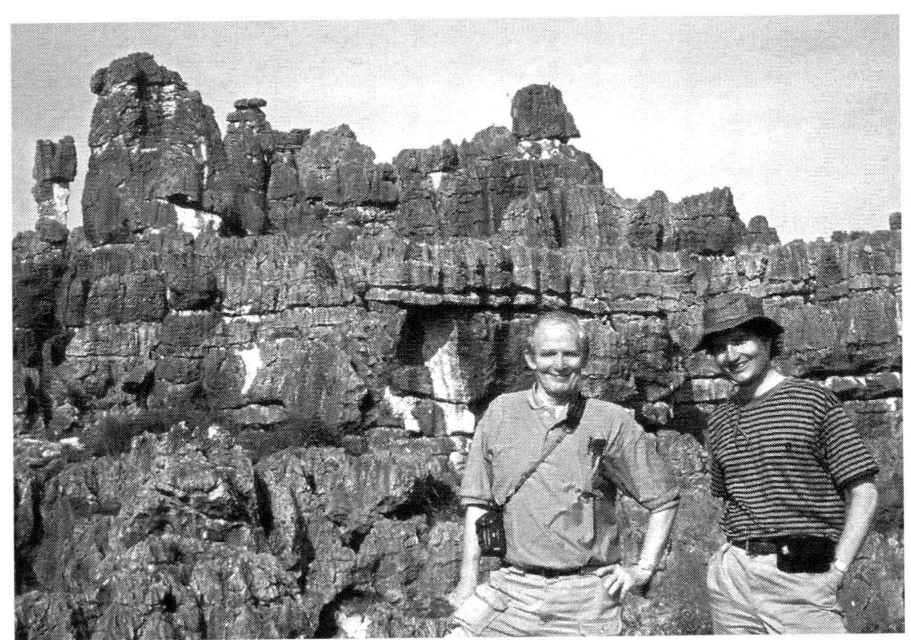

Exploring the Stone Forest of Kunming

Kunming is most famous for its Stone Forest. We climb steadily on a wide road, its red earth bright against very green rice patches and shining irrigation trenches. People are toiling in fields that are often steep terraces. Water buffalo drag plows. Then we begin to see great, monolithic spires of stone thrusting up in the fields, then denser groupings. Finally we come to the Stone Forest village, jammed with tourists and aggressive lady hawkers. These women are Sani, part of the Yi nation. They look Tibetan and are in costume, which they wear all the time, including as they work in the fields.

We hike through the Forest, with formations that look like stalagmites but outdoors; they're 270 million years old, created by water erosion. We find ourselves crawling through tight, dark places and circling shadowy pools. It's all a bit eerie.

Then Bel, Steve, and I go off on our own. At the embroidery stalls, we get to talking with a young woman with a baby strapped on her back. She offers to take us to her Sani village, away from the city clamor, and then invites us into her house. It's spacious but almost completely dark, with a dirt floor. Her only furniture: three tiny stools, a sewing machine, and a TV with a religious icon sitting on top (the Yi are mainly spirit worshippers). We crawl up a ladder to see a rumpled bed and a loft "for changing" and cooking. We wait while she feeds her baby, and then, just as we're leaving, she flings open a gate to a courtyard and our eyes pop.

Suddenly we're in a realm that could be straight from the Middle Ages. Breugel-like, there's sun shimmering on golden wheat, people of all ages bustling about in the Sani costume, chopping, threshing with a foot-pedaled machine, and binding sheaths of grain. Pigs and chickens are wandering freely. Bathed in the brilliant late afternoon light, we feel we've been transported to another world entirely. It's absolutely magical.

The little miracles do not end with the sunlit courtyard scene from another era. Our group is up the next morning before dawn to stroll into the countryside amid the rock outcroppings. It's totally silent except for strange birdsongs (such quiet is a great rarity in China, at least in the parts we've seen). Whole families are hoeing; some farmers are hacking the orange soil, others are collecting bundles of twigs for firewood and piling enormous loads onto horse carts. The horses gather steam and then gallop full-tilt up the hills. We come upon an open pagoda on a little knoll, and spontaneously we all gravitate there. We sit quietly on the benches to survey the ancient peasant rituals unfolding around us, to breathe in the fragrant country air, and to meditate in the silence. I think for most of us, this morning stands out as one of the more memorable experiences of the trip.

More of the "Unreal"

We'd all seen paintings of the jagged, solitary peaks soaring skyward around the south-central city of Guilin that seemed pure, stylized fantasy. But we have to sail up the Li River for a day to see for ourselves that these odd karst (limestone) formations are indeed real—ancient rock companions to outcroppings of stunted trees that march down their steep sides like stubble. They are fingers sticking up from the otherwise flat landscape in an area that 300 million years ago was sea.

One of many tourist groups (with only a smattering of Western "round eyes" among them), we're hustled onto one of a whole fleet of boats whose captains honk furiously as they jockey to be the first out onto the river. We watch the busy cooking crew at the stern, chopping vegetables that go into baskets they dip "to clean" in the muddy, swirling waters. Baskets are lowered into the river and brought up a minute later filled with snails, stirred from the bottom. We find luxurious, soft chairs and carpeting for passengers, yet there's also the ubiquitous plumbing arrangement: an oval, porcelain-lined hole with a raised platform for feet, over which one squats. You flush into the river where all the dishes are washed in blackened garbage cans and where, probably, water is drawn for tea and cooking.

The blasting, echoing horns quiet down as distances lengthen between vessels. The scene becomes more serene as we float past forests of the limestone peaks and fjord-like giant cliffs plunging straight down into the water. We drift past fishermen on rafts; some, with nets, are snaring turtles and eels. Others have giant, black cormorants tied to their boats; the birds dive for fish that the fishermen then retrieve from their mouths. Dilapidated junks rock at anchor near little villages of clumped, thatched huts. Sheep and goats are being herded on the almost-vertical cliffs. After a very good lunch of fish and vegetable soup, one of the best of the trip, despite dubious cleanliness—we loll lazily on the deck in the hot sun, soaking up the mysterious anomalies we're floating past. Back in Guilin, there's a hike through the Reed Flute Cave, and a farewell banquet before flying off to Hong Kong and home.

Reflections

Trying to make any kind of summary of my two (or Bel's four) trips to China is almost impossible. It was clear, though, that the back alleys we glimpsed in the early 1990s in pockets of Shanghai and Beijing—where people were still living in labyrinthian warrens in disintegrating wooden and tin hovels without water or toilets or kitchens—were on the way out. Some may be sad that the antique character of these cities is disappearing, but I suspect now, twenty years later, that most of those old structures may be gone.

The first thirty years of communism were defined by poverty and no market economy. During the Cultural Revolution, the bourgeoisie and intellectuals were persecuted and sent to farms in the provinces "for reeducation." Now, for the first time, there is a generation in their twenties and thirties coming up in an economic system that has been broken wide open. They are the first generation to strike out on their own; they're scrambling to be entrepreneurs, to get rich. Some are suddenly *very* rich.

China actually has a long tradition of entrepreneurship. Before the nineteenth century, it boasted one of the more advanced economies in the world. After several decades of stringent collectivism from the mid-twentieth century, in 1978 economic reforms were started within the Communist Party, led by Deng Xiaoping. Deng began to dissolve the collectives and opened the country to foreign investing. Then, by the late 1980s and 1990s, there were more changes: many of the state-owned businesses shifted to private ownership. By 2005, China's economy had grown exponentially until it became the second largest in the world after the United States. As a result, poverty has been reduced, but inequality has increased.

As part of this remarkable boom, where young people are clawing their way up the status and job ladders, we also hear that they're starting to feel as stressed out as their counterparts in the West. We're even hearing that some in the competitive marketplace are beginning to long for the simpler times of their forebears. In the early days of the economic opening, the first private cars became a huge status symbol, and bicycles were scorned as evidence that one was stuck in poverty. Now the affluent and stressed-out entrepreneurs look on bicycles with a bit of nostalgia—they hark back to a slower, more peaceful era.

When we visited in the late '80s and early '90s, despite the economic loosening, authoritarian oppression still hung heavy, and the most hope for real freedom centered in the academic and research communities. It was there that the teachers and scientists strove to keep their independence from a government that effectively muffled any assaults against its buttoned-up, communist orthodoxy—as witnessed by the events in Tiananmen Square.

Through our contacts with the various institutes, we found that as they sought to join the rest of the world, they were eager for technological exchanges and joint ventures. Academic exchanges were a good way to understand the cultures of others and to truly cooperate.

The wisest know that on many fronts China is growing too fast to unfold as a healthy, sustainable culture—one reason that twenty years ago they were so anxious to have us share our American ideas about the unsustainability of fossil fuel societies. They knew their coal dependency and the demand for cars and refrigerators for over a billion Chinese could lead to future disaster. It's why China is now blowing the whistle loudly on ecological issues and is starting to make remarkable strides in exercising its historically astute gene pool that stimulates them to innovate and achieve.

The articulate voices emerging courageously from the odd mishmash of old Maoist proponents and stock market "hot dogs" are the ones who may begin to bring about the true freedom of expression that those hopeful and doomed students were pushing for in the spring of 1989.

At our meeting at the Institute for Contemporary Foreign Relations in Shanghai, the professors were looking at the collapse of the USSR and communism and saw that capitalism didn't necessarily triumph for them at that point. The Chinese leaders had studied the experience of their fellow communists, and they proceeded cautiously in another direction with, as they said, "socialism with special Chinese characteristics." The professors predicted that both China and Russia would have a more prominent role on the future global scene. After 1979, when China began to rejoin the world community, it grew prosperous, opening wider to the world. Its culture has become distinctly different from that of Russia, which has no history of freedom and entrepreneurship; China is learning that privatizing business is useful for modernization.

For our group, the president of the International Technology Institute, also in Shanghai, pontificated:

> Let us have cooperation, not only competition, so that we will all win. We are all brothers and sisters on this ship. If one person is threatened, we are all threatened. Compromise is essential. I want to cooperate closely with foreign scholars. You have come to us at the right time. Our government tends to separate problems into small units, but our thinking at the Institute is more on the same wavelength as yours.
>
> China doesn't retain its older philosophy as well now as it did. We need to integrate the old *and* new ways. This can be China's contribution to an international think tank.

This was the concept that Bel pushed in all our official meetings.

We came away with great empathy for the Chinese we met as they tackle monumental challenges—challenges that are hurling into a brand-new era a society entrenched in an ethos and customs that go back thousands of years.

St. Basil's Cathedral in the Kremlin: "But what about animal fur?" "How else would we stay warm?" When in Rome . . .

Citizen-Diplomats in the USSR

JANUARY 1990

Backstory

If I were to continue with the correct chronology of our socio/political adventures, Bel's and my citizen-diplomat stint in Moscow in 1990 would have been sandwiched between the two reports from China. But because the 1989 and 1992 China trips were part of a closely related, four-year sequence, they needed to be looked at together. The theme of the Moscow Summit was "Restoring the Global Environment: Sustainable Development for the New Millennium."

As alluded to in my discussion of the Shanghai conferences, a major interest of Bel's was to create a holistic, global think tank to strategize action that would contribute to building a more peaceful, sustainable world. This would be a counterbalance to several think tanks that were already effectively guiding and deciding conservative, nationalistic US policy coming out of Washington.

At the New Synthesis Think Tank Consultation in New York in 1987, which Bel helped to put together, it became clear that fresh winds were starting to blow through the Soviet Union. Mikhail Gorbachev had come in as general secretary of the Communist Party in 1985 and had boldly introduced his concepts of Perestroika (restructuring the economic and social life of his country) and Glasnost (openness). Just as our science professor friends in China had told us, Gorbachev also was pressing the idea that everyone in the world is "in it" together—that we must begin to respect and support each other, not only for mutual survival, but for the mutual benefit of all.

The Cold War that for decades had threatened to explode in a nuclear confrontation between the United States and the USSR was winding down. Exchanges between private individuals from both countries were quietly beginning to take place when it was still difficult or impossible for officials and governments to meet in in-depth ways.

Our longtime friend and peace activist Barbara Marx Hubbard had recognized the need for rapprochement between these two major powers, and in 1988, she helped to organize the "Soviet-American Citizens' Summit I" in Alexandria, Virginia. A hundred delegates from the USSR flew over to dialogue with several hundred Americans. When Barbara and her associates proposed a follow-up gathering in Moscow for January 1990, she tapped Bel to cochair with a Soviet counterpart a "US-USSR Think Tank Task Force on Global Perestroika." This would be one of many working groups commissioned to come up with concrete proposals by the end of the meeting. I was invited to come along as one of the two hundred American delegates.

Bel's task force of thirty, international but mostly Soviet, came up with one of the more exciting projects: establishing a Global Think Tank for an Interdependent Sustainable Future. Initially it would have five members: USA, USSR, UK, India, and China. It would focus on policy formation and research, communications, and education and consultation. Individual task force members volunteered to take the lead on specific projects, such as establishing a global electronic network, environmental assessments, dialogues on new thinking, and a series of retreats to train Russians in grassroots democracy. Concrete plans were initiated, but soon thereafter the USSR experienced revolutionary changes that brought new leadership, so these projects did not go forward.

Orienting for Another Culture

Our huge, unwieldy American contingent of two hundred assembles in New York and flies first to Shannon, Ireland, for a three-day orientation. Our leaders stress the delicacy of international relations at this very unsettled time—it's the eve of fighting between Armenia and Azerbaijan in the south, and also the precarious testing of Gorbachev's Perestroika initiative. For these reasons, the country is wide open, vulnerable, and under tremendous pressure. It could go either in the direction of relaxing further into individual freedoms, or the situation could provoke a hard-line clampdown. Our Summit, our massive presence, has the potential for providing a small but critical impetus for real change.

We're told:

> The Soviet system, how the people think and perceive, is essentially "Byzantine or Eastern, but in Western dress." On the surface, we may imagine great similarities, while actually differences run deep. For them it's the whole setting, the *context*, that's most important. In the West, we tend to stress the components, the *content*. The Soviets will be euphoric when we first meet—an emotional response—but then may express disappointment when we want to get down to concrete details and communication breaks down. They're highly intuitive and don't hear words. They're apt to see us as too intellectual and "dry as pie crust." Not understanding the nitty-gritty content of what we're saying, partly because of language barriers, they'll relate mainly on an eye/heart level, so we'll need to work constantly to get our feelings of compassion and love across.

Our purpose will be to identify long-range planetary goals with the Soviets and to develop specific joint projects with our counterparts in some twenty task forces.

Landing Behind the Iron Curtain

On a Saturday morning in Shannon, we gather in the dark with our five hundred pieces of coded luggage to be gotten through the airports to Moscow. We take off in two aging Aeroflot planes.

It's mid-afternoon, dusk in this land on the edge of the Arctic Circle. We dip through the clouds to see vast expanses of dark forests rimming white snowfields. Scattered clumps of tall apartment buildings rise out of nowhere. Only one main highway appears to be plowed; the little roads are snow covered, and there are virtually no vehicles. At the Moscow airport, we zip in over the now-distinct evergreens and birches crowding the runways.

On the twenty-mile ride into Moscow, along deserted stretches of the main road, are long, glass enclosures with knots of fur-hatted people waiting for buses. In the city are lovely winter scenes: skaters on small ponds; figures strolling through shadowy, snowy, unlit parks; parents pulling kids on sleds.

As we wait for room assignments in the enormous Cosmos Hotel, the whole world passes by: heavily made-up young girls of many nationalities in miniskirts or skin-tight pants. The open cloakroom displays hundreds of fur hats perched on special hooks over their respective coats. We get our first dose of signs in the Cyrillic alphabet and the Russian language; I'm frustrated and decide I'll need to learn this if we're to continue working in this country. (In fact, I study Russian for the next ten years back in Wisconsin.) Despite dire warnings of food shortages, our first supper belies this—with three kinds of lamb, mashed potatoes, baked beans, Kaşha, cold salads of fish, shredded cabbage, and beets, and cooked apples. Of course, it's probably a very different story outside the international hotels. We almost never see fresh fruits or vegetables in the USSR.

The Plenary Sessions

We take over the thousand-seat Congress Hall and wide lobby outside it with our giant Citizen Summit II sign and information booths with troops of facilitators, runners, and some thirty translators. The conference is organized by the Center for Soviet-American Dialogue and the Soviet Peace Committee—this latter liaison questioned by some because the Peace Committee is considered to be a holdover from the pre-Gorbachev/Brezhnev era. Still, it's the only group able to pull off a huge, weeklong event like this with five hundred participants, and it has over a million members who contribute to it (not voluntarily).

Each morning is spent in the big hall for Plenary Sessions with three or four major speakers. I won't attempt to report the proceedings in any detail, but to give the flavor of the conference, I will paraphrase from my notes some of what a few of the notable presenters are saying.

Noel Brown (North American Environmental Program of the UN, from Jamaica; he kicks off the sustainability theme of the conference). The United States and USSR are the greatest technological states, and are also the greatest producers of pollution, so it's appropriate that we take the lead in reversing this. We need to ask: What can we do personally? How can we encourage our own governments? What can they do bilaterally? Globally? We need: 1) a covenant that sets standards for the Earth; 2) targets, achievable goals for sustainable development; 3) commitment; 4) equity, sharing with the Third World; and 5) costing and financing.

David Brower (twice nominated for the Nobel prize, fifty years with the Sierra Club, founded Friends of the Earth and the militant Earth Island). It's time to heal and restore the Earth. When you've reached the edge of an abyss, the only progressive thing to do is to step backward, or turn around and step forward. We're already fighting and winning World War III, against the Earth. If we don't question what we're doing, I give us only thirty years more. If, for instance, the nuclear power station at Le Havre were destroyed, Western Europe would be uninhabitable. Is electricity worth this risk? We're losing species at the rate of one every minute; years ago I knew a child with four days to live who was cured by a plant now extinct. We need to "tranquilize" our developers, and then give them a shot again when they wake up!

Sergei Tolstoy (grandson of Leo Tolstoy). It is science that's befouling our planet; Oppenheimer and Sakharov were aghast at what their inventions caused. My grandfather created a new spiritual path, a religion based on brotherhood and the true teaching of Christ. "Thou shalt not kill" must be obeyed absolutely, my father said. There must be no death penalty. Perestroika must be spiritual as well as economic.

Mikhail Milstein (retired USSR general, author of the Palma Commission Decision). We must get rid of all nuclear devices; any war is unthinkable in terms of damage to the environment. We need a "Common Global House" to orchestrate disarmament so we can all feel safe. I can see the possibility of exchanging whole military units between our two countries.

Daniel Ellsberg (tried for treason when he spoke out during the Vietnam War and, incidentally, Barbara Marx Hubbard's brother-in-law). I foresee a very clear possibility of all Soviet arms being removed from Europe in the next five to ten years. We could eliminate entirely our US military budget in Europe in one to three years because our presence has been based on a possible Soviet attack there. Over a trillion dollars would be saved to use on social and environmental programs. The Soviets must lead the way in disarming, though, or the United States won't follow.

Yuri Zamoshkin (prominent professor of sociology at the USSR Academy of Science, associated with Perestroika and restructuring the Soviet Union). There are real contradictions in our society: the need for individual self-expression and uniqueness and personal goals—and also the need for organized, institutionalized action, collective movement, and the subordination of the individual to common needs. In the democracies, people want to have their cake and eat it, too. People need to take responsibility and shoulder the consequences of standing on their own. At this point, our resources are exhausted, so how can we pay for this, and what will be the cost in human labor?

(I see firsthand a small-scale example of the curious contradictions the professor is noting. In our hotel, a lady stands at the top of the escalator, and when someone wants to go down, she switches it on; then when it's needed to go up, she presses a button to reverse the direction. When she isn't there—much of the time—people simply walk. It never runs all the time; a waste of energy? Yet all the rooms are kept at a stifling 75-80 degrees, day and night!)

Hazel Henderson (a leading US economist and futurist). The economies of the world are having great trouble surviving Western "progress." Governments can no longer protect their people from pollution or from other global ills, including economic upheavals. Economists see only prices as valid feedback, not real costs, such as to future generations. We debate what is valuable under the new conditions: Air? Water? We hear about leveling the global playing field to fit into a global idea of efficiency. But economies are only rules and games of a particular culture or country. We tell Japan it must pave over its land and build shopping malls and have its people drive twenty minutes to work, but these are *our* conditions. We need to "raise the floor of moral standards"—protecting the health of workers, the environment. As the GNP goes up, the poverty gap grows wider, and the United States uses more than twice as much energy as does Japan and the USSR. So we need to compete on energy efficiency, not use.

Work in the Task Forces

The twenty task forces meet each afternoon. Bel's Think Tank for an Interdependent Sustainable Future labors hard with a handpicked group of

Americans and a talented Soviet contingent (writers, political activists, academics, businesspeople, new-town planners, half of whom speak English). They come up with twenty-seven projects, with the global think tank mentioned above as the most dramatic.

My group, the Environment Task Force, brings out a lot of ideas for projects—seventy-eight. There are only a dozen Americans to some sixty Soviets, few of whom know English (though we all have headphones for translations). Each of us gets up to speak. Most of the Soviets bring up life-and-death issues, such as cleaning up rivers where the government has been dumping huge amounts of radioactive waste. My issue is identifying anyone working with small-scale, safe, sustainable technologies. However, in a country where everyone is trying to get more and catch up to the West in appliances and "the good life," it may be going against the tide to exhort people to slow down and maybe to sacrifice.

It takes three days to hear all the proposals and it's pretty chaotic; we find that no one wants to "stand under anyone else's umbrella," so it's questionable how much follow-through may be possible. The Soviets conclude that ecological problems stem from the fact that it isn't a priority for human beings to see themselves a part of a living nature; thus, massive educational work in schools and for adults is needed. In the end, we come up with a Covenant of Resolves that mesh the ideas of each side, Soviet and American.

Connecting with the People

One afternoon I take off to participate in a Childrens' Vigil in front of the Peace Committee building. About ten of us join a hundred kids to stand with candles and signs saying "Don't Kill Our Fathers" (in the Armenia fighting). There is lots of media coverage, and a Radio Moscow reporter tapes an interview with me, asking what I feel about the conflict, then my opinion of the Green Party, Greenpeace, and so forth. I talk about the intentional community in America (High Wind) that Bel and I founded, and our ecological ethic. The reporter, Tanya Petrovna, is very excited and comes back on the bus to the hotel with me to attend our environment group. She also invites me to her home, but unfortunately there isn't time. We speak in French.

The Soviets are generally very eager to get close to us, inviting Americans to their apartments for fancy spreads and drinks, and to exchange gifts. In the dining room, there is nonstop connecting and conversation. One evening I find myself chatting with a matronly Muscovite across the table. It turns out she's a noted parapsychologist, Barbara Ivanova. To my many questions about the current situation, she closes her eyes and consults her "sources" before giving her views:

> My guess is that Gorbachev will still be around a year from now, but he may have less power. There is still tremendous strength in the KGB, the military, and the conservative wing of the Communist Party. These groups enjoy many privileges, have more money, and are not ready to give up such advantages. The USSR is not a "classless society." The sad thing is that, aside from the small number of writers/intellectuals/radicals—some of whom are here at this conference—the great mass of people may prefer to keep the old guard in power. They say that Perestroika isn't working, and they don't like Gorbachev, who brought them the worst of Western "development"—poverty, unemployment, scarcity of commodities, violence, crime, drugs. This is a country with no history of democracy, no tradition of freedom. People tend to look at independence with more fear than hope. Many would prefer the tight

control and security of being taken care of that goes with this. Some think that Gorbachev, who is the hero/savior in every country except his own, may only be accepted and his ideas carry real clout in the USSR when he is no longer around. Most of the "good" people have been killed off—the thinkers and artists—and only the hacks are left who are too timid to question what's going on.

We hear many of these opinions on the streets ourselves, so there isn't a lot of optimism. There is very much the mentality of living only for today, grabbing what one can now, rather than tightening one's belt for a greater future good. Widespread polluting certainly fits with this. Soviet history has been so dark and tragic that the people don't know how to be optimistic or to plan for their children or grandchildren. My new friend, the psychic, nearly wept with the pain and frustration of voicing her fears, and she made it clear that she'll do everything possible to further contacts with the outside world to catalyze the changes.

Bel reports that a very attractive woman follows him around and gives her telephone number as a place to stay when he returns to Moscow—a secret agent?

A week after our return, when I was writing up my notes, it was the day of Gorbachev's crucial test. He was about to propose the most radical break in the Soviet political system to date: to take absolute power from the Central Committee and allow a multiparty system. I heard reports of unprecedented crowds gathering outside the Kremlin walls shouting encouragement and support for the president. Juxtaposed against the gloomy thoughts of my friend at the conference, one can surmise that despite an inbred lack of faith born of bitter experience, many of the people desperately do want to join the thawing process of their Eastern bloc neighbors. They can almost see the light breaking through and will give to this precious moment all they can to further human rights, individualism, and perhaps ethnic autonomy within the Soviet Union.

Getting around Moscow

To my mind, we are trapped altogether too much in this big, Western-style hotel. It's old and a bit creaky, with a heavy, smoky atmosphere (everyone smokes; a cab driver literally won't stop unless you flash a pack of American cigarettes as an incentive). The way I get the feel of a new country is by walking the streets, seeing people going about their ordinary lives, and traveling to villages and the countryside to touch into the land—so our confinement is definitely getting to me!

We do manage to escape several times, however, to Red Square, with spectacular St. Basil's church where Ivan the Terrible had its architect blinded so he could never design another, and where there are perpetual long lines to view Lenin, perfectly embalmed in his tomb. Then we step inside the magical confines of the walled Kremlin and its assemblage of old Orthodox churches, with their onion domes and spires, steep roofs, riotous colors, ornate carvings, gilded icons, and paintings. On one outing, we tramp around some back lanes and along Arbat Street, the artists' quarter. Paintings are sold on the sidewalks, and we wander into little cafés, bookstores, and handcraft and poster shops. Another day someone in our delegation has a wallet stolen there, and purses are slashed, an influence, some would say, from the West.

A couple of times we ride the metro, plunging hundreds of feet via fast-moving escalators so long we can't even see the bottom in the strange blur of lights. Deep in the earth, the platforms are lit by crystal chandeliers and decorated with huge, classical sculptures and frescoed ceilings. We can travel anywhere in the city on this efficient system for five kopecks (one cent).

The weather turns out to be much warmer than we'd been led to expect for January. We haven't had to dig out our stacks of long underwear after all. In the overheated buildings, even sweaters are often too much. Outside it's foggy or drizzling by day, though frequently at dusk, the temperature drops and we get a soft, wet snow. Mostly we tramp around in slush. Great numbers of Soviets wear fur coats and nearly all have fur hats. When we question the killing of animals, they shrug and reply, "But it gets very cold here, and this is the only way we can keep warm."

Experiencing the Soul of the USSR

A number of spectacular entertainments are arranged for us, starting with a great crush of a cocktail party with exotic food and drink (champagne and exquisite pastries). There is a concert in an old church with zithers, mandolins, balalaikas, pipes, drums, and accordion; the superb musicians start out wearing tuxedos to play classical numbers, then switch to bright ethnic costumes for folk music and dance. Our people hop up to join in. Another night they treat us to Gypsy theater, with the highly emotive drama of these peoples' history told with singing and dance.

A final gala is offered at the Hall of Columns, where Lenin lay in state when he died and where, eight years later, his widow spoke out for women's rights. This is an enormous space, with Parthenon-like white columns gleaming down corridors lit by thousands of lights from mammoth chandeliers. Very elegant, it reminds me of Versailles. Precocious children whirl and stamp their way through regional dances, and forty more stand up to play violins in unison. Finally, three hundred musicians come on stage to perform the "Ode to Joy" from Beethoven's Ninth Symphony.

A Secretive Meeting

On our last day in Moscow, Gennady Alfarenko slips quietly into the conference to meet with a small group of us. Gennady is one of the brightest leading political activists in the country. (He shepherded Boris Yeltsin around the United States and to the White House on Yeltsin's infamous 1989 trip, the year before Yeltsin was to spearhead the democratic revolt against the USSR.) We hope to work with Alfarenko on a Soviet-US retreat that would contribute to opening the USSR to greater freedom. Gennady is in "maverick" garb (i.e., jeans and

Bel and Roger Doudna (from Findhorn) are taken by activist Gennady Alfarenko to hush-hush Moscow headquarters

sneakers rather than the formal suits that most of the others at the conference are wearing). Because he's a true radical, he doesn't publish or identify himself publicly, because then he would be controlled by the bureaucrats. He opts to stay underground to move freely. He has little use for the Peace Committee and its touchy-feely meetings and exchanges with the United States. He asks, "How is this really stopping the fighting in Armenia?"

Gennady leads our little group surreptitiously through back streets to a small room in his simple hotel where his Foundation for Social Innovation is based. The desk clerk and cleaning ladies are all fervent supporters and coworkers. Bel explains our aim: to transform values and make basic changes in society—all societies. They discuss which groups in the USSR could help to bring this about globally. Apparently the prestigious Peace Committee is reactionary or tainted, not tuned into real problems and suffering. Gennady suggests inviting to future planning meetings the president of Latvia, an important key thinker, along with businesspeople who can transform and reach millions of people. The real leaders are hard workers and are not the ones out front meeting foreigners.

Conference Conclusions

A wrap-up of the Summit summarizes the joint projects coming out of the task forces. There are 122 projects mentioned formally, and undoubtedly others will blossom in time as the connections deepen. Among a great many intriguing ideas, here are a few that seemed promising to me—besides those Bel or I would he involved with directly:

- Clean up the environment with the armed forces, worldwide (the armies on land, air forces for the air, navies for the seas and waterways—a "civilitary").
- Create an "ecology army" of young people who, before going to college or careers, could be paid to clean up the land and rivers, which would give them financial independence.
- Send out, free of charge, a UN-sponsored crisis/disaster corps (as for the Alaska oil spill): an "International Green Cross."
- Get every child in the United States and USSR and in twenty other countries to plant two trees a year; this would be a billion trees.
- Replace the Berlin Wall with trees and flowers.
- Restructure all institutions and aspects of social, political, economic, and cultural life so that women and men may serve as equal partners, nurturing and protecting our children and all life on Earth in joy, with unconditional love, on a healthy, boundaryless planet of "green forests, blue rivers and smiling suns" (the Soviets are ever the poets!).

One project is completed by the end of the conference. A member of our delegation with family roots in the Ukraine, Margie Joy, visits Kiev. She identifies deeply with those who suffered in the pogroms of the early nineteenth century, a feeling heightened by the terrible trauma for both the land in that area and the people uprooted after the Chernobyl nuclear accident in 1986. One hundred thousand people had to be removed from the afflicted area. During the conference, Margie Joy is delegated to deliver a gift in Kiev, a quilt made by children, parents, and teachers in the state of Washington. This follows a tradition of people joining together to make a quilt for a family that has lost its home in a disaster; this one is to go to a group of Chernobyl refugees in one of their resettlement villages. The children have traced their hands on green fabric, cut out the patterns, and appliquéd them like leaves onto branches of "The Tree of Life" depicted on the quilt—a symbol of compassionate hands reaching across the world for the regeneration of life.

Margie Joy travels with a group by train to Kiev, and, after some red tape, is able to set up a meeting with some of the refugees in a room behind a barn. About a hundred peasants come, most of whom had never seen Americans; they half expect them to be fierce and evil. By the end of the presentation, however, the Americans and Ukrainians are all in tears, including the stiff, dour, KGB-type guards standing around. The barriers melt, and those who went tell us that the outpouring of emotion and warmth was extraordinary. This experience becomes a perfect culminating symbol for the Summit, a blessing on the mission our two cultures have undertaken together. After the report, someone notes that we don't actually need nuclear weapons because we see that three percent of the contaminated material at Chernobyl caused all the damage. The plants themselves have become nuclear deterrents; if they suffer damage, the proliferation of radiation from them will be lethal.

Escape to Leningrad

By the end of the week, we are all saturated. We've had enough of being tethered to the heavy atmosphere of the Cosmos Hotel, and are getting overloaded with tension-provoking topics. Bel and I, with seven friends, make arrangements through one of the brand-new, private, entrepreneurial travel agents to see a bit of Leningrad. It costs us a quarter of what the government Intourist package is offering conference-goers.

Traveling overnight by train, we crowd into cramped compartments with berths for four (mixed sexes; if a woman wants to undress, the men in the compartment step out into the corridor). We're rocked to sleep, and when I look out from the curtains from time to time, there is only frozen tundra. I'm reminded of *Dr. Zhivago* and almost expect to see a troika drawn by its three horses racing across the snowy fields or a shadowy wolf pack. In the morning, glasses of tea are served in our compartment in silver filigree holders. While I stand in line for the toilet, I'm propositioned for dollars with souvenirs. We're met at the Leningrad station by an outstanding guide who actually edits radio news and is just going off to London with the BBC to report on the war in the South.

Over two short days, we're bussed around this stunning city—the "Venice of the North," with its graceful European architecture and canals everywhere. Much too rapidly we whiz through the Hermitage Museum, climbing the grand, marble ceremonial staircase and being rushed through room after room of alabaster and malachite, with inlaid tables and, of course, some of the finest paintings in the world. It's a delight to see the originals of some of my favorite impressionist pieces: *Place de la Concorde* of Degas, *The White House at Night* of van Gogh, and whole rooms of Monet and Pissarro, many of these hidden during the war and thought lost.

We drive out into the countryside to see where the Germans ringed the city for more than three years of siege during World War II, when one million Leningraders died of hunger. Everyone we meet lost relatives in the siege. It's why no one wants to fight again and why they think Soviet-American dialogue is so critical. What people are mostly talking about right now, though, are issues of private property (there are some private houses allowed on public land) and democracy (more than one party). They fear, though, that it may take twenty years before there is real change. They

Approach to the Summer Palace of Czar Paul I in Pushkin, near Leningrad

have no faith in Gorbachev's initiatives. He started well, our knowledgeable guide says, but with fifteen republics, each with its own language and culture and historical development, the unification he seeks may be impossible.

Then it's on to the village of Pushkin with its wooden houses and dachas, and through the blue-and-gold palace of Catherine II. We lap it all up, even though midwinter is not the ideal time to be here, with its excess of darkness and cold. On a frigid morning, we watch a bride clutching her windblown veil near a Leningrad bridge where her wedding is taking place—apparently a sacred tradition.

One night, the president of the travel agency overseeing our Leningrad tour and his wife invite Bel and me to a performance of the Kirov Ballet, where we're stunned to be seated in the box of Czar Nicholas. The next day they drive us in their car to their coop apartment on the city outskirts. It's one of the many huge, monolithic buildings clustered on a desolate, treeless plain. Inside, however, Vladimir and Svetlana's apartment is clearly upper middle class. They have a comfortably furnished living/dining room, good-sized kitchen, two bedrooms, and bath and toilet rooms. We feast on meat jelly, smoked fish, cheeses, champagne, wine, vodka, cognac, and meringue cream cake. Bel and I are puzzled (and uncomfortable) as to why we happen to have been plucked away from the rest of our group for this dose of luxury and ostentation, and afterwards are happy to rejoin our friends for beers in our hotel bar.

We reverse our steps—train back to Moscow, by car at sixty miles an hour to the airport, two different flights for our large contingent to Ireland, and home.

Reflections

We were well aware that we were going to the USSR at the very moment when a historic struggle for control of that country was unfolding minute by minute. That's exactly why the Citizens' Summit was planned for this critical time. Gorbachev was a brave hero to the West, taking on the task of reforming several badly slipping systems throughout the USSR. He was trying to keep the Union together when the newly empowered future republics were pushing for autonomy, and the rigid centralization, a holdover from the Stalin era, was stifling new businesses in a time when technological innovation was blossoming worldwide. By 1989, Gorbachev's people were restless and dispirited, with a stagnating economy that was rife with corruption and waste; terrible losses in the Afghan conflict; and then the ongoing civil war. Most of the Soviet farms had no means of storing crops, which meant huge amounts simply rotted—a critical problem for a chronically undernourished country. Already, when we visited in January 1990, Gorbachev was battling unpopularity at home and hanging on to his power and influence by a fragile thread.

André Melville, Bel's Soviet counterpart co-chairing the Think Tank Task Force and an astute and respected academic, summed up the situation:

> We're seeking a new relationship between the State, the society, and individuals. Independent impulses and projects must be fostered. The USSR is more democratic than ever before, but also we've never seen so much gloom and pessimism. Not only is the economy in crisis, but a civil war is brewing and the basic Union is being questioned. There's a debate as to whether we should go back to the old socialism or support the new efforts toward democracy. Gorbachev has begun unilaterally to disarm the Soviet Union, but as yet the United States hasn't reciprocated. It's disheartening that both sides are still "modernizing" (testing) their nuclear weapons.

With all these sparks flying and threatening to ignite at any moment, we in the American delegation felt that every effort to create friendship and trust and support with those idealists who came out to meet with us was beneficial. Just as we were leaving, word came in that the fifteen Soviet republics were staging a massive demonstration against Gorbachev and clamoring for independence. It was an exciting time to be experiencing the last of the shadowy repression of the old regime but at the same time to be meeting face-to-face with some of the brilliant thinkers who saw clearly the failures and shortsightedness of their system and were working hard to inject positive strategies.

A number of small, collaborative projects resulted from the Summit. In the end, we found how similar Americans are to the Soviet people. We're both quick to connect on an emotional level. We appreciate each other's spontaneity; we lead from the heart. Yet it's also clear that ingrained in the Soviet personality are all the strains of living under repressive regimes. Subsisting under pervasive surveillance is all they've known. The pursuit of independent or democratic initiatives is almost unthinkable, and they live with a centuries-old legacy of always being told what to do. They've never experienced real freedom. Now, with interaction with the outside world, they're just beginning to get a taste of this.

Bel speaks at Awaji Conference

Incense brazier at Nara shrine: with Swanny Voneida

Dreaming the Future in Japan

AUGUST 1993

Backstory

At our conferences in China and the USSR there was a lot of fevered speculation about the future of the world—both good and bad. On the one hand, knowledgeable leaders pointed to catastrophes on any number of fronts that loomed imminently. On the other, more optimistic scenarios described steps that could lift us to a new era of sustainability and civilizational well-being.

Kaoru Yamaguchi had been a Japanese delegate to the 1991 Shanghai conference, the second of the three that Bel co-organized. After a week of discussions exploring the relationship between the environment and economic development, he suggested to Bel the possibility of carrying these ideas to an even greater depth by looking at how they might necessitate an entirely new kind of education. He offered to convene such an exploratory meeting in Japan.

Over the next couple of years, Professor Yamaguchi, on the Faculty of Management Sciences at Osaka Sangyo University, identified a group of leading scientists, environmentalists, activists, and forward-looking educators from around the world. He invited them to bring their expertise to his hometown on Awaji Island for the first of a series of brainstorming seminars to begin to imagine a different model for higher education. Held in August 1993, participants were to design "an international network university of the green world—dedicated to the continuing study of human values." The gathering would be the First World Futures-Creating Seminar. Its theme: "Renewing Community as Sustainable Global Village."

The Japanese central government recognized the creative energy and potential of Awaji Island, located in the Seto Inland Sea in eastern Japan. In the flush of its halcyon economic bubble of the early 1990s, the government had awarded huge sums of money to each town in the nation, including the villages on Awaji. Some of the island's towns focused on establishing resorts for tourism or sought other ways of growing their economies. One of them bought a big mound of gold for the villagers to look at. Yamaguchi persuaded his own village of Goshiki-cho to use its grant—$100,000 a year for ten years—to fulfill his dream: to create a University of the Future. The first step would be this gathering of major thinkers in August 1993. It was an idea close to Bel's heart, and he readily accepted the invitation. "Housewives" were included, and I was delighted to tag along.

I should note that now, well into the twenty-first century, some ideas that emerged as cutting edge at this seminar in 1993 will now seem old hat. Twenty years later, many of the ideas have been disseminated widely. A number have been implemented. Bel, and I jumped onto this track in the early 1970s; you will hear more about those explorations and experiments in the next section. But, as a page from what may seem quaint history, I include a bit of what transpired in Japan when our little group of world leaders proceeded to imagine what a healthy, viable future could look like.

Opulence and Elegance

Bel and I bus from the Osaka airport to Kobe and find our way to the very chic Shinkobe Oriental Hotel where conference-goers are to gather. It's the tallest building in Japan, a needle soaring high up against the Rokko mountains at Kobe's back. (In retrospect, we remember that Kobe was the epicenter of a horrific earthquake in January 1995 when huge numbers of buildings collapsed and more than five thousand lives were lost. The city has since been rebuilt in glittering splendor.)

We find that the hotel costs an awesome $1,000 a night, but fortunately we aren't paying. The young women we see there are rail-thin and beautifully dressed; there are lots of minis and shorts suits as well as long, pencil-slim skirts. Shoes range from stiletto heels to chunky gym-type shoes and sox (worn with elegant dresses). There is water everywhere, playing in fountains, running along as indoor brooks, cascading down several stories of stone walls in patterns made by outcroppings and graduated raceways. From our room, we look out on a fleet of cable cars going up and down the mountain.

We begin running into some of the conference participants, and meet our leader, Kaoru Yamaguchi. With Brian Tokar of the Green Party from Vermont, Bel and I hunt down a place to eat in a vast, underground warren of shops. Our dinner is noodles dipped in a sauce we make by grinding sesame seeds into spicy condiments, along with crisp shrimp and seaweed on rice, washed down with tea.

Crossing the Inland Sea with the Presenters

The next morning, our group of twenty-five piles onto a bus bound for the port. After a lunch cruise on the misty Inland Sea, we drag our luggage onto a speedboat for the hour-long ride to Awaji Island.

We begin to meet the presenters, an impressive bunch. Here is a very partial list: Besides **Professor Yamaguchi**, there is **Albert Sasson** from UNESCO in Paris; **Jim Dator,** president of the World Futures Studies Federation and a professor at the University of Hawaii, where he heads the Alternative Futures Option within the political science department; **Jerome Karle,** Nobel laureate in chemistry who worked on the Manhattan Project in Chicago, and then before retiring, became chief scientist of the Laboratory for the Structure of Matter; **Roger Sperry,** scientist, teacher, philosopher, humanist and artist, who won the Nobel prize for his work as a neuropsychologist specializing in split brain research—left and right brain hemisphere functions; because Sperry is ill, his former colleague from Caltech, neurobiologist **Theodore Voneida,** will read his paper; Ted created the Northeastern Ohio Universities College of Medicine where he chairs the department of neurology; **Tony Stevenson,** a futurist from Australia who is director of the Communications

Centre at the Queensland University of Technology, and who studies and writes about communication and interconnecting communities; **Nandini Joshi,** managing trustee of the Foundation for Constructive Development in Ahmedabad, India, involved in grassroots efforts and introducing "The Prosperous Village in India"; **Brian Tokar**, director of the Institute for Social Ecology at Goddard College in Vermont and a national leader of the Green movement; **Michael LaFontaine**, director of the Community Land Trust Project, seeing the New Hampshire Community Loan Fund as an antidote to failing market economies; **Howard Didsbury**, active member of the World Future Society, who offers WFS seminars and anthologies for futures studies curricula; and Bel—**Belden Paulson**, professor at the University of Wisconsin-Milwaukee, relating personal experiences with higher education and community development in Wisconsin, and offering ideas to undergird the global village concept.

Landing on Awaji, we're whisked across the scenic island in vans, passing villages of wooden buildings with black tile roofs, some upturned like those in China. It's hilly with rice paddies and bamboo forests. On a high perch, our Galaxie Awaji Resort hotel is brand new with art deco themes, lots of marble, and exquisite flower arrangements tucked into shrine nooks. Its dining room is a semicircle of glass hanging off a cliff above the sea.

Mayor Mitsugu Saito of the town of Goshiki-cho is on hand to greet our group with a welcoming speech. It is he and the village who have invited us and paid our way.

We'd hoped to sample fine Japanese foods, but, instead, they are trying to impress us with haute French cuisine. Some of the best beef in the world comes from Kobe, and our first night we're served tenderloin that cuts like butter, with gourmet wine sauces. There are also tiny bits of vegetables, sashimi (raw fish and seafood), and pickles—only three or four items on a plate, artfully arranged. The more minuscule servings there are, the more elegant the meal is considered. The finale is a pear sherbet with whipped cream.

Primal Drumming

After dinner we scramble to get off to Goshiki-Cho to help celebrate the anniversary of the end of World War II. Looping down the mountain, we land amidst throngs of villagers, bright lanterns, and concession stands, and then are led to a large hall. As we kick off our shoes, we're given slippers and are ushered to chairs; the townspeople sit on the floor. As soon as we arrive, our group is invited onto a stage, lined up under klieg lights, and subjected to television cameras, which stay with us all through the conference.

The mayor speaks again and hands us gifts of locally made cotton jackets that we put on in 110-degree heat; we nearly wilt in the steamy, packed auditorium. Then out come fantastic drummers in a spellbinding performance that, for me, might be the most exciting experience of our trip. Some twenty young people pound on various-sized drums, some ten feet tall. It's an amazing feat of primal energy and precision—syncopated, deafening, and tribal, almost to the point of frenzy or delirium. The players twirl their drumsticks and kick and leap around their instruments in an astonishing display of virtuosity. I imagine them as the ferocious samurai of old.

The Marathon of Talks Begins

The next morning we're bussed to the town hall for the opening conference sessions. About three hundred people show up—townspeople and some sixty foreign students, mostly from China but also Africans and Caucasians, housed by local families. After speeches by officials, with simultaneous translations and the ubiquitous TV cameras, the papers by our group begin—taking up a good eight hours each day.

Three days of discussion yield a dense panoply of ideas where we examine the momentous shift taking place from the industrial age to the information age. We hear about community-based socioeconomic systems and the building of sustainable communities globally. The group begins to design a higher education institution to address concerns about the environment and about the future generally—which could be key in setting up an entirely new framework for community economies of scale. I won't attempt to report the minute details of the sessions, but think an abbreviated, somewhat scattershot paraphrasing of the proceedings needs to be included here because the concepts are critically important, if not prescient, for 1993. They also express much of what Bel and I have believed in and worked for over a number of years. For the most part, I won't assign talks or ideas to specific speakers, partly because there is some overlap and I want to keep the points concise.

The New Education

A few of the opening comments: A failure of education in the fading industrial age was that it focused on fragmented specialists and their narrow fields. "Futures studies" is to "normal" academia now as Copernicus and the first scientists were to traditional academia in the Middle Ages. This a time of merging events, trends, images, and actions, arising largely because of the new technologies. Now we're moving beyond simply forecasting to clarifying positive visions of preferred futures. We must consider these futures constantly anew, not with technology alone but anchored through ethics and shared community participation. We need to return to the idea

Bel with Mayor Shiki Cho Saito and conference friend Kazuki Nishioka

of broad scholarship, as in the 1920s and 1930s. Futurists need the widest knowledge of the history and culture of as many cultures as possible. Teaching futures must be the heart of all academic disciplines so that goals will be held in common. We can't assume a deterministic future. Linear extrapolations are becoming impossible.

If we don't instill "character" at a young age, a humane society will be difficult. When there is self-respect, laws to prohibit bad behavior won't be necessary. The new education will be an exercise in criticism and discernment, but one that also provides practical solutions. This becomes a globalizing task, essential for a green world. It is compassionate and, unlike most of academia, it delights in what sometimes looks absurd.

Among the disciplines to be included in a future curriculum, besides the basic essentials such as hard sciences and math, would be humanities and language that challenge science. The social sciences and political science would tilt toward a more positivistic stance than what we see currently, and there would be a stronger emphasis on performing arts and self-expression. Applied science would be key—agriculture, medicine, architecture, law, social work, and business (not theoretical studies *about* business but exposure to practical experience). Students will be able to view all these fields connected as a meaningful, sustainable whole.

The future of education is to be a *network*, not a place. Information will be compiled in world databases and disseminated to everyone. UNESCO is planning to handle this. It is collecting, sharing, and transferring wisdom, and organizing seminars worldwide to speculate creatively on where the culture is going. It strives to join economics and art by bringing cultural knowledge to the practical arts, blending craftsmanship and cultural heritage with everyday life and entrepreneurship. A database on a mainframe computer will hold the experiences of all future-oriented groups. Decentralization and communication will be key, with thirty-five or more civilizations networking and sharing. It could begin here in Goshiki-cho.

Scientists are beginning to address the impact of the cognitive revolution. The controversy between the behaviorism of the materialistic era and the new consciousness lasted until the late 1960s. But now that science/values dichotomy is ending. Subjective input plays an important role in mental cognition. A more holistic paradigm is emerging that is based on the patterns of nature. Solutions will come primarily through science and the green revolution. Subjective human values are key to saving the planet. We're starting to understand that less is better, not multiplying. We need bright new utopian goals, biodiversity, and a sense of the sacred at the very top.

Restructuring Society

Some feel that the mass production of the industrial twentieth century will not be as prevalent in the twenty-first; in fact, it may be difficult due to great population growth. A number of speakers emphasize that the most ominous trend is overpopulation. They ponder the question: Are we past the point of no return for our Earth and for retaining quality of life?

A representative from Awaji Island steps in with his thoughts about the local future. He reiterates many of the ideas of the previous speakers. Essential, also, will be a garden or park where people can meet and connect with nature. Awaji is believed to be special as one of the first islands supposedly created by the gods. Currently there is a monumental project underway: constructing a very long bridge to connect Awaji to the mainland. A "Communication City" is planned here, with the aim of establishing a truly sustainable community that is not just the island itself but which will include the 35 million in the region.

The mayor of Goshiki-Cho adds, "Good health is much in the public consciousness here. We're creating a community where everyone looks after everyone else, where no one is left out, especially the elderly. Our village can be an example of mutual support for the rest of Japan and the world."

Imaging the Global Village to Come

After these initial talks, the speakers gather for a roundtable discussion where they look at the shape of the community of the future. Some of the comments:

Do we assume there will be more leisure in the future? Environmental pessimists would say no—a green world where we might no longer need to work traditional hours may not be possible. They say we must brace for huge, difficult changes.

Full employment is not what we are bound to, but how will we be able to share jobs? It is a different picture for both rich and poor countries. What we need is *gainful* employment, not full employment. If it is full, there is too much manufacturing, production. Standards are disappearing. It isn't the intellectuals who are making decisions now, but those with power. We can talk wisely among ourselves, but if we can't reach people, nothing will change. Governments are deaf; it's better to try to interest a broad spectrum of people.

We'll have to redesign the role of the state. Decentralize so there is less state and more community, more bottom-up participation. Find a balance of power and control between the state and community.

A worldwide CCC (Civilian Conservation Corps) is a worthwhile plan. Also preventive healthcare. People working for nothing, like Patch Adams, the doctor-clown who volunteers his free medical services and created a free hospital where greed and competition are replaced with compassion, generosity, and interdependence. Barter is part of the picture. Serving the community and receiving services. We've got to get out and actually do these things, not just write papers about them.

People are part of nature and when we destroy it, we destroy ourselves. We cannot conquer nature. Before we build our ideal village we must restore beautiful, nourishing nature.

After this marathon session finished, there is a ceremony where some thirty foreign students come forward with their hosts, shake our hands, bow many times, are applauded, and get their pictures taken. During our noon break, while we are devouring tiny, artfully arranged items in little wooden *bento* lunchboxes, many of the Japanese come up to talk with us and try out their English.

Ideas on Community, Connecting, and Work

In order for the economy to continue, we must push for minimum consumption. The market economy of the past two hundred years is not appropriate for the future. Economies have collapsed in a number of places because they did not take into account environmental destruction; they only looked for profit. There must be Muratopia: information-sharing, self-management, participatory democracy, and sustainable development. (Mura is the Japanese word for village.) A new economic system would be global self-similar villages where people help each other and respect nature's way. Because the villages all share values and approaches, together they make a cohesive whole. The information age is an age of synthesis.

We have the technology to reach around the world in every field and circumstance. We can see everything with great clarity and can alter images, blurring the consumer/producer dichotomy. It's all happening as we approach population saturation and ecological overload. Industrialists are threatening world harmony and contributing to the extinction of human life, but new global networks could emerge to counteract their influence. Villages are the key to revitalization. For instance, sixty thousand Australians are currently living in alternative lifestyle communities (there are a hundred such enclaves in Australia). The communities need to communicate with each other and with the world. We need broad, philosophical underpinnings. There is great value in diversity and in fluid, open relationships, a lot of face-to-face communication, and folk wisdom. Intimacy and conviviality to facilitate major communication and bring innovation and change. Responsible enterprise; empowerment, not power. We need knowledge of healing, not ruling. There is a study of human networking; it is called "Local Global Netweaving" and is based on four principles: connection, participation, communication, and action.

In India, there is much violence, idleness, and inequity resulting from lack of work in its big cities. One key would be to revive traditional Indian villages, and, in particular, revive village-based cloth production, bringing back the spinning wheel and pit loom. Both the raw materials and markets are always available. Modern technology and international trade are why the present economy is not viable. It's causing unemployment, especially in the underdeveloped world.

The new system would look something like this: I spin nine yards of fabric for my six-yard sari and have three yards left to pay for vegetable dye and printing of the pattern. Any unskilled person in any place can do this easily. It's the first step to full employment, using cloth as the medium of exchange. With the cloth, people can get food and roof tiles. In our present economy, when we buy a shirt, we're paying for management, profit, transport, machines, advertising, shops—plus banking and wars. Why do we carry such a burden? India needs not funding but intellectual and moral support. Work must be for joy; it is the purpose of life, along with service to others.

On the future of work, a fraction of the labor force will supply all the goods and services needed in the future. Ten years ago we talked about the need for a radical way to distribute wealth. We redefined the nature of work, with a growing underground economy and more employee-owned businesses—a situation that politicians will have to recognize and address.

There are basic faults also in the university system; it has become a dinosaur. Departments are isolated fragments that have no contact with each other; they have difficulty dealing with visions and values; they lack imagination. The future is an image in our minds only; the social scientists, who should be tackling this issue, are especially deficient.

The United States leads the world in unsustainability, waste, greenhouse gases, and consumption. One in four Americans is born in poverty, yet we also lead in wealth. Effects of toxicity are causing high rates of cancer and birth defects. When the arms race was still going strong, schools and hospitals and other services were without financial support and became very demoralized. The upper echelons of both the government and the environmental movement were losing touch with the grassroots and making unconscionable decisions.

Then, in the 1960s, a different environmental consciousness emerged in unexpected places. Ordinary people started working to take over the destiny of their communities—such as the anti-nuke, anti-industrial, anti-pollution movements—along with radical wilderness activism. Groups were decentralized but coordinated. We found that racial and ecological issues can't be separated, since most of the toxicity occurs in poor areas where there is racial diversity. Now we see loggers working with environmentalists toward creative solutions.

One of the most visionary thrusts today is the bioregional movement, defined by topography, soil, weather, and vegetation. For example, people in Vermont live differently than those in the desert or southern United States. Bioregionalism is concerned with small-scale economies and self-reliance. The green politics movement is dedicated to a global vision for change and to eliminate unhealthy government pressures. It interconnects ecological and political issues, championing the causes of social justice, nonviolence, community-based democracy, decentralization, feminism, and respect for diversity.

But there are international implications: now corporations and politicians are using environmental language to further their own ends. The US government does this to hide its anti-ecological actions. Powerful institutions decide how much ecological action is necessary to preserve their own activities. Some organizations, such as the World Bank, are using the crisis for its own ends; it has given funds to fight ills after it has caused much of the damage in the first place.

The goal of the Community Land Trust movement is to acquire land and hold it safe forever. This applies to housing and businesses as well as land conservancy. It is available to individuals, farmers, and cooperatives. Long-term leases are passed on to heirs, but individuals cannot profit. It keeps housing affordable. Community land trusts fall between public housing and private rental housing; they are neither entirely public nor private.

Some of the speakers express concern about the direction of the talks as the catalogue of societal ills is rolled out. But others say we need to look at where we are now, start from there, and then strive to improve and change. There are too many theories, when what we need is action and real problem-solving. Yet we mustn't destroy old theories and patterns before we have the correct path for the future. The challenge is that we have six billion people to feed, not that we're ruining the ecology—a cart-before-the-horse situation.

One speaker lists some unhelpful but widespread attitudes:

- technological optimism; we're working on the pollution problem, so don't worry
- gloom-and-doom attitude: it's just too late
- nostalgia: we create a romantic distortion of the past, longing to recapture the good old days of the 1930s and 1940s.

Then the same speaker looks forward to possible futurist topics for discussion: the aging population, genetic engineering, and the global scene of the future. History is important when thinking about the future. All the ideas we're discussing today were once thought to be crackpot and impossible dreams, yet one way or another, they are coming to pass. With wit and will we can create the world we want.

Goshiki-Cho Mayor Saito and Yamaguchi announce that they are planning to raise a million dollars above the yearly government allotment for the new university project.

This concludes the formal discussions where I've passed on just a smattering of the thinking presented, from my own notes. Yamaguchi edited the complete transcripts of the talks for a book that came out in 1997 (Adamantine Press Limited, in England). It is called *Sustainable Global Communities in the Information Age: Visions From Futures Studies.*

A Barbecue with Squid and Octopus

By the end of the second day of the seminar, everybody is ready for a respite from all the cerebral activity. We're bused back to the hotel to change into casual clothes, and then back down to town to a large, open shed for a huge barbecue. Some twenty metal barrels filled with burning coals are grills for thin-sliced beef, squid, octopus, chicken, hot dogs, sweet potato slices, carrots, cabbage, and mushrooms. As soon as the perfectly seared food is cooked, it is transferred to dozens of trays and the barrels are restacked. Armed with aluminum plates and chopsticks, we load up and roam around socializing with townspeople, the foreign students, and our own delegates. Tubs of ice are filled with bottles of Saki and beer. The heat in the shed is sauna-level, and periodically we escape outside for air. Exhausted after the long day, our group calls an early night and is off to bed by 8:30.

Onions, Puppets, and a Long Bridge

Swanny Voneida, Ted's wife, and I opt to skip the next day's proceedings and are given a driver for an outing around the island. Kazuki Nishioka is a local friend of Yamaguchi and has helped to organize this event; he sells medical supplies, was trained in America, and is a fine, knowledgeable guide.

We set out, passing numerous sheds for drying onions; most of the onions for Japan are grown on Awaji. Driving along the sea, we stop at a botanical garden and an animal preserve; several shy pandas are hiding in bamboo trees, and some animals are for petting. Everybody who enters is handed a container of 3 percent milk.

In the town of Fukura at the bottom of the island, we take a small boat out for an hour—cruising in the Naruto Strait under a huge bridge where, when the tide is right, the Pacific Ocean meets the Inland Sea and it roils and forms myriad whirlpools. Our boat pilot brings us samples of green seaweed to taste.

We drive a bit into the interior, weaving back and forth through its pine-clad mountains, and then pop out again for spectacular cliff views out over the sea. It feels something like the Amalfi Drive in Italy. Then the piece de resistance: a puppet theater. This very ancient tradition started on Awaji. The puppets are about four feet high; each puppet is manipulated by three people dressed in black with black hoods over their heads. After a few minutes, we aren't aware of the puppeteers at all. Seated off to the side is a woman in ancient costume who tells the highly emotional story of love and violence. A man near her provides accompaniment on the koto (harp). As the sad tale unfolds, the storyteller's singsong voice rises and falls and sobs. People in the audience become very engrossed and begin to cry, too.

The following day, after final speeches and ceremonies, we're off for an island tour with our entire group. We stop at a high point overlooking the two main support pillars for the new Akashi Kaikyō Bridge to Kobe on the mainland. The pillars are a thousand feet tall and are already in place in the middle of the sea. The bridge is expected to cost 4 billion dollars. They anticipate forty thousand cars a day will cross when it's completed in 1998. We shudder to think what this access will do to change the magnificent, wild quality of the island.

Kyoto: Shrines, Temples, and Tranquility

We say our farewells to Mayor Saito and the seminar group, and after a horrendously hot, sticky rush to the railroad station in Kobe, we're on a speed train to the sacred city of Kyoto. With Bel and me for this next adventure are Ted and Swanny Voneida. In Kyoto, we have a hard time finding taxis; several refuse to take us, not wanting our dirty bags on their fine, white, embroidered seat covers. The cab drivers also wear white gloves. We have to corral two taxis because of all the luggage, and both drivers get lost because we have no exact address for the guest house the Voneidas have booked.

Finally, on the remote outskirts of the city, we find the house in a narrow alley. Our hostess is Machio Horie, a pleasant lady who speaks fairly good English. She hurries out to greet us and to give extensive instructions about not proceeding past a certain step in our shoes. From there we're to go barefoot or in socks. She provides slippers to wear on the wood floors, but again we're not to wear even slippers on the tatami mats in our rooms. It's an old house with high, dark ceilings and cypress beams. We're ushered into Ted and Swanny's room to sit around a low table for green tea and peanut-butter-crunch cookies and a chat with Machio. After supper and an evening stroll in moonlight and shadows through the nearby temple grounds, a magical oasis of silence and peace, we repair to our rolled-out futons. Everywhere are sliding doors with paper or painted cloth panels. Each room has a little shrine area.

The next couple of days are mainly spent hunting the many magnificent holy places for which Kyoto is famous. Machio fortifies us with a full breakfast of omelet, bacon, toast, a big pot of rice, pickles, bamboo, grated daikon radish, fruits, juice, and tea.

One of our favorite temples is Taizo-in, with mysterious paths through lush trees and foliage, flowers, pools and little streams, resting pagodas, and rocks artfully placed. At the mammoth Heian

Serenity in Taizo-in gardens, Kyoto

Shrine, huge koi swim in pools in the heart of the city. This is one of the fascinating features of Kyoto: here is a large, bustling metropolis of a million and a half, but sprinkled throughout, every few blocks, are many, many oases of tranquility—Buddhist and Shinto temples and shrines built in the eighth and ninth centuries, each with its enticing, immaculate gardens where water and vegetation mesh in perfect artistry. At the Jisho-ji Temple (Ginkaku-ji Temple), bright moss covers the ground, and we walk the Philosopher's Path along a tree-shrouded canal flanking a posh residential area. At the Gion Theater we sample the ancient arts of the tea ceremony, flower arranging, and puppetry, as well as Noh and Kabuki theater, with old instruments and colorful dances.

Bowing Deer and a Huge Buddha

The next morning we catch a train for the town of Nara, forty-five minutes away. We'd thought Nara would be a quaint, rural village, but it turns out to have a population of 350,000. As we're asking for directions at the information center, a fiftyish woman at the desk volunteers to be our guide for the day—for free. Amazed and delighted, we find her an encyclopedia of knowledge and very gracious and kind. She's a widow; her husband had been manager of a steel company.

We spend the day at Nara-Koen Park, a huge complex of temples and grounds. A thousand deer, considered sacred messengers, roam freely and aggressively. They come up to us to beg for deer cookies. We say "Bow" and they dip their heads for rewards. Some have great antlers, some are babies; all are reddish brown with white spots.

The park is vast, with mysterious tangled jungles of cypress and twisted wisterias and giant ferns. It's very hilly, with tree-lined walkways and steps bordered by thousands of stone lanterns that are lit on holy days; twenty-foot bamboo torches are also lighted and carried.

The temples are mostly Buddhist, but we also see some Shinto shrines. Twenty percent of the Japanese people are Shintoists, 65 percent are Buddhist.

We enter a tall, wooden gate with two thirty-foot wooden statues of Deva Kings fiercely guarding the enormous Buddha inside. Then to the great hall, Kaibutsuden, the largest wood structure in the world, 157 feet high. The entire complex comprises the Todaiji Temple. Kids are squeezing through a hole in one large pillar inside to ensure getting into Paradise. There is a fifty-three-foot bronze Buddha, commissioned by the emperor to unite the country.

On to the Kasuga-taisha Shinto Shrine. These are rebuilt every twenty years to purify the site, and the old temples are moved to the countryside. We notice that Shinto shrines often have fortunetellers and astrologers available. They have no images of gods, believing that divinity is manifested in nature. We find that the white papers we see tied in bows to trees, like Christmas decorations, are fortunes that people buy; if the fortune is bad, they tie it to a tree and the gods will commute it to a better one.

Around the big Buddhist temple are smaller surrounding ones, one for each month. We climb a small mountain to the February temple, Nigatsudo. From there, there's a panoramic view of the park and city from a lantern-lined balcony. After a visit to the National Museum filled with Buddhist treasures, masks and statues, we take the train back to Kyoto. We spend our last evening with the Voneidas over beer and chips, swapping stories of our lives, seated on tatami mats around their low table. Ted tells a story of standing in a crowd and seeing a 1,000 yen bill ($10). Others saw it but no one picked it up, so he did. A Japanese friend said probably the others thought it dirty and so wouldn't touch it.

We say goodbye to Ted and Swanny. On our own now, we catch a bus to the Golden Temple, Kingkakuji; after it burned down in the 1950s, its exterior was entirely gold-leafed.

Then we trudge a mile down to Ryoanji Temple, distinguished as the most famous garden in Japan. There are fifteen stones set in raked gravel, but one can see only fourteen at any one time. These represent land/earth/island in the sea of ridged sand waves. We're encouraged to sit and contemplate the idea of nothingness. After taking off our shoes to walk in the temple, we stroll around the lovely grounds, with more paths, artfully placed rocks, moss dappled by sun filtering through a dense forest. There are little stone altars, clumps of blue flowers, ponds, running brooks—all extraordinarily tranquil.

Checking out of our quiet guesthouse, we taxi into the city. By now I've given up looking presentable and just let the sweat pour off my face, hair soaking, clothes wet and sticky. The Japanese carry washcloths to mop off. We stagger about in broiling sun and finally retreat to a nearby McDonalds to revive in the air conditioning. It's mostly filled with students. Classical music is playing, and there are Juan Gris prints on the walls. As in Russia, there is an appreciation of good art by the mass of people.

We hear that the most frequently stolen objects in Japan are umbrellas and bicycles. Actually, we feel very safe everywhere. This is because the penalty for crime is excessive; we're told about terrible prisons, bad treatment, and often torture. If you're arrested, it's almost guaranteed that you'll be found guilty. You may not be allowed to see a lawyer or make a phone call.

After lunch, we wander the Palace grounds, resting on stone benches among the tall trees. It reminds us of steamy summer days long ago in Rome when we took our boys to Villa Savoia, the royal park, and everyone moved slowly in the heat. Here, fathers come on bikes with their three-year-old sons to kick a soccer ball and eat ice cream cones. It's Sunday, the only time they get to see their kids. We learn that a forty-hour week would seem like heaven to the Japanese. Even given two weeks of vacation, they seldom take more than a couple of days because they might lose out, or it would be considered impolite to make someone do your work while gone.

We also hear that it's normal (a perk) for businessmen to go to hostess bars after work, and for the wife to have to be up and ready with a hot meal for her husband whenever he gets home, even at 2:00 a.m. If women are serious about a professional career, they can forget marriage; a working wife would be too threatening to a man. Most women aspire to marriage, even though their status drops behind the man with his job, and also behind the children. A good job for young, pretty women is "office lady." These may earn $35,000 a year and get a vacation; they wear a uniform, make tea, handle little ceremonies, and generally take care of their bosses.

We check into our hotel, rather seedy, though $127 a night. It's heaven to have a room with a private bath. We guzzle lots of water (safe everywhere), and climb into fresh sheets in the ubiquitous, neatly ironed robes provided. In hotels, they give two pillows: one down-filled and one filled with rice hulls that are harder, cooler, and make a crunchy noise.

A bus takes us to the Osaka airport, cutting through mountain tunnels. Rising above the industry and sprawl, the hills are green. We fly off for a few days of unwinding on the island of Kauai in Hawaii, where we hike around Waimea Canyon with friends. Among other sylvan pursuits, we gather banana poca vines and make baskets of them, taught by a Korean woman. We learn she is married to the assistant production manager for the filming of *Jurassic Park* (who also operated the right front foot of the wounded triceratops puppet). And so home.

Reflections

We've watched a good many of the ideas expressed at the Awaji Island seminar gradually being addressed and actualized over the subsequent twenty years. In 1993, however, we had the unique opportunity of seeing them collected in one place, one gathering, which shone a spotlight on important hypotheses—a planetary wish list that would begin to lift our culture quite a few notches toward a more humane, civil society. By highlighting just a few of the points made by that august group of participants, I wanted to remind readers of goals that in the trajectory of our collective life are worth fighting for.

The discussions on Awaji may look simplistic now, but there was something brave and rash in those earlier declarations. These were pioneers in their fields who were setting out new standards. Now there are more refined, sophisticated arguments, and scientific data to back them up. Examples of greatly accelerating consciousness are encouraging. We see most clearly among the young people coming of age today that they are in a very different place from those of even the previous generation; it's almost as though they carry a different DNA. Suggestions that were suspect or rejected only a few years ago are easily taken for granted now by an idealistic and determined cadre of twenty- and thirty-somethings. They are enthusiastic champions for issues of environment, gender, race, health, participatory community, and much more. We see young, assertive, innovative women in the workplace. When these young people find existing businesses and institutions lacking, they become entrepreneurs and jump in to create their own.

Speaking from a personal perspective, as I am recounting the journeys Bel and I have taken over the past sixty or so years, this one to Japan is certainly one that fits the rationale for why we committed to a life journey together.

As for our experience of Japan generally, we were impressed with a great sense of order and what seemed to be a universal appreciation and love of beauty in all its forms and the inspiration for all this: nature. Even in crowded cities, we felt an unspoken homage to the ancient traditions of the culture, where regularly seeking tranquility in forests and gardens and beside reflecting pools is not a frill but a necessity. If we were going to discuss the urgent need for global sustainability, with all its ramifications for our human species, Japan seemed a good place to be.

Transport in Cardenas

Cuba
Delightful Anachronism or Pariah?

March-April 2003

Backstory

Here is another trip where other family members joined Bel and me. Our son Steve and my brother Doug had expressed interest in going to Turkey, and we were scheduled to go in March 2003 with an adventure tour group. But then, just at that point, the United States decided to invade Iraq, and there was a strong chance that our troops might go in through eastern Turkey. So, a bit apprehensive, we canceled out.

All of us were disappointed, but almost immediately Bel heard through his university grapevine about a group scheduled to travel shortly from Milwaukee to Cuba. We sounded out Steve and Doug—both politics and history buffs—and they were excited at this new prospect. The four of us signed on.

This was a study tour, organized by the Institute of World Affairs of the University of Wisconsin-Milwaukee. It was called "Inside Cuba: Does the Revolutionary Beat Still Go On?" Our three very competent American leaders were William, Raúl, and Ljiljana. At a briefing in Milwaukee, we met the others in the group—forty-six of us altogether. In Cuba, we were joined by Alberto and Carlos, our local guides whom we found extremely warm and knowledgeable.

In 2003, the strict US trade embargo against Cuba was in effect, and no Americans were allowed to travel there without permission for a particular legal purpose. Raúl had been taking medical supplies to the island for a number of years, which provided the rationale for taking along other people who would each carry supplies not available in that country.

Just Getting There Is Problematic

It almost seems an ominous omen when my suitcase disappears on the first lap from Milwaukee to Fort Lauderdale. Then in Miami, we encounter what seem like Gestapo security tactics; we're spread-eagled and given the wand treatment, the men are ordered to unzip their pants and remove their belts. Every piece we are taking is thoroughly rifled. Maybe this is because we could be traitors going to the land of "the enemy"? Because I've lost my luggage, I scurry around in the terminal to buy a pair of shorts, warned that there's little chance my bag will be found and forwarded to Cuba.

We wait for an hour aboard a stifling little turbo prop while William explains to top airport authorities why he's carrying $30,000 in cash: in Cuba all transactions are in dollars; credit cards and travelers checks are not accepted, ATMs nonexistent. While waiting, somebody kicks the plane's tires and twirls the propellers by hand to see if things are working. A baggage cart careens around a corner, and a suitcase flies off unnoticed and is not retrieved—perhaps the fate of my bag?

The ninety-mile flight takes an hour as we lumber south in the dark, spotting the lighted thread of highway linking the Florida Keys. Finally there are the lights of Cuba, and we're down in Havana. While we wait for a bus that never arrives, throngs of Cubans press against the fence and stare at us, the "aliens in the cage." Outdoor TV screens all around are blaring war news and showing Al Jazeera footage of the horrible death and damage caused by American troops. We're shoved into taxis and our driver zooms into the city, clocking 120 kilometers an hour, zigzagging around cars and barely missing shadowy bicycles and pedestrians.

We reach the Sevilla Hotel, enormous and once very grand. The lobby is spectacular, with marble columns and delicate grillwork and ornamentation. There's a photo gallery of past greats who have stayed here: Joe Lewis, Errol Flynn, Al Capone, Graham Greene. . . . Bel's and my room is large and Spartan, with shaky plumbing (our toilet requires eight flushes).

Our first breakfast is fabulous on the equally fabulous ninth floor of the hotel. Ceilings are ornate, with inlaid squares and dropped beams, reminiscent of Italian palaces. Fifteen-foot windows look out on the ocean; they're open and birds fly in to perch on our tables. As we fall on the omelets, many varieties of meat, vegetables, rice, and fruit dishes, a black violinist serenades us with nostalgic, quavering renditions such as "I'll be Seeing You," from *Casablanca*. In fact, at nearly every meal on the trip, there are live combos. As Carlos says, Cubans are born with music in their bones, and they learn to jiggle and dance early on.

Revolutionary Heroes, Bicycle Taxis, Horse Carriages—and Old Havana

In our two buses, we're off for a tour of Havana. We barrel down the main boulevard, the Prado, to the sea, where there's a fort, battlements, moats, and prisons. We pass hundreds of amazing colonial, baroque, and neoclassical buildings, many with great arches forming shaded colonnades and galleries, towering Greek columns and fine-filigreed, wrought-iron balconies. The facades of virtually all these buildings, however, are peeling or crumbling, many fallen to ruin but nevertheless inhabited.

The condition of the structures is partly because of weather and water damage, and also because there simply has not been money for upkeep and restoration. In other parts of the world, such wrecks have simply been knocked down. Here they must continue to suffice and are laboriously patched together. Foreign historical architects cry that the buildings must be saved; they make the entire country a museum of authentic treasures.

On the city outskirts, we find some elegant, well-kept villas and grounds; these are now mostly foreign embassies (the biggest is the Russian). Some are headquarters for the few joint ventures. There's one millionaire Cuban, we're told—an old woman with an interest in Mercedes-Benz. When Castro's band instigated the Revolution in 1959, sweeping out the dictator Batista, many of the wealthy and middle class fled, abandoning their fine homes. Their servants and the liberators took over these houses and were given the right to live in them; by law they can pass such property on to their heirs. We see crowds gathered under the shade trees in the middle of the Prado, where exchanges of houses and apartments are negotiated daily. There can be no buying and selling and no private ownership of houses; they can only be sold to the government, which also owns virtually all businesses in Cuba.

Carlos tells us there are no homeless here; people are taken care of by their large, extended families. If we see people who seem to be living on the street or are begging, it usually means they are mentally ill, and there are programs for them. Medical treatment and education are free—two exemplary state programs where Cuba shines worldwide.

When the USSR pulled out in 1990, all the big subsidies that had supported the economy disappeared. Carlos was a university teacher, but when academic pay dropped to only $15-$30 a month, he resigned and trained for a year to be a tour guide, with access now to American dollars. The only way Cubans make it is either by being connected to the growing tourist industry (from countries other than the United States) or with funds sent by relatives in the United States (this latter brings in billions). Other Cubans are in bad shape.

We stop at Revolution Square to see the huge statue of José Martí (the hero who began the war to liberate Cuba from the Spanish in 1868, the War of Independence). There's a towering monument, which we understand also houses Castro's office. Across the square is a black, bas-relief sculpture of Che Guevara that covers an entire building. Che is the real hero for Cubans—the dashing, visionary Argentinean who linked up with Castro to bring equality and justice to Cuba, fought from the Sierra Maestra mountains and in the Congo, and finally was killed in Bolivia. Dying young, he remains a hazy, romantic, iconic figure, his image on billboards, T-shirts, and postcards. Castro, on the other hand, has been around forever and is the more staid, accepted administrator of this communist regime.

The capitol building, constructed in 1926-29, is impressive, bigger than ours in D.C. It's used primarily for the Cuban Ministry of Science and Technology. Parked outside are ranks of 1950s cars, many used as taxis. Some are rickety, some are shining and beautifully maintained. As we see them here, and rattling around everywhere throughout the country, it's this more than anything else that makes us realize we're in a time warp where almost everything stopped in 1959, where there has been no modernization, no way to get parts to repair machines. For a while, there was help from the USSR, but the US embargo now effectively cuts Cuba off from the rest of the world and to this day stops it from participating fully in the world economy. Even though trade is possible with other countries (as with Europe and Japan), in order to buy goods, Cuba must turn its dollars into other currencies at terrible exchange rates, tariffs, and taxes, so they lose heavily.

Much taxi service is with three-wheeled motorized mini-cabs (that look like little amusement park bumper cars), three-wheeled pedicabs (bicycles), and horse carriages, some of them like our black Amish buggies. We marvel at the monstrous "camels"—two buses (the humps) joined by a lower section and pulled by what looks like the cab of a Mack truck.

We see long queues waiting at the bus stops; the camels hold up to three hundred people, as Carlos says, "belly-to-belly—the place for sex, violence, and bad language."

We stop for lunch at a noted restaurant, La Bodeguita Del Medio. First they bring mojitas, the ubiquitous national drink (rum, sugar, soda water, and lots of fresh mint that you tamp down into the sugar) followed by platters of dark rice and beans, plantain, and more vegetables. As everywhere, a lively trio of musicians hovers over our table and plays requests for our dollar bills, then sells us CDs.

We go out to explore the colorful streets of Old Havana in 95-degree heat. A costumed band of noisy street musicians advances on us on high stilts, waving banners and passing the plate. Older women lounge picturesquely in doorways in richly colored dresses and smoking cigars. We four break away from the tour to examine the big artisan market until we're wilting from the sun. Back at the hotel, there's a note that my suitcase has made it to the Havana airport after all (hallelujah!), and I arrange to taxi out the next morning to collect it with Ljiljana.

Political Ping Pong and the National Sport

We're told that because of a sensitive political incident, happening just at this moment, our planned visits to the various diplomatic posts and the library are canceled; our presence, en masse, could create a problem and jeopardize those entities. Some one hundred Cuban dissidents have been arrested following a meeting at the home of James Cason. He is the top US diplomat here at the US Interests Section, located in the Swiss embassy. We no longer have an embassy of our own. There is talk that Castro may expel Cason, accusing him of paying the dissidents to create trouble. (A week later, when I was back home, newspaper articles were coming out saying that some seventy-five of the prisoners have been sentenced in a kangaroo court to twenty

A visit to Hamel Alley to experience the religious art and rituals of Santería

to twenty-seven years or more in prison.) Several of those detained are journalists, and all care deeply about their country—they simply want to see it flourish again. They are not "traitors" as Castro calls them.

Fortified by ice cream cones (the ice cream in Cuba is wonderful), a contingent of our group buses off to a baseball game. For $3, we have front-row seats along the first-base line. It's Saturday night, which we understand accounts for the low attendance, though loud enthusiasm makes up for sparse numbers. Cubans are passionate about their national sport. It turns out to be a rout, with the powerful Industrials team pounding their opponents. There are beer and peanuts to be bought and loaves of a sweet honey bread that we pass around, tearing off pieces. Steve and Bel are in their element talking sports with Raúl, who is Cuban American (he's head of Milwaukee Public Television.) Our Steve, a Wisconsin Public Radio producer-interviewer, tapes a lengthy interview with Raúl, with the shouts and cracks of the bat as background.

Alberto suddenly becomes an entrepreneur (I'm American," he says), making hilarious deals with the players who run by our box; he gets them to sell the caps and shirts off their backs, and balls autographed by the whole team. He jokes about negotiating next for home plate. Like everybody else in Cuba, these professional ball players make a maximum of $30 a month. The team, of course, is owned by "the people"—aka the government.

Gods of Nature and Primal Energies

On Sunday, while I collect my bag at the airport, our three guys are off to Mass at the Cathedral (low attendance, but worship is allowed). Then the whole group is taken to Hamel Alley for religion of another sort. First, we look at the colorful outdoor wall murals by famed painter Salvatore González. These are strong representations of Santería, the religion where the many African deities were brought to the Caribbean and given the names of Catholic saints so that the two beliefs became merged. This is similar to what we saw in Brazil with Macumba and Candomblé. All these are dominated by the spirits of nature and of the dead.

There's a powerful maternal energy of the goddess of the deep sea and other prominent gods, called *orishas*. Drums are played to evoke the spirits of the deities. One of González's apprentices comes out to explain the history of Santería and its art. He passes out sprigs of basil, to be worn for protection. Then a truckload of musicians arrives and sets up under an olive arbor; they bring mostly drums and other percussion instruments. Singers and dancers start slowly, then work up to a frenzy, some gyrating wildly.

With our spiritual nourishment taken care of, we proceed to a private home for lunch. These *paladors* are opened up to a few guests on condition that all who work there are family members, since there can be no hiring. It's a sumptuous feast of calamari, red snapper, vegetables, chocolate mousse, and the finest rum, drunk straight as a liqueur.

We're on our bus again, traveling east from the city, past plantations of mangoes, bananas, vegetables, sweet potatoes, sugar cane, and then military installations and a plastics factory. We learn that there are two-and-a-half million people in Havana, with eleven million total in Cuba. The population is 66 percent white, 32 percent black and mestizo (European and American Indian mixed blood), and one percent Chinese. In the mountains, there are people with reddish skin and straight hair, descended from the Arawak Indians; their medicine men practice natural healing.

Hunting Hemingway

We're on our way to Ernest Hemingway's Finca Figia (farm), a lush estate in a village of low bungalows. It's pouring torrentially, so we don hats, clutch umbrellas, and march up to the house. Cameras are forbidden, and we can only peer in the windows and doors, but we get a good feel for this larger-than-life figure and his lifestyle. There are animal heads on the walls—elk and buffalo—collections of knives, tables of liquor bottles, a minuscule typewriter (we hear he wrote standing up at his desk). The décor is austere, definitely masculine. Bookshelves everywhere hold ancient, leather-bound and old paper-covered books. Someone spots boots of an enormous size.

We forge on to Cojimer, the simple town of poor folks, fishermen whom Hemingway hung out with and often helped financially. These people adored him, and after his suicide in 1961, they sold pieces of their boats to pay for a memorial bust of him displayed near the ocean. We leap through puddles into the famous seaside bar where he held forth and downed his daiquiris. This is the locale for his *The Old Man and the Sea*. The book is modeled on his good friend, the fisherman Fuentes, who died seven months ago at age 104. Steve pays homage by posing at the bar with glass raised and cigar in hand.

We return to Havana. The wind has whipped up fiercely; Carlos learns that his wife's taxi flipped over three times and the roof blew off a "camel." The gutters are all running full. Our evening program is the noted cabaret, Tropicana. It's setting in dense woods in the suburbs is magical, where statues of dancing nymphs form a lighted fountain. Usually the show is held outdoors, but because of the threatening weather, it's moved under the "crystal ceiling," a glass roof where you see out and at the same time twinkling lights overhead guide us to our table.

Champagne and a bottle of rum appear, and a spectacular collage of fast-moving color begins, one act tumbling on to the next, for two hours. There's song, jazz ballet, rumba, and acrobatics, all suffused with salsa, the infectious Cuban beat. Costumes are flamboyant: giant lampshade headdresses, feathers, flounces, pasties, thongs that don't really cover bare bottoms. Everybody is shaking and leaping. The orchestra is deafening, the pace rapid-fire. The women performers are stunning, some 95 percent of them black or mestizo. Carlos grabs his beautiful wife and they jiggle provocatively in the aisle for us. We're glad to see this world-famous production (mounted for foreigners), but once is probably sufficient.

A black filmmaker comes by our hotel to chat with us about the culture of Africans and women that lives on in Cuba. Many of these people originally arrived from Bantu and Yoruba tribes on the passports of their owners. The Haitians here mostly entered illegally. They all worked on the sugar plantations. In the 1920s and '30s, Cuba was very rich, more so than the other Caribbean islands. Before the Revolution there was more racism and separation of blacks. Castro fought for equality, though, we're told, there is still subtle color discrimination.

At a premier rum factory we see thousands of barrels piled of the "handmade" drink—pure, natural, filtered with charcoal and silica. We're plied with generous samples. Many in our group also buy liqueurs, gourmet coffee and cigars ($85 a box). Lunch, then, at the Catalina Lasa mansion, an elegant setting with a sad Romeo-and-Juliet-type history of thwarted love.

Political Rumblings—A Front-Seat View

Happily, strings are pulled and we're able to visit the United States Interests Section after all. We're to be briefed by Rick Weston, head of public relations. As we approach the building, there is heavy security by Cuban guards who keep us on the opposite side of the street until we're processed and cleared at the checkpoint; our leaders must show copies of all our passports. The United States built this embassy for $5 million and owns it still, though it's officially the home of the Swiss delegation. Weston has been here off and on for some twelve years and, clearly, is fond of the country.

We had expected a pat American propaganda line but are pleasantly surprised to find him offering frank answers to the tough questions from our politically sophisticated, mostly ultra-liberal group. It's evident that he is not a George H.W. Bush fan. He speaks of "Black Spring," referring to seventy-eight dissidents now sitting in jail, to be charged under Article 88 that carries at least a twenty-year sentence for "sharing information with the United States." Their crime: wanting to explore the idea of democracy and more freedom.

Most of the detainees are associated with the Varela Project, the daring petition put out by physicist Oswaldo Payá and presented in May 2002 to the Cuban National Assembly with 11,020 signatures (10,000 were required). The petition called for a constitutional referendum on free speech and elections, as well as giving all the US rights we take for granted, such as operating a business. This coincided with President Carter's visit to Cuba. When Carter brought up Varela in his speech on national television, it was the first time the Cuban people had heard of it. Payá was awarded the European Union's Sakharov Award for human rights. In retaliation, the Cuban government collected enough signatures (supposedly 90 percent of the people) to make socialism irrevocable. Now the Iraq war gives an

Crumbling colonial architecture in Havana

excuse for Castro to round up dissidents, journalists, and librarians. He brushes aside the desire of his people for the end of the travel ban.

The Interests Section functions like an embassy, helping with visas for Cubans to escape their oppressive government. James Cason was doing what his mission demands: meeting with citizens who wanted to plan a different future, to discuss their aspirations and goals. No Cubans were coerced to attend the workshop held at Cason's home, and supposedly he wasn't talking to them about how to overthrow the government. On the other hand, it probably would have been more prudent for meetings with dissidents not to be held by US officials.

Until eight months ago, it was possible to buy computers here. Then the devices were quietly removed, possibly to thwart easy communication. It costs $150 a month to subscribe to the Internet, but when most citizens earn $10-$20 a month, this is obviously out of reach. No Cuban would even consider owning a computer. Satellite dishes are illegal. All news is filtered. Cubans are told we're in Iraq for oil.

Weston tells us, "Castro doesn't really want the trade embargo lifted. He wants or needs to be able to stand up in defiance to the world, to prove that the United States is imperialist. Probably no American president will lift it now." When Clinton was considering ending the embargo, Castro shot down the US planes.

Weston invited a spirited question and answer period:

Q. Why does Bush associate with the most rightwing Cuban exiles?

A. Politics. Cuba is classified as "terrorist" because it is said that people from around the world in terrorist organizations are given safe haven here.

Q. Why is there an embargo of Cuba and not, for example, of China or Syria?

A. Because those other countries have goods we need. Also, other countries have become more open than Cuba. We thought if economics improved in China and Vietnam, Cuban politics would change, but they remain totally closed.

Q. Why doesn't this trouble other countries?

A. Bush is influenced by South Florida and Jeb Bush. It's hard to lift the embargo after the planes incident, and also there's a two-year wait for Congress to pass it with a two-thirds vote. Bush opposed this. Relations between Cuba and the United States are bad right now. This Interests Section might be asked to leave, although we doubt it. Castro won't do this because then we'd evict the Cuban presence in the United States. The Helms-Burton law punishes countries dealing with Cuba and denies them visas; companies are subject to seizure. If Cubans were to have their property confiscated, and then they later emigrated to the United States, Helms-Burton gives the right to sue for restitution in US courts. This is a very controversial part of international law. Because Castro wants to control all the economy here, he's not interested in opening up free entrepreneurial activity. No Cuban can employ another Cuban. All hotels are 51 percent owned by the government, even if others put in all the investment money. Many companies are not pulling out because Castro would create a huge hassle for them.

Q. Who will be Castro's successor?

A. For now it's his brother Raúl, aged seventy-one, but there are a couple of younger ones

> who are possibilities. We're closer to a "transition" now than ever before. The government is scared, which is the reason for throwing the seventy-eight in jail now.

Breaking Waves and Cuban Education

Steve, Bel, and I head out for a walk on the Malecón, the legendary esplanade and roadway following the shoreline. We want to see the enormous waves—fifteen feet high—breaking over the seawall and spilling into the street following the big winds. We cross to the wall to get photos and have to leap away to dodge the spray; Steve stays for a spectacular shot and gets drenched. Then we stroll up the Prado to the Ingleterra Hotel to catch the view from the roof bar. Later Doug and Steve launch out to take in some late-night Cuban jazz.

Next morning we bus to the University of Havana for a meeting with the vice-rector. This impressive collection of buildings is situated on a high bluff. It is 275 years old. There are research exchanges with sixty-seven US universities, with American students coming for a semester and receiving credit back home. Presently 108 US students are here. Twice a year there's also a semester at sea: seven hundred American students and professors arrive on a cruise ship and come ashore for three days at the university for informal exchanges. Fidel meets with them as well and welcomes their questions—which is always interesting to the Cubans present (some of it televised). The university can't spend too much time on this program, or expand it, because its first job is educating Cubans. However, they feel it's valuable in preparing for a future they hope will afford a freer, more "normal" exchange.

The history and philosophy dean speaks to us next. She says:

> Since the early 1990s, there's been a crisis of jobs for young people. A school for social workers was started, sending them out into the villages and provinces to bring dropouts back to study. They especially need teachers and nurses. Since Cuba guarantees jobs for all university graduates, there had to be a drastic reduction of students accepted after the economic crisis of 1994; previously 90 percent of high school students were accepted. Now only 70 percent of those who apply get in. It's all free, including books, food, and lodging, and even a stipend to visit their families. All students can use university computers, including Internet access. The University of Carlton in Canada, which carefully encourages the Cuba-Canada relationship, pays for this.

Bel and the dean exchange business cards for possible future collaboration.

The Other Side of the Political Divide

Next is an audience with Gustavo Machin Gomez, the deputy foreign secretary of the Cuban Ministry of Foreign Affairs. Though eagerly friendly, he also clearly is giving us the Party line. He claims there is no anti-American feeling, but also says that we may be the last group to visit Cuba, because the United States just passed a new law prohibiting Cuban-American exchanges. Gustavo was at the Cuban diplomatic mission in D.C., his main role being to normalize relations. He thinks that politically we're at the lowest point of our relationship but sociologically at the highest (in terms of people-to-people programs). He says:

> In the United States, Republicans and Democrats have united in dealing with Cuba. Cuba wants to cooperate on drug trafficking and terrorism, but the United States has declined. You have to remember that Cuba is

a third-world country; it's under great pressure from you because of the embargo, so has no credit anywhere else in the world. No ship docking in Cuba can land on US shores for 180 days afterwards, so the Cuban people suffer and pay three or four times the usual price for goods.

As at the US Interests Section, we're invited to ask questions. Our group doesn't hold back:

Q. Does the embargo help Cuba politically?

A. No! But we're not ready for business competition, not ready for five million tourists.

Q. What about James Cason?

A. He has violated diplomatic law, he's acting against Cuba and is financing revolt. Diplomats are supposed to promote relations between their country and where they are serving. Cuba has been patient with his violations.

Q. Why doesn't Cuba respect its citizens in questioning their regime?

A. US foreign policy is to topple Cuba, so we must be on our guard. We have to fight for our views. We can't allow dissidents supported by the United States.

Q. Were relations improving before the planes were shot down?

A. Yes, but then in 1996, US leaflets were dropped on Havana, violating Cuban air space, provoking Cuba. We're not proud that we shot down the planes, but we warned Clinton.

Q. What does Cuba think about the US presence in Guantánamo?

A. The United States is there illegally. The Platt Amendment lets the United States intervene whenever it wants. The United States gave Cuba independence in return for Guantánamo, and Cuba accepted because it wanted independence above all. But when Taliban prisoners were brought there, Cuba objected.

Q. What did Cuba think about Carter mentioning the Varela Project publicly?

A. We like Carter as a peaceful friend. We gave him freedom to say what he wanted, including Varela.

Q. What plans does Cuba have to normalize relations?

A. Whatever we do, it's because we think it right. There are no bases for terrorists in Cuba. We do what we can to normalize, but we don't discuss independence.

Q. What are your plans for succession?

A. We are a republic; there are elections, not succession. No one has been chosen. There are no term limits.

After we leave this session, Raúl tells us that just two weeks earlier Gustavo was ejected from the United States for spying, which, of course, he never mentioned. Clearly he was walking a fine line and talking very carefully with us.

The False Calm of Cuba's Former Luxury, and Then Fallout From the Current Regime

In our last few hours in Havana, the group descends on a former Biltmore Hotel on the city outskirts, now in Cuban government hands. It used to be an exclusive private club and is now rented only to those with impressive means, meaning no Cubans. It is indeed elegant, and William splurges, springing for three hours of open bar with mojitas and daiquiris and a sumptuous buffet. We mill around on a wide veranda overlooking white sand and ocean, and descend a grand stairway leading down to the beach.

We settle happily into the vast dining room with paintings of Greek mythic figures on the ceiling. It's said that Castro has an estate up the road.

Back in the heart of Havana, our family four sally forth for a last walk down the Prado to the Malecón. Waves are still high, but not crashing over the wall. Steve has his tape recorder out to pick up street sounds and kids singing and playing ball. We notice many older men sitting in one dilapidated doorway after another, absorbed in games of chess or checkers.

We learn that earlier in the day a Cuban plane was hijacked on a flight from a small Caribbean island to Havana; the pilot held the passengers hostage at the Havana airport, supposedly with grenades, while he demanded fuel to get to the United States. After several tense hours, he got the fuel and took off for Key West. Under US ruling, if Cuban escapees set foot on dry land, they are offered asylum; if caught at sea, they are sent back. We don't know how many of the passengers, if any, decided to stay.

Dancing with a Snow White Dwarf and Delivering Medicines

We're off on a ten-hour bus ride east to Camagüey, our chance to see the interior countryside. Farmers are hoeing their little vegetable plots. Large cattle herds graze among stunted trees and brush on the flat, scrubby land; they were all imported and cross-bred—we see the white, humpbacked, floppy-eared African variety. There are citrus plantations, some rice paddies, crocodile farms, and fields of sugar cane, though the market for sugar is way down.

We see almost no heavy machinery; the very few tractors are tiny and rusty. Groups of men are scything the grass next to the eight-lane highway. Open trucks rumble past, packed with workers standing up. Lots of people are walking or waiting. Covered, horse-drawn wagons and occasional cowboys galloping by on the wide plains recall what the American West may have looked like 150 years ago.

We drive past huge billboards (never advertising products), mostly political or admonishing about lifestyle, e.g., "What is Revolution? Power, Freedom." "Don't Drive After Drinking, Says Fidel." "In Cuba There is No Corruption." "Cuba—How Beautiful is Cuba!" "No to the War, Stop the Massacre, Down with Imperialism and Zionism." "For Country and Liberty." Many signs show pictures of Che or Fidel. One with Che exhorts: "Follow His Example, Continue the March."

Now mountains with conical peaks are poking up on the horizon to the south. We stop at the little village of Santa Clara, where tobacco is grown and workers are cutting cane with machetes. Here, out in nowhere, is the large monument and mausoleum for Che. His body was recovered only in 1997 in Bolivia, and now he is buried here.

We stop at a *rapido*, a fast food place where, as always, there is live music. These musicians are especially good, and they pull out one from our group to dance. I note a pig on a leash, strolling through a park. Beyond the pineapple and papaya orchards are fields with more and more goats along with the cattle; white egrets follow the cows' droppings. At every little shack, there's a horse tied up and usually a buggy. *Vaqueros* (cowboys) ride through the fields. We spot a gleaming bust of José Martí in the front yard of a ramshackle shanty. Some roofs are thatched with palm. Many fences are constructed of crooked saplings laced with barbed wire.

In late afternoon, we arrive in Camagüey, sister city of Madison, Wisconsin. Our two buses squeeze into a narrow street in front of the Gran Hotel, the best in this city of 325,000. The town seems more intimate than Havana. We're hustled off to a Young Pioneer center, where a host of grade school kids wave as we arrive, then grab our hands and reach up to kiss us. This is a school for specialty training, here emphasizing the arts.

The Pioneers, with their red neckerchiefs, are the communist youth organization; they propel us into a makeshift auditorium where a lively show begins, "Fantasy of the Dolls," with ballet dancers, acrobats, all in splendid costumes. At the finale, the performers grab our group members out to dance; I find myself doing a samba with one of Snow White's dwarfs who comes up to my waist. Speeches and recitations are translated by a young man who pleads for peace and unity between our countries—for a joining of hearts. He also makes a political pitch for the release of the "Cuban Five" imprisoned in isolation cells in the United States after being accused of spying on Cuban Americans planning to overthrow Castro.

The following morning we hike through the spotless streets of Camagüey. In one building we hear about the famous nineteenth century medical researcher, Dr. Carlos Findlay. Then we climb to the second floor, where a dozen singers of Haitian descent hold us spellbound in a surprise, hour-long concert that runs from wild, rhythmic thumping to Negro spirituals. Their voices are stunning; we hear they are in demand worldwide.

Another hour on the buses brings us to Nuevitas, Milwaukee's sister city, small and run down. Officially the purpose of our trip is to deliver humanitarian materials here, and Raúl has brought two hundred pounds of medical supplies. He's been coming down three times a year since 2000 with groups, always carrying badly needed materials. Each of us has also brought scarce items like vitamins, medications, soap, and pens (we hear, for example, that each person is allotted one bar of soap a month). Young Pioneers welcome us with flowers, we give our gifts, and the mayor and William exchange official greetings. They invite us to a spread of coconut milk sucked through straws, crusty fish sticks, stuffed baked dough, and tropical fruits.

Ugly Americans?

Now the official part of our trip is done and we have a day and a half of real R&R. We retrace part of our route on the only east-west highway, then veer north to Cardenas, famed as Elián González's hometown. You may remember the dramatic story, several years ago, of the little boy who was fleeing Cuba in a boat that capsized near the US shore; his mother drowned, Elián was rescued and subsequently snatched forcibly from his Florida relatives and returned to his father in Cuba. Now he's a propaganda spokesperson for Castro's regime. We note his little green bungalow.

After eight more hours on the road, we arrive at Varadero, exclusively a resort town with numerous joint venture hotels lining one of the loveliest beaches we've ever seen—fine white sand with absolutely clear, turquoise, pink and silver ocean shimmering and undulating slightly. During a day on the beach, we chat with Canadians and Germans sunning near us; we see no other Americans. Other nationals, of course, have no problem entering Cuba, and many have discovered it as a delightful and intriguing playground.

Our farewell dinner is booked at Xanadú, the former DuPont mansion on a bluff, now used for private parties. Built in 1928, it's exquisite, a mix of colonial, Chinese and early twentieth-century American. Its terrace hangs over the lapping ocean far below.

Then it's back to Havana for a final night. We're a bit spooked about strolling too far along the Malecón; we hear that the day before, Pat (in our group) was out walking with Raúl and was mugged, her passport, money and camera snatched.

A last billboard on the way to our plane at 5:30 a.m. reads: "We Are All Revolutionaries; The Future is in Your Hands." There's a horrendous, sweltering, four-hour wait in the terminal; we sit on the floor, propped on our bags. We were scheduled to fly out at 8:00, but the staff in this major, international airport doesn't even show up until after 9:00. We learn that our charter had arrived earlier but was not permitted to land, probably because the field personnel were not yet on duty, so it had to go back to Key West. Pat is informed by customs brass that she can't fly without a passport, even though copies are shown. Tearful and tense, she leaves with Alberto to return to the US Interests Section for a new one, hoping to catch a later flight. Our plane returns, and finally, close to noon, we lift off. No further mishaps, except that in Miami an alert beagle sniffs out my forgotten banana, which is duly confiscated.

Reflections

My impressions of Cuba? A friend asked if any of my preconceptions had changed. Actually, I went with very few. I guess I'd always felt somewhat sympathetic toward Castro and his lofty, idealistic aims, and his courage to stand up against the hostile behemoth to the north. He had managed to stick to his guns and not get sucked into the darker excesses of capitalism and consumerism. There was a kind of brave purity that's rare these days, certainly in America. I felt that the United States was especially unreasonable and heartless in continuing the embargo that was primarily hurting the Cuban people by crippling their economy. After visiting there, I still held some of these thoughts.

But I also saw that there was a rigid game of chicken being played by both Castro and Bush; neither one would give an inch, and their extreme attitudes were only becoming more entrenched. Certainly Castro had made important strides toward equalization in the health and education fields that could be examples for the world.

Yet we sensed the innate longing of so many in Cuba to be freer. This was not only in terms of a generalized, across-the-board equalization, which had been accomplished with the Revolution. People also wanted the freedom to express their creativity and drive for personal independence by becoming even small-time entrepreneurs, claiming the results commensurate with work they put in. The squeeze since the USSR pulled out its aid in the early 1990s has placed a heavy burden on Cubans in that they don't have access to even the simplest amenities and goods.

Almost everyone we spoke to believed that the situation in Cuba would change in the next few years. "It might be through some kind of coup," they said, "but probably will happen more gradually. We're sure that when Fidel leaves the scene, something is bound to shift." We Americans would hate to see a McDonalds on every corner there, and certainly some of the older Cuban values and culture of frugality—that have gone by the wayside in our country—are important to preserve. One would hope for a bit of accommodation or leeway at both ends of the spectrum.

Our tour itself was fascinating, affording rare glimpses into a country that in many ways is an anachronism largely cut off from the rest of the world, with much that showed a rich and sensitive culture. We saw people vibrant, brave, and

Three-wheeled taxi, Havana

ingenious in the way they've adapted to severe deprivations. In juxtaposition to our own society of excess and waste, with our lust for "more" and "bigger," Cuba—awash with obvious challenges—has sobering lessons for us.

As I was finishing this wrap-up, I heard that three of the hijackers of a ferry in Havana harbor last week were summarily executed today. A journalist reported that the situation there was getting more tense by the minute—that Castro may believe that when we're finished with Iraq, we'll go after him, and that the Varela proponents could be ready to initiate a coup.

Because of the cataclysmic political events ("Black Spring") that coincided uncannily with our trip, the United States immediately tightened the rules of travel between our countries. We realized that in the new climate, we might not have been permitted to go at all. It was a historic time to be there, and the four of us felt very fortunate. We were glad to see Cuba before the eventual end or dilution of communism.

Now, a decade later, Fidel's younger brother, Raúl Castro, has taken the reins of government, and we are seeing seismic changes. Self-employment is now permitted in some sectors, so that people can augment their very meager government stipends. Cubans can travel more freely. Obama has changed a ruling so that Cuban-Americans may send as much money as they want back to their relatives on the island. Most significant is that just within the past year, Raúl has instituted legislation allowing Cubans to buy and sell property. It's been pointed out that this will have a huge effect on the demographics, especially in Havana, where we'll begin to see sharper class distinctions. Such a shift must have been an enormous shock to Cubans who, since the 1950s, had gotten used to the slogan, "Socialism or Death"!

Part II

Traveling with a Vision

Search for Enlightenment

Eric and Bel in the Findhorn dunes above the North Sea

Findhorn
The Trip that Became a Quest

October 1976

Backstory

Part II of this book launches off in quite a different direction, a different kind of traveling. You might say that almost all of our trips were colored and undergirded by curiosity, a need to know more about unusual spots or situations around the world. But those in Part I were primarily motivated by a sense of *mission*. We—with Bel usually taking the lead—were drawn to settings where we felt we might contribute ideas or elbow grease that, on some level, could alter the circumstances of those we joined to work with. At other times, we were simply intrigued by a critical moment in the history of a locale and wanted to bear witness to what was unfolding there, such as our visit to Cuba and the travels across China. All of these, whether we were on the ground working or going in a study capacity, loosely fit under the umbrella of *socio/political journeys.*

Because I've divided our trips into categories, the story I'm about to tell must go back in time, slotted in after the experience in Brazil in 1967-68. The following few years marked the beginning of my own need, after just scratching the surface, to peel back some of those layers of transpersonal mysteries hinted at in the Brazilian hinterland. I also felt compelled to dig more deeply into my own particular life purpose. In a lot of ways, since meeting Bel in 1952, I was following *his* star, *his* compulsions to stir up the societal soup in ways he hoped might contribute to a more humane world. But there came a time—a midlife realization?—when I had to find a path that was uniquely mine.

Sure, I had been a contributing member of our "team"; I had raised two sons and managed households in some pretty challenging parts of the globe. My own particular "adventures" included getting shot up for a plague of boils by a Sardinian doctor who brought his rusty needles wrapped in newspaper, giving me a nasty, year-long bout with hepatitis B. At a Roman hospital, the baby nurse transmitted a virulent staph infection to our newborn Steve, who passed it on to me for a year of surgeries for multiple abscesses. In Brazil, apparently I was zapped by a voodoo priestess with an evil eye spell that paralyzed me and addled my head for a while.

All of these I've already recounted in previous chapters. I had also exercised my amateur talents in various (less life-threatening) fine arts. Not that all this was boring, but I wanted more. I was driven to search for meaning and purpose that would be mine alone. This next section is about vision and idealism, with a different twist on these terms that takes the adventure into the realm of "spirit."

More than anything else, it was probably my continual encounters in both Italy and Brazil with intimations of another layer of existence or knowing that pushed me to explore further such metaphysical conundrums.

In summer 1968, following the year in Brazil, our family returned to Milwaukee. Bel plunged back into running his Urban Community Development department and teaching political science at the university. At the same time, we also discovered an intriguing new school in the city. Called Psy-Bionics, it was offering a course teaching "altered states of consciousness." We thought this might be a way to continue our exploration of the transpersonal areas that had opened to us in Brazil.

Bel and I and our two boys all took this course in mental imaging. The results for each one of us were so compelling that I jumped in to work with the instructor to develop the school. We had found that at a subconscious level apparently one could direct outcomes for health and other life conditions by imagining specific goals while in a deeply relaxed state—and believing them possible. We also saw how these techniques might be accessing some of those supernatural realms I had glimpsed in Brazil.

Among the mushrooming activities of Psy-Bionics, we sponsored a number of large conferences, bringing in from around the country noted medical researchers, psychologists, and investigators of paranormal phenomena. Interestingly, over and over, we heard these people talk about an unusual place in Scotland called Findhorn. This was a community of some two hundred people engaged in

Lisa with Peter and Eileen Caddy, Findhorn founders

what the scientists were calling "one of the most important spiritual experiments in the world."

I listened, fascinated by wild stories of how oversized and unusual plants were being grown in beach sand not far from the Arctic Circle. What made this possible was the step-by-step instruction received in meditation by the founders of this group. In 1962, a middle-aged British couple, Peter and Eileen Caddy, and their Canadian friend, Dorothy Maclean, had been instructed to drag their ancient trailer to the dunes near the fishing village of Findhorn and to plant a garden. It seemed that direct communication had been established with the patterning life force in each species of plant. The response was so remarkable that, as word got out, people from all over the world converged on this desolate corner of northeast Scotland to find out for themselves what this "Factor X" might be and to practice living in this kind of conscious cooperation with nature.

Quickly I boned up on Findhorn, read the few published books about it, and realized that I simply had to go there—by myself. It was an essential next step for me. It would be a quest to clarify the next steps of my life.

The reader might be wondering what this tangent has to do with "trips," unless possibly a psychedelic one. But I'll get to the connection.

Now, as I look at my journals from this episode nearly forty years ago, I see that the account of my first encounter with the Findhorn community may come across as florid, excessive, and probably ingenuous. Two years after the 1976 trip I went back, and this time (see the 1978 report that follows) I had crashed down to earth and was looking at the whole phenomenon with a much more critical eye. I could see the very human challenges and flaws, and yet I remained convinced that the basic message—the lesson—was important, maybe unique, at that time.

It was the essence of what I experienced on all levels that I brought back to America. I have no doubt that it was my initial euphoria that was responsible for the excitement I could communicate, which apparently touched so many people in our region. It was what drew them to be a part of a new worldwide movement that had the potential to move societies to a heightened awareness around sustainability and even survival issues.

Stepping into a River of Energy and Knowing

It's October 1976, and after months of dreaming, plotting, and corresponding, now it's really happening. As the Glasgow-Inverness train speeds northward, I first glimpse thickets of bracken and yellow broom. Then misty forests of larch and towering fir give way to high, frowning crags and bare moors. The sense of nature in command, demanding recognition, grows clearer. The feeling gathers momentum as we rattle past the foothills of the Cairngorm mountains, and then, as we officially enter the Scottish Highlands, comes an odd and almost heart-stopping realization: I'm home.

So begins a visit to the Findhorn community, one of the more astonishing three weeks of my life. Beyond all the stories of mystical happenings, what I actually experience far exceeds any expectations. Immediately I am aware of the purpose of the community: "to redress the balance between people and nature," recognizing the intrinsic interrelationship and interdependence of all the elements of life on Earth.

More is going on than simply growing unusual plants. In the time I live and work in the community, I begin to observe old personal habits and constructs in clearer perspective, and for the first time can actually step away from them. Letting go of my usual chewing over baggage from the past and meticulously planning for the future, I sense that I'm stepping into a river of energy and "knowing." I let myself be swept along in the present moment—trusting that whatever the outcome, it will be the right one. This is a switch from fixing goals, as we had practiced at Psy-Bionics. I begin to see that there are intelligences at work—perhaps an unconscious part of myself? Whatever it is, it seems to know better than I what needs to happen, better than I might "program" on my own.

Intimations of a Challenging Future

For the first couple of weeks, I plunge into a packed schedule of plenary talks and breakout discussions at two back-to-back international conferences: "World Crisis and the Wholeness of Life" and "Creative Renewal: A Spiritual Approach to Social and Economic Problems." It's the first time that I've heard serious discussion about impending, planetary environmental crises such as climate change and dwindling fossil fuels. (Remember that this is 1976.) Three hundred visiting participants have been attracted by a dazzling panoply of world-class thinkers/speakers. We hear Buckminster Fuller's pronouncement: We are foolishly living off our "principal" (nonrenewable resources) when we should be living on the "interest"—renewables like the sun and wind.

Fritz Schumacher, author of *Small Is Beautiful,* stresses the need for "intermediate technology." We still have what he calls "stage one" tools like shovels and hammers, but have progressively discarded all the subsequent technological improvements to the point where, for instance, we now rely on multi-million-dollar field machinery that eats up energy resources and makes it impossible for any but the very rich to farm successfully. As the Chinese found, it is better to upgrade the skills of the midwives in the villages than to send out university-trained doctors who are accustomed to costly hospital equipment. Schumacher also points out that humans have become "gap-fillers"; we merely pull the levers while our elaborate electronic computers do all the fun, creative work. There's a terrible urgency to begin to humanize work again, to "reconstitute the middle" before the soul is literally destroyed.

We hear sophisticated analyses of the challenges facing us, individually and collectively. We listen to intelligent solutions that are light-years beyond where the mainstream stands. It becomes clear that to have a future at all, as much as possible we must learn to conserve and recycle, share tasks such as the growing and preparation of food, pool tools and equipment, and live with common walls and land and wells. One can do this more easily in an "intentional community" such as Findhorn. Intentional community is defined as a group of people who come together with a shared vision and purpose and a commitment to live and test these values together.

Along with the practical exhortations during the conferences also spring homilies that relate such ecological, economic, and social measures to immutable esoteric principles. David Spangler points to one of the prime Laws of Manifestation, on which Findhorn was founded and through which it has operated successfully for fourteen years: every need met perfectly through faith—belief in these mysterious forces. The energies and gifts given must be recycled back to the source. If I receive, I need to return the gifts; nothing must stop with me. I own nothing, not even land I may have bought, but am simply given stewardship of it for a time. The energy exchange must be kept flowing.

Being Present, Listening with the Heart

For my third week, I've signed up for the basic Findhorn program, "Experience Week." At the edge of the sand dunes, I settle in among the jumble of bungalows and aging trailers that make up one part of the Findhorn community. Sharing my bungalow are four other short-term visitors: an effervescent Londoner from a center for homeopathic medicine who recently had cared, alone, for a woman dying of cancer in the countryside; an empathetic TV producer from New York involved with the Inner Peace Movement and esoteric studies; a widow in her sixties from Kansas City conducting parapsychology experiments for a master's thesis; and a quiet girl in her mid-twenties who had been growing vegetables in California and plans to stay on in Scotland to plant an organic garden.

The thirty participants in our group listen to community members talk about the philosophy and initiatives of Findhorn, and then we can put these ideas into practice immediately by pitching into the daily life. We hear often about how "work is love in action."

I find that people come here from every belief—or nonbelief—system. They're drawn to this place of palpable power and energy in order to learn the practice of being constantly mindful of living in harmony with all they touch, bringing gentleness and caring to every task and interaction.

One way all of these diverse paths converge is through simply being together in silence. Each person listens to his/her own quiet, inner voice that connects to a wisdom or intelligence transcending individual beliefs. A bit like a Quaker meeting, this is also how the community makes group decisions—coming to consensus intuitively, rather than voting from a conscious, mental level. This way they are able to sidestep personal bias, which might get in the way of coming to clear answers in the highest interest of everyone.

The Sanctuary, a charming bungalow set among clumps of brightly colored flowers, has designated group meditation times, and may be used throughout the day by individuals to work quietly through private questions or to be replenished. The heart of what Findhorn is about, it is a busy place. One might see this as Western mysticism. The idea of communing with the intelligence or divinity in nature is what some would call animism. Much of the philosophy of oneness, of universal energies present in every animate and inanimate being and object, is also what the Sufis talk about. Findhorn has found an eclectic approach to spirituality, recognizing that all beliefs must in the end come down to some very basic principles of acceptance, cooperation, and love.

"Work Is Love In Action"

In the early 1970s, the emphasis at Findhorn shifted from the glamorous myths about big vegetables to "growing people with a new consciousness." An extensive array of educational offerings has been organized over the years, so that now there is a continuous stream of visitors coming for shorter or longer stays to investigate any number of topics. There are programs in various languages. To date, thousands of people have had the chance to experience a very different and eminently graceful way of life.

The idea of living with integrity and honesty in relationships with others, and seeing sacredness and beauty in the ordinary, means approaching both grand and menial jobs with equal enthusiasm. It means caring meticulously for the materials and tools one works with. Any line between work and play vanishes, because everything one does is seen as important and exhilarating. This is what I experience during my visit, letting go of old patterns and opening up to entirely new modes of thinking and being. I spend days in the garden happily digging a trench for a pipeline in freezing sleet and rain; then, at the end of each session, my cohorts and I carefully wire-brush and polish our pitchforks and shovels with oily rags before hanging them up on designated hooks in the shed.

The famous Findhorn Garden, incidentally, isn't one huge mass of flowers or vegetables. One must remember that the total area where two hundred people live is not much more than three acres, jammed with trailers and bungalows. So the gardens are hundreds of brilliant little patches of color, lavishly and artistically arrayed around the myriad walkways and surrounding each building. I keep running into rock gardens, reflecting pools, splashing waterfalls. The variety of plants is breathtaking—the attraction for horticulturists who come from all over the world to marvel at species they say simply should not be growing in northern Scotland, and certainly not in this "non-soil."

I work in the kitchen, where I take utensils from drawers labeled "wooden beings" and "metal beings," and I mix dough in a huge machine named "Hobart." There is recognition that *everything* contains natural material that on some level holds a kind of consciousness—which can be communicated with and influenced. The attitude with which one approaches a task is critical. Someone tells the story of how the giant Gestetner copier in the publishing building shut down cold every time a certain guest walked past, which it hadn't done in weeks. One day, while we're eating lunch outside and I'm about to set my bowl of steaming soup on the lawn, a member reprimands me: "Please, nothing hot on the grass!" You know how some people are in tune with their cars, or how some have a "green thumb" when it comes to making plants grow? Findhorn folks understand this, pay attention, and nourish their relationship with all they touch.

Not a Cult

If I'd had a preconceived picture of two hundred glassy-eyed cultists, euphorically soaking up "the power," it quickly dissolves. Instead, I'm impressed with a tremendous amount of dignity, maturity, and sophistication. Solid, practical thinking, and hard work. Understatement and restraint. A straining to "hear" without ears because no one is preaching. There are no visible gurus running the community.

Of course, eventually I see (to my relief) that Findhornians are also mortal and can feel harassed and insecure at times, especially this month under the enormous strain of running several weeklong conferences. But the point is that they become ruffled far less than would have been thought possible. As educator Sir George Trevelyan puts it, "It's a question of acting, not reacting." This is noticeable; clearly they've all done a lot of interior homework on the subject of inner-versus other-directedness.

An interesting phenomenon: besides an almost palpably different or more alive atmosphere, I begin to notice the synchronicity of events, uncanny "coincidences" that follow one after another. When the experience needed for understanding how to cut through to new insights—when the right contact is needed—it just happens. I might be reeling under a soul-splitting problem and suddenly the answer, the way to deal with it, the peace, is right there. Mealtimes become a kind of game: I'm drawn to a table of strangers and find myself seated next to the person who fills my need of the moment exactly.

Getting into Community Life

Every day after breakfast in our respective bungalows, our group meets in the Community Center, attunes, and discusses the day's program with the two focalisers (coordinators) of our guest program. Each of us volunteers for work in one of the various departments according to the number needed that morning.

A word about the concept of "attunement": Whenever we gather as a group—for a lecture, a meeting, a work project—hands are joined in a circle and there are a few moments of silence when each person tunes in to the others and to the task at hand, recognizing our interconnection and immediate purpose. We can actually feel we *become* the seedlings we're about to plant, or are an integral part of the printing press we're operating, or one with the vegetables we're scraping in the kitchen.

The first morning, with an Oxford law graduate, I wash lettuce and scrub beets at Cluny Hill (the large hotel in the nearby town of Forres, purchased recently to house many of the education programs). Midmorning there's a half-hour tea break. Tea is always prepared in the work location (in the gardening shed, publications . . .) and provides a chance for guests to get to know community members and focalisers. Here they can really feel the pulse of the particular project and can articulate questions.

Another day I make soup in the Findhorn kitchen and put together one of the twenty or more types of raw or cooked salads for lunch. When I ask the focaliser what he wants in the soup or how much, he keeps saying, "Put in what feels right; you'll know when it's enough." And so it is. There isn't a feel of "work" or drudgery, even for the dirtiest, most exhausting jobs. An effort is made to see repetitive tasks as completely new each time. When I think it's "me versus a nasty job," I may feel disgruntled and tired. But if I'm part of the same energy and consciousness and process of a plant growing, a soup being created, there's a rising crescendo of satisfaction. I find this feeling everywhere. When a group of people joins together on a project, they are offering their labors and themselves. It becomes an adventure, and a collective high lifts it out of the plane of "work."

Another day I report to the publishing plant. It's a delightful, low-key spot, with tapes playing the New Troubadours (a polished Findhorn music group) and Celtic and classical music. Our job is to check through the just printed *Onearth*, Findhorn's top-quality, semiannual journal. In this efficient yet totally informal department (an area with work counters, drawing boards, a darkroom, a Heidelberg Press, duplicators, and other machines), one is aware of the highest professional standards, the talent and creativity.

After the work period, everybody pours into the Community Center for lunch, picking up soup and salad fixings and cheeses from huge, Findhorn-produced stoneware bowls. Findhorn members then go back to work while we visitors gather for special programs—talks, discussions, group exercises to loosen people up, trips to places of beauty or significance. There's free time to go off to explore the ancient Findhorn fishing village, two miles up the road, or hike to the beach. Then back for afternoon tea.

Exotic vegetarian dinners are served at night. Cluny Hill is slightly more formal, with wine and candlelight. Magnificent flower arrangements adorn all the tables; it's a full-time job just keeping up with these. In the evenings, after another Sanctuary period, are talks, audiovisual presentations, movies, folk dancing, concerts, skits, and other offerings by the performing arts department.

The special alchemical combination of ingredients at work here can't help but cast a spell. First, we're exposed to raw, violent nature in this remote part of Scotland: the closeness and power of the sea in the salt spray and sand blowing up from the gorse-dotted dunes; the wild expanses of purple moors; the mercurial changes in weather—ferocious winds that one day tear out whole beds of geraniums by the roots and topple trees; torrents of icy rain giving way half an hour later to brilliant sun and cobalt skies and an exquisite gentleness. Then there's the Findhorn community itself—a living being, pulsing with a quiet spirit of joy and light and infinite possibility. There's the strong sense of the divine in all life—in nature and animals and people—over-lighted and fused by a vision and awareness of our oneness.

Reflections

My last day in Scotland found me struggling against a tempestuous wind and driving rain to the top of a sand dune that overlooked the roiling North Sea. I was wrestling with the knowledge that I could not go back to America to the same life I'd left just three weeks before. My life had turned upside down and changed me irrevocably. It became clear at that moment what I had to do. I would take these strange, powerful experiences back and try to translate them for folks in Wisconsin. I had my marching orders!

Now, almost forty years later, I look back at the exploding trajectory of events. When I returned to Wisconsin, I found audiences eager to learn about that weird experiment in Scotland connecting humans and nature. When we brought the Caddys (Findhorn founders) to speak in Milwaukee in spring 1977, an astonishing crowd of twelve hundred flooded into the university to hear them. Clearly the timing was right, and people were popping out of the woodwork to question decades of ingrained beliefs. I've written at length about what happened next in my 2010 book, *An Unconventional Journey: The Story of High Wind, From Vision to Community to Eco-Neighborhood.*

Briefly, Bel organized university classes to examine new ways of looking at the future, attracting a core of devotees that coalesced to create a rural intentional community in 1981. We called it High Wind. It would combine the spiritual approach I had found at Findhorn with the cutting-edge work with alternative energy technologies of the New Alchemy Institute in Massachusetts. A government grant to build a demonstration passive solar building, based on New Alchemy's "bioshelter," attracted volunteer carpenters. Some stayed on to form the nucleus of the embryonic community. We instituted educational programs on our land, as well as in the city, addressing the issues of sustainability on all levels. Our ties to Findhorn strengthened over the years as their people came to High Wind, and we took study groups to live in Scotland and in similar communities in the United States and Europe.

Findhorn itself has continued to evolve. Its state-of-the-art ecological village is perhaps the strongest and purest model in Britain—reportedly with the smallest carbon footprint in the country. Gradually members have put into practice more and more energy-saving methodologies. Four giant wind turbines supply more than 100 percent of the community's electricity (generating a total of 750 kilowatts) and feeding the excess back to the local grid. A biological waste treatment system in a greenhouse purifies raw sewage by running it through a series of tanks with fish, plants, and bacteria to produce almost-drinkable water. Recycled wood chips from a nearby sawmill are burned in an efficient central boiler to heat most of the major buildings in the trailer park—saving some £15,000 a year and reducing carbon emissions by eighty tons that previously were produced by gas and oil units. The boiler also heats the water for a large outdoor hot tub.

Some members operate relevant private enterprises within the community, and staff running the guest programs now receive remuneration—all steps to ensure personal sustainability as well as that of the community work with the public.

Universal Hall, Findhorn Conference Center

The trip I undertook to wrestle with the next steps in my own life led Bel (a reluctant convert at first) to shift his priorities. He moved from confronting urban crises of race and poverty to "futures studies," to teach what universities were not dealing with at all. His co-instructors were David Spangler and other ex-Findhornians who, years before, had articulated what that community was about and had created its educational thrust.

Scores of people came to live and work at High Wind, and thousands more have visited the model, energy-wise homes we've built and to participate in learning programs.

We also managed, here and there, to stir up controversy and suspicion in our conservative township. High Wind was a radical departure from the typical nuclear farm family raising cows and taking pride in doing things just as they had always been done for generations. When some neighbors were threatened by our difference, I tended to take this personally. We were a group of mostly young singles from the city, pioneers ahead of our time. It was hard for me when High Wind was questioned because I believed so deeply in our purpose. I had to grow tougher skin to stand firm in the face of these pockets of local opposition.

The community has morphed into an "eco-neighborhood" of folks living carefully on the land, secure in their shared previous experience in the intense earlier years of intentional community, but freer now to pursue their own creative dreams and projects. Currently High Wind is giving grants for regional sustainability initiatives.

I'm still astonished when I remember the warnings I first heard at Findhorn back in 1976 about world crises and challenges—warnings that have proven ever more prescient and pressing. It is such earnest little community enclaves around the globe that often have sounded the warning notes most clearly and have taken concrete steps to point our sluggish culture toward a better way.

Cluny Hill: Education Hub

Findhorn houses of recycled whiskey barrels

Findhorn Revisited

May 1978

Backstory

Over the two years since my first Findhorn trip, interest in Wisconsin was ratcheting up fast. High Wind had already incorporated as an educational nonprofit, even though we had only a general idea about where it was going. We hadn't yet applied for the government grant to build the demonstration bioshelter, the catalyst that would coalesce a solid energy experiment, not to mention beginning to form any sort of community.

Bel was organizing courses and workshops and conferences through the university based on ideas triggered by my exposure to Findhorn. David Spangler, Milenko Matanovic, and others of their Lorian group (sparkplugs at Findhorn in the early 1970s) had moved to Milwaukee to teach with Bel, sensing that this was the right place and time to put down roots. They particularly recognized that their grounding in esoterics could provide an important balance for Bel's knowledge of politics and economics—complementing the practical with the transpersonal. Both Bel and the Lorians had much to give each other, and together they created the first of several years of very popular events. "New Dimensions in Governance" met twice a week for a semester in an off-campus venue, drawing participants from across Wisconsin and Illinois.

Perhaps readers are wondering why they don't see the term "New Age" in connection with our recent adventures. Clearly these would seem to fall under that label. Frankly, though, I can't bring myself to associate with the gross misrepresentation, misuse, and ridicule the term has generated—even though Findhorn and High Wind have aspired to New Age principles in the best or purest sense, which David Spangler spelled out eloquently long ago. In fact, David has sometimes been called "the father of the New Age." I felt that because this is a travel book and may attract a different clientele than did my book *An Unconventional Journey*, I would stay away from the term. Instead, I talk about "the new era" or "the new thrust."

By this time, Bel was realizing that he needed to visit Findhorn himself, to get that experience first-hand hand and to meet the dynamic leaders in the community I had talked about. We hatched a plan for me to fly over in early May 1978 to spend three weeks as a "working guest." Then, while I attended a workshop, Bel would come in for Experience Week.

Moving Inward

> Just back from a glorious Sunday, prowling alone among the gorse-covered sand dunes and along the beach. After a week of fortyish temperatures and rain, today it was suddenly summer—warm winds whipping cloud wisps and gliders around the sky, the North Sea crashing dark blue and white. Spent six hours alternately drowsing and "listening" in the sand between spiny golden hummocks and crawling through acres of brilliantly colored, striped, conglomerated stones, sculpted and painted by God and the sea—appreciating, feeling drawn to find this jade one with the bands, or that scarlet speckled egg. Feelings of disembodiment, slight madness, and a consuming joy.

This is a note from my journal written soon after I arrived back at the Findhorn community. I'm finding it a totally different experience this time. Instead of the vibrant energies and glamour surrounding that first international conference—the frenetic high, with every minute programmed to the point of psychic saturation—this time I'm fitting into the community's normal routine. As a working guest, I'm trying to blend with the rhythms of the members and to absorb as much as possible their ways of seeing and moving.

It seems so low key, in fact, that I'm feeling quite isolated, which, after the initial surprise and pang of loneliness, is providing a splendid chance to just relax and be. Besides working in various departments, I have also manifested a trailer to myself, backed up against the pines and dunes on the periphery of the community. Not for as long as I can remember have I really had an opportunity like this to daydream, read, reflect, let events and the elements and energies wash over and take me from one moment to the next. No planning, no major responsibilities—fantastic!

As Eileen Caddy pointed out the other day, this is obviously the experience I need. First, though, I am having to get over the uncomfortable feeling that I should be keeping my inner ear cocked for pithy cosmic nuggets. What, curl up in front of the coal stove with a novel when I'm living on a *power point*, for heaven's sakes?! (Power points, in this context, are strategic spots across the globe where it is believed powerful energy streams converge.)

In addition to the leisure to examine the shape of my life, another important gift is that I'm thrown into intense relationships with those forces near the sea, taking me directly back to identical feelings and experiences with nature that were part of my childhood. Running to the sea twice a day becomes a sacred ritual. I never speculate as to whether I'm connecting with devas or elementals (the supposed creative, formative forces in nature). I just know I have a "thing" going with the gorse bushes, dunes, rocks, beach, wind, and sky as clearly as I do with humans. To me, Findhorn is what it has become precisely because of its position and relationship to this dramatic corner of Scotland, this particular piece of nature.

The Work Departments

My first two weeks are split each day between the Findhorn kitchen and Publications. My connection to the Earth remains strong, since every time I step out of a building, I'm in the midst of the garden. Myriad spring flowers are blooming, and the perfume of hyacinths and the delicate coconut scent of wild gorse are everywhere.

Collating and checking books in Pubs is a meditative process. It's hard to believe that first-rate products roll off these presses at a prodigious pace while the atmosphere is so low-key and casual.

The gentle radiance of Irene, the Swiss kitchen focaliser, lights the whole operation and captures for me Findhorn's strength and beauty. It seems quite miraculous that the most complex menus always get finished exactly on time; I never see anyone frazzled, irritable, or rushing. The work is hard, yes; sometimes we stand at the stainless steel tables for two or three hours chopping vegetables, but always there is time to decorate the huge salad bowls with flowers sent over with the lettuce by the gardeners, or to create mandalas from shredded beets and carrots. To assure an interesting variety in the vegetarian diet, each evening meal is dedicated to a different nationality. An accordion player provides Neapolitan songs on Italian pizza night, and I really get into the spirit of Israel as I fry five hundred falafel balls. One image of the kitchen sticks in my head: Irene on the floor on hands and knees, up to her elbows mixing cake batter in a giant bowl by hand.

As I work in the departments with members, there is little need for conversation in order to feel at ease. I watch people moving, thinking, acting in ways that have become instinctive through practice, but what is automatic for them is still very foreign to most of us on the outside. Because they believe and speak of food, plants, materials, machines, and tools as responsive beings, there is always a special gentleness and respect. Jobs are done as perfectly as possible. Shortcuts and shoddiness have no place at Findhorn.

This seems particularly apparent in Universal Hall (the dramatic building being constructed for large, public gatherings) where I work for a week. The construction department sees the organic process of its completion as producing the kind of energy Findhorn is meant to be demonstrating. This won't emerge, it is believed, if expediency or utilitarian needs are put first, but only when and how the higher intelligences decide things must unfold. It is up to the crews to tune in to these directives.

When not away traveling, Peter Caddy keeps a finger on the pulse of the community, silently orchestrating the dozens of simultaneous operations. Every day, whether I'm holed up in the control room of the Hall helping connect wires to floating plugs, or running a sander in a dusty corner of the basement, Peter invariably pops in, constantly aware of how the mass of details fits into the whole. He is not asserting any direct authority in this spirit-directed community, but, as a founder, continues to feel ultimately responsible for what happens.

Findhorn's extraordinary sensitivity and consideration for all things keeps showing up. Bel and I are gardening in the Pineridge section one afternoon, and Dick Barton shows us how to turn and cover our footprints in the loose earth as we hoe down a row, leaving nature as little disturbed as possible. (After we had returned home to Wisconsin, I found that while we weeded and forked mulch at our farm, I was remembering these bits of awareness. Through our own garden, I was suddenly at Findhorn again, not three thousand miles away. Findhorn, indeed, had become a "state of mind" rather than a geographic place.)

What Makes a "Centre of Light"?

The third of my four weeks is spent participating in a workshop titled "Creating a Centre of Light." After free floating in the work departments, I really appreciate the sense of belonging in the tight group that we guests develop. The emphasis is on learning

"Hobbit house" sanctuary for meditation and Taizé a cappella singing

to internalize the basic principles so that we might function more automatically with the right consciousness, both as individuals and collectively.

The heart of the workshop is a series of sharings by the three focalisers and resource people (community members) invited in. Though we've all read David Spangler's books, or have gotten pitches about attunement, manifestation, relating to nature, and co-creation, I, at least, find myself hearing with fresh understanding. I need to hear the principles in the context of living in a place where they are practiced. Here are elaborations on the basic premises:

Attunement, Guidance, and Meditation. (Helen Rubin) Attunement is a resonance (equate this to sounding a "C" note and then hear someone else's "C" in another octave). Unlike more traditional spiritual concepts, where the guiding force may be perceived as being outside oneself entirely, we're talking of something within oneself that can tune into everything else. Chances are that you'll feel this as an intuitive hunch or a creative idea. It is important to believe that this is part of a universal flow, which might be called "spirit," and that it is valid and available to everyone. Learn to trust and act on what you feel, but also practice wisdom, especially when it involves others, so that you don't act irresponsibly. Learn to tell real guidance from wishful thinking by looking at how emotionally attached you are to the outcome and how it will affect others. It's when we're allowing, tapping into a flow, not willing and expecting things to happen, that we begin receiving. This means releasing personal desire. It's not what you do that matters but how. What counts is quality. However, there's also a danger of flowing too much with the environment and not being the prime mover of your own life. It comes down to a "knowing," a sense of inner direction and then having the perseverance to stay on the path.

Manifestation. (Jim Maynard) If things aren't coming to us, what aren't we doing right? The old laws have us going out to find where a need can be satisfied. The new law is finding a way to meet the need within ourselves, tuning into our higher self. Resources, of any sort, will come when there is: 1) *Right Identification*: seeing yourself as a cause, creating your own reality, a response to your own divine creativity. Identifying with the wholeness of unlimited resources; being conscious that there is an abundance that can supply exactly what you *need*, and also recognizing that extra luxuries are *wants* (personality-level desires, which are quite different). If you expect poverty or second best, that's what you'll get. 2) *Right Imagination*: tuning into real needs through meditation. Look at your motivation; is it honest and valid? An intuitive flash may give the answer. 3) *Right Attunement*: aligning the physical, emotional, and mental levels to the vision. Emotionalism can involve doubts, so the universe can be getting two orders and becomes confused (I need this but don't think I deserve it). Give thanks and hold the vision, even if it isn't happening; time is irrelevant. Harmonize your own personality with others. Building a genuine unity in a group is absolutely essential. Growth stops when there is friction and you must wait until there is unity again. If you do not use what's given at the time, it will be taken away. Be appreciative. Complete a cycle: for example, finish constructing one building before starting another. Know when to release when a cycle is finished. Above all, don't focus on the form of how a need will be met; for instance, don't see money as the biggest obstacle if a house is needed.

Starting a Centre of Light. (Peter Caddy) (Because Peter's guidelines for beginning community have appeared in several publications, I'll pick only a few highlights.) Basically, creating such a centre involves a group learning to function with the laws of attunement and manifestation before starting to build community; otherwise the venture is based on the mental or personality levels rather than the spiritual. If a group comes together for economic or political reasons, it probably will not last. If there is a common spiritual vision, there is a real grounding. The hallmark or test of this new kind of community: Does it cooperate with others? Does it have a wider world vision, and is it dedicated to world service? Does it recognize the need to network? The foundation for any new undertaking demands a balance between love and light (light being discrimination—if you let in everybody by loving everybody, it will fail; you will draw disruption, disharmony, freeloaders). But also, if there is too much exclusivity, the community will dry up. People may come wanting to live in a spiritual atmosphere, but unless they master the physical, then the emotional, and finally the spiritual (intuitional) challenges and ways of functioning, they will remain unbalanced. One of the most important lessons: "Love where you are, what you are doing, and whom you are with." By thinking positively, positive things will result and come out in balance. Remember the esoteric principle: Know that we are responsible for what happens to us; we draw experiences to ourselves.

Changes Afoot

The community is beginning to talk about decentralization, with more responsibility assumed by individuals and separate departments. This has to do with independence on an operational level as well as members becoming more philosophically aware of their reason for being here. Several departments, such as Universal Hall, have begun to raise money

Bag End ecovillage at Findhorn

for specific projects of their own. If Findhorn is to be an example for the rest of the world, maybe it can't remain a "pure" demonstration of manifestation—in the sense, for example, of relying heavily on donated gifts and labor. People are speaking of creating autonomous small industries that can bring in revenue for the community and perhaps make it possible for long-term members to earn money. Up until now, it has been strictly understood that all members are full-time volunteers; everyone must be equal.

If Findhorn evolves from the rather isolated enclave that it has been to this point (quite deliberately), the "city of light" envisioned will surely need to interact in more conventional social, political, and economic modes with its Scottish neighbors. Already there is energy going into dialogue and exchange visits and joint projects with nearby villagers, but the community is realizing that a full-scale diplomatic effort may be necessary to develop trust and support as it gradually expands. Within the past year, Findhorn has acquired two adjacent manor houses, partially donated, one of which is to become an experimental farm. They've also been made custodians of the tiny island of Erraid near Iona off the west coast of Scotland, where an embryonic community has been started by a handful of members.

Challenges after Leaving Findhorn

As greater numbers move through the "mystery school" training of Findhorn and then go out to apply the principles, the challenges of "reentry" become increasingly apparent. Often the culture shock is more difficult when going back into "the world" than when adjusting to the rarefied yet shared questing that the community offers. Findhorn supplies a supportive atmosphere where people can look at themselves clearly, stripped of game-playing and masks, where they can be more open and vulnerable.

But as they leave this cocoon of mutual trust, sometimes they find that when talking about honesty and love and unconditional service, there is a proportionate rise of suspicion and discomfort in others. It can be a blow to realize that all the world doesn't see the common sense in joining this new era—that proliferation of the ideas can take place only in very subtle ways that don't immediately threaten to destroy ingrained behavioral patterns and beliefs. How to keep the new values clear and high while working with others who are not in that space at all is a very real question—which recently has included explaining the difference between "cults" that operate through an absolute authoritarian figure and groups guided by an individual inner authority.

Besides communication, a major challenge for Findhorn "graduates" is making and handling money. This is one reason why more cash-producing enterprises in the community could be valuable preparation. At Findhorn, I sat in on several meetings on the subject of money—how there are two ways of dealing with it: on the personality level, where we receive according to what we merit or earn, and on the soul level, where we give and serve with no thought about what we may receive in return, not worrying about how our needs will be met. It was agreed that obviously there is value in demonstrating to the world that the latter way is possible. Yet strategies to bridge the chasm between such lofty standards and life "outside" need to be formulated.

Another principle has been making inroads in my consciousness for the past couple of years: the idea of people coming together in couples or groups from a point of individual wholeness and balance rather than from need. Support systems may not be healthy if perpetuated to fill a lack or void in their members. Interdependence has positive meaning when we think in terms of cooperating with nature, being one with everything, and parts of smaller wholes creating a greater one. Dependence implies emptiness that one is demanding to be filled.

Repairing Holes in the Honeymoon

Toward the middle of my fourth week (the midpoint in Bel's visit), I drop unexpectedly into a low-ebb period. Because I've loved and believed in Findhorn for so long, because it has been an anchor around which to focus my own life over the past two years, I've wanted especially for Bel to love it too. All of a sudden, I'm seeing it through his eyes, matching the reality with the mystique being built across the globe and with the descriptions I myself have been perpetuating. The "honeymoon" euphoria that most members experience intensely during their first couple of months for me have been telescoped into a much shorter time, and with little warning, I fall hard from that, all the challenges and shortcomings looming up at once. I'm the kid disillusioned when she first discovers that her parents are human.

Happily, the gloom lasts only for a few days, and I stop sharpening my negative darts. I recognize that the community is "divinely human," and that if every aspect ran perfectly, there'd be no reason for people to come here to live, no chance for them or the community to grow.

Dealing with the "God Stuff"

Though intellectually I had previously accepted the idea that divinity lies within, that *I am God*, it didn't really sink in until this visit. I am helped to see myself differently here: I find that I need not feel at one of two opposite poles—either having minimal value in a situation where I am making little input, or egotistically taking credit for a positive event that I have facilitated. I see that I can be comfortable simply as an instrument through which "God" (or "spirit" or "the universe") is working. I can give the divinity in myself the credit for a job well done. I can see this not as my power, but that I am just a neutral channel.

Conversely, I needn't feel responsible for the experience of others when something I set in motion seems to turn out negatively. I have to remember that people attract to themselves what they need in order to grow. They are responsible for their own experiences.

One member, a Methodist minister, found that he had to come to the eclectic environment of Findhorn to discover the essential Jesus. As a Christian clergyman, he had found Jesus to be somewhat of an embarrassment whom he tried to sweep under the rug, feeling that Jesus represented an uncomfortable exclusivity within the Christian institution. Only in this community did this minister see that Jesus embodies the real principles of Findhorn, and perhaps (heretical?) couldn't be termed "Christian" in the sense of the established institutional church. Since leaving Findhorn, this minister has been touring the United States, sharing these discoveries from various pulpits. Another prominent member, long estranged from religion of any sort, recently accepted Jesus as her "master" as a result of her meditation, to her own as well as her friends' astonishment. Strange happenings in what is sometimes viewed as an animistic or even pagan enclave!

Reflections

Bel's experience of Findhorn was as positive as mine had been two years earlier. He seemed to have gone through several phases. First, trying to comprehend the community's deep qualities, its real essence, which in its larger ramifications could point to a new kind of culture. Second, digging into its various effective practices, such as its governance process where the leaders (focalisers) are selected through attunement and recognition of "evolved consciousness," not through conventional elections. And, third, beginning to imagine how we could adapt some of the Findhorn experience to our budding High Wind in Wisconsin. Always in character, his response was to begin thinking about how he could translate the ideas into practical projects.

He reported that during his Experience Week (Findhorn's basic program), he had swapped notes with a high-level hospital administrator from New York. Both agreed that if they tried to inject the Findhorn ways of thinking and running the community into their own large, conventional institutions back home, they would never get to first base; it would be unthinkable in the culture of traditional systems. Very gratifying to me, though, was that Bel and I could truly begin to talk the same language between ourselves. We kept finding opportunities to reexamine the concepts vis-à-vis our personal interactions. It was the subtle differences in the outlook at Findhorn, responses infused with love and kindness rather than surface parrying (or equivocation?) that were most impressive and durable and translatable to our own situations.

We continued with familiar tasks and initiated new ones. Bel organized a series of futures-oriented courses and conferences run through his university department with academic credit, always being careful to describe the programs in non-threatening terms. With Lorian involvement, we established a core community of consciousness-embracing ideas of living more gently and self-sufficiently on the Earth, both in the city and country. These values and goals created a new impetus that we sensed was taking charge in our lives.

Now, thirty-five years after our 1978 visit, Findhorn has made enormous strides in establishing firm, friendly partnerships in its surrounding Moray area. For instance, the Scottish government recently gave them a grant to provide some fifty schools with

Tour of High Wind bioshelter, 1985

"eco-kits" modeled on experiments of the community—teaching ways to work with nature to provide clean water and power, and so forth, as a response to climate change. The early suspicions or outright hostility, so prevalent in this stern Presbyterian corner of Britain, has definitely lessened. (In 1976, when I told my hosts at a B&B in Inverness that I was going to Findhorn, they stiffened visibly and warned that I would be exposing myself to devilry and blasphemy.) However, now those fears have been allayed to a considerable extent. It is also clear to the local population that the hundreds of thousands of visitors have brought substantial financial benefit to a struggling region.

And, lest the reader continue to wonder whether Bel and I had gotten lost in the Brigadoon mists of some witchy, religious fad, one has only to look at the caliber of visitors, members, and trustees, and at the Findhorn Fellows roster (those who have come to speak). They include world leaders in finance, politics, education, environment, and social/cultural analysis. Trustee and Fellow Jonathon Porritt is a member of the British Parliament, author, and long-time leader of the UK Green movement. A no-nonsense group and good futurists all.

As I wrap up this chapter, I realize that it does contain a fair amount of esoteric Findhorn jargon and is pretty heavy on the definitions and directives. There's not much "traveling." But think of this as "inner travel," and then look forward to the next chapter as, armed with insights about personal equilibrium, we pull on our Wellington boots to stride into the mists of the Inner Hebrides on the west coast of Scotland to deal with some practical issues of living simply and sustainably.

Rugged Isle of Erraid

Isle of Erraid
Rugged Findhorn Outpost

March–April 1979

Backstory

By 1979, we had gathered a solid constituency in Wisconsin. This group, the local "cream" of the new ecological/spiritual thrust, was anxious to create some kind of response to what we had seen as alarming blind spots in our culture. Well steeped in the problems and possibilities, these folks, aged seventeen to seventy, also had studied "Western Esoterics" with David Spangler over the winter. By now, Bel and I , the Lorian group, and these students were all close comrades-in-arms, and the students were angling for a trip to Findhorn.

The Findhorn community was enthusiastic about hosting a two-month study expedition, especially since creating a link to an academic institution would break new ground for them. Bel worked it out that participants could earn university credit. Twenty-three people signed up, most from the Milwaukee area, but some from across the country. I was designated to accompany them, and Bel would come in for a week in the middle of the stay.

The second week of March we lifted off from Milwaukee. After a minor mishap—a duck flew into our plane's engine—we had to land hastily in Detroit. As a result, I had to scramble to get our large contingent onto a flight to London—not part of the plan. When we finally arrived, hours late, at Prestwick on the west coast of Scotland, we stepped out into a freak, raging blizzard. Michael Lindfield, our Findhorn focaliser, was there to meet us with a bus, and after a harrowing ten hours traversing the country on bad, snowy roads, with accidents on all sides, we slid into the familiar trailer park on the Moray Firth.

Witnessing a Critical Juncture in the Community

I'm assigned to the primitive Block House; maybe it is assumed that the Wisconsin group's leader is already acclimated to hard living and can cope with what is easily the most problematic lodging in the community. There is no heat; my two housemates, Grant Abert and Keith Symon (good Wisconsin friends, also accustomed to rugged conditions), and I can never get the coal fire lighted, and the loo (toilet) doesn't work.

The first night I hike to the dunes in half-light at 10:00 p.m., greeting my favorite gorse bush. It seems to be telling me that now is my time to be whole, not to need others for approval. Don't try to fill anyone else's expectations, it intimates; don't be anyone else's vision of me. If I take time to tune in to who I am and what's working out through me, this will be the finest gift I can offer. On the way back via the Findhorn fishing village, the wind is roaring and sighing in the pines. A bonfire whips up near the restless horses in their paddock.

A packed schedule of activities has been planned just for our Wisconsin Group ("Wiskies"). We will have access to all the major figures in the community, an unusual privilege. There are talks, discussions, briefings, The Game of Life (a board game where players get a chance to identify and deal with challenges in their lives), and, of course, work projects, such as the gardens and kitchen.

One day I break away for a solitary walk to the beach through a fairyland of white cotton and swirling mists burning off in the sun. I luxuriate in the unusual stillness and balmy, spring-like air despite snow on the ground. Another day there's a nature trip to the Auchindoun Castle ruins south of Elgin, encouraging me to let go briefly of the intense life in the community and my feeling of responsibility. It's also a chance to reestablish my roots, my love affair with nature in Scotland. Dazzling snow, hard blue sky, whistling wind. We climb a mile up a moor to the castle, and then scramble down to the River Fiddich; the Glenfiddich distillery is nearby.

It's a lucky stroke that we happened to come to Findhorn at a critical turning point for the community. The Core Group is a self-appointed leadership circle whose task is to sense the tenor or will of the community (and of its over-lighting entity), and then set in motion the next steps to be taken. At this moment, Core Group is wrestling with questions about paying for or acquiring new buildings, and a particularly delicate decision to move away from Peter Caddy's strong leadership. It is clear that Peter does not wield power from his own ego needs, that he simply sees himself as carrying out "the will of God" (and making sure members are doing this as well). But now it's felt that the community is coming into its "adolescence"; members need to stretch their own judgment and creativity, take real responsibility, and become their own authority. This push-pull is both exciting and painful, and our focalisers rush out of the meetings to give us firsthand reports on the proceedings.

There is also the perennial challenge, as in all communities, of balancing the need for individual independence and growth with the needs of the group, the whole. In America, feisty intentional communities may tend either not to cooperate well at all or to surrender totally to a guru—or they may choose to vote. Findhorn is supposed to be a democracy, run by "spirit," but there has not been much chance for the entire community to have real input in decision-making or for members to feel free to exercise their own creative impulses. There are rumbles of change on many levels.

Bel arrives from traveling around Europe, where he has been touching in with innovative education projects. In the week he is here, he deepens his connection with the thinkers and movers at Findhorn and gives a talk in Universal Hall on his thoughts about "transformation"—fundamental societal change. Our Wisconsin folks are anxious to meet with him to pour out what has been happening for them, their insights and challenges. Meetings are called to relate how the experiences here may contribute to what we may together create back home.

The Real Adventure Begins: Erraid

A month flies by, and it's time for some of our group to leave for the Isle of Erraid (see the Glossary for the pronunciation of Scottish names used in this chapter), part of the Inner Hebrides on the west coast of Scotland. This is a tiny island owned by a Dutch family, which has recently given Findhorn custodianship over a cluster of buildings there. We're up at 4:00 a.m. for a gorgeous drive down the length of Loch Ness. Suddenly we're under Ben Nevis—at 4,406 feet, the tallest mountain in Britain—white-on-white, draped in mist. We ferry across the water to Movern below Fort William, sun shafting through lowering clouds. Then we're treated to the full spectrum of the Scottish landscape: gnarly, moss-covered trees; long, deep lochs (lakes) with craggy hills sliding into them; bald rocks humping out of heather-covered moorland. Lots more snowy peaks and slopes.

We swoop down to sea level, loop into the second ferry crossing at Lochaline and onto the island of Mull. Through dense evergreen forests, and then it is bleak and bare as we go off onto an indistinct track and out to the water's edge. Erraid residents are waiting for us. It takes two trips across the little channel in the dinghy, then relaying the luggage and supplies up the hill to the "village"—four granite houses in a row.

I settle into half a "duplex" with Beth Herbert, my close Milwaukee friend, in her late twenties and wildly irreverent and funny, and Betty Wilson, the feisty, warm, seventy-year-old who is a leading champion for our unfolding Wisconsin dreams. We learn the intricacies of a gas water heater

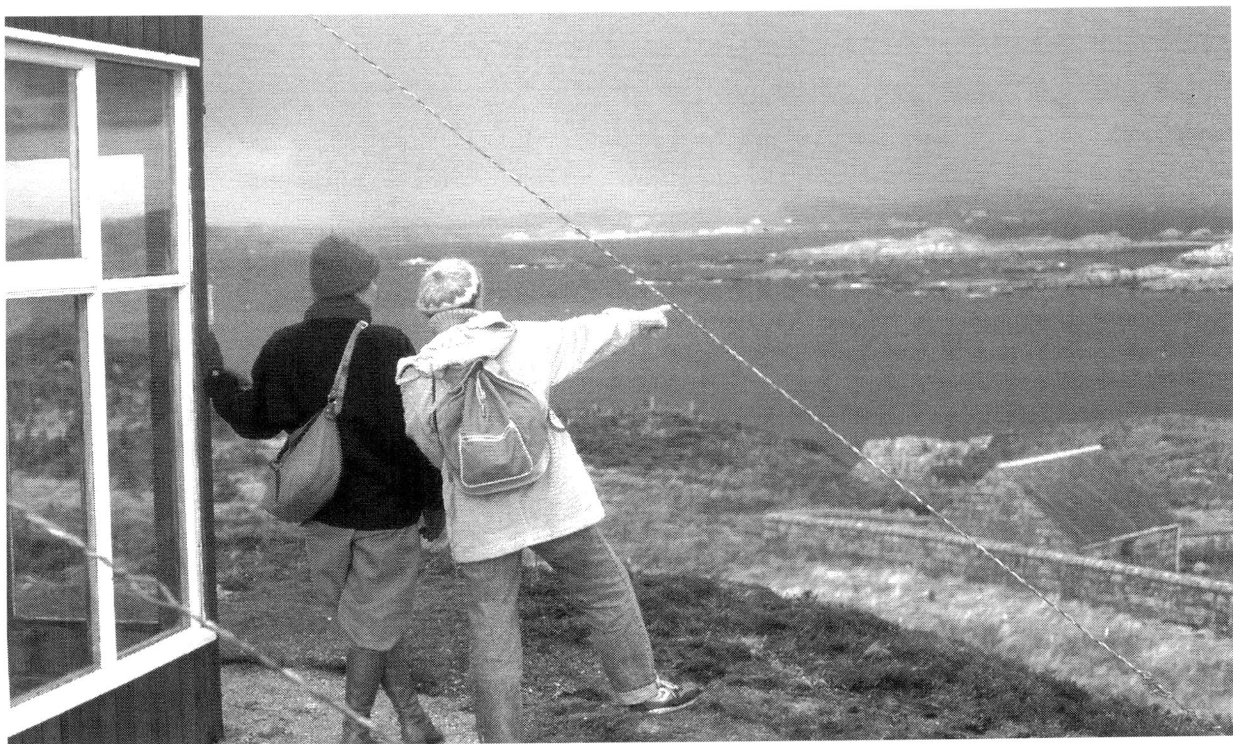

View from the sanctuary on Erraid—looking to Iona

(not working because the storage tank is dry), gas lighting, rainwater spigot outside, and wood and peat supply for the fireplace. The one cow is drying up, so we have to use powdered milk. There are few eggs because the chickens are not doing well. Two inquisitive Saanan goats complete the livestock collection. In the main kitchen, we dig into thick vegetable soup and scones Laurie Nicholson (in our group) has just made and meet the twenty-some folks living here.

As soon as possible, I tramp up to the top of the island. Erraid is just a mile long. From a tiny sanctuary of glass and wood, anchored by guy wires against the fierce gales, I look down to the sea and spot the Isle of Iona across the sound. Higher up on the crags, the east wind is howling. The late afternoon sun catches the green water and silhouettes dozens of tiny, surrounding islets. From this grand height, I can see Balfour Cove, figuring in Robert Louis Stevenson's *Kidnapped*, which was written on Erraid (his father was the lighthouse keeper here)—white sand against emerald water. Scrambling up and down cliffs, I startle a huddle of sheep. Cattle graze in a lower pasture. The capricious sun dips under clouds and a stinging rain begins.

The Challenge and Exhilaration of Living in Survival Mode

We're coping with homesteading simplicity, tasting what it's like to live in survival mode. Materially, everything is marginal. The members (who have opted to strike out from the larger Findhorn home base) are always short of cash, equipment, and good tools, and yet there's also a quiet serenity. It is all very relaxed. Unlike Findhorn, there is total informality and no structure. We sit around the warm kitchen in the evenings to chat and drink tea.

Findhorn outpost: stone cottages on Erraid

One glorious day we're told to leave our chores; we're free to go off exploring the island. Laurie takes a couple of us to Seal Bay, where eight curious seals keep popping out of the water. They swim close, attracted by Yolanda's red coat (she's one of the children living here). It's warm in the lee of the wind, but it's blowing full strength on the high cliffs. We all open our coats and lean off into the wind—it feels like flying. We play zany blind tag, chasing each other with our eyes shut in the white curve of sand of Balfour Cove, and collect scrap wood.

Home to a wonderful oatmeal quiche for supper. At the sanctuary afterwards, I get: "Don't be afraid, don't be other-directed or hold expectations. Just live now, with love and gentleness for all." This place is stern, the work is tough, but there is palpable peace and satisfaction. There's a feeling that people are not only going within, but are living from within all the time.

All week I work happily under a cold frame spading up turf, then spreading compost and topsoil. I'm crawling around in rubber pants in earth and manure. Life is a poem, I decide, and at this moment, I could stay here forever.

Beth, Betty, and I sit around our peat-and-wood fire. We get it going with used toilet paper we keep in a plastic bag next to a can of sawdust in the "bathroom" that is for urine only. Other business is down the alley in an outhouse moored down with ropes.

A great dinner: kale and potato soup, spaghetti with Brussels sprouts cream sauce, and apple pie. Today we ran out of bread, tamari, meusli, oranges, and milk, so we just do without, and that's fine. The atmosphere is light, the spirits are high. It's exciting to be pioneers together.

My best day yet. I'm really in tune with my work; there is no fatigue as I get into a rhythm of digging up turf, then smashing and sifting and throwing the weeds out of the little cold frame. I come to love being alone for hours. There's excellent parsnip pizza for dinner, and then we dash up to the sanctuary/observatory to watch the red fireball drop over the horizon, painting the heavens crimson. Our triumvirate repairs to our stone cottage for good talk over a bottle of Drambuie and chocolate before we fill stoneware bottles with hot water for our icy beds.

A holiday is declared and a trip announced. We take rowboats to Mull, walk to the landing at Fionnphort, and then ride the little ferry across choppy water to the Isle of Iona. We hike around, inspecting the venerable Abbey on this famed sacred island, and take a look at the cottage that Findhorn uses for retreats. In the sixth century, St. Columba and his band of monks sailed here from Ireland. They created a base on Iona, and are credited with introducing Christianity to the West. There's a soft, gentle feel to Iona, its spongy, green marshlands a contrast to the harsh rocks and prickly bracken of Erraid. Ewes with their new lambs wander freely everywhere. Back home, it's an evening of wine and Scottish folk dancing.

Rescuing the Tractor from the Bog and Full Moon Fishing

One lunchtime Jonathan Caddy (one of Peter's three sons) rushes in to announce that the tractor is stuck in a peat bog and sinking fast. We leap up from our plates, throw on waterproof gear, grab boards and logs, and stream out to the southern tip of the island. We find the tractor and wagon, loaded with blocks of freshly cut peat; they're both mired in the mud, their wheels half buried. An hour later, after various schemes—levering, ballasting, pushing—eighteen of us lift out first one vehicle, then the other. A scouting party walks ahead, identifying the driest land, but we get stuck again. The wagon lurches over mounds and peat flies off. We gather it up and race after the tractor to reload. Three hours later, black and soaking, we're home. A thoroughly exhilarating adventure—a team effort in a real crisis!

It's 11:30 at night, and we're going fishing. Mark Stevens has waited for low tide and a full moon. We carry a huge net down to a couple of small boats and row out. After stringing the net across almost the entire mouth of the bay, everybody proceeds to throw stones and slap the water with paddles to scare the fish into the net. The sky is full of stars, it's cold, and we're fortified with thermoses of an oatmeal drink laced with whiskey. We all get wet, but we catch salmon and sea trout—breakfast the next morning.

After a week, our Wisconsin group separates, some to go back to Findhorn. Beth and I decide to spend a week on Iona. We book into the St. Columba Hotel, a lovely, airy building with views to the sea and surrounded by fields of daffodils and black-faced sheep. On Easter Sunday, I join fifty people to climb Dun I, the highest point on the island, for a sunrise service. The clarity is superb, the puffy clouds gold-edged. Iona and its neighboring islands are spread out all around. The group sloshes through rivulets and mud, pushing in and out of sheep gates, and then into the Abbey for a rousing anthem.

The St. Columba is a bit too elegant for Beth and me, so we move to Mrs. Black's more modest farm B&B. Immediately we take off for the south end of the island and St. Columba's Bay. We trudge over the Machair, an expanse of springy turf that we hear is a sometime golf course whose grass is kept short by grazing sheep. Arriving at the beach, in the lee of towering red-and-green cliffs, we crawl feverishly, scouring the sand and tide pools for colored stones. These are the unique, legendary prizes we've heard about and seen displayed here and there. Returning, we bushwhack the three-mile length of the island to the north end. The stillness is almost deafening, the air clear and the sun hot. Off on one horizon is a snowy peak, and hundreds of feet below us swirls white sea foam. At times, the Iona landscape appears flat, like a Japanese painting, the two-dimensional delineations painterly and unreal.

Laden with our precious stones, we discover the one restaurant on the island, serving fish and chips, and then rush back to Mrs. Black's in time for the flaming sunset. The sea glints metallic silver, holding the last light. We find cake and Tia Maria waiting for us in front of a friendly coal fire. Any thoughts or concerns about our recent community involvement seem far away. Suddenly it's pouring rain, and Mr. Black brings his new lambs inside the house to warm and dry out. When it clears, layers of steaming mist rise from the turf. After another compulsive expedition to St. Columba's Bay, by myself, I crawl into bed, exhausted, and from our window watch lambs jumping under a pink-and-blue sky. The great lifesaver here is the electric blanket under my bottom sheet, heated to roasting before bedtime, and then switched off as I hop in.

Back at Findhorn, a Solitary Retreat

We bus back to Findhorn. Beth has arranged to babysit our focaliser's kids while he and his wife fly to the States for an unexpected emergency. I decide I want private space and rent a room in Dorothy Corney's house in Findhorn village, the ancient fishing enclave of whitewashed buildings that crowd the few narrow streets. It's a twenty-minute walk from the community. Dorothy's house is a quaint, old cottage with stippled white walls

Erraid family sorting potatoes

and stained, wainscoted ceilings. One day I surprise myself by hiking fourteen miles round trip along the beach to Burghead, in the rain. While walking, I begin to ruminate on what may be next. I practice "listening." Over and over, though, I'm "interrupted" by the stones on the beach, which call, beckon, and speak to me. They're like a mantra, pulling my focus back from thinking to the pure meditation of searching for pebbles.

I'm shown an orange-pink, translucent marble
that takes me back to the same color and quality
of a gauzy, chiffon flowered dress my mother wore
in the 1930s—forty years ago. Long forgotten,
but I had loved it as I cherish this stone now.
Then the polished blood-red of a chiseled heart.
Amber-and- white, perfectly round pearls. I vow
not to look down, to walk only on the sand, but
then am drawn back, over and over, to the piles of
multi-hued jewels. I consider again my decision to
stay in the village; it may be testing my compulsive
tendency to do the "right thing," to plunge in to
help somewhere in the community. Then I realize
that I would have blown this chance to cut loose
from everything and be really free. Here there's no
excuse for not dealing with the listening/purpose
agenda; I can't postpone it by keeping busy.

I stroll to the community to find a fat letter from Bel, who had gone back to the United States when we left for Erraid. Eileen Caddy invites me to her house for tea and to talk about her complicated relationship with Peter, and mine with Bel—the little clashes or misunderstandings that are universal but not catastrophic. Several people remark that I seem to glow, that after Erraid I'm markedly more relaxed, as though the weight of responsibility for the group I'd felt before was gone. How true!

Home to my cottage, past the still, mirror surface of the bay, boats rocking at anchor, fishermen casting lines, two swans sailing by. I inhale deeply the pungent coconut of the gorse and the loamy arborvitae forest.

One evening Beth and I check out a Ceilidh in the village. Some two hundred people jam into the town hall for marvelous impromptu singing, mostly in Gaelic, with our community people joining in with the villagers. I reflect on the richness and balance and versatility at Findhorn, where many members hold two or more very different jobs: distributor of coal to the trailers and writer of BBC programs; focaliser of both community maintenance and an upcoming conference; author and switchboard operator; house cleaner and personnel counselor; bus driver and artist; actor and cook.

Amusing lesson: hurrying from the village to the community, I trip and fall on the sidewalk, sprawling out, my bag flying. My only thought: how humiliating. I pride myself on dexterity and coordination way beyond my age—I never fall. I scramble up, caring only that no one will see me. Good, the road is empty. Three minutes later, as I near the church, a lorry zooms up from the village and stops, and a man hands me my glasses case, grinning. Don't be too proud!

Last days. After a day of violent stomach flu, I test my shaky legs and venture out in a freezing

Rocky heights on Erraid and the Sound of Iona

blizzard to the community to pick up the group's mail and to say a few farewells. I feel strangely now that I should be gone. People seem more distant toward me. But Scotland blesses me with her most radiant show: sun shafts guild the edges of cumulus clouds and turn the sea to liquid fire. I'm standing on the point where the boats come in, and I take in the whole, placid village arcing around the bay. Then, across the Moray Firth, rise layer upon blue layer the majestic mountains of the upper Highlands. Is this a parting gift, proffered especially for my delight—a final signal that I'm done with my "work" here? I sense that I'm ready to move safely and surely to the next chapter. There's a deep sense of gratitude.

The final day. My deliberately narrow pattern is ending: washing and shivering into my clothes each morning in the 50-degree house, packing the poncho into my bag for a long walk. Returning to read in my electric blanket (Iris Murdoch novels are my treasures). It has been a very solitary existence, quite on purpose, but now I'm ready to go home, to connect fully to the family and friends I love. Where I expect to find purpose, promise, vision, and opportunity. Where there are no limits to what, together, we may accomplish. I sense strength and support. I will lean on that strength and give it back, too.

Reflections

This time at Findhorn, more than previously, became very much an inner journey for me, full of challenges and tests. At the end, there was the unique opportunity to be utterly alone, to sift out the lessons, to review my life to date, and to see how all this might fit into a future agenda. What started out as a hazy vision quest turned gradually, over three years, into a clear nuts-and-bolts mission.

The bits of wisdom that I had been picking up at Findhorn since 1976—and that I thought I had "gotten"—were not really internalized until this trip. For the first time, I actually found myself just flowing, minute-by-minute. I was listening more "without ears." There were no "wise ones" to lean on, I found. Inner wisdom was available directly when I slowed down to listen.

For the first time, I could begin to scrape away years of protective armor, the barnacles of self-doubt, and could see what I could contribute.

Most of all, I saw in retrospect that my scary challenges turned to blessings and moved me up the ladder of "growing." I found courage to be more open with people whom I'd found difficult to agree with; I could take initiative in resolving sticky situations. I also saw that it wasn't fatal but human to backslide on any of these lessons. The important thing was to be able to acknowledge the glitches and start again.

Of course, all such pompous conclusions from my 1979 diary, reviewed now, many decades later, look presumptuous indeed. When I reflect on the adventures generated during our own stab at creating intentional community in Wisconsin, I saw a lot of these conclusions go out the window, again and again. Now I can look dispassionately at the harrowing low points and glorious highs in the life of our community venture, High Wind. I can see that it was an experiment that had to be undertaken, an experiment that hopefully was a modest wake-up call to those who came into our orbit. It certainly had a lot to teach our little group of idealists about our own level of consciousness, our ability to live cooperatively, and our facility to interpret what we believed in.

Ruins of Urquardt Castle on Loch Ness

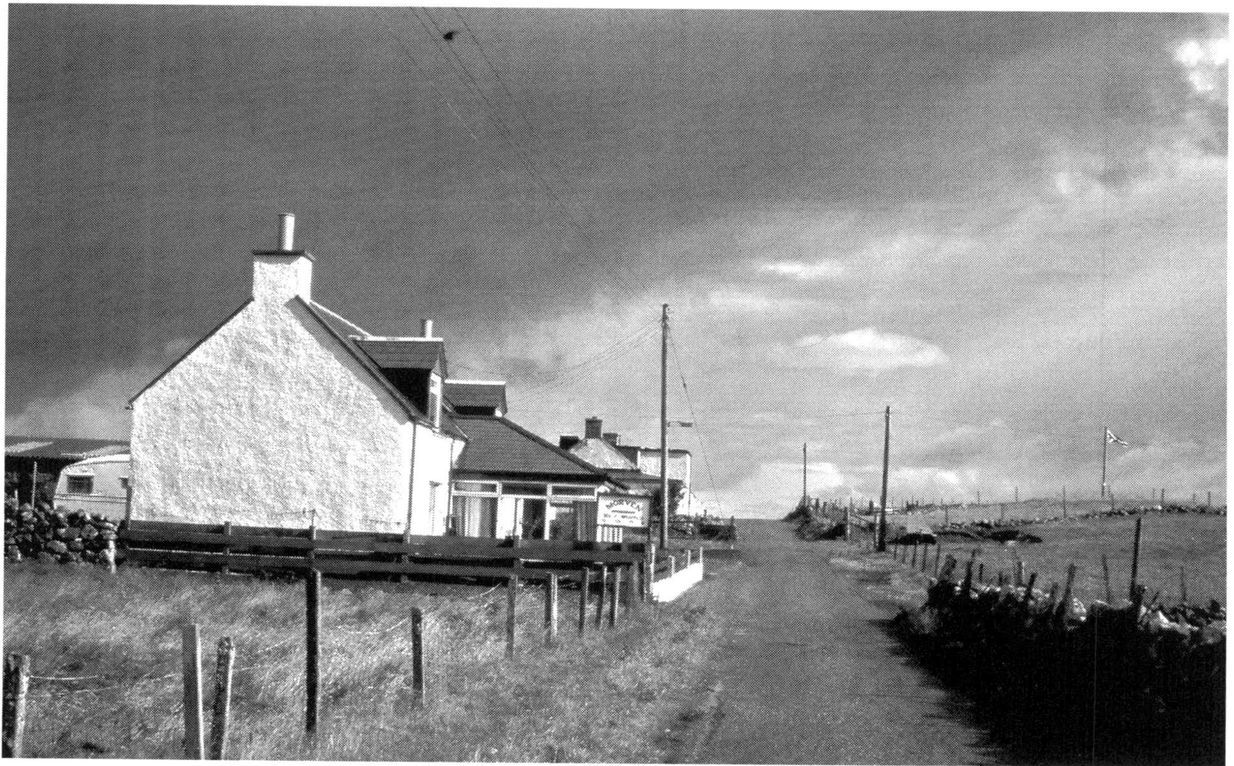

Durness on the northwestern tip of Scotland

Stranded at Cape Wrath
Another Adventure in Scotland

AUGUST 1994

Backstory

If readers are exhausted or bewildered after the "inner journeys" of the past three chapters, they may take heart. From this point, we'll tramp actual trails, push back new horizon lines.

It would be difficult to leave Scotland, though, without a last glimpse of this magnificent land. After 1978, Bel and I visited the Findhorn community half a dozen more times. We usually came to attend or speak at conferences or to bring study groups, and then would take to the road to explore our favorite haunts up and down the west coast.

In August 1994, we planned to look in quickly at Findhorn, catching up with Eileen Caddy and other long-time friends, stalwarts of the community. A bonus was learning that David Spangler and his family were in residence for a month. We found the Bag End ecovillage flourishing—the sharply pitched roofs, renewable timber construction with nontoxic materials, and "breathable" walls were all unusual in Scotland. There was a new cluster of round dwellings made from recycled whiskey barrels.

Walking around, I noted several houses with sod roofs and a group putting up a straw-bale building (where bales are smeared with an earthen or lime mud, a technique that offers remarkable insulation value and stability). The first tall Vestas wind generator (supplying 20 percent of the electricity for the community) was whirring away in the Bicken field. In just twenty-four hours, we managed to cover all the bases. It was exciting to see the community making major strides in pointing the way to many more sustainable living practices than I had seen back in the 1970s when Findhorn, even then, was a radical pioneer. But we were itching to move on.

To the Top of Scotland

Retracing roads we'd discovered previously, we head toward the Ullapool area, well up the northwest coast of Scotland. A strategic fish processing center, it is located on The Minch, the sea that separates the mainland from the Outer Hebrides; large factory ships from Russia and elsewhere dot the harbor. We book into Mrs. Stewart's B&B, one of a tiny cluster of houses in Rhue, just north of Ullapool. When we had come in 1988, we stayed next door with Mrs. Campbell

Mrs. Campbell's B&B in hamlet of Rhue above Ullapool

and climbed over the rocks to the lighthouse on a nearby promontory.

The only other habitation we saw then was artist James Hawkins' little house and studio. We loved and bought one of his semi-abstract landscape paintings that caught the wild spirit of the region. Ten years before, James had left the busy art scene in Oxford to find his own inspiration and "voice," where he would not be distracted by mainstream artistic trends. Now we discover that his work is hanging in the best galleries across Europe and in New York, but Rhue continues to be his home and inspiration.

From our window, we see the ferry to the Hebridean island of Lewis chugging past, and then watch a couple of border collies expertly round up the white-faced sheep in the yard and escort them to the barn. Later, after stuffing ourselves with mussels and crab at an Ullapool pub, and our pockets with pretty pebbles from the Rhue beach, we head north. The convoluted coastline dips in and out with innumerable little bays, and we pass Stac Pollaidh, the peculiar landmark mountain we climbed years before, its funnel peak soaring out of the plain.

The terrain becomes more desolate and beautiful. Wide, sweeping moors, towering peaks, high lochs brimming full. Mountain streams tumble down through rock outcroppings and past patches of purple heather. When the lochs turn from black to sea-green, we know we're approaching open ocean.

We book a B&B in Scourie for the return trip, when we'll make a side excursion to Handa and hope to spot the puffins and guillemots that famously nest on this island.

Finally, our destination: Durness at the northwest tip of Scotland. The last twenty miles is single track; only one vehicle fits on these narrow roads, and drivers must pull into one of the frequent "passing places" to let an approaching car go by. Navigating these single tracks at night in mountainous regions can be especially exciting!

The Roof of the Island

Durness is a tiny village with a scattering of cottages set on bare slopes. We dip down to an expanse of emerald-and-indigo water. Bright green grass is spotted with cement pillboxes, the low, concrete emplacements for machine guns and antitank weapons left over from wartime defense of this northernmost coast of Great Britain. Marvelous white sand beaches tuck into the cliffs and moorland. We wander in search of a B&B, finding one run by a Mrs. Morrison on a "wee" road near the high headland. Our snug room overlooks the water, where a rainbow appears regularly as each heavy shower moves away.

Between the sudden downpours driven by sixty-mile-an-hour gusts, we risk a picnic lunch at famed Smoo Cave. Its name is from the Norwegian for "hiding-place," and it is thought there may be some supernatural association here. Rounding a corner, we're drenched by a torrential, sixty-foot waterfall that thunders down from an open stream above. The yawning cavern is 120 feet wide, 45 feet high, and more than 250 feet deep—the largest sea cave in Britain. Archeologists have found Norse, Neolithic, and Iron Age artifacts here, and they believe it may go back to the Mesolithic Age. We manage to finish our picnic despite finicky skies.

The next morning we're off to Cape Wrath, the *real* northernmost tip of the British Isles. Little do we know what is in store—a totally unexpected adventure. Sixteen of us have signed up for the excursion to the Cape. We gather to board a "ferry" to cross the Kyle of Durness to the isolated peninsula, but we find that the tiny motorboat holds only four people. It takes an hour-and-a-half to get our party over the channel, twenty-five minutes for each round trip. We're met by a military van with all-wheel drive, and we bump along a rough, grassy track for eleven miles to the huge lighthouse. Four servicemen live out here in virtual isolation on one-month rotations to tend the strategic post. The lighthouse—another one built by Robert Louis Stevenson's father (in 1828)—sits on a barren point with sandstone cliffs and grassy verges. The winds blow so hard, our guide tells us, that they can easily lift a person off the ground.

From 620 feet above the Atlantic Ocean, we take in the extraordinary views to sand dunes and beaches far below. Cape Wrath is a major breeding site for sea birds, such as kittiwakes, puffins, razorbills, guillemots, and fulmars. Periodically tourists are kept away when it also becomes a practice bombing range and site for military exercises (also disturbing the bird and animal populations on the peninsula, and angering the locals).

After exploring on our own for several hours, the group assembles at the appointed time down on the dock, weary and ready to call it a day. But there is no boat waiting for us. Across the water, we can spot a teenager standing next to it. He removes an obviously dead motor and drives it away in a truck—several times over the next two hours—presumably for repairs.

No Boat, a Forced March

Eventually we conclude that he isn't coming for us at all and that we'll have to walk back. This is a long peninsula, and we're out at the end. I'm a little dismayed. Shortly before leaving the United States, I had broken my foot, and am still limping and being careful about putting much stress on it. But apparently we have no choice.

It turns out to be a nearly five-mile trek across very rugged terrain. There is no trail, so we bushwhack and just hope to make it through the daunting obstructions. Everybody scrambles up and around steep cliffs, through marshy turf, over boulders and rivulets. It's a vigorous, cosmopolitan group: Germans, an Australian, a Norwegian, a couple of Londoners, and Glaswegians. No one slows or stops. The younger athletes in the lead travel very fast, and those of us in the rear must concentrate and race to keep up and not get lost among the rocks. As it gets rougher, we draw closer, watching out for each other, making sure everyone is accounted for. There's no way I would dare to stop to unpack my camera and record some of the spectacular sights.

At one point, the London stockbroker gallantly carries me across two rivers on his back, fireman's-hold, while Bel takes off his soaked shoes, rolls up his pants and wades through icy, knee-deep, rushing water. One woman falls and twists her ankle but trudges on. My broken foot doesn't improve, but I puff, hobble, and make it to the end. After two hours, we come in sight of a farmhouse near a tiny footbridge that would take us across the river to the mainland. The farmer rolls up on his tractor and tries to order us off his land, but eventually our guide persuades him to let us phone for a van to be sent for us. We wait another forty-five minutes at the road, mercifully able to sit on the ground. Near the bridge an angler, standing mid-river, is artfully casting his fly rod. Someone tells us it costs £100 pounds a day to fish this river.

Just as the skies open to pour, the van arrives. Filthy, soaked, and exhausted, we ride back to our car and stumble into our B&B for hot tea and to wash muddy clothes.

Reflections

And so, a dramatic finale to dramatic Scotland. I realize that this exploration to the northern tip of the island—just one of many trips around a beloved country that I, or Bel and I, took over twenty-two years—doesn't really fit the title of this section. It isn't exactly part of the Findhorn "vision quest." It doesn't immediately conjure up "enlightenment." And yet I have always felt the sacredness of this fiercely lovely landscape. As I said earlier, it became clear to me that here nature is truly in command. Scotland, for me, is a worthy chalice, an enchanted land that holds and bestows holiness. And with every blast of its furious winds, or when a blinding sun suddenly pierced dark, racing clouds, I got an unmistakable message.

Part III

Traveling for Fun
Worldwide Family Adventures

Reconnoitering at Lauterbrunnen in Switzerland

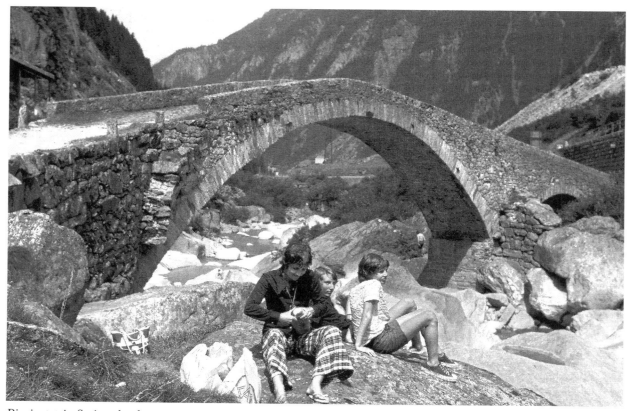

Picnic stop in Switzerland

Poppy Fields • Old Stone • Stars in the Sea

Our early years of travel abroad were primarily focused on serious work or study projects. In the aftermath of World War II, Bel and I found ourselves thrown into dealing with dire human needs. Then we were drawn to exploring strategies that might help lift the global society in terms of values, spirit, and practical paths to greater sustainability.

A small portion of our current travel destinations still relate to such agendas, but along the way we began to tilt our trips toward what could be called exploration into pure delight and to satisfy our curiosity about off-beat places. There was a hunger to "feed our souls." We wanted to strengthen the bonds between the two of us, with our growing family, and then our extended family—against backgrounds of periodic peregrinations, mostly abroad.

Ever the chronic note-taker, I kept daily accounts of these adventures, over some thirty years. Now I'd like to balance the often intense, earnest tone of the previous two parts of this book with a section that is lighter, less goal-driven, more in the spirit of going just to see what's there. Such foreign trips began in 1973 when we took our two sons, Eric and Steve, then sixteen and thirteen, back to Europe to revisit the places where we had lived and worked, and to discover some new ones together.

The chronology isn't exact because the "work-related" journeys I've already described went on, interspersed, for a couple of decades after that. The method and tone of this part are different. I've skipped lightly through the narratives, picking out scatterings or condensations of episodes that I think were unusual, or descriptions that I felt were particularly enchanting or exciting.

The reader will ride with us in a tippy boat on a dangerously flooded river in Costa Rica as we're suddenly in danger of being dumped overboard. She will climb down the Imbrose Gorge in the White Mountains of Crete and then wind up a dizzying, unguarded cliff road of hairpin turns to the tiny village of Anopolis that hangs above the sea. She will join our family as we bunk into cells in a crumbling, deserted Italian monastery and hunt for ghosts in the chapel burial vaults. Year after year, the adventures unfolded—from a dolphin hunt in icy seas off Key West to tuning in to the spirits of prehistoric artists in the caves of southwest France.

Switchbacks in Switzerland

Hunting ancient pottery shards in Phoenician ruins of Tharros, Sardinia

A Six-Week Ramble through Europe

Summer 1973

Ancient Pottery Shards and Fish Heads in Sardinia

In the summer of 1973, Bel and I decide that it's about time to take Eric and Steve to Europe, back to see some of the places where they began their lives. They will experience the locales the two of us had struggled in and had grown to cherish. We cram our two leggy teenagers into the backseat of a little yellow VW bug that we buy in Luxembourg. For six weeks, we tool through Switzerland, France (for Mont Blanc), and then across into Italy, the "home of our hearts." For starters, in Pisa, the boys terrify us by racing around the outside concentric circles of the leaning tower with no railing, shrieking with delight. We can't stand to watch, which, of course, is their aim.

We find there is a general strike throughout Italy, so at the moment there is no government in power. Everybody is taking advantage of the complete chaos to walk off their jobs and go on vacation. Because of the strikes, we're lucky to secure berths on the overnight boat from Civitavecchia to Olbia in northeastern Sardinia. Our car swings on board in a net. On docking, we drive down through the center of the island to Oristano, checking the now-dingy apartment buildings where we had lived and worked while resettling refugees in the late 1950s. Quickly we continue out to the sea on the west coast to the isolated fishing village of San Giovanni, our remembered favorite place to swim off great white beaches. I'll spend a week here with the boys while Bel catches up with the refugees still left in our HELP project.

The big attraction is Tharros, the deserted, Pompei-like ruin on the tip of the peninsula, where we can still wander freely and pick up interesting pottery shards. These were left from settlements of Phoenicians (dating back to the eighth century BCE), as well as others coming by on a trade route from the East and North Africa—Greeks, Romans, Carthaginians.

We settle into the two guest rooms of an unpretentious *pensione* in a small cove close to the water. For six dollars a day, with full board, we savor marvelous, fresh seafood. At first, the kids are reluctant to cut off the fish heads and tails, tear off feelers from the large whole shrimp, or dig out clams and muscles from their shells with their fingers, but they get pretty adept. A bit squeamish, Eric still opts for the tough beefsteak, while Steve adores the fried calamari or squid. One day I stand amidst the broken columns on the Tharros hill and watch the two of

We hunt up our 1957 young helper in Sardinia— now, in 1973, she's married with kids

them swim the half-mile back to our cove, little dots in the placid Mediterranean.

Back on the Italian mainland, we head to Rome. From our base in a convent at the top of the Spanish Steps, we hit the major sights, the boys poring over history books to identify every ruin in the Forum, and the sequences of paintings in the Sistine Chapel, and to relish the rows of skulls deep in the bowels of the Priscilla Catacombs. They never miss opportunities to climb every precarious wall and cliff or kick a soccer ball around the vast Villa Savoia park near our old apartment.

There's an evening at the opera in the Baths of Caracalla to see *Aida*. It's a gorgeous night, with a full moon hanging over the gigantic ruins of the Baths. The outdoor stage showcases all the splendor and pageantry of the production, complete with fires burning, explosions of colored smoke pouring into the sky, wild primitive dances, and the traditional camels and horses prancing down the hill onto the stage. Steve manages, barely, to stay awake until 1:00 a.m. when it finishes, but complains grumpily, "It wasn't really worth it because the only thing I was interested in was the animals, and they were here hardly any time at all."

Beware the Swans: Tranquility May Deceive

An afternoon excursion past the travertine marble quarries to the Alban hills takes us to the Emperor Hadrian's villa. The sun is starting to go down, and there are few people in the park. We have a couple of hours to wander, and Steve latches onto a scrawny little dog that follows him everywhere. Eric, as is his custom, immediately disappears to explore the greatest heights. He covers ten times the territory anyone else does, always off the tourist paths, into distant olive groves or onto surrounding summits. We see him half a mile away, loping along a ridge, then shinnying up a broken column. He stops to watch an archeologist with his large, scrolled maps, scratching into dark recesses with his pick and broom.

The extensive villa, where Hadrian brought copies of some of the finest architectural ideas and designs from Greece and elsewhere, provides an atmosphere of great peace and grandeur. Dusty avenues of canopied plane trees become silent, shadowy tunnels. There are subterranean passages and beautifully tiled baths, some two hundred feet across. Then, coming upon quiet pools surrounded by statuary and columns, we sidle conspiratorially up to the edge to greet a fleet of swans sailing languidly toward us. We lean out to one that unexpectedly snaps his neck down and bites a very surprised and aggrieved Steve. So much for staged tranquility.

Waterfalls Are for Getting Soaked

We drive on from Hadrian's Villa to Tivoli to see the lighted Villa d'Este fountains. The atmosphere is unearthly, with illumination under and behind every jet of thundering waterfalls and delicate spattering into stone basins. The boys lean over the statues at the top of the hundred-foot-high cascade to touch the falls, then they rush down to walk behind them to get soaked. We sit beside the long, rectangular pool—absolutely still—that perfectly mirrors the trees and flowering bushes surrounding it, so quiet that staring down I imagine there is no water but a shadowy green jungle hundreds of feet down that I could easily climb into.

Ravello: Celestial Sounds in a Moon-Washed Garden

Driving south, we look up our old Casa Mia colleagues in Naples (where Bel and I met in 1952). Dr. Teolfilo Santi, who brought Bel into the Italian Service Mission to minister to the postwar homeless of the city, takes us around to see impressive advances in his Evangelical Hospital, then invites us to an evening concert in nearby Ravello.

After two hours of climbing and winding up the steep mountain above the tortuous Amalfi Drive, we arrive at the little town of Ravello three thousand feet above sea level. A German symphony is performing Beethoven and Brahms in the gardens of Villa Rufolo, a sumptuous estate literally hanging over the precipice. Its walls are banked with flowers and punctuated with classical statues, umbrella pines, and spreading cedars of Lebanon.

We find chairs in the formal garden near the edge of the cliff. Fountains splash around us. We look up at the orchestra silhouetted against the rock peaks to the west—obscured now by pink-and-gold clouds as the sun drops from view. Then lanterns flick on to bathe the gardens and trees in rose and silver. Far below, the Mediterranean Sea mirrors the many dots of sailboats. The lights in the arc of the bay blink and shimmer like the stars coming out overhead. When the music ends, the thousand spectators (perched on walls and stairs and in trees several tiers up the cliff, as well as in the rows of seats), won't let the musicians go, and we're treated to an extra half hour of Wagnerian passion. Finally the spell is broken, and we head for the tiny exit arches and tunnels. The players have to fight their way through with the rest of us, holding their fiddles over their heads so they won't be crushed.

We're "Monks" in a Monastery

Continuing the rendezvous with old friends and colleagues, we proceed to the strongly communist town of Genazzano southeast of Rome. This is where Bel stayed for several months following his United Nations stint in 1960 after the boys and I returned to the United States. He joined forces with Athos Ricci, former Communist Party secretary, now more a delightful, eccentric poet-type who has seen first hand the hollowness of the promises of the communists. Back then, the two of them tramped together around the vineyards and back streets interviewing a cross section of the townspeople to get a sense of their current politics and opinions and aspirations. A book resulted in 1966: *The Searchers.* Now Bel and Athos want to go back to see what some of their former interviewees are thinking about a dozen years later.

Athos, in his late forties, has become more roly-poly, but has the same florid, cherubic visage. He relishes a reputation as the town maverick and seems oblivious of the fact that his sartorial choices are outlandishly out of step with the current mode.

He has arranged for our family to stay in the third-century mountaintop monastery where Bel lived when he was in Genazzano in 1961. This is where Athos stayed up most of every night transcribing the tape-recorded interviews they had conducted by day. Bel's fellow residents back then were a group of Irish Augustinian priests, with whom he was encouraged to fraternize and explain the local political situation in return for meals and a cell to sleep in.

Now we find no priests. Except for an English family and the caretaker who lives next door, the building is abandoned, and we have fun picking our own quarters from among nearly a hundred crumbling, monastic cells. It seems to us much like a castle or great house in the Wuthering Heights tradition, with shutters and windows that on the day we arrive are creaking and banging with fierce winds, rain, and thunderstorms. "When I lived here thirteen years ago, on nights of the full moon, I would hear the local 'werewolf' howling below my window—which definitely added to the creepy atmosphere," Bel tells us. The boys lug an extra cot and mattress into their private lair. I sweep out the dust of years and clear cobwebs to make the rooms fairly livable.

Scorpions in the Sink and Coffins under the Floor

The monastery, San Pio, commands a superb outlook. It towers above the medieval village of Genazzano that hunkers into rock cliffs, and whose precipitous streets are so narrow they are one way going down and drivers must circle the periphery of the town to get to the top. Beyond the valleys on each side rise even higher mountains, so that from our windows we look up to steep slopes.

We discover delightful amenities—a pergola covered with grape vines to walk and read under, a sparkling swimming pool where Eric and Steve practically live (underwater most of the time). Inside, we become accustomed to a five-minute hike to the nearest functioning john, though spigots of water empty into ancient stone bowls that adorn the corridor walls. We're told that the pitted marble sink in the cavernous kitchen where we heat water and eat some meals was in use in the time of the Caesars; it is decorated with stone medallions. One morning I find a two-inch scorpion crawling in it, and the boys delight in watching it snap at a prodding fork.

We're in a slightly newer part of the monastery. The older section has uneven, cobbled floors, and in the central part is a grassy courtyard with graceful galleries and arches built around it on both the first and second floors, all open to the air—cold and very still at night. Our footsteps echo as we trudge to the bathroom, trying to see our way by the starlight shining in. It's a bit eerie, and we're told the priests keep out of one supposedly haunted room where strange things have happened. With experience as something of an investigator of unexplained phenomena, I buy candles, and Eric , Steve, and I hold a brief midnight séance in the room. Disappointingly, we get only good vibes. Spookier, however, is the smallish chapel with burial vaults under the floor. The boys find they can lift iron plates and reveal the coffins below. They're anxious to climb down. Pope Pio, from the time of the Empire, was buried here, as well as an aristocratic family that later owned the monastery.

The boys kick a soccer ball down the corridors, whose walls are rich with religious frescoes in faded orange and blue, as well as on the vast roof terrace where I hang my laundry. They explore a series of rickety, cobwebbed ladders to the top of the bell tower, inspect the caretaker's beekeeping operation, and chase shy kittens. At first they grump about "wasting time" here, but they manage to keep occupied. It's a welcome respite from racing around on the tourist circuit.

Philosophy, Prosciutto, and Spumanti

Bel and Athos take an afternoon off from interviewing and we all descend on Athos' good friend Bruno. He lives at the top of a four-story walkup that opens out onto a delightful park where Eric and Steve are lured into a soccer game with other kids—Steve finally quitting in shame when they shout directions to him that he can't understand. (Since then, he's been diligently studying his

Italian grammar, concentrating on learning irregular verbs.)

Bruno is a unique specimen, on a par with Athos, always a proud original. He jabbers passionately and nonstop about everything for four hours, displaying a vast knowledge of politics, philosophy, theosophy, mysticism—a real Renaissance thinker. His vast proportions bulge out of an undershirt and shorts as he presides over the proceedings in his garden. I imagine that he could have been tapped for a Fellini movie. Waving a huge carving knife, he slices prosciutto off one of his own home-raised hams to offer us a sandwich, along with oceans of his own wine and spumanti. His great pop-eyes roll heavenward to make a point about the necessity of reestablishing the art of humanizing one-to-one contact between teachers and students. His sixteen-year-old plays a guitar and sings, inviting Eric to come join in on a Beatles jam session (alternated with Bach cantatas on the phonograph).

We're meeting next to Prince Colonna's castle (the famed landmark that brings tourists to Genazzano), so Steve and I duck out of the party to stroll through the pines for a closer look. Crossing the bridge spanning the town square below, we stare up into the blackened, vaulted recesses of the castle in the gathering darkness.

Fashion note: After several weeks now in Italy, we recognize the ubiquitous uniform for young men: navy blue shirt, with sleeves turned back at the cuff and unbuttoned nearly to the waist; medallion on a chain; tight-fitting, flared jeans or white pants; and a small, leather shoulder purse (all men carry these). The young women lean toward tall platform shoes, jeans, or miniskirts, and embroidered blouses of rough-woven Indian cotton.

We head north with quick visits to Florence and Venice, and then cross into Switzerland.

Near Death (or So I Believe) and Mortally Wounded Pride

All the hotels around Grindelwald are full, and a fierce thunderstorm is just letting loose. We end up descending into a valley to little Lauterbrunnen. We find there an inn opposite the minuscule German railroad station that reminds me of illustrations in Ludwig Bemelmans' *Hansi,* an enchanting book from my childhood. We've arrived on August 1, which turns out to be a big national holiday. After dinner, a brass band assembles in front of our hotel, performs loudly, and then marches up to the other end of the village followed by girls in Tyrolean costume and dozens of kids holding aloft lanterns and flaming torches. The entire town trudges behind to listen to speeches despite a cold drizzle. There is singing and fireworks.

The next day we take the funicular straight up the mountain and hike for four hours to the tiny hamlet of Mürren, which no cars can reach. As we climb, there's a superb view of the Jungfrau, though when it rains occasionally, the peak flickers in and out of cloud. The crushed stone path leads past goats grazing, a few barns, rushing falls, and a ski lift. It's not the boys' idea of real climbing, though, and Eric suddenly breaks away to slide down a slippery grassy slope to dangle over the knife-edge of a sheer drop of over a thousand feet. When Steve leaps out to follow, I envision sure death and snatch him back. He is so outraged at this indignity that he refuses to speak to anybody for the next twenty-four hours. "You've ruined my trip to the Alps!" he screams at me because I prevented him from looking over the cliff. "Better to die doing what you want!" (Five years later, during a college semester in Denmark, he returns to this spot and finally, defiantly, hangs over the edge. Closure achieved.)

Liechtenstein is all mountains

In Search of Beauty and Tranquility

Cinque Terre, The Dolomites, Liechtenstein

October 1990

Bel and I set out alone on a trip that starts as something of a throwback to the European "Grand Tour" of a century ago. It's definitely designed to be a switch from the frantic, socially meaningful junkets of recent years that were packed with meetings and strategizing. What it actually turns out to be is an odyssey in search of natural beauty and tranquility. Yearning to be laid back and lazy for a change, we find ourselves deliberately avoiding the crush of major cities and, instead, seek out the sea and mountains, with distinctive village cultures that punctuate each area. Our best times turn out to be unplanned stops in unfamiliar places.

For so many years we have gravitated to crisis situations around the world and often have found ourselves in the midst of urban ugliness and pain. Now we are in need of the opposite.

We have to start in Paris, though, where we pick up our spanking new, little Renault Clio—which we come to love. Inching our way through interminable stop-and-go traffic, every vehicle belching asphyxiating black fumes, I'm actually choking and nauseated. It's a cruel change from the idyllic times we had there in the early 1950s, and even 1973. Eventually we crawl onto the Autoroute going south, but the thick smog doesn't clear for a long time. Finally the sun emerges and we can smile (and breathe) again in the lovely, peaceful Bourgogne countryside.

Cinque Terre

We cross into Italy and make a disappointing, heavily touristed stop in Santa Margherita on the Riviera (because we're forced to wait for word on lost luggage, finally forwarded to Genoa—eureka!). Meandering south again, we leave the toll road for the less-trafficked sea route and find ourselves in the Cinque Terre region. There are signs for Vernazza, one of the five famous medieval towns in this cluster, all of them more easily approached and viewed from the sea. Soon we're leaving the paved road altogether for a rough path of dirt and solid rock. We crawl along the single track, hugging the side of the mountain with dizzying drop-offs. More hairpin turns down to Vernazza, where all cars must park outside the town. It's a marvelous village, with a castle, streets less than twelve feet wide, and a tiny, sheltered marina where people are swimming off rocks. Hikers of all nationalities have converged here. We meet a party of fourteen Swiss who get together every two years to walk somewhere; today they've hiked seven hours from La Spezia. Looking almost straight up from sea level we get the full view of the houses and terraced vineyards pasted onto the precipice.

We drive on, again up and up, stopping periodically to cool the car's engine. Finally we descend into Portovenere on the tip of the peninsula—not one of the five Cinque Terre towns. We're surprised to find available a stunning room right over the bay in the Belvedere, the only hostelry still open this late in the season. Portovenere becomes my idea of heaven: few people, no cars (totally pedestrian), so quiet we almost whisper. Our footsteps ring out on the irregular cobbles. The air is soft and warm, water lapping. Cats everywhere. A black-and-white striped church and a castle on the bluff. We step through an opening in the wall of an old ruin, finding ourselves in a lighted grotto with night fishermen and waves crashing against huge rocks; it's a spot dedicated to Lord Byron after he swam here and rhapsodized about the grotto. Dinner is at the simple Antica Osteria del Carrugio, with long plank tables where we devour a minestrone of beans and grains dressed with olive oil and pepper, then mussels and calamari and anchovies.

It rains all the next day, so we read, I study Russian, and lazily we watch fisherman on the water from our window. The sun finally comes out, and we drive along the high ridge, then down to the sea to Riomaggiore, another Cinque Terre town. From there, on the Via del Amore, we hike to the third town, Manarola, again built spectacularly into sheer rock cliffs, returning for our car by tiny train.

The Italian Alps

Next we're heading southeast, passing Cararra, where that unique marble is gouged out of a huge, white cliff in the Apennine mountains. We enjoy a short stay at a convent in gridlocked San Gimingano and exploration of the amphitheater in Siena. We head north again and past Lake Garda, where windsurfers are out despite choppy water and icy rain. Finally to the Dolomite Alps, where we came for a vacation from Sardinia in 1959. Eric was two and I was unexpectedly pregnant with Steve (and horribly nauseated). We find the same clusters of villages with their curious, onion-domed churches and Tyrolean chalets, all with red and pink flowers tumbling out of window boxes. The trees are shimmering autumn gold against bright green pastureland. Climbing to the little village of San Pietro, we're just in time for the procession of an oompah band with players in lederhosen.

We discover the scenic Brenta Dolomites, a well-kept secret, I think, where all the locals go for nearby outings. Unfortunately, it's a murky day, so the sharp spires and peaks (over ten thousand feet) are shrouded in mist. We hike into a forest primeval—Val di Genova—a nature preserve with a wild river, great boulders, ravines, and the Cascata di Nardis, a falls that plunges hundreds of feet. At the top of the pass, the dense fog that had completely enveloped us breaks slightly for a few dark trees to emerge along the ridge across the valley. As we cut our bread and cheese and apples, suddenly—way above the ridge and disembodied in the sky—appears a great, snowy crag. It comes and goes with patches of blue sky; then everything shuts down again. At the bottom, we find a country house to stay where the talkative owner agrees to cook us a meal. We finish with *tiramisu* ("pick me up"), the heavenly dessert of cream cheese, eggs, sugar, chocolate, and rum.

Pause on a hike above Triesenberg, Liechtenstein

On Impulse: Liechtenstein

Into Switzerland. With the European Community, there's no serious border control now, and we cross the Bernina Pass, where marvelous yellow larches gleam against a cloudless sky. We climb and climb to the mountains that are topped with snow. Checking the map, we notice that we're passing close to the tiny principality of Liechtenstein, to us an unknown. Impulsively, we decide to investigate.

Up through the Julierpass, a very long stretch of moonscape—stark and grand with only barren rocks and no trees, much like parts of northern Scotland. Past Chur, across the Rhine, and into Liechtenstein, the only remaining true monarchy in Europe where a prince actually rules. They say it's the best of both monarchy and democracy (with an elected parliament). Apparently everyone is happy and hardworking, and there's no poverty. The entire country is only fifteen by three miles, with a population of thirty thousand. There are five thousand in the capitol, Vaduz.

We wander around Vaduz and secure the name of the Hotel Kulm in the town of Triesenberg. It perches high above on the side of a mountain (everything is on a mountainside), and we set off on yet another switchback drive. After Vernazza, Bel is switchback shy, so I do much of the mountain driving. The Kulm is new but built like an old Swiss chalet with *bierstube*, gleaming pine beams against white plaster. Our room has its own balcony overlooking the valley and peaks of Switzerland. We bounce on the feather bed and drink ice-cold Vernaccia wine while hearing 24-hour classical music on the radio. Then we venture out to explore Triesenberg and find a cozy restaurant for *spaetzle* and veal.

After a night of rain, the next morning the sun is gloriously hot and the air swept clean—the kind of thin crispness you find only in high mountains. We drive at 15 percent grades up to the smaller town of Menasche, and then even higher. Leaving the car, we get out to hike dirt tracks that crisscross

Hiking in Liechtenstein

expansive, very steep meadows and woods. We're almost to the top, with bare rock and where hawks are wheeling, when suddenly a hang glider sweeps by. While we munch our picnic in an upland pasture, taupe-colored cows graze all around us, their bells a constant symphony echoing across the valleys and competing with the periodic clanging of church bells. We watch three more hang gliders soar languidly around us for an hour. Anywhere you step off a road there's danger of falling off a cliff—ideal, of course for this sport where one can simply spring effortlessly off into space at almost any point.

Everything in this country is vertical. It's virtually impossible to grow vegetables; they only raise milk cows. The farmers are out cutting or raking hay on their vertiginous parcels. They must use weed whackers; it's too steep and dangerous for bigger machines. More than any place we've discovered so far in Europe, Liechtenstein turns out to be the perfect and unplanned finale for a trip whose purpose was to leave the noisy world behind.

Regretfully we wind down the mountains and cross Germany into France, skirting the battlefields of World War I, for our flight home.

Reflections

Instinctively we have sought out and found some of the few places in Europe that offer the only tranquility left: the more remote mountains and water, where nature still remains more or less intact. The historic beautiful cities, sites of youthful romantic idylls forty years ago, are now too often blackened by smog and choked with evil-smelling vehicles. We could literally see Earth dying here and could only wonder how long it can continue to withstand the punishment humans are inflicting for our selfish, immediate ends. An apt symbol of the frightening *1984* kind of nightmare: a man waving a flag for us to slow down for construction on the Autostrada—who, we discovered on approaching, was actually a robot, life-sized and mechanically raising and lowering its arm.

Costa Rica
The Flood

MARCH 1997

Eric's family felt a particular pull to the nature opportunities in Costa Rica, so he, Angelynn, Lark, and Niko suggested that Bel and I join them for a tropical midwinter expedition. With only a week allotted, we decided that the highlight should be a trip down the Sarapiqui River, offering probably the most varied and intriguing scenery.

Basing in San José, we explore the city a bit first. Lark (a bird expert and afficionada since she was about four), hunts for a tropical bird book. Angelynn is whipping around efficiently on crutches, having torn a calf muscle the week before, but didn't see a doctor, determined to go no matter what the verdict.

On the day of the big adventure, we gather for the bus at 7 a.m. There are fourteen of us with our able guide Marco, and driver Jesús (for luck, he tells us). Ominously, it's raining lightly, and the dark mountains ringing the city have all but disappeared in cloud. Leaving San José, we climb toward the northeast, and it begins to rain seriously. Marco explains that there are twelve microclimates in Costa Rica, and we'll be passing through several. First is the mountain area where the great coffee plantations flourish. We pass fields and fields of coffee bushes (which last twenty years, the fruit ripening every fifteen days to be hand picked). As we climb, it also grows colder, and after a couple of hours, we pull up at a high, very windy, open-air restaurant for breakfast. By this time, the rain is driving; at the last minute, we had opted to bring our heavier coats and are very glad. Breakfast is hearty: rice and beans (these are always left over from the main meal the previous day), scrambled eggs, fresh pineapple and papaya slices, a frothy strawberry fruit drink, the ubiquitous tortillas, and good coffee.

Fortified, we drive on, climbing still higher. The white, humpbacked Brahma bulls (for beef) are grazing, along with Holstein milk cows. Rolling hills are dotted with palms and the fast-growing *jual* trees used for reforestation. Here and there we see prosperous ranch houses, along with tin shacks.

It rains even harder, and the cloud cover closes in completely. Gradually we descend into more tropical rainforest vegetation and another climate, the trees more lush and dense. There are

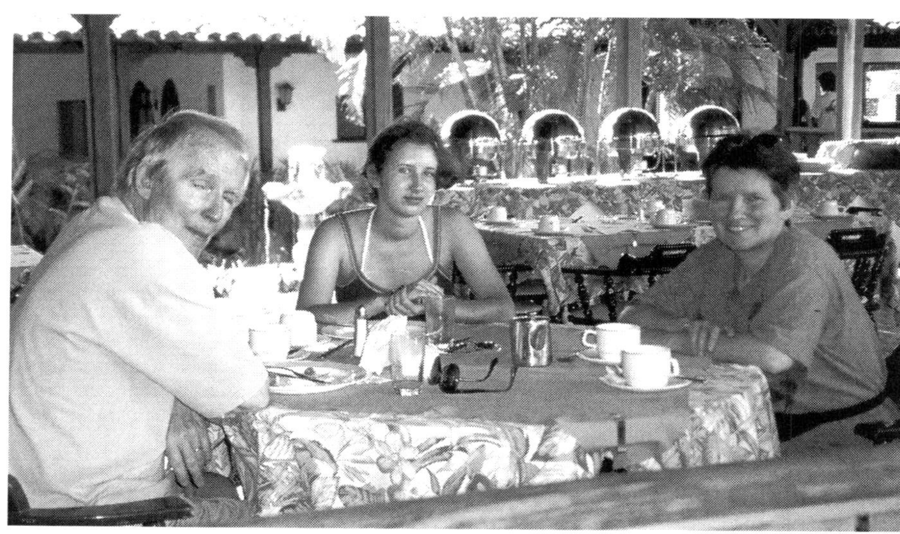

Open air breakfast

lots of umbrella leaves, the biggest in the world, at least a yard across, scalloped and round. It's a bit warmer here. As we're driving, Marco notices that all the waterfalls are pouring more forcefully than usual off the mountains into swollen streams. "Very peculiar in this 'dry season,'" he says, a bit apprehensively.

At one point, we stop to look at a towering, triple falls; running out with our cameras, we're drenched. Occasionally Marco warns of a "holy bridge": "You must pray before crossing and then give thanks if we've made it to the other side." Mountain brooks and rivers are thundering under these bridges that have no rails—definitely sobering. Marco has an encyclopedic knowledge of nature, stopping the bus often to point out birds or plants. Lark lists all the birds she's spotted; by trip's end she has some forty new species.

Onto the Water

We arrive at the banks of the Sarapiqui. On the dock we climb down a steep flight of steps to a twenty-five-foot-long skinny, tippy boat with a canopy top. Marco carefully balances us on the seats on either side. We slide off into the muddy current that swirls us downstream. Howler monkeys are perched in the tops of tall ficas, from which sloths are also hanging. Yard-long iguanas stretch out along the branches. Toucans, vultures, and innumerable other impressive, colorful birds pop up everywhere. We zip past banana plantations where bunches of the fruit (wrapped in plastic to speed growth) are so heavy they must be tied up.

We travel for about an hour and a half, the rain getting heavier all the time.

Arriving at our lunch stop, we clamor up another long stairway from the dock and dash through torrents to reach the open restaurant. Barbecued steaks, plantain, and hearts of palm await us. This is where we were to ride horses, but the downpour has not let up and the lawn has widened into a lake. One lone horse shows up, its rider holding an umbrella. Spray blows in over our lunch tables. A talking parrot makes friends with Lark, who lures him onto her hand.

Clearly the weather isn't improving, and Marco is worried. "I think we'd better get back upstream fast," he says. "You can see that since we arrived our dock has disappeared and most of the steps." Everyone helps to roll down the canvas flaps on both sides of the boat to keep out the deluge. Almost immediately, though, as we head into the center of the river, we see that the water has risen a great deal; at the end of the voyage Marco notes that it has come up thirty feet. The river width has doubled, and many trees are now out in the current, their branches catching in the eddying stream.

Most alarming now are the great rolling waves that set our fragile craft twisting and rocking. At this point, Marco gets down the life jackets and orders us to put them on. And even though we'll be drenched, we help to roll up the canvas sides so that if the boat capsizes, we'll be able to get out and swim—along with the crocodiles and snakes that inhabit the river.

Each of us is eyeing the current we're struggling against and figuring out strategies for reaching shore. The boatman has his hands full maneuvering around the huge logs and trees that are coming swiftly at us. Sometimes he has to stop and run the engine backward to dislodge debris from the propeller. At one point, Niko is so frozen that Eric takes off his own jeans to wrap around Niko's neck to stop his shivering. I've been wet through for some three hours and am more or less numb. Suddenly the large cooler parked in the bow of the boat tears loose and is gone in an instant. We meet a couple of other boats coming toward us downstream; their occupants seem puzzled by our life jackets. Soon they'll find out what they're up against.

After an hour of nearly unbearable tension, our starting point comes into view, now almost unrecognizable, because both the dock and steps are submerged. Standing sentinel is a soldier in camouflage hefting an uzi. What, I think, we're going to get shot, too? At one point, apparently, we were twenty miles from the Nicaraguan border, and Costa Rica has trouble with refugees and Sandinistas slipping across. We climb shakily out of the boat, enormously relieved, and dash to our warm bus. Eric, always up for life-and-death risks, is totally happy: "This last boat ride was definitely the best part of the day." Later we all have to agree that between imminent submersion into the jaws of waiting reptiles and the paralyzing cold, this took the prize for dramatic adventure of the trip.

Angelynn and Eric in lush garden of Costa Rica

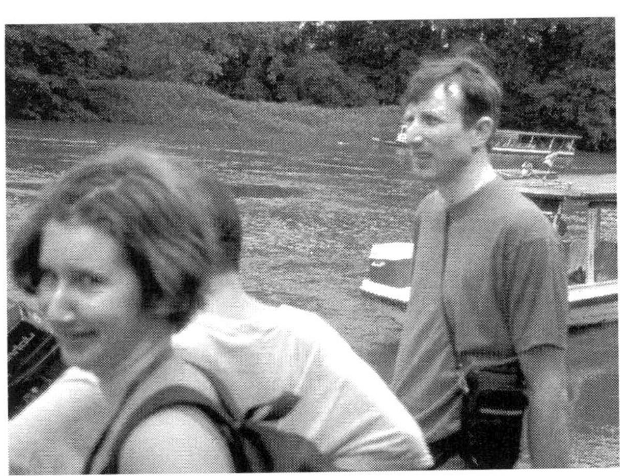

Lark and Eric disembark from our boat on the flooded Sarapiqui River

A late, dreamy supper on the back terrace

Ed, Susie, Anne with Katie, Steve, Bel

The slothful life at Fonte Vecchia

Italy
A Tuscan Idyll

May–June 1997

Backstory

This became the first of the really big extended family trips abroad. The Strainchamps clan (Steve's wife Anne, with her father Ed, mother Susie, and sister Emily) had lived in Florence for two years in the mid-1970s when Ed received grants to research Renaissance music. They had come under Italy's spell, as had our family with our own long-cherished ties and memories. So Bel and I, Steve, Anne, their year-old Katie, Ed and Susie (who have become close friends), and Emily, all decided that it was time to go back. We were excited about resurrecting our language skills and allowing ourselves to fall into all the familiar cultural mores and idiosyncracies that we had learned and loved many years before. Anne (our travel genius) signed us up for two weeks in a renovated farmhouse in Tuscany, not far from the medieval hill town of Cortona.

The Caravan from Rome

Everybody converges at the Fiumicino airport in Rome, and we collect three rental cars. There are some comical delays when Steve can't figure out how to back up his car, and Bel and I, with a defective card, can't get the airport barrier to lift and let us out. We nearly lose the others as they speed out of sight.

All is resolved, and we're off in caravan on the Annulare circling Rome, then cut north on the Autostrada toward Florence. Mad Italian drivers in the fast left lane are doing at least one hundred miles per hour, while we putter along on the right at seventy-five. Gradually the feel of city drops away and we climb into the hills. The first hay crops are standing in golden bundles, fields are dotted red with wild poppies, and bright yellow patches of broom line the roadsides. I'm suddenly overcome with nostalgia seeing the familiar austere, tall, stone houses with their red-tiled roofs—the ancient towns crowded onto hillcrests, surrounded by fortress walls and spiked with cathedral towers.

The first night we stop at a working vineyard in Orvieto where we're too bleary-eyed from jetlag to appreciate the many courses of a gourmet dinner and our host's lecture about his grapes. The next day we enjoy a bread-and-cheese picnic at Chiusi across from the little museum with Etruscan artifacts. Suddenly we're inundated with the age-old, homely details of Italian village life: roses and geraniums against buildings that line the unpaved streets, glimpses of luxuriant vegetable gardens through iron gates, the smells of wood fires and fresh bread—all evoke our time here over thirty-five years ago. I find in the grocery that my Italian is still intact.

We push on, changing to smaller roads, finally coming off a steep mountain into the village of Mercatale di Cortona. The last lap, to our farmhouse, is three miles farther. Following instructions, we turn abruptly onto a primitive dirt track and start to climb. And climb. The write-up had mentioned a forty-five-degree pitch, and I think that's close. Susie develops a phobia about the abrupt, acute-angle turn onto our long driveway where her wheels spin on the gravel and the car starts slipping backward toward a drop-off. Terrified at this point, and having noted the little roadside crosses with dead flowers signifying mortal crashes, she jumps out to walk. "No way am I doing this!"

But after bumping over cavernous ruts, we all make it safely, Ed bravely taking the wheel of their car. Emerging from a wooded grove, we're welcomed by the ubiquitous cypress sentinels (which I discover the locals bind to keep them skinny). Then, suddenly, here is Fonte Vecchia—a castle! (or at least a very grand manor).

Our Own Shangri-la

The views in every direction from Fonte Vecchia are astonishing. Anne exclaims, "We should have brought hang gliders; we could step or float off at any point!" A valley of silvery olive trees stretches out beneath us, with more mountains at our back. There are stone steps and terraces at different levels around the house. One terrace, covered for dining alfresco, looks over a stunning blue pool.

We wander through the house in awe, unable to imagine that this is ours for two weeks. None of us is accustomed to grandeur on this scale. The walls are two feet thick, with white plaster setting off the crude, aged bricks and mortar—how buildings were traditionally constructed in Tuscany. The floors are large, weathered, uneven bricks or tiles. The stairs are blackened ancient planks with no risers. Arched lintels over low doorways are of exposed stone (the men keep bumping their heads). Great, hand-sawn ceiling beams support smaller crossbeams with the chinked brick floors of the upper story visible. Lovely paintings and pottery pop out in every corner.

I explore the many gardens: huge bushes of lavender, rosemary, and sage, roses everywhere, pots of geraniums, a lemon tree to pick from, flowering trees I can't identify. In the evening, the heavy perfume of climbing jasmine greets us as we open the front door. Honeysuckle invites us onto the back terrace.

Gradually we uncover the history of Fonte Vecchia ("old well"). The owner lives most of the time in Belgium, employed by Reuters. Several times when we call him in frustration to report the persistent failure of the hot water system, we picture him on his cell phone just rushing off to his private plane, perhaps to cover a visit by President Clinton. He has delegated Ada (the elderly signora from up the road, who speaks no English) to be caretaker of the house and show us the ropes. She comes by every morning for a cursory cleaning, but we think it's more to make sure we're behaving. Ada tells us that she used to live here years ago when it was a *casa colonica*, a tenant farmhouse. Her family stayed in the south end, and their animals bedded down in the rest of the building.

Fonte Vecchia dates back to the fourteenth century when it was probably a watchtower guarding the valley below and the approaches to Cortona from the east. Once it marked the frontier between the Grand Duchy of Tuscany and the Papal States, the two frequently at war. Before that, the Romans occupied the area. We learn that near here the Roman Empire suffered its single greatest military defeat when Hannibal wiped out the Roman legions during a daylong battle near Tuoro on Lake Trasimeno, over the mountain from us. They say the lake ran red with blood. Earlier still the area was ruled by the Etruscans. Restoration of the house and its seven acres (mostly olive groves) started in 1975 and has been going on ever since.

What's so enchanting is that this magnificent house and grounds are perched in the middle of a wild, primitive mountain—where Ada insists vipers abound (she comes daily through the woods to clean in knee-high rubber boots), as well as foxes, wild boar, and wild horses.

We take memorable day trips to the medieval towns of Cortona, Assisi, Gubbio, Montepulciano (for Brunella wine in the famed caves), Montalcino, and Florence, all within handy distance. More often than not, wherever we travel, we spot castles on the numerous conical peaks. Intrigued by our local castle that we always see looming just outside Mercatale, one day we drive up the steep lane to the minuscule village of Pierle. We want to examine up-close the edifice that has stood guard over the region since the thirteenth century. Glowing in the late afternoon sun, now the castle is mostly an imposing ruin engulfed in weeds, though still it dominates the valley it once protected. Fewer than twenty houses make up the hamlet within the wall that circles the castle's base. Groups of Pierle ladies are parked on chairs in their yards, chatting and crocheting. Others are no doubt busy behind their closed shutters, while a few of the men are still hoeing in the vineyard just below, taking advantage of the evening cool.

In between these forays, we hustle home to our secluded eyrie—*our* mountain—to practice serious sloth. We collect piles of books, head to the pool, and, with sighs of bliss, settle into deck chairs. The great valley drops off immediately from the edge of the pool. Fourteen wild horses snuffle and snort behind the rear fence. One afternoon two cuckoos sound off, one in a grove of trees near us and the other answering from the forest at the bottom of the valley.

When we feel ambitious, with Katie in a backpack, we puff up the dusty road above our drive. We discover a rushing brook, and I tick off the indigenous flora: poppies, yarrow, viper's bugloss, lots of gold broom, wild primroses, daisies, a version of Queen Anne's lace, and spiky purple lupines. The vistas become more majestic as we climb. Sheep graze near a ruined farm.

Susie and Anne are our premiere cooks, concocting splendid pasta meals with the tender, new green beans and other ultra-fresh vegetables from the market, or snaring a share of *porchetta*, the whole pig spit-roasted once a week at the butcher's. Local wines (two weeks' supply, purchased on arrival, to the astonishment and delight of the Mercatale grocer) are happily consumed at lunches and dinners. After one such "buzzy" feast in the damp dusk on our back terrace, Steve slips into the pool and floats on his back, balancing his fruit bowl on his chest. Such decadence doesn't come very often! The fireflies are winking all down the valley and the stars take up where the fireflies leave off, sparkling overhead, illuminating cloud wisps shifting over the nearer mountaintops.

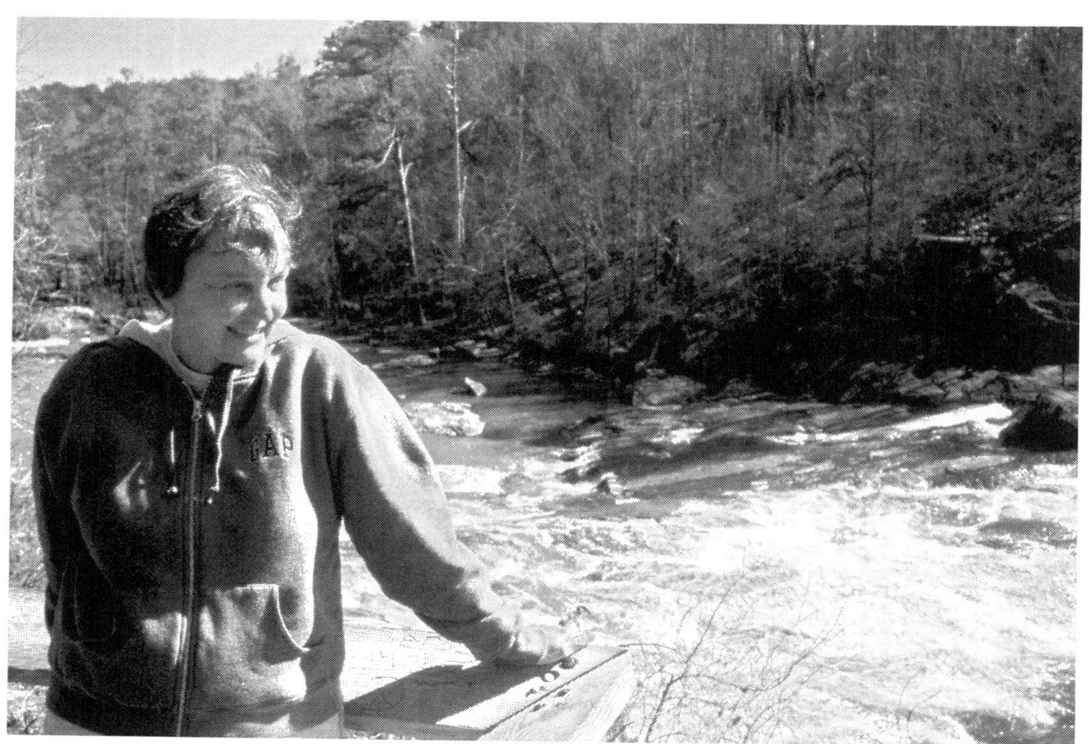

The trio at High Falls, Georgia

Wisdoms

Dolphin and Otherwise, Southeast United States

FEBRUARY 1999

Backstory

It was unrelenting winter in Wisconsin, and Bel and I felt a sudden urge to get away. We found that Eric, whose landscaping business allows him to take the cold months off, was game to go with us. He helped map out a route that would take us south along the East Coast, touching areas we didn't know at all. For him, it would be a coming home; he had hiked the Smokies in his college and post-college days and had vacationed in Florida. "I realize that I became a Wisconsin landscape gardener because I don't live in the mountains," he has said. "It's my way of being in touch with that elemental earth force absolutely essential to my life and well-being."

I can relate. I feel the same way about the necessity of being out in nature. I got this from my father, who craved mountains desperately. After moving east, when he could no longer climb in his beloved Sierra Nevadas, every weekend he got out the maps and organized family outings. When I asked Eric what he'd be doing for a living if he lived in the mountains, he answered without hesitation, "I'd be taking people into them." And so, for our first stop, he will take us into the wilds of North Carolina.

Hunting and Gathering Isn't Just Romantic History

We find the town of Waynesville on our map. A dirt road leads us to a sprawling, cedar-sided house that takes guests. It's set in a meadow beneath steep, grazed slopes and wooded peaks—Jonathan Valley. We're soon ensconced in cozy attic rooms, and the rising half moon blinks in through skylights. While Bel and I succumb with books in bed, Eric tries out the Jacuzzi outside; the water is a sizzling 100 degrees against temperatures now dipping into the frosty teens.

We wake to first light creeping down the mountain. Breakfast is sausage and eggs baked into a golden biscuit, creamed potatoes, stewed apples, a warm loaf of dark, sweet bread, and cocoa. Our host, Les, regales us with stories of the local fauna: packs of coyotes take off his neighbor's calves, black bear and wild boar are thick. Everybody hunts. He recommends a drive up the mountain for the view. "But don't go past the end of the road," he warns. "The hillbillies live up beyond and shoot anybody who trespasses." He traverses the mountains on his ATV.

He also has a corner on all the archery in the region—has a range and shop in his barn where he sells new bows with scopes for $1,400 and finely made, old-fashioned ones for $500. His wife Gail has won the championship for the area with one hundred fifty bull's-eyes in a row. Les shoots all his meat (either with bow or rifle), and so with their granary and vegetable gardens they're almost self-sufficient. He says, "Once, four of us were chased up a tree by a wild pig. Bear will run away but boar will chase you." Showing us his arsenal, he speculates, "If the Indians had had bows like this, the pilgrims would still be on Plymouth Rock."

Les hasn't read a newspaper in six years ("So I don't have to worry"), and doesn't go to movies.

We do venture onto the mountain trails, battling thick vines like witches' hair that choke out the young saplings. The skyline undulates with worn peaks, sprouting bare bristle-brush trees along their spines.

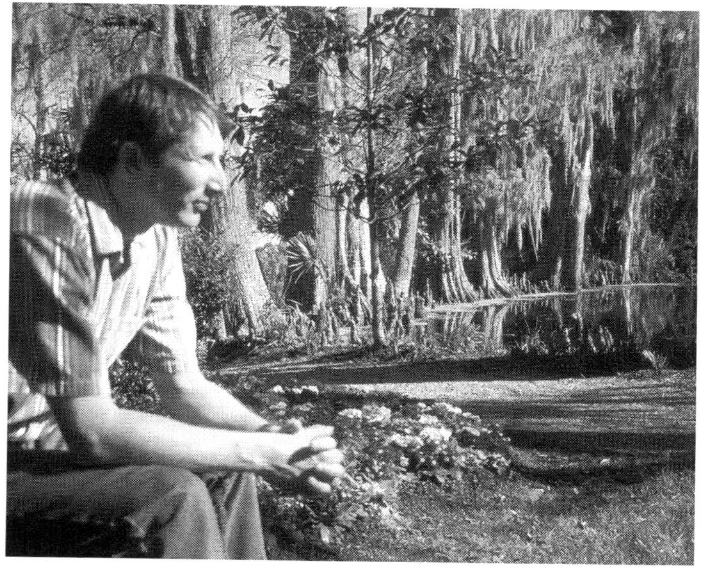

An alligator-infested plantation near Charleston

Dripping Moss, Murder, and Alligators in the Deep South

Proceeding southward, we take in the stately, historic quarters of Charleston. Three hundred-year-old live oaks and magnolias fill the gardens of a plantation where hundreds of slaves once produced highly profitable rice and indigo (for blue dye). Alligators with bulging eyes float lazily in the ponds or suddenly appear and scuttle across our path. They are protected, along with all the other wildlife on the property—calculated to keep the natural balance—so they are not considered a threat to people (presumably because they find enough satisfactory food without bothering the human variety).

Having just read John Berendt's *Midnight in the Garden of Good and Evil*, we're primed for dark doings in Savannah. We get the sense of an old European city, with rickety stone steps descending to dungeon-like caverns that used to be cotton warehouses, all with grimy, blackened walls. Then we work our way back to Bull Street, which every two or three blocks is interrupted by a lovely square. Towering oaks are draped in moss. Shaded walkways lead past fountains or heroic statues and flowering shrubs. We're curious about famed Monterey Square with Mercer House, where Jim Williamson apparently murdered his young male lover. The stately, red brick edifice stretches to take up an entire block, set back from the sidewalk by an ornate black iron fence. We are a bit disappointed that nobody appears at a window or comes out the door.

We've heard about Mrs. Wilkes' famous Boarding House. The protocol is to wait outside on the street until summoned through the unassuming basement door. Rooms are filled with long tables that seat about a dozen. At our table, we chat and swap information as we pass the big bowls of food. I count some twenty different dishes: mashed potatoes, sweet potatoes, yellow squash, cheesy broccoli, green beans and bacon, lima beans, fried chicken, sausage, melon cubes, gravy and biscuits, cornbread, and more. There are pitchers of very sweet iced tea. We fill our plates over and over. It's all superb and we feel like gluttons, happily stuffing ourselves as though it's our last foreseeable meal. They come around with desserts: banana pudding or peach cobbler. Everybody carries their dirty dishes to the kitchen, and we pay at the desk, where ninety-year-old Mrs. Wilkes presides, as she's been doing for fifty years. At ten dollars apiece, it's the bargain of the trip.

Into the home stretch—Florida, old and new. St. Augustine with Revolutionary War relics and the Kennedy Space Center, where we gawk at the 149-foot shuttle and the "crawler," that carries it. The largest on-ground vehicle, the crawler transporter—a pair of tracked vehicles—is as big as a baseball field and requires a bed of crushed rock seven feet deep to support a weight of six million pounds creeping along at one mph.

We come away imbued with the spirit conveyed here: nothing is impossible, humans can go anywhere and do anything. Even though the goals are an exact science with known technologies and skills necessary, the end result and where it may all lead is still very much a mystery. It's stepping into the universe to discover places and conditions never before charted. It's these elements and qualities that one can see as a transcendental experience, even though they are never referred to openly as "spiritual" by employees at the Space Center.

This is also on the mind of a distant cousin of mine we visit. She and her husband are active in the space program and say they and many of their fellow workers are convinced there must be life "out there." They go regularly to Star Trek camps.

The Dolphin Hunt

Right up there on our agenda is a longing to swim and communicate with dolphins. We're at the tip of Florida now, Key West. After sampling the daily sunset pageant on the waterfront with street performers—jugglers, weight lifters, a bagpiper—along with noisy mobs of exuberant young people and leathery-faced, aging hippies with ponytails, we're ready for a more thoughtful exploration.

It's Eric's nineteenth wedding anniversary, and as a special treat we've lined up Captain Victoria for an all-day ocean trip to look for dolphins. Vicky is loading her boat, *Imp II*, as our other three shipmates arrive. After stowing our stuff, we roar off in the twenty-seven-foot canopied craft. Passing one island, Vicky tells us, "This is where Navy Seals train to kill and shoot from under water. They use the dolphins for explosives research."

Alternately, we ride full-speed with bone-rattling winds and spray soaking us (wrapped up in our warmest coats and hoods), and then we idle in strategic spots where Vicky says dolphins hang out: the "bedroom," "the playground," "the dining room." We travel out into the Gulf and then to the Atlantic Ocean, about thirty-five miles. At one point, we wade ashore to beach comb on a deserted island; we eat sandwiches in the shade of a mangrove swamp with herons, ibises, cormorants, and ospreys—a spot attractive to birds because of masses of tiny bait fish along the shore.

Then, even though we're shivering in heavy sweatshirts and parkas, it's time to snorkel. We're fitted with masks and fins. Stripping down to bathing suits, we flop into the water. Nearby is an old

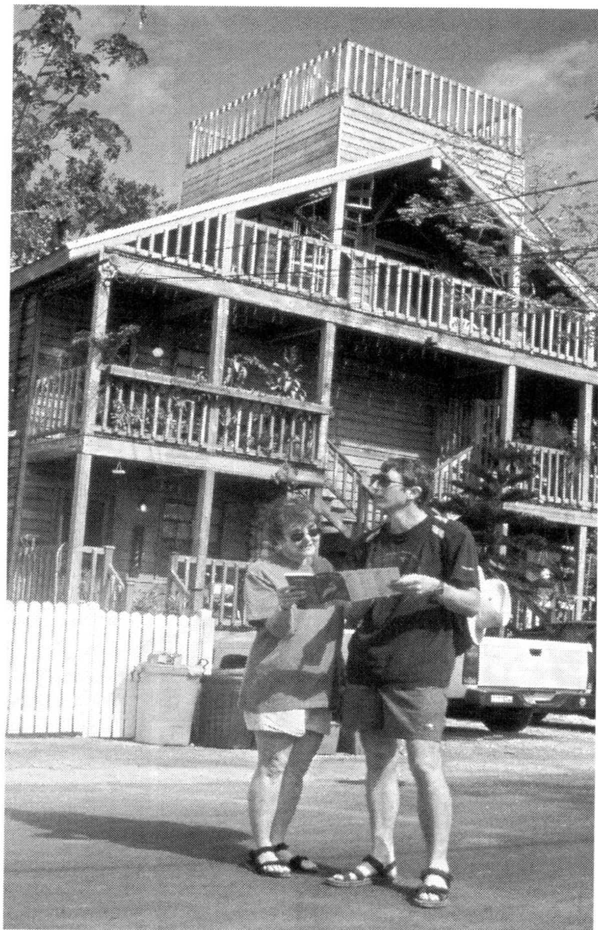
Checking the map in Key West

shipwreck, and we inspect the fish gathered around it. Then we grab wood paddles (two swimmers on each), and the boat tows us quickly into deeper water to see giant corals and forests of waving seaweed. I'm the first to signal that I'm ready to come out, frantically trying to get Vicky's attention; I haul myself along the line and clamor aboard, chilled through and shaking. At first it wasn't bad, but gradually we were all freezing. Eric says his hands were numb.

As we travel, Vicky plays music to call out the dolphins: reggae, didgeridoo with drums, German oompah, shaman chants, Itzhak Perlman's violin. She says they're sometimes so fascinated that they stand up out of the water and prick up small ears to listen. She knows them all and has named them according to habits, temperament, physical characteristics, and sense of humor. She swaps names with the other captains who take people out for dolphin-watching. Captains get their licenses only after three hundred hours of tests on the water.

But we never do find dolphins, nor does another passing boat. They're either staying out of sight or "aren't home today." Often dolphins travel fifty miles in a day, and they hang out in certain general areas for different purposes. Vicky is active with a local environmental group, puts out a newspaper, and lectures on this work. She makes several points: "Dolphins can tune into peoples' expectations and desire to see them; if this is strong, they're *less* apt to show up. Our human way is to want to make something special of an experience and build on it to further knowledge. The lesson here seems to be that dolphins function differently. If we're unattached to outcomes, being playful and nonchalant, this is when they're most likely to come out to frolic and be with us."

She continues, "Too often people try to save animals and environments, but the dolphins' message is: The earth can take care of itself and regenerate; you need, instead, to clean up the *human* species, look to your own failings." This is a reason Vicky is an activist for homeless children and other causes. She observes that dolphins take special care of their own young, elderly, and sick.

The new scientists who come out with her are actually "shamans," as she puts it. "They listen to nature and try to learn from it."

Full of these gentle thoughts and close to the many manifestations of nature working continually to balance itself, we complete our seven hours at sea and come back to shower and go out for an Italian dinner to celebrate Eric's special day.

I note the definition of VISION tacked up on the wall of our Spartan little hostel room: "A vision without a task is but a dream; a task without a vision is drudgery; a vision with a task is the hope of the world."

Ruminating in my journal that night about our boat trip, I know I'd been trying to see it all in a positive light. Now I wonder if maybe it was also a test: putting me through actual pain, making me face several weaknesses, both physical and mental. First, there was the apprehension of a long trip on the water and forecast of high waves (I suffer badly from seasickness). We found it was really cold starting out and bundled up in our heaviest clothes. The wind was unrelenting, and periodically we were drenched with spray. Despite my wristbands, there were twinges of nausea.

When it was snorkel time, I had to swallow my trepidation about the cold, show bravery (making up for missing out on the dolphin part of the adventure), and strip down to my bathing suit "polar bear" fashion to leap into the water as people do in January in Lake Michigan. It wasn't too cold, though, and when I got the hang of the snorkel and fins, I paddled off happily. The fascination lasted until Vicky suggested that we grab the line to be towed. Suddenly the water was deeper and much more frigid. Pretty soon hypothermia (I imagined) began to take hold, and I wanted to get out fast, but couldn't attract Vicky's attention for some ten more minutes. I was a little panicked that I wouldn't make it out.

All these physical challenges added up to a somewhat different outcome than the blissed-out romp with dolphins, lured by music, that I'd expected. There had to be the release of those anticipations, as well as a pride in managing something distinctly tough.

Eric, too, keeps scribbling his thoughts. As he says, he realizes that this is a unique journey, maybe the first time since he was very small that he's been alone with Bel and me. Many times there have been trips with both Eric and Steve, but the dynamics now are different. He's sensing things about our relationship and his own life, all against the backdrop of our tourist activities and hanging out together. In fact, he talks about this as a "womb experience"—going back to a much earlier time that connected him to us.

Reflections

After we were back home, Eric told us that this may have been the best trip he's taken, especially because it opened up for him a different perspective, knocking loose something that exposed a whole new vista of possible future directions of thinking and acting, which in his ordinary routine he couldn't leap to in the same way. He appreciated the way we traveled, balancing seeing and doing new things with time to absorb and reflect and write. The dynamic of the three of us together he found really pleasurable, he said.

For Bel and me, too, it was an unusual experience: both traveling with this kind of stop-and-go rhythm into new territory, and particularly making the trip with Eric—enjoying him as a wise, resourceful, always light and light-filled companion. It stirred us out of *our* usual travel patterns *a deux*.

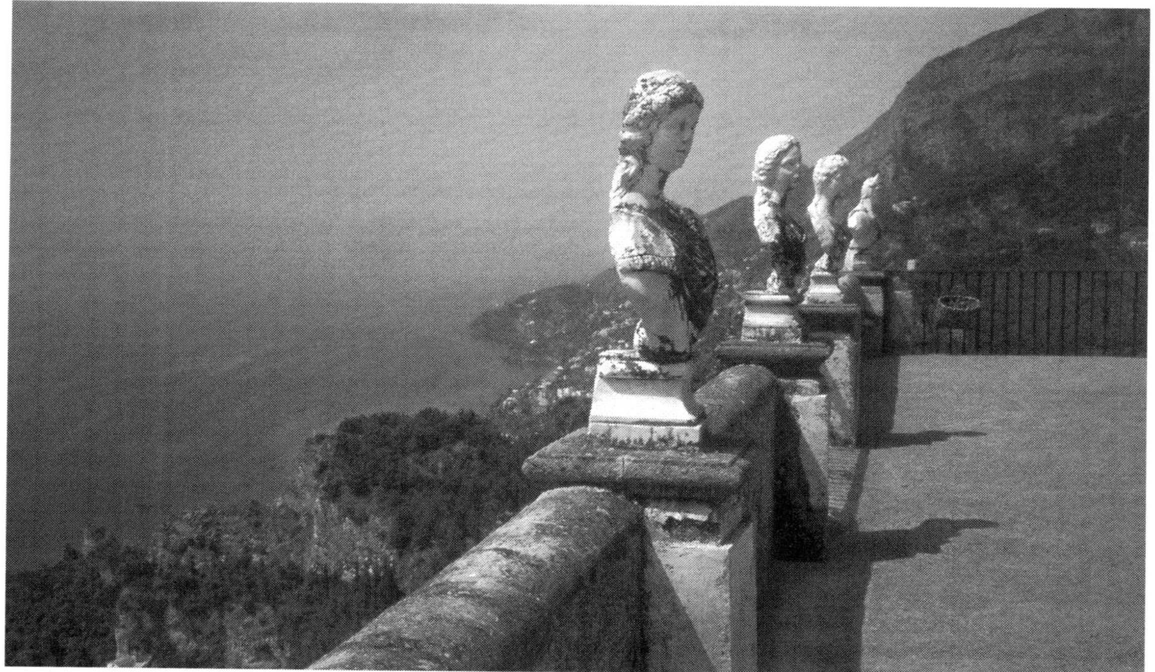

From the terrace of Villa Cimbrone: "Best vista in the world" (said Gore Vidal)

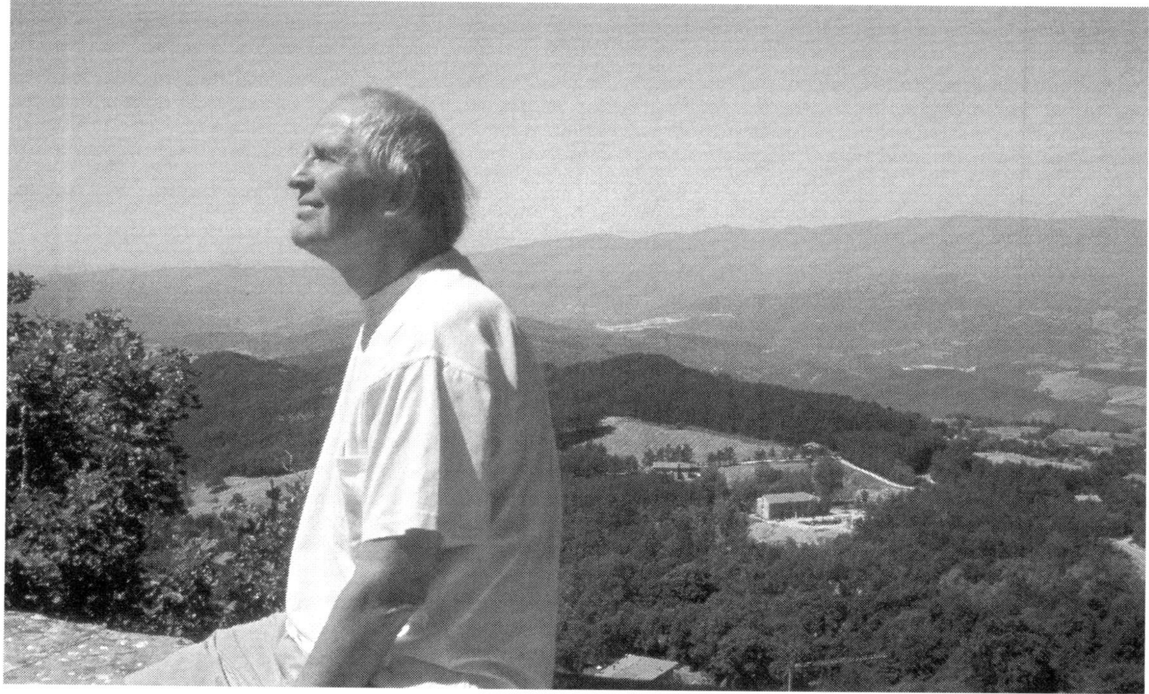

View down the mountain from La Verna

Italy Again
Retracing Past Steps

June-July 1999

Backstory

The die-hard Tuscan enthusiasts decided to replicate the Fonte Vecchia idyll—Steve's family of four (now Nicky had appeared on the scene), plus Ed and Susie Strainchamps, and Bel and I.

First, though, Bel and I wanted to take the honeymoon trip we never had time for in 1954 when, between Bel's graduate classes at the University of Chicago, we shoehorned our wedding into a short weekend. We felt it was time for just the two of us to revisit haunts that have been favorites over the years since 1952.

Honeymoon in South Italy—Where We Met

Remembering the moonlight concert in Ravello in 1973, we reserve space in this enchanted little town for three days at the convent of Chiesa Santa Chiara. Bypassing the touristed Amalfi Drive, we cut across the high interior to reach Ravello, hanging above the Mediterranean Sea on its high cliff.

We almost give up trying to get into the fortress-like convent. When we call from next door, a cloistered nun says she'll unlock the great wooden portal. Once we're inside, she talks to us, but through a grill so that we never see her. This is a "closed" order where the nuns are not allowed to be seen by the public—a little tricky when you're running a rental facility! A lazy Susan swings out from a wall where the hidden nun passes us keys and a pile of sheets and towels. We're instructed to go up the street to the locked guest entrance. For ten minutes, we wrestle with the keys with no luck, and again almost give up, expiring from heat, hunger, and frustration. Suddenly we discover the trick: kick the door hard.

After a breather, we hike down to the famed Giardino Rufolo, built in and around thirteenth century structures. There are terraces with little pools and fountains, towering cypresses, and white Roman pillars silhouetted against the sea below or mountains above. Ravello is a major music/art town, and when we hear a piano, we duck into a little concert garden, a ruin with Moorish arches and chairs set among the pines. The performer for that evening is practicing a Mendelssohn sonata, with birds accompanying loudly, along with the Duomo bell chiming the hours.

Back to our Spartan but spotless cell for a luxurious icy shower, then next door to Villa Amore for dinner. Pots of red geraniums are massed on the marble walls of our terrace. Jagged mountains press in, and gradually the misty sea below merges with the haze of the sky. Lighted lamps illuminate the switchbacks winding up to Ravello, but we see no cars. No sound reaches our rarefied heights. Even our fellow diners are speaking in whispers.

Later, at the convent door, we race up the stairs to the second floor before the one-minute timer light shuts off. Around 10:00 p.m., a thin plainchant floats up.

Next morning we explore the second famous garden, Villa Cimbrone, vast and eclectic, with shaded tunnels of trees and vines leading to a spectacular viewing spot—a terrace wall studded with the stone heads of Roman emperors overlooking the vertical drop. Gore Vidal, who lived in Ravello part time, claimed this to be the most beautiful vista in the world.

We follow an innocent-looking circular path, but its steps take us straight down to the sea and up again—a hike guaranteed to develop muscles. Then a final feast amidst giant hedges of lavender and roses as the evening mists begin to swirl and a stiff breeze flairs.

From "The Old Ways" to Modernity in One Generation

Now we're off to Naples to catch the night boat to Sardinia. It steams out of the bay, past Capri, like a silent grey battleship, on our left, and then past the lights of Ischia winking on the right. Bel thinks he spots Granili, the horrific monster building that in 1950 housed twenty thousand homeless Neapolitans bombed out in the war, from which came most of our Casa Mia clientele.

After fifteen hours, we inch up to the dock in Cagliari, capital city of Sardinia, and head northwest toward Oristano, our home from 1957-59. This is where we created the farming village for Eastern European refugees with film actor Don Murray. The changes in Oristano are staggering, even more so than when we came back in 1973 with the boys. Long gone are the days when water buffalo shuffled by pulling wagons, and the peasant ladies in their long, pleated skirts relieved themselves in the streets. In our day, the only phone in this fourth largest city on the island was in the central bar; now nattily dressed urbanites hurry by chattering on cell phones. The dusty alleyway where we lived has vanished.

After hiking in circles, thoroughly disoriented, we give up the search and drive out through swampy flats to San Giovanni Sinis. This spit of land sticking into the sea was a favorite get-away spot we'd bounce out to on our only vehicle, a Lambretta scooter (Eric and I on the back), and it's where we returned with both boys in 1973.

Inquiring about a place to stay, we're pointed down the road to the Agriturismo Domenico. Housing tourists on farms is newly popular throughout Italy. A friendly old guy emerges from a grove of eucalyptus and shows us simple rooms with a bathroom block a hike away and al fresco showers. We help set the dinner table, a twenty-foot slab of marble under palm trees. There are twelve of us: Swedish, German, Swiss, northern Italian. It's all very friendly and informal, and the food, served family style, is incredible: spicy pasta, grey mullet cooked whole in the huge outdoor wood oven, shrimp in shells, and the great Sard dessert—*seadas*, a pancake stuffed with fresh pecorino cheese and lemon and then deep-fried and drizzled with honey. Local wine and perfectly ripe cantaloupe and soft peaches, espresso, and many kinds of liqueurs, including the fiery aqua vita ("good for digestion"), and amaretto cookies complete the meal. We linger over conversation in several languages while the cook and proprietor's son wash dishes in an outdoor tub under the stars.

We're off to Simaxis, the village outside Oristano where the refugee project unfolded. I inquire at a grocery store for Angela and her husband Anselmo. Angela lived with us in those early days, and together we scrubbed Eric's diapers in the bathtub. Angela is amazed and tearful to see us. They're both worn looking, yet robust and handsome in their early sixties. Angela still has the erect carriage once needed for carrying large water jars on her head, and there are hints of a classic beauty that made her the belle of our project when she was nineteen. She wears over-the-knee skirts, telling us that twenty years ago her kids decreed the traditional full-length taffeta costume all older women wore to be too antiquated. Anselmo still works as a builder. When we visited in 1973, their shack was primitive, with an outhouse. Now it has been transformed into a fairly grand abode with airy rooms, an inner courtyard garden and huge kitchen. Intricate Sard baskets that Angela weaves hang on the walls.

All but one of the original refugees are dead, but we find a number of the wives and seventeen children still around, in the houses we built with them. There are lots of group photos to look at, nostalgic reminiscences and joyful tears.

The dolce *lady and friend are delighted to meet us in Tonara*

Back to San Giovanni, where we find skinny girls in string bikinis on the beach. In one generation, Sardinia has succumbed to modernity with the rest of Italy. Many have come in hiking boots or high-top air sneakers and T-shirts with slogans in English ("The Beach is a Philosophy"). Mobile phones are hooked to their waists. There's now a pay gate to view the Phoenician ruins at the Tharros tower where once we could freely pick up bits of ancient painted pottery. We peer through the fence at the excavations to check out the Pompei-like rooms, aqueducts, millstones, and *amphore* (jugs)—and the lonely white columns thrust up against the dark blue of the sea.

We're on the road again now, heading up along the coast to Santa Caterina. We remember this as an enchanted spot with a ruined tower on a high promontory. We could look down on the bizarre limestone formations just offshore, with holes and tunnels worn by the sea. As a two-year-old, Eric used to race up and down the beach collecting sand dollars and the prized spine-covered sea urchins that Sards crack open and drink (the juice resembles raw eggs). The hillsides are still covered with wild rosemary, but otherwise the area is not recognizable—it's a dirty little sprawl of houses.

Into Bandit Country

On to Cuglieri, a medieval hill town. In 1958, we ventured into the mountainous interior with great caution; there were outlaw bandits hiding out who would barricade the roads and then rob motorists. We hear it's relatively safe now, except for Orgòsolo, the one town notorious for drug traffic (where Don Murray considered making a bandit movie).

We pass crumbling nuraghi, the odd towers of unmortared stone from the Bronze Age we used to seek out, many now reduced to just heaps of stones. There are very few sheep. Fifty years ago we saw old men and young boys everywhere on the roads and in the hills, wandering with their flocks twenty-four hours a day, always seeking fresh pasture, with only umbrellas slung over their shoulders. Fencing was unheard of.

I revel in this rough landscape—knobby granite pinnacles thrusting up from steep olive groves, and the taller blue peaks of the Gennargentu range in the distance. Stone walls snake straight up the mountainsides through stubbly fields to denote property lines. Our way twists and climbs, then hairpins down into gorges. Tall wheat feathers, red poppies, and candles of wild foxglove line the roads.

Our destination is the mountain town of Tonara. We have great memories of ordering our now-faded dining room rug there in 1957. That was a time when all the women wove in their homes and you walked from house to house meeting and buying directly from the weavers. Armed with the names of a couple of hotels, we hunt the Belvedere and book into a light, airy room. It has a balcony that looks out over tile roofs and down the slope on which the village is built. Bare rock crowns the peak. Our hotel padrone suggests a hike: "Why don't you go all the way up to the top? From there you can see all of Sardegna."

After supper, we amble into the main square to join the promenading crowds. There are festive banners and a bandstand in front of the principal church where a loudspeaker booms with popular songs. It's the *Festa* of San Antonio. I see older women in the ornate, traditional costume, and when I snap a photo, a couple of them hurry up to introduce themselves. One of them is "Assunta Floris, *chi fa dolce*" (who bakes sweets). "You must come to visit me tomorrow," she beams.

We'd planned on an early night, but can't resist strolling to the church for the *Festa* concert. By 10:30 the musicians are warmed up and the whole town (pop. 1,500) dribbles in. We perch on a stone wall and chat with everybody within earshot, then are introduced to others. The music alternates between slow songs and fast dance numbers with wild rhythms—Sard music has a flavor and tonalities that seem to be a cross between Bulgarian and Irish. The performers are professionals, up from Cagliari, all in costume. They play guitar, kazoo, penny whistle, eighteen-inch pipes, tambourine, drum, two kinds of accordions. We're hoping to see real Sard circle dancing, but it seems everyone is too shy to start. Many little kids are tearing around despite the hour. Long-legged teenage girls wear tight pants with high heels or long, modish shifts split to the upper thigh.

Next morning, considerably restored, we drive with the padrone to the top of the mountain, stopping to help him fill his water jugs at one of the many springs. He tells us we're only the second Americans to visit Tonara this year. He leaves us at the bald, rocky summit to hike down. Layers of mountains and valleys and villages are spread out around us, from interior Nuoro to Olbia on the northeast coast.

Back in the town, we hunt up the weaving cooperative where we buy table linens from a lady busy on her loom. "Ten years ago," she tells us, "there were seventeen women in the coop; now only five are left. None of the younger girls know how to weave or embroider, and they don't want to; these are dying crafts. In fact, they don't want to work at all. They just want to stay home or get married and have babies."

Our padrone climbs one of his trees to pick cherries for us.

Next, we find the *dolce* lady's house. She kisses me warmly. "*Viene, viene*—come into my bakery!" We're plied with *amaretti* and other confections and inspect her huge oven and the machine that grinds the almonds.

After a breakfast of ripening sheep milk on our bread, we hug and thank the padrone and cook and drive off north to Nuoro and Orune. The thick vegetation disappears, and the trees become stunted and wind-twisted. They're mostly red cork, recently stripped of their bark. Eventually we're in an eerie moonscape of scattered white granite rocks. At one point a pack of snarling, mangy dogs stops us dead on a desolate road. They circle our car and leap at the windows, guarding a herd of fat pigs, swaggering along, prodded by a boy on a donkey.

Sardinia continues to intrigue us because, even though many of the old ways are gone, there is still a primitiveness very different from the cultivated, almost effete antiquity on the Italian mainland that mesmerizes tourists. We stop for spaghetti in Orune, the tiny village stuck on the top of a jagged pinnacle we visited forty years ago. We were with a film director from Rome, Pino Fina, who was hunting a picturesque location for a movie.

A night in Dorgali, noted for its handcrafts and where we once bought another fine rug. Our hotel proprietor tells us at breakfast that sadly Sardinia is losing its uniqueness. Also, the new European Community regulations are killing them economically. Legally they can't even offer guests wine and jam made on the premises. There are huge taxes and inspection costs—to make sure cheese made where the animals live isn't contaminated. For these reasons, many Sards have emigrated to France, Germany, North America, and Argentina.

Fonte Vecchia, Déjà vu

Sailing back to the mainland, we're now on a fast track to join the rest of the family. In Pienze, we find everybody and line up the three cars for the procession to Mercatale. In the two intervening years, Fonte Vecchia has assumed mythical proportions. It doesn't disappoint. In fact, it's even more stunning with a new third-floor tower sprouting from the roof. Ada's illiterate daughter rushes out to throw her arms around us. The kitchen is fabulously remodeled.

We start off our two weeks with the gargantuan Sunday "lunch" at Mimmi's, our illustrious but simple local eatery. Everybody gets the same food at the same time: crostini with foie gras, ravioli with ricotta and sage, spinach gnocchi, lasagne, veal, roast chicken, lamb, fries, salads, lemon custard cake, great slabs of tiramisu, red house wine, espresso, lemon liqueur. After two and a half hours, we stagger out and wobble home to digest by the

Steve's family at the ruined castle, Pierle, near Fonte Vecchia

pool. Three-year-old Katie shows off by dashing off down the driveway, then solicitously comes back to monitor her younger brother Nicky's happy gallop; he wouldn't have remembered his first time here in "Mommy's tummy."

In Cortona, half an hour away, we run into Frances Mayes and her husband in the main square. Steve has been trying to reach her to confirm their appointment to talk about her book *Under the Tuscan Sun*. Later that day he's back to see the house she described renovating and to record an interview for his and Anne's PRI radio show in Wisconsin.

Prussian Pomp

Bel and I join Susie and Ed on one of several real estate quests—not that we're ever serious about buying property, but it's a fun way to see what's happening in the foreign market, and we get into backcountry. Because this offering was advertised in *The New York Times,* we should have been alerted that it was somewhere in the oxygen-thin stratosphere.

A self-described Italian count, Antonio Bolza grew up in Hungary where his family had settled after leaving Italy. Schooled in England and Germany (where it's rumored he became enamored of the Nazis), eventually he saw an opportunity to make money back in his ancestral land. He bought two thousand acres in Umbria on which sat thirty-two decaying old farms. One by one he is now renovating the buildings with his architect/interior designer wife, exquisitely and faithfully restoring them to pristine splendor.

When we show up for our appointment, Count Bolza receives us very cordially in his elegant office with dark beams and antique pottery. He's wearing a chic silk jacket, foulard, and Armani shoes. As he drives us in his huge 4 x 4 over the rough fields, his German riding master (body guard?) canters alongside in smart jodhpurs and boots. We get the feeling that he's sizing us up and concluding—despite our academic credentials (and Ed's always "sophisticated intelligentsia" demeanor), plus staying at Fonte Vecchia where he has dined with the owners—that probably we are sub-aristocracy and not worthy candidates for his snazzy Reschio development

We watch one villa being readied in a hurry for a German family moving here in two weeks.

Sixty-two workers swarm around: an artist painting authentic ancient designs on the stair risers, four men planting an eighty-year-old olive tree, a crew completing the swimming pool with automatic electronic regulators. Others are installing thousand-year-old statuary and fountains. Gardeners and landscapers are creating something akin to Versailles. Apparently the count and his wife haunt the antique dealers and completely furnish the houses, down to selecting the "correct" books with handsome bindings to line the living room shelves. The price tag for this estate (the guest house is maybe triple the size of our house at home): $2,000,000.

This is a condominium where everyone submits to the count's endless regulations—such as garbage out and milk picked up at specific hours. He clearly revels in his fiefdom, privileged and closed, where he's the reigning padrone/big brother. We run into a couple of recent American buyers who, so far, are happily playing the game. A castle on the property will become a hotel where folks "like Prince Charles" will vacation.

We're thankful to return to our homey, utterly private retreat to savor our own dusty olives and to sink back in our beach chairs, dozing to the soporific buzzing of bees nosing into the purple lavender.

Another real estate foray takes us to Murlo Mountain in Umbria, not far from the Tuscany border. The house is grand, complete with its own beamed, vaulted chapel and brick floor—which Ed fantasizes as a venue for chamber music concerts. Four hundred years old, squeaky clean with splendid views off toward Assisi and an adjacent golf course, it has been renovated recently. Singer Luciano Pavarotti's ex-wife is anxious to unload it for $500,000.

On the drive back, we note two scantily clad, tall Nigerian prostitutes standing out on the deserted road. Our English realtor says that when they first saw these (it's apparently a Russian mafia operation), and her ten-year-old wanted to know why the women didn't have many clothes on, Jill thought fast and replied, "They're probably on their way to the pool."

It's our last night. I'm about to go off to bed but feel there hasn't been enough time today to enjoy the magic outside. I tiptoe out to smell the night perfume, then amble around to the back to see the pool glinting like a thousand stars in the pale light. The water is very warm and, impulsively, I drop my clothes and slip in, floating weightlessly under the low-slung real stars.

Genazzano

Italy, Return Engagement
A Writing Assignment in Genazzano

May–June 2001

Backstory

Bel has been commissioned to write an article for the *World Policy Journal*, updating the political and cultural tenor in the village of Genazzano that he first described in his book *The Searchers* in 1966.

As before, his collaborator will be Athos Ricci, former Communist Party head, now a major critic of the empty promises of that movement. Athos is retired from a clerical job with city government in Rome. The two of them have also contemplated writing another book together to update *The Searchers*. Bel and I will make the trip alone, and have earmarked several other points around Italy to explore when the research is done.

Finding An Old Stomping Ground

We're four hours late getting to Genazzano because my purse is stolen at the Rome airport. A thief watches us cashing money and follows us to the car rental office. I look away from the baggage cart at my elbow where I have laid my purse to talk to the agent. When I turn back, seconds later, it is gone—and there is no sign of the culprit. It is a tiny room and we never dreamed it could be vulnerable. The purse contains every important document and item of value for the trip. Sufficient to say that if we hadn't spoken Italian, it would have been many moons before the police could get our testimony. A valuable lesson learned about believing blithely that "it could never happen to me."

We find Athos hovering in his doorway. His wife races down the steps, we all embrace, and Giuseppina immediately insists on cooking us an elegant lunch. They watch as we devour. Athos, in his floor-length brown raincoat (his ubiquitous theatrical costume), sits and chatters away.

Athos has found us a spot in a hotel on the outskirts of town. We'll lodge here for the next week while he and Bel resume their old routine of clomping around with a tape recorder to interview representatives of the various cultural strata. I do a lot of sketching and translate some of the transcribed interviews. One day I hike into the town to see the first rituals of a celebration honoring the early Prospero Colonna and the revolutionary hero of Genazzano, Bartalotta. The huge city portals, draped in banners, swing open, and horsemen in medieval costume gallop through, trying to grab a hanging ring with a stick. TV cameras whir. Italians do love their *festas*.

The Left-Wing Fashionista

After a Sunday lunch, we pick up Athos and snake our way to the top of the town to park near the Colonna castle. We amble down the street to wait for Athos' sister-in-law Maria, who wants to show me her house. She arrives (from a funeral) in a chic yellow redingote with flying tails over a tight black dress and jaunty scarf. She's an haute couture seamstress-designer, so I feel properly disheveled in khakis and jeans shirt and huraches—just another sloppy American tourist.

Maria shows me around what is truly a museum from the tenth century: little lighted shelves illuminating intact artifacts from Roman, Phoenician, and Etruscan tombs; silver services and candelabra from the royal families. Great carved beds, chests, and chairs. Windows of scalloped stone, red marble floors taken from the San Pio monastery. Ceilings of ornately carved squares. We peer into a small study where one of the popes worked (he also lived here). Out of the window, a mountain looms in our faces, just across the deep canyon beneath the precipice that edges the town. Maria offers us Campari in delicate flutes and fine chocolates wrapped in gold in a gold filigree basket.

A lively political/social discussion ensues. Maria is vehemently *sinistra* (leftist) and hates the newly elected right-wing president, billionaire Silvio Berlusconi. Perhaps because of this, she's recently estranged from her rightist husband. Two of her three daughters breeze in, both movie star-pretty with curly long hair. Both wear skin-tight black pants and tight tops with deep décolletage—modish like their mother. We make our exit and climb back down some one hundred worn stone steps to Maria's gate.

More Glimpses of Local Values and Mores

Another evening we're invited to dinner at the home of Athos' daughter. Katia has married well and lives in an elegant new suburb. We enjoy aperitifs in the garden, lush with huge roses and masses of daisies, flowering vines, and *lawn* (mowed grass in Italy is rare). Giuseppina is already here, helping with the Lucullan feast coming up.

Athos Ricci (left), Bel's research partner in communist Genazzano

There's a lively discussion around responsibility for household chores in America vis-à-vis Italy. Katia's husband Gian Marco has never participated in kitchen or housework, but is a devoted husband and father. He gets up at 6 a.m. and drives to Rome at 100 mph in his Alfa Romeo; he's an engineer and also designed and built their fairly opulent house. Then we watch a video that Athos has brought: one of his theatrical philosophical discourses in the main piazza where he's surrounded by an enthusiastic crowd and accompanied by classical music.

There are notes of levity at dinner. Athos has arrived in his princely, long raincoat and doesn't remove it in the house. When we're ready to sit down at the formal table, Gian Marco firmly pulls off the coat to hang up. Athos is left in his ragged old sweater. At one point, we're talking about modern appliances and Athos states, rather proudly, "I am without electric typewriter, without computer, without car—without money." Katia's attractive seventeen-year-old daughter, also at the table, tells us that she plans to enter law school and has never used a computer. In fact, she writes all her papers in longhand. An entertaining family!

By the week's end, Bel has talked non-stop for twelve hours or more every day, always in Italian. He has interviewed some fifteen people with Athos, including idealistic communists from another era; those of the political Right who applauded the recent landslide election of Berlusconi; Genazzano's first woman mayor, a leftist; a local "historian" who owns three bars in town; the now elderly intellectual/philosopher we met in 1973, obsessed with proving that UFOs exist.

Especially telling are discussions with a number of single young people in their twenties and thirties. Sitting around a crackling fire pit one night after pasta and wine at a former aristocrat's run-down country estate, a group of these young people are vociferous in declaring that they have no interest in politics. Some have never voted. They're fed up with the mess of the leftist parties and muddled rule. "If Berlusconi can deliver even some of what he's promised—to eradicate crime and corruption and other ills—this will be an improvement and he deserves a chance," says one.

These young folks are more interested in hang gliding in the nearby mountains, but their deeper yearnings and values begin to come out when they all emphasize that though they work in Rome (in sales or business and relying heavily on their computers), what's really important to them, for their sanity, is keeping a home base in Genazzano—owning a bit of land in the countryside.

A Blacksmith Symphony

We say goodbye to Athos and are off to the north. Slicing through the Monti Sabini with gorges and white cliffs, we touch into favorite craft towns like Deruta and Gubbio. Our destination is Montone in Umbria, the tiny gem of a village we happened upon two years ago while staying at Fonte Vecchia. There is a room reserved for us just outside Montone that opens onto a panorama of patchwork fields—gold, green, and brown, marked off by hedgerows of dark green trees.

Parking near the wall at the top of the town, we hike down steps—one of several narrow "streets" that are spokes converging in the little central piazza. Everyone walks, so it's blessedly quiet. We stop in the abbey museum with 11th century paintings, sculptures, frescoes, and tapestries, admiring again this nearly vertical, spotless village with streets swept clean. An old lady invites us into her house to chat.

For several days, Bel reads on the ramparts while I draw the old buildings and arches. We discover that this is a week celebrating the art of blacksmithing, and we're in time for a demonstration of the Grande Fabrici Forgiatori, an extensive open-air display of iron craftsmanship brought from forges all over Italy. The pieces range from small, utilitarian implements to giant pieces of abstract art. While sketching near the top of the town one late afternoon, I begin to hear music in the piazza. Packing up, I trot down to find the tiny square filling with a stylishly dressed crowd. A concert is underway.

A black-suited maestro is conducting an all-brass orchestra, and a women's chorus emerges periodically on a balcony hung over the piazza to sing lovely baroque pieces. Two trumpeters blast from another balcony, and a virtuoso violinist solos from yet another. In the center is an amazing timpanist who, symbolic of the occasion, attacks a great iron kettle with an iron hammer. Off and on, he whacks brass chimes with red glass mallets.

Most remarkable is an instrument that requires three people: a woman marches in with what looks like a hollow rod twenty feet high, held vertically. It attaches to a device at the bottom that a man blows into while a third man pours water into it, which dribbles over the woman's shoes. The sound is something like a very deep and loud Australian didgeridoo. At the end, a balloon pops.

Later, there are two trumpeters playing from the bell tower that chimes every quarter hour. Most of the music is not familiar. Some is heraldic, and the chorus is medieval in tonality, but much of the program is very avant garde. I expect it may have been composed for the occasion.

Venice: Water, Water Everywhere

Next we head west to Lucca, with its Roman wall and reminders of Puccini everywhere (it's his hometown); then a quick round of museums and parks in Florence after a nail biter rushing to return our car before the clock runs out. It's a relief not to have to figure out the highways and mazes of city streets any more. For a change, someone else can be in charge, and we climb gratefully onto the crowded train to Venice for the trip finale.

The railroad station opens directly onto a Venice wharf so that we can conveniently board a *vaporetto*—a waterbus to take us into the city. From there, it's a sweaty marathon of dragging our bags through alleys and over little humpbacked bridges that span the labyrinthian system of canals. Settling into a cramped, second-floor room in the Locanda Fiorita, we set out to explore what appears to be a chaotic tangle of passageways.

Clutching our city map, it becomes a game to find a destination, hiking through myriad lanes and over canals, with red-cushioned gondolas gliding past. The twists and tunnels and dead ends are so numerous that we give up being rational and just drift in a general direction and hope we arrive eventually. But it's utterly enchanting—houses of every color with red geraniums in window boxes, water lapping. There's an aspect of grandeur, and the constantly moving water creates a sense of drama, from the smaller canals splashing against the canyon walls of tall buildings to the great oceanic expanses of the Grand Canal.

There are days to hunt carnival masks and Murano glass beads near the Rialto Bridge (so that I may replace some of my stolen jewelry). Vivaldi and Pachelbel and Albinoni are performed by musicians in full eighteenth century dress and wigs. We come across a fight on the Accademia Bridge—a man and woman shoving each other and shouting, apparently a gambling dispute. Everything is moved by water: people, produce, merchandise, construction materials, police and fire control brigades.

Shades of The Titanic

For our last night, we plan a celebration in the great San Marco piazza. It starts to sprinkle, so we grab jackets and an umbrella. There is indeed the legendary magic, but not exactly what we'd pictured. The water table in Venice is precisely at sea level, so that even this gentle rain has flooded the square. Half of San Marco is under three inches of water. All the major restaurants with tables outside have shut down, and there's limited seating under the covered arcade circling the huge piazza. Competing orchestras on opposite sides play bravely on.

As the rain pours down more insistently, I shiver at an eerie sort of déjà vu and turn to Bel: "The gypsy violins remind me of what it might have been like during the last moments before the Titanic went down—the musicians continuing to fiddle in the face of the inevitable deluge." Everything glistens under the many street lamps. Tall, well-groomed women sweep past, along with tourists in parkas and sneakers and backpacks. Young lovers embrace or dance to dreamy waltzes. Sweet-faced young Indian boys stop couples to offer long-stemmed roses.

Bel and I recall our brief few hours in Venice forty-seven years ago, on our way back to Naples from our Middle East trip—the place where we more or less realized we were going to marry. There was never a formal proposal; after traveling together for a month it had simply become clear that we were ready to commit to sharing adventures for the rest of our lives. Taking shelter under the vaulted colonnade, we savor the historic and romantic significance of this return journey. But the rain in stronger now, and we realize it's not going to let up. We step out and begin the squishy trek back to our room.

A canal in Venice

After a couple of plane changes, we relax for the final homebound flight. I find, though, that the adventure is not quite over. Blissfully I drift off to sleep for a couple of hours, then wake for a trip to the rest room, only to have Bel whisper tersely: "I wouldn't do that—they're about to take over the plane!" I gulp and go down the aisle anyway. I figure that if shortly we're going to be in the clutches of terrorists, I'd better make that trip.

When I return Bel explains, sotto voce, that the fierce-looking guy across the aisle from us, with his leg in a cast with many metal buckles (to fool the metal detectors?), has been signaling five other Middle Eastern men ever since we took off from Milan. All of them are circling the cabin and communicating continually. Periodically they huddle to confer. Bel hasn't slept at all.

I concentrate on positive thoughts, and shortly we land uneventfully in New York. There's no sign of our man at the baggage claim; he and his friends have vanished. Feeling a little foolish, Bel calls the FBI anyway. An agent listens to his story, but we never hear anything further. Was it simply our paranoia, a jittery, unconscious buying into racial stereotyping? Interesting that this was three months *before* 9/11.

The Seine in Paris

French Impressions
Down the Rhône River

October-November 2002

Backstory

Bel and I had managed to get this far in our years of overseas jaunts without succumbing to either guided tours or cruises. Those were for the timid, the infirm, or people needing popular entertainment. We didn't figure we fit into any of those categories.

In a weak moment, though, we decided to take a break from heaving heavy bags and being responsible for every move on a trip. We were curious and wanted to experiment, especially after our last time in Italy with a few nightmarish rides through gridlocked cities in a rented car. There was a trip offering a week on a small cruise boat floating down the Rhône River in France. There would be three days first in Paris, and we'd wind up with another three days on the Côte d'Azure in Nice. We bit.

To Paris and Giverny

Liliane, one of the directors, meets us in New York and divides up the 108 travelers into three manageable groups. In her mid-fifties, Liliane is a sophisticated Israeli who has also lived in the United States and France. She entertains us continually with a wry, dark sense of humor. She describes a very good time dancing with King Hussein of Jordan (short and shy) when she was twenty, when he knew that her father was a Mossad agent tracking down Adolf Eichmann.

We arrive in Paris in the same warm, golden, autumn haze that Bel and I remember from long ago, in the early 1950s. We leave the group to wander past the familiar bookstalls along the Seine, then head to the Musée D'Orsay, where our favorite impressionist paintings are housed. Standing next to us in line is a voluble Anglican priest from England who holds forth loudly, "I want you to know that I'm much more ritualistic than even the local English Catholics. I'm absolutely opposed to women priests. After all, Christ was a *man* who administered the Eucharist, and it would be entirely too unseemly and jarring to see a woman in this role!" He's come to Paris because it's only about $40 on an intra-European flight.

For hours, we're captivated by the paintings we once saw at the Jeu de Paume, the gallery that originally showcased the greatest impressionist paintings (later moved to the D'Orsay). The Jeu de Paume was renovated and reopened in 1986 as the foremost collection of contemporary art in Paris. The D'Orsay is deeply satisfying, especially for me, a newly resurrected painter looking closely at how these artists piled on their pigment. Then it's a hike to our distant hotel, past the old buildings, many with a dozen little pots in one chimney, each pot signifying a different fireplace in the home. Like teeth in a comb, they recall the time when everyone relied on coal fires for heat. One truly modern Parisian image: a young girl whizzing past on a skateboard, talking furiously into a cell phone as she dodges in and out of traffic. We notice that students from the Sorbonne are still trysting in the Luxembourg Gardens, but now they all have backpacks slung on their backs.

A day at Giverny! Our special guide for the day is Ghillene. On the bus ride from Paris, she proves to be an encyclopedia of information, reeling off intimate details about Claude Monet's life, work, struggles, and complicated (maybe scandalous) family relationships. How he decided to move to this rural village in upper Normandy in 1883 after he spotted it from a train. We hear how he and fellow painters attempted to see and paint light and color rather than meticulous detail—revolutionary thinking in the art world then.

We're spinning through deep fog, and when we arrive, the little stream, the famed lily pond, and bright green Japanese bridges, all of which he created, are overhung with mist. We're looking at the same water world where he painted hundreds of pictures to capture the surface of the water, what grew beneath it, the growth around it, and what was reflected in it. Then on to his beloved

Monet's lily pond at Giverny

garden, as much a passion as his art, now lush with dahlias, roses, cosmos, and cropped balls of lavender—all organized with the colors just as he laid them on his palette. The large country house is exactly as he prescribed: the dining room walls, woodwork, and furniture are painted bright yellows, the white kitchen accented with blue Delft tiles and hung with rows of shining copper pots. Every wall is crammed with hundreds of fine Japanese prints—first discovered when his wife Alice came from the market with vegetables wrapped in one. There's the lumpy little bed where he died, with Alice glaring sternly down above it.

On the way back to Paris, I pump Liliane about her background. She has just returned from a month on an Israeli kibbutz where she was shepherding a group of Africans. She says no one in Israel worries about suicide bombers. They're too busy living and working. The cafés are full. She lived there through the Gulf War ten years ago and isn't concerned about Israel's survival with any new Iraqi threats. In fact, as a recent widow, she's just bought a house at the Israeli seaside.

Leaving Paris the next day, our bus rolls south. There's a walking tour through Dijon, mustard capital of the world, lovely with half-timbered buildings, ornate grillwork on the balconies, multicolored roof tiles in intricate geometric designs, and soaring turrets on the gothic cathedral with seventy-two devilish gargoyles.

Our Floating Hotel: Wine, Pickets, and Tummy Bug

At Chalon-sur-Saône (where the demarcation line was drawn between Free and Occupied France during World War II), we pull up to our ship, the *Debussy*—our home on the Rhône River for the next six days. It's sleek and spiffy; our cabin resembles a luxury hotel room in miniature.

Every day we disembark to explore important winemaking operations. At Nuits S. George, vine roots go down fifteen meters, picking up moisture naturally. Irrigation is not allowed; it has to be a natural process, with the soil condition determining the correct wetness. Wine quality depends on soil and microclimate, which are excellent here. The best growth (*Gran Cru)* is usually found higher up on the plain. At Château du Clos Vougeot, one of the superb winemaking houses, we stroll under great vaulted ceilings. Its giant presses operated with a screw twelve feet high that the monks had to hang from to apply greater pressure.

In Beaune, capital of the Burgundy wine trade, the centerpiece of the city is Hôtel-Dieu, the imposing Gothic masterpiece erected by a philanthropist in 1443 as a hospital for the poor. The patient ward has thirty-foot ceilings "so germs had air to disperse in." Red velvet curtains surround each truncated bed—short because the patients sat up (two or three to a bed). If they were lying down, it meant they had died.

Steaming southward again, the surrounding terrain is progressively hillier. Leaning over the bow at the first of fifteen locks, we watch the water drop thirty feet. During the trip, we pass under some two hundred bridges, most of them so low we must crouch or even lie flat on the deck. There's a shout "Low bridge!" and everybody ducks.

At Lyon, we come to the confluence of the Saône and the Rhône rivers and dock for a walking tour. A crowd of feisty picketers thrusts signs in our direction telling the United States to keep out of Iraq: "No U.S. war!" Our guide nervously hustles us away. All along, we've seen graffiti with similar messages but have had no direct confrontations. Tourism is bread and butter here.

There are more side excursions, one I take alone on a single-gauge steam train up into the Ardèche, "Deep France" (meaning a remote, little-traveled area of the country where the culture is more authentic), with deep gorges, ancient aquaducts, and prehistoric caves (where munitions were stashed in the war). I go solo because Bel is depleted from a bad night of upchucking. We learn that a third of the passengers have come down with this virulent and very contagious stomach bug.

One evening at dusk, we dock at Viviers, one of the high points of the trip for me. After dinner, we stroll through this tiny, mysterious, fifth-century town. We enter through a magical tunnel of plane trees (cousin of our sycamore), many of them a hundred years old with trunks more than a yard across. We scuff through huge leaves drifting down onto bumpy cobbles. The village is lit by yellow lamps, which illuminate the skinny, four-story, sixteenth century houses. Some of the dwellings are built into the towering rock itself that looms two hundred feet high. All the shutters are closed tight. We see no sign of life.

I'm reading *Charlotte Gray* by Sebastian Faulks, and find that there are several concurrent realities blurring pleasantly into each other for me: the fact that we're floating down the Rhône River with Cezanne-like scenes rolling past, which are also the landscapes of the painter Sisley (whose superb exhibit we've just seen in Lyon). We also found there the Café Lion D'Or that Sisley painted and that Faulks mentions; and then Faulks' references to the encroaching dangers of the Germans suddenly entering Free France in the *Massif Central* that we've just been through, along with descriptions of little village streets exactly like those we explore each day. Perfect!

Now it's my turn to be hit by the rampant stomach bug, and it's also our last night on the *Debussy*. I have a rocky time trying to hold it together on the all-day bus ride next morning, and when we arrive in Aix-en-Provence in the heart of Provence, I crouch weakly on a park bench while others go for lunch and to explore the graceful, tree-shaded boulevard.

Preserves of the Rich and Famous: Nice, Monaco, Monte Carlo

Finally, we're off again and entering the Côte d'Azur. The soil has turned pinkish ochre, and umbrella pines abound. Past neat rows of grapes and olives into Nice, which we glimpse from a ridge that looks down on the blue Mediterranean.

I'm healed, and we're ready to launch out in Nice—to the astonishing flower market, with acres of stunning blooms, plants, trees, vegetables, herbs, fruits, and preserves. There's lavender in every form, a major crop. We dodge the flow of in-line skaters, bikes, scooters, and joggers on the promenade circling the Bay of Angels and munch sandwiches on the beach. Then it's on with the group to discover an exquisite Russian Orthodox church, Matisse's house, the Chagall museum, and numerous palaces. On top of Mt. Boron is Elton John's yellow villa (with helicopter pad).

Our bus skirts the shore, and Liliane points out the estates that have been summer addresses for Somerset Maugham, Winston Churchill, Bill Gates, David Niven, Greta Garbo, and Tina Turner. Approaching the Principality of Monaco, we note the little road snaking high above us where Princess Grace plunged to her death. We're told that in order to live in Monaco (just one-and-a-half square miles), which many would love to do to avoid taxes, you have to be at least fourth generation and obscenely rich.

To reach the town, we mount two escalators, then march through a rock cave to elevators, then ascend further with more escalators. Tramping past the Cousteau Oceanographic museum with Jacques's ten-foot-long yellow submarine, made famous by the Beatles, we come upon the Cathedral of Monaco, a soaring white vision with Romanesque arches. Inside, an organ thunders dramatically (somehow a mad Boris Karloff comes to mind). This is where Grace was married. She is buried beneath the stone floor, her grave the only one with perpetually fresh flowers. Hiking on, we reach the royal Grimaldi palace just as the guard is changing, preceded by flourishes of trumpets and drums. Eating our lunch on a bench under a window, we wonder whether Prince Rainier might be peeking out from behind one of the closed lace curtains. Does he ever get a chance to stroll privately in his own gardens, lush with bougainvillea and acacia?

Last stop: Monte Carlo, a bit further east. Again we must park below and take elevators to the top of the cliff, coming out onto the square with the Grand Casino. This is also the home of the opera and ballet. We poke our noses into a couple of the casinos. The focus in Monte Carlo, not nearly as lovely as Monaco, is clearly on gambling and very conspicuous consumption. The best hotel suites go for $17,000 a night. It's a show just watching the fancy cars wheeling in and out—rows of Mercedes, extreme sports cars, the odd Bentley, and the new little Smart Cars. We watch a wave of hang gliders step nonchalantly into the air from one cliff and float idly above the sea.

Reflections

So what's our verdict on cruises? We found that virtually all our fellow passengers (a hundred of us) were indefatigable travelers, taking these trips several times a year. We wonder whether it's curiosity or fear of emptiness? Most were more or less retired, some not. Some were obviously well-to-do, while others saved their money from precarious, low-paying jobs (truck driving, maintenance) because this was important.

What we found most irritating, and even embarrassing, was to find ourselves in front of some attraction (Notre Dame in Paris, for example), struggling to keep track of our guide's blue flag as our group of thirty-two was jostled by a large contingent of Japanese nearby. Herded like sheep. Every time we broke away to wander on our own, or retreated to the solitude of our snug cabin to watch the French landscape sweep by silently, we felt "reconstituted," or pleasantly cut loose.

A further hazard was being trapped in close quarters with a large group, especially on a ship, where germs multiply and spread inexorably. On the other hand, for a change, it was rather nice to be completely taken care of—tickets and travel handled, luggage collected and delivered wherever we went, superb meals that we didn't have to scare up on our own, and ample cultural information and sights offered.

Nevertheless, I'd think carefully about doing this again. We've discovered that we're pretty independent mavericks, and even as the years catch up with us, we still relish making our own discoveries—and missteps.

Climbing down the Imbrose Gorge in Crete

Above Anopoli in Crete

A Greek Odyssey
Celebrating Our Fiftieth Anniversary with the Paulson Clan

May 2004

Backstory

Bel and I figured that arriving at this impressive milestone called for gathering as much of the family as possible and launching off all together for an extra-special adventure. Angelynn suggested Crete, and we all happily acquiesced. Included will be Eric, Angelynn, Lark and her then-husband Brannon, Steve, Anne, Katie, and Nicky. Niko can't make it at the last minute because of work obligations.

First Stop: Athens

Luckily, because it's 5:00 a.m. in Athens, we'd arranged for transfer help, and a couple of cheerful reps from a tour company are at the airport to meet us. Loading our sixteen pieces of luggage onto a bus, we whiz through the pre-dawn city, taking in modern and ancient buildings and the partially finished arches of the Olympic stadium (which our escorts assure us will be done for the summer Olympic games, with workers toiling through the night). We get out several blocks from our hotel and grab our bags for a final trundle through cobbled pedestrian streets. Katie and Nicky skip along pulling their own suitcases—surprisingly peppy despite two nights with almost no sleep because of canceled and missed flights.

Lark and Brannon (in their early twenties—ah, youth!) opt to hike directly to the Acropolis for the sunrise, but the rest of us snatch a couple of hours in bed.

The families split up to go off in the morning at our own pace. We climb the hill under the shadow of the Parthenon, a steady breeze keeping us refreshed under clear skies. Soon the familiar proud columns are looming above us, soaring (along with a giant building crane) against cobalt blue. As we get closer, we see that half the building has disappeared, and desperate measures are being taken to brace and preserve what's left. There are rock heaps—bits of carved lintels and capitals and grooved columns. Some may be used to shore up the edifice, being damaged now even more swiftly than usual by heavy pollution. Archeologists are raking and sifting in the lower areas, and construction workers are perched on high scaffolding.

Crete

Next morning it's an hour by jet-prop plane to Chania, one of the three main cities on the island of Crete. Angelynn has researched and booked us for a week into three little cottages on the Akrotiri Peninsula—"Alma's Villas." Alma's husband and daughter Peggy are at the airport to welcome us.

While waiting to sort out the rental of three cars, I ask Peggy about her opinion of the United States/Iraq situation (Bush's war is just a year old). She's emphatic in her opinion: "Because we experienced so much horrific bloodshed in World War II—at least one entire village was massacred by the Germans in reprisal—and for centuries before that, all we Cretans want now is *peace—no one* carrying arms." She's wrathful about W's bellicose administration, but doesn't lump us or ordinary Americans into that camp.

"But I have to say that much as I hate the US military encroaching on my island," she says, "there is NATO and a big US naval base on the southeast end of Akrotiri—which may be all that keeps the Turks from sweeping in to take over." Peggy, herself in her thirties, dreams of attending flight school in Florida to become a pilot. Her family built their cluster of small villas three years ago, and they also own clothing stores in Chania. They're very worried that the tourist business in Greece may be permanently depressed as a result of 9/11. People are incredulous that even with the Olympic games fast approaching, there has been no upturn in vacation bookings in Crete. We see everywhere half-finished construction, apparently abandoned.

Alma's Villas sit alone on the side of a hill covered thickly with flowering scrub bushes and endless varieties of aromatic herbs in clumps and tufts. It reminds Bel and me of Sardinia. Straight down from our pool is a serious gorge that clefts the hill to the sea, all spread out grandly below us.

With several cars, we can go off to explore in shifting groups. There's a temple of Artemis discovered, the spot where *Zorba the Greek* was filmed, beaches of tiny white shells, caves in the sides of a saw-toothed grey mountain, Minoan excavations in progress in the heart of Chania. Chania is considered the spiritual capital of Crete. In 1645, it fell from the Venetians to the Turks after a terrible siege. In the nineteenth century, Crete struggled for independence until, in 1913, it finally united with Greece. Chania fiercely resisted the Germans in World War II, when much of the city was destroyed. It was the site of a massive German parachute drop early in the war.

A Canyon Hike and an Ascent into the Stratosphere

The most ambitious day of the trip is hiking the Imbrose Gorge. All but Anne, Katie, and Nicky are off early, heading south. We zoom through mountain villages, tiny and charming, with enormous roses in the gardens. The roads are lined solid with pink oleanders and yellow broom, and often we must stop for masses of sheep blocking our way. As we proceed, the peaks are higher and more barren and majestic. These are the White Mountains, the Lefka Ori, which dominate all the views in the western part of the island. Some are snow-capped, soaring to eight thousand feet. At the top of the gorge, Eric and Steve, our two drivers, drop the rest of us to wait while they take the cars to the bottom so we'll have them at the end of the hike, eventually reappearing in a cab.

The sun flirts with a few dark clouds, but mostly it's bright with fresh mountain air, perfect for hiking. We set off down a path filled with jagged stones and must circumnavigate monstrous boulders. Gradually the pale limestone canyon sides grow taller, and at one point are just two meters wide. Black goats are lying around or nimbly scaling impossible ledges. There are masses of poppies and daisies. A few other hikers hurry past us—mostly Germans—and a few are panting their way *up* the gorge. We're glad to be going downhill.

Continuing down the mountain, three hours later we arrive at Chora Sfakion on the south coast. We find this village, with its small harbor on the Libyan Sea, packed with climbers. By now we're definitely primed for a fine seafood lunch: stuffed tomatoes and eggplant, squid, and various kinds of fish. We toss bread to hungry schools of fish swimming just below our table.

Then it's off to Anopolis, an extremely harrowing twenty-five-minute drive up and up around hairpin turns where there are no guardrails between us and sheer drop-offs hundreds of feet down. For a while, we're following the cliffs directly above the water. Steve, who seldom gets rattled, admits afterward that he found it pretty alarming. Further inland, it's really bleak—a moonscape with only strewn boulders. The minuscule village of Anopolis, with just a coffee house, a few farmhouses, and sheep roaming, is so quiet we hesitate to speak out loud. The epitome, though, is a short, nerve-wracking drive even further up on a dirt track so narrow a single car barely fits. We scramble the last bit to the summit on foot to a tiny, well-kept Orthodox chapel. It holds six chairs. A ruined church overlooks the great sweep of sea and the layers of switchbacks snaking up.

Twelve hours later, after ice cream and a caffeine fix on the road north, we're back home.

There are more excursions—to the isolated Gouvernétou monastery where we hike down to Arkouda Cave, an important Minoan shrine where

Steve and Nicky hike at Gouvernétou Monastery

Eric turns on his headlamp to spot fat stalactites and stalagmites and a dank baptismal pool. Anne is in heaven with the landscape—the stony path leading down a cleft through colorful wildflowers to the Katholiko monastery, the oldest in Crete, built directly into the rock. Eric continues further to the glittering sea to swim off the boulders.

Another day Bel and I join Angelynn and Eric to find Lissos on the south coast. A little motorboat takes us to a remote peninsula to wander among Dorian ruins—caves and tombs galore, an amphitheatre, a third-century BCE temple of healing beside a curative spring.

Gods and the Minotaur in Knossós

Time to leave our little villas and head east to Iraklion, the island's capital, the fifth largest city in Greece. As in most of Crete, the landscape is constantly gorgeous, with surprises around every curve of the reputedly deadly west-east coastal highway.

About two-thirds of the way across (some 150 kilometers total), the desert scrub and terraced olives give way to evergreen spires. Patches of snow streak down from the higher peaks. From our perch on the winding heights, there are periodic glimpses of shining seas. We find the Cretans' habit of using the right shoulder as a driving lane a bit unnerving, and if they want to pass, they insistently push us over onto that non-lane.

Then commences a hair-raising hunt in Iraklion for our hotel. There are numerous false turns on streets so skinny and congested we have to fold in our side mirrors. At one point, the three cars are separated and hopelessly lost, but eventually everyone finds the hotel. We notify the car company to come pick up the vehicles. It can hardly be fast enough!

After a spin through the Archeological Museum, with twenty rooms of artifacts from digs all over Crete, from 6,000 BCE Bronze Age relics up to Roman-era statues and sarcophagi in 300 AD, we're primed for the real thing. We hop a bus for legendary Knossós.

For hours, we wander the impressive ruins, discovered and excavated by Sir Arthur Evans in the early twentieth century. The hill was thought to be originally a Neolithic settlement. Then in Minoan (Bronze Age) times, from 3,000 to 1,100 BCE, with its palace complex of over a thousand rooms, it was the nucleus of a town. Later it became part of the city-state of Knossós (2,000 to 1,700 BCE), perhaps serving as a place of worship dedicated to Zeus's mother, the Goddess Rhea.

The myths we all grew up with come to life here and blur with reality. Legend and history become delightfully tangled: King Minos was supposedly the son of Zeus (born and raised in Crete) and Europa, a Phoenician nymph. Also, the labyrinth that Minos supposedly constructed to imprison the Minotaur—a creature half man and half bull—morphed into the intricate maze of palace buildings. The story goes that Theseus, one of the Athenian "bull leaper" youths decreed by Minos to be sent periodically to Crete to be fed to the Minotaur as a blood sacrifice, was helped by Minos' daughter Ariadne to enter the labyrinth and kill the Minotaur and find his way out. Daedalus built the labyrinth, then was imprisoned there and escaped with his son Ikarus with wings he built for them with feathers and wax. Despite warnings, Ikarus flew too near the sun, the wax melted, and he fell into the sea.

We find buildings and walls of great stone blocks, and rocks of striated marble. Ingenious skylights at once let in air and light. Often the lowest floors (some buildings were five stories deep) were the choice dwellings because they stayed cooler in summer and warmer in winter. Clay jars ten feet tall, used to store oil and grain, are still scattered about.

We all explore at our own pace, from time to time bumping into each other. At one point, Anne gathers Katie and Nicky under a shady tree to reread to them the story of Theseus.

Ghosts of Atlantis

Next morning we scramble to assemble three cabs and rumble down to the port to board a hydrofoil. There will be a final three days on the nearby island of Santorini, an over-the-top, flamboyant fantasy of domes, curves, and arches. Each of its tiny towns, with dazzling white buildings trimmed in harsh, purplish blue, is cantilevered out from the sides of the cliffs. In counterpoint, there is always the black specter of a live volcano perched just out in the bay.

Some of us pursue the artisan shops or photo ops with electrifying views from every twist of the steep little streets of Fira and Oia. With Eric and Angelynn, Bel and I seek out the wilder parts of the island, hiking around red volcanic boulders, admiring bushes of purple oregano, herbs, and what look like giant buttercups clinging to precipitous slopes. We lunch on a tiny balcony from which we look directly onto islanders on the next layer down playing in their pools or hanging out laundry. At the bottom of the cliff, people are swimming off the rocks at the "naturist" beach.

Lark and Brannon sail out on a small schooner to swim in warm, thermal waters and to hike around the volcano island. They report seeing smoke in the crater and learn that molten lava starts two kilometers below the surface and goes down another two. Even twelve inches beneath the surface, it would be too hot to touch. The volcano last blew in 1,450 BCE. Some believe that Santorini is where "the big one" erupted, which destroyed the advanced civilization of Atlantis and everything else around, including Crete. Bits have been found as far away as Greenland.

The "kids" have organized a celebratory lunch for Bel and me at the Socrates restaurant in Fira. Angelynn pins a corsage of roses on my T-shirt. Eric and Steve read poetic reflections, each having to stop frequently to mop their eyes—as do Bel and I and others. Here's a bit of what Eric offers—ever the long-view philosopher:

> For me, there is a sense of coming back to the Mediterranean, not merely as a vacation but as a pilgrimage in honor of our beginnings within a civilization and within a family, since it was not far from here that Mãe and Pai [the boys' Portuguese names for us, adopted in Brazil] truly met, planting a tree of which, in one form or another, all of us here today are fruit. And it is a part of the world where I have had a lingering love affair since I was very small—with its history, with what lives in the stone walls and inside the ancient olive trees. It's a sensual memory and a tactile embrace of a land and a sea that have softly whispered to me across time and experience, so that I remember at least a piece of it even as I lay stones in a garden in Wisconsin.

What comes out clearly in this moment, and indeed throughout the trip, is the great love and caring we all hold for each other—a sense of our deep connection that becomes increasingly precious. We eat splendidly and the wine flows. Little thimblefuls of ouzo end the feast.

Reflections

So finished a journey we'd envisioned and planned for over a year. I think we all agreed it was everything we had dreamed of. How it would work with such a large and varied group had been a question, but somewhat to everyone's surprise, this never became an issue. There was a graceful and effortless way in which we flowed together for some parts of the expedition, and also a tacit acknowledgement of when we needed to be alone as couples or families. Each one of all the families brought a unique contribution: his or her own distinctive viewpoint and way of seeing history, personal yearnings, and agendas that opened new vistas for the others. Personal agendas were reflected in satisfying side trips: Anne went off to bargain for exquisitely painted icons, Eric and Steve excitedly engineered the gorge hike, and Angelynn sought out any remnants of real or mythic figures of antiquity.

Bel's and my anniversary was the perfect excuse to lure the entire family off on a grand, shared adventure. Already we're dreaming of a repeat for our sixtieth.

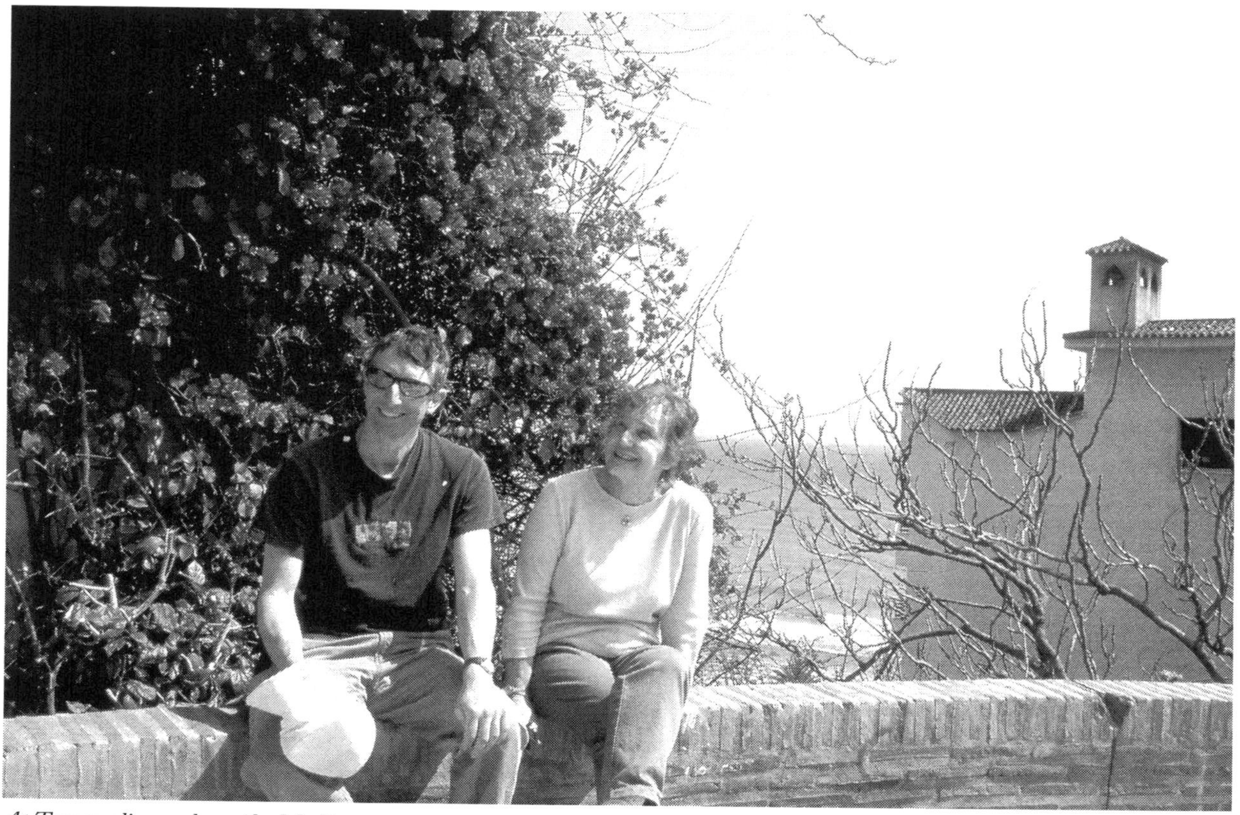

At Torremolinos, above the Mediterranean

Andalusia, Spain
Moorish Alhambra and Christian Santa Semana

MARCH 2005

Backstory

For years, Bel and I had expected to explore Spain, the only Latin area of Europe we'd missed, and we found a willing companion in Eric.

Always leery of latching onto a group trip, we nevertheless discovered an enticing package through Grand Circle that offered access to unusual experiences as well as allowing for plenty of free time. This included four days when the three of us rented a car to explore the area around the southern coast by ourselves. Eric not only didn't mind getting snarled up and lost in city traffic or navigating impossibly narrow streets and precipitous mountain roads—he always relished the challenge. This way we could feel truly independent and free to roam at our own speed and to tackle destinations too difficult or remote for the big buses.

Our Base on the Costa del Sol

The town of Torremolinos centers around vertiginous steps lined with shops that showcase fine Moroccan and Turkish, as well as Spanish, craftwork. Our hotel is directly on the beach, where we look down on the Mediterranean Sea and hear faintly crashing waves at night through open balcony doors. We can almost see Africa. Rarely (happily) are we with more than twenty others from the tour at any one time, and when we are, it's with a truly superb and lovable guide, Eduardo.

"White Villages" and a Precipitous, Foggy Wilderness

Our first solo driving destination is Ronda, important from the time of the second Punic Wars. Soon we're climbing amid sharp peaks that seem to press in, and past deep clefts and drop-offs dotted with broom and gnarly olives. We're continually surprised at the very craggy terrain all through this southern part of Spain—red rock punctuated by white limestone outcrops. After Ronda, we continue into higher country, ending up in the tiny alpine town of Grazalema, one of the famed "white villages," where all the houses are whitewashed, making each cluster a dazzling gem set against surrounding slopes of green. It's siesta time when we sit down in the plaza for ice cream, and very quiet until a few backpackers straggle in.

Keeping the car overnight, we set out the next morning to the northeast. At the top of the town of Antequera, there's a castle with massive crenellated ramparts and topiary gardens where we wander in a silence interrupted only by muttering doves. We head on to El Torcal, a wild area of curious natural limestone sculptures formed by the winds where we plan to hike. We're on a narrow road with rock towers all around but whose tops are increasingly obscured by swirling fog. Some standing stones are forty feet high.

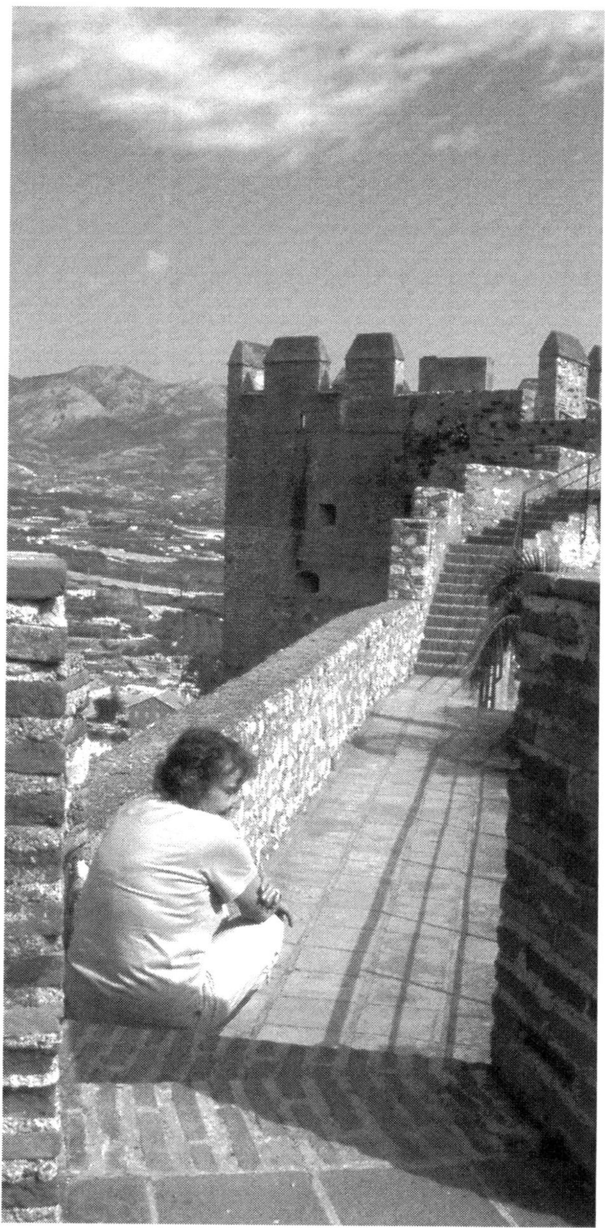

Castle at Antequera near El Torcal

We get out for photos and are nearly knocked over by icy blasts. When we reach the Torcal and accidentally land on a single track road, which climbs even higher, we're soon navigating hairpin turns and find ourselves totally and perilously blinded in dense fog. It's far too inhospitable to walk. On the return, we take a small "donkey trail," as Eric says, with grades probably prohibited in America. Coming on a farmer's car stuck in a ditch, Good Samaritans Eric and Bel hop out to help, which encourages a couple of other drivers to stop as well. Eventually a mighty group effort involving a jack and stones for leverage lifts the car back onto the road.

Alhambra, the Fairy-Tale Moorish Palace

Our first group trip is to Granada and fairy-tale Alhambra. For protection, Granada was built on three hills: one for the Moors, one for the Jews, and one for Spanish royalty. Supposedly the city goes back to about 2000 BCE and was the last stronghold and longest-running kingdom of the Muslims in Spain. Under assault by the Christians, in the thirteenth century, Ibn al-Ahmar, as Mohammed I, moved his capital to Granada and founded the Nasrid Dynasty, ruling for the next 250 years. For some seven centuries in Spain, there was a uniquely compatible and peaceful confluence of Moors, Christians, and Jews (Jews were the philosophers, doctors, diplomats, and often generals). Then Ferdinand

and Isabel sought to unite the entire country under Catholicism. In 1480, the bloody Spanish Inquisition was set up and effectively expelled or destroyed the other two groups. The Inquisition lasted until the nineteenth century.

Passing gypsy caves in the mountainsides outside Granada, we look down on the vast complex of Alhambra—built between the twelfth and fifteenth centuries. Its location was chosen because of the quantity of artesian well water pouring down off the Sierra Nevada mountains. The Alhambra is an Islamic city in miniature, the culmination of a vision of Arabic imagination and artistry that brings to mind *One Thousand and One Nights*, often referred to as "tales of the Arabian Nights." We stroll past the Renaissance palace of Christian Carlos I, then into the Palace of the Nasrids, an unfolding series of splendid rooms, catwalks, balconies, and courtyards, all interwoven with abundantly flowing water. Tiny canals run indoors and out.

The intricacy of detail is astonishing: delicately carved wood ceilings, lacy, deeply honeycombed reliefs chiseled in plaster walls. Complex arabesques are repeated everywhere—on slender Arab columns and archways dripping with ornamentation. Floors are inlaid with tiles and river stones or parquet bricks. "This was meant to signify Plato's idea of Paradise," our local guide tells us. Outside, past reflecting pools and fountains, in the complex Generalife Gardens, we see where oleander, wisteria, magnolias, and roses will soon burst into bloom as rich accents against sculptured topiary "rooms" and arches.

Christian Solemnity: Holy Week in Málaga

The highlight of the entire trip for me is the night we attend the Holy Week (Santa Semana) processions. Eduardo leads a small contingent of us up the steps to the top of Torremolinos where we catch a jammed train to Málaga, a half-hour away. (Málaga is the birthplace of Picasso.) Disembarking, we hurry to the major Avenida Alameda and maneuver our way to good viewing positions. Forty-one processions are mounted by competing "brotherhoods," or neighborhood parishes. Each brotherhood enters two floats, the first one with a giant Jesus, the second with the Virgin Mary. They work the whole year to update and burnish their displays, paying attention to the tiniest details, such as the angle of a handkerchief. Some neighborhoods have devoted themselves to their processions for three hundred years.

We hang out long enough to see four floats pass. The processions begin at 5 p.m. and go to 6 a.m., from Monday through Good Friday. The marching in Málaga is very slow and deliberate. Each neighborhood takes about seven hours to walk its float from its local church along the route and back to home base.

First comes a vast number of marchers, all with green velvet Ku Klux Klan-style hoods covering their faces, with eye holes and pointed, yard-high hats. They wear black robes and white gloves and carry thick, four-foot tapers. Children in the throng run out continually to catch the falling wax from the candles to pack into huge balls. Led by a solemn drumbeat (dum dum, da-da-dum dum dum), the marchers are all walking slowly in synchronized step. Young boys come next, swinging censers and sending a huge fog of incense rolling over the immense crowds and up into hazy streetlights and treetops. On their heels the marching band appears, its dirge lugubrious, grieving—multiple drummers and a screeching, wailing brass ensemble.

Finally the first Jesus float appears, and when it passes in front of us—regardless of personal beliefs—I think everyone feels a rush of emotions. It's a startlingly powerful moment. The float blazes with the light of hundreds of candles and is carried by close rows of maybe fifty perspiring men in black, wearing white gloves and shouldering heavy metal poles. We estimate that each man must be carrying maybe fifty pounds. Eduardo tells us that some floats are a hundred feet long, needing two hundred men each to carry them. Next comes Mary's float, always grander and more spectacular than the Jesus ones. Gilded details shimmer gold in the candlelight. The twenty-five foot train of Mary's cape is made entirely of solidly packed blue flowers.

Another procession is waiting to enter the avenue on our other side. It begins with small children in white robes—some as young as three—then horses and riders in sixteenth century red uniforms, with matador hats and cascading plumes, swords and hammers strung on their saddles. We speculate that these are policemen. Eventually the two floats appear and pass. Two hours later we're exhausted. Our little group hops across the marchers' path to catch a late train back to Torremolinos. "While the float bearers in Málaga walk in full view," explains Eduardo, "in other cities they must crouch, hunched, under a curtain around the float, with only their feet visible." It must be killing—a real penance, which is perhaps a major point of the entire exercise.

Spanish Sherry and Olives, Brave Bulls, and Lunch with a Family

There are other excursions. In Jerez, we go to see the González Byass winery—second biggest in the world—famous for its sherry; to see the renowned dressage spectacle where riders in elegant period costume "dance" their horses; and to see the "brave bulls" grazing in fields (those larger black bulls with horns thrust forward, which may be chosen for contests in the ring). *Ferdinand*, from my childhood bookshelf, comes to mind.

Another day our bus barrels through terraces of olive culture. Eduardo tells us that olives were brought to Spain twenty-seven centuries ago by the Phoenicians because here was the best climate. Trees must be ten years old before they produce and only after thirty years are they fully productive. One tree can yield two to three hundred pounds of olives every two years. "Spain is the top producer of olive oil in the world," he says. "Most is shipped to Italy for packaging, so the labels you buy are always Italian." He adds that eight pounds of olives are needed for one liter of oil. The best olives are hand-picked, but now trees are mostly shaken, often mechanically, and olives fall onto plastic sheets.

We pass little enclaves of black pigs and learn that these porkers are a cross between domestic and wild. Again, Eduardo: "These are leaner because they are allowed to free-range, and they give the best prosciutto. This is because they graze under oak trees and eat acorns for five years. The ham is cured in salt, then hung in the dry air of the mountains. You would pay 50 euros a kilo. People eat it with dry cheese and red wine. Look for the black hoofs hanging in the market."

Our destination is a small town where groups of half a dozen of us are invited into modest homes for lunch. It's pouring rain, and our hosts greet us with umbrellas. No one in our family speaks English, but we manage to communicate, more or less. The wife seats us at the table (heated beneath, lovely for my frozen toes after a soaking at an open olive oil factory), and proceeds to bring out course after course of hearty food. We could have stopped after a big plate of antipasto and a heavy garbanzo soup, but then come platters of fried zucchini and other vegetables, pork cutlets, flan, cookies, and candies. We all pass on the coffee and brandy and can barely waddle out.

Seville for the Ghost of Carmen, Catholic Gold, and Fierce Flamenco

There's one overnight trip away from our base on the sea, to Seville. On the way, passing a cemetery, Eduardo points out:

> You always see cypress trees here; the cypress has sad connotations, but also it's the tree of life, pointing to the sky. There has been a huge convulsion in the Catholic Church; finally cremation is sanctioned. In fact, recently there had to be new regulations about where ashes can be scattered when swimmers at beaches found themselves with mouthfuls of who knows who. Just in the past ten years, the birthrate has dropped drastically to 1.24. In the 1960s and 70s, there were *no* divorces; now about half of all marriages fail. But even divorced parents keep the family close, and college kids stay home until age twenty-nine (saving up for a mortgage because it's all-important to own property). At thirty, they either marry or go off to independence. There's excellent care in Spain for "third-age" folks, with hospitals and medicines covered when you're over sixty-five. Most transportation is free and there are paid holidays in special, very nice hotels where widows and widowers often meet and hook up but don't marry—a great advance for a Catholic country!

In Seville, we're hauled around to see the cigarette factory where Carmen worked and past

Triumvirate at American Square, Seville

the governor's palace, where gypsies are selling bunches of rosemary in the streets. Our local guide meets us at Santa Maria, the Cathedral with the largest square footage in the world. It took one hundred years to build, finished in 1505. Construction started as an Arab mosque, but then the Christians took over and turned it into a purely Gothic structure. Most striking is two thousand kilos of gold ornamentation in the main chapel alone—obscene when one ponders the needs, through the centuries, of the very poor.

Along with lots of Japanese groups, we crowd into a small theater and watch a polished flamenco company—four gorgeous women dancers, four male dancers, a gargantuan singer, a couple of guitarists, and two men who sing and wield castanets. In each dance they work up to a frenzy, with ferocious clapping, shouting, and stomping. (As a result, I'm inspired to work on my castanet skills to accompany very private dance efforts.) There are continual changes of gorgeous costumes—the women in tight bodices over the hips, then flounces and trains they kick out of the way. The men wear tight black pants and vests.

To the Remote Snow Fields of the Alps

Our fourth day with a rented car is for a trip the three of us have anticipated: into the high Sierra Nevada mountains. We start east along the coast, following an escarpment above the sea. The first stop is Salobreña, a tightly packed little town with a great Arab castle on top. Bel and I hold our breath as Eric navigates streets so steep and narrow we nearly scrape the walls on either side; turning around is a near impossibility.

Turning inland, we begin to climb north. Huge mountains in the distance are topped with snow. There are three little white villages hanging off bluffs, a couple of hang gliders, and almonds blossoming on the terraces around us. An hour from sea level, we're up to eight thousand feet, looking way up, almost overhead, at cars crisscrossing the hairpin curves. Our destination is Bubión, the next-to-last village before the snowfields. We hear that a few years ago the incarnation of the new Dalai Lama was discovered in Bubión—an eleven-year-old Spanish boy. Apparently he was whisked off to the Himalayas for training but then decided this wasn't the vocation for him and he returned to Spain. Bubión and other isolated mountain villages in the vicinity were the last areas where the persecuted Moors fled and hid, accounting for a still-strong Arab feel here. We pull out sandwiches to picnic on a grassy promontory, sniffing the clean, alpine air, listening to cowbells and communing with the sheep grazing around us.

Starting back, we pause several times to take pictures. Once, as we're rolling away from such a stop, we're all just about to re-buckle our seatbelts when a motorcycle cop zooms up and pulls us over. Result: $100 fine for Eric. "This is lenient," says the cop. "For Spaniards it would be considerably more. And if you were caught talking on a cell phone while driving, it would be $200." It's a slight damper at the end of a marvelous day, but probably a good lesson.

Our final day is a group excursion to Mijas, stopping en route at a brand-new Buddhist temple—soaring above the sea—dedicated just a few days before by the actor Richard Gere. Clearly there is a lot of money in Mijas, with lavish villas where a number of foreigners have settled. The streets are spotless, and there are lovely old buildings, exuberant fountains, fine shops, and a bullring. We crowd into a tiny grotto shrine—the Virgin of the Rock—devoted to Mary and her healing assistance. It's carved out of stone, and Eric turns to us: "Can you feel the vibes here? To me they're really thick compared to what we found in that pretentious Seville cathedral." We munch sugared almonds boiled in a big pot and watch the progress of pilgrims climbing to a mountainside chapel.

Reflections

I'd always thought we *should* visit Spain. After all, we've gone so many times to Italy and also France. Maybe we went to Spain as much out of guilt as curiosity, thinking we needed to be informed, more well-rounded about the Latin world we seem to have gravitated to over the past fifty-plus years.

For me, in the end, some of the things I least expected turned out to be the most endearing. Instead of a sun-soaked mass of tourists thronging the beaches along the fabled Costa del Sol (which a couple of weeks later in the season it may well become), the Spain I discovered consisted of vast expanses of craggy, chaotic landscapes, wilder, more majestic, and seemingly more untouched than I had imagined. There was that "zing" of connection I felt to something elemental and untamed that perhaps matches the fierce dignity and pride of the Spanish people, their capacity to survive thousands of years of assault and servitude and change.

In contrast to gregarious and laid-back Italians we've known who rush to expose their hearts and emotions, I found the Spanish more reserved, solemn, reflective, intense. They also seemed more vigorous and motivated—perhaps anxious to catch up with the rest of Europe? We also found a strong impulse toward sustainability—wind generators strung along mountain ridges, tiny compact cars, exhortations in public places to conserve water. Lights went out in our hotel room whenever we pulled the door key out of a wall slot.

Eric jotted down a few notes along the way:

> This afternoon's lecture on flamenco and gypsy culture in southern Spain mirrors my understanding of how the Moors (from North Africa) entered and left their mark on Andalusia. These gypsies originated in India and migrated over the last seven hundred years across the Middle East and North Africa into Spain, absorbing even Irish and Celtic idiosyncracies until now they are a blend of so many cultures that a source point or direct cultural lineage is hard to trace. I could feel this eclectic heritage expressed in a small guitar riff or an anguished facial expression.

Similarly, the Moors' occupation of Spain is a story of adaptation and inclusion. Coming to Spain as conquerors, they ended up preserving and translating a good piece of classical antiquity. They created a multilayered and diverse peace for many centuries at a time when the rest of Europe was besieged by disease and the downward spiral of feudal parochialism. For me, the Alhambra in Granada is the shining symbol of what political, philosophical, religious, and artistic harmony can create. I marveled at the impeccable workmanship and how the Arabic language merged seamlessly into the architectural details, as if words themselves could hold up walls, and columns and waterways were the punctuation of some poetic verse. It blew me away.

Drinks at the Bencistà, Fiesole

Our pool in the Garfagnana

The Tuscan Alps and Umbrian Assisi

Touching Spirit

June 2005

Backstory

Here was an adventure that divided itself neatly into two parts. Two distinct themes colored most of the innumerable excursions and discoveries. Again it was a family affair, the third time we had traveled to Italy with Steve's crew of four and Anne's parents, Ed and Susie Strainchamps. For the first part, we were joined by my brother, Doug Hill, and his wife, Marge Bradley. There were ten of us in all.

Initially it was a complicated arrangement of logistics, with the four families converging in Florence after flying in from various parts of the United States at different times. Steve and Anne and the kids came early to see Venice, as did Susie and Ed, who wanted several days in Florence where they used to live and where Ed still carried out his musicology research.

Though we had crisscrossed Tuscany many times, none of us had been to the Garfagnana, a mountainous region west of Florence, sandwiched between the Apuan Alps and the Tuscan-Emilian Apennines. This was our first-week destination. For the second week, we arranged to return to Fonte Vecchia, the idyllic villa south of Cortona where we had stayed twice before. This time our sojourn was flavored strongly by Steve's compulsion to explore the life of St. Francis and to follow his footsteps in and around Assisi.

Rendezvous in Florence and a Shaky Start to Our Western Trek

We all converge at the imposing Bencistà, a spacious, "modern" (sixteenth century) ochre B&B the Strainchampses know in Fiesole, a little village above Florence. As we're relaxing under the lemon trees, Steve's group, the last contingent, rolls in. All our rooms open out onto the majestic panorama of the city spread below, some eight miles away. In the evening, we can savor the lights winking on without the congestion and noise of the crowds. We hear birds singing well past midnight. Gardens are tucked around several levels of stone stairways, with pergolas of wisteria and roses, jasmine and rosemary.

The second day we cram into two large taxis taking us to downtown Florence, where we line up to claim our three rented cars. The plan is to drive west in caravan, but immediately we lose each other in the fierce traffic that weaves at breakneck speed around the one-way streets. Each vehicle is suddenly on its own. Miraculously, when we manage to exit the Autostrada an hour later, we all notice a McDonald's and pull in almost simultaneously to reconnoiter. From there we stick close together for the last stretch that's mostly steep hairpin turns as we lurch upward through dense chestnut forest.

An Alpine Paradise

Instructed not to arrive at our two rented villas before 4:00 o'clock, we while away a couple of hours in thirteenth century Coreglia Antelminelli, the nearby village that becomes our supply center.

Our fabulous garden near Coreglia Antelminelli

Then, making a proper entrance to Belvedere and Paradiso, our adjoining homes for the next week, we find housekeeper Nora and master gardener Robert, both British, standing at attention to welcome us. It's all far grander than we'd imagined, the splendid buildings set in extensive, manicured gardens something akin to the famed Giardino Rufolo in Ravello. There are endless terraces, boxwood hedges, a profusion of enormous white roses climbing blackened walls, topiary bushes, exotic trees in pots, flowering shrubs, and purple blooms trailing over trellised archways. Everywhere we look there is a new garden, a hidden "green room," classic statuary, pools, fountains, columns. Gravel paths and shallow, lichen-covered steps lead to secret surprises at every turn. Our villas are situated on a high and very narrow spine that drops off abruptly on all sides—clearly visible from a number of surrounding towns that we explore.

From a sparkling, solar-heated pool set in a stone terrace, we look west to see, just across the Serchio River, white rock cliffs and the jagged peaks of the Apuan Alps—looming almost in our faces and soaring to six thousand feet. This, then, is the key aspect of our Garfagnana stay: being situated squarely in the midst of rugged mountains. There is certainly antiquity to study in the scattered towns, but it's the spirit found in the mountains and the alpine valleys that dominates, and that has determined all settlement and life here through the centuries.

Our days alternate between lazily reading in old-fashioned steamer chairs "at home," staying out of the way of serious lap contests in the pool, reveling in grilled feasts and flowing local wines on the terrace accompanied by Ed's soft jazz CDs. There are walks in the gathering dusk down the road to Coreglia, the eastern peaks receding into misty lavender layers.

Ode to Joy!

There are major expeditions too. We climb up and up to the Grotta del Vento (Cave of the Wind), blowing our horns constantly on the sharp curves. The road is barely wider than a single lane, and there are no guardrails. Torrents swirl far below. When we step inside the enormous cavern, we understand its name: an icy wind caused by a startling temperature change blows relentlessly through a hole in this six-thousand-foot mountain until a metal door clangs shut.

Another day Steve offers to drive Doug, Marge, Bel, and me for an outing into the western mountains. First, it's to the thirteenth century Hermitage of Calomini. A quick turn off the main road takes us up a steep drive until we reach the white Franciscan monastery, dwarfed by the towering cliff into which it's constructed. The chapel and hallways are actually caves excavated out of rock; the courtyard is draped with netting to protect against falling stones.

Our destination, farther north, is Arni, famed for its marble quarries. Supposedly this is where Michelangelo found some of his stone. The whole area was also the site of fierce fighting in World War II, where communist partisans were very active against the Germans. The road twists, but like all our roads so far, it's in excellent condition. Italian drivers are agile and aggressive with their little cars and, as Marge notes, there are no dented fenders that we see.

Suddenly the evergreen forests vanish, and we're in a desolate moonscape. Grey rock that turns white in spots reaches far down the slopes of serrated peaks. Now we're in the village of Arni: a paltry half dozen buildings on a bend in the road. Is this it? We're about to turn around in disappointment. But something propels us a bit further. Shortly we're entering a dark tunnel, one of several punched through the mountains. As we emerge, suddenly we're blinded by brilliant sun and a huge arc of sky. Spread below us are vast green folds and just beyond, the blue Mediterranean.

Most spectacular, though, is a gigantic, gleaming, sheer wall of white marble, with huge squares where the stone has been cut and removed. We scramble out of the car and stumble up a swath of marble fragments that leads to a plateau of flat, pure white stone. Enormous twenty-foot blocks stand at the edge of a cliff. We leap about, snapping photos and begin collecting marble chunks to take back to Katie and Nicky. It's clearly a high moment—all the more so because it's such a surprise. At one point, we

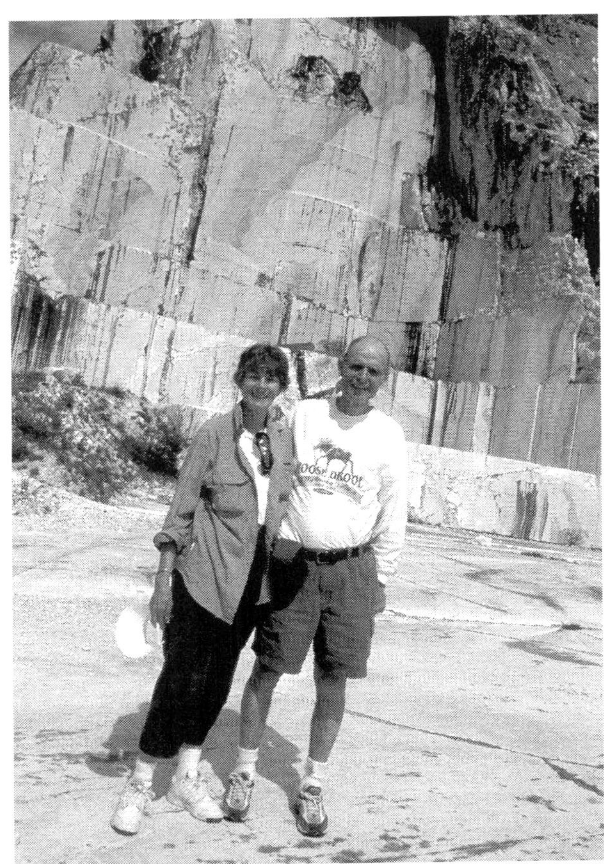

Ecstasy at Michelangelo's marble quarry above Arni—Doug and Marge

hear a yelp and a tremendous yodel that reverberates against the rock wall; it's Doug, lifted to heights of a spontaneous ecstasy we all feel.

On the Road Again

Now it's goodbye to our hosts and a special appreciation for the glorious garden creation that is Robert's passion. Doug and Marge, off to Venice, wave goodbye at the train station at nearby Lucca, and the rest of the group speeds south past Livorno and then east. We approach the familiar rolling Tuscan hills with golden wheat fields alternating with squares of dark green. Fat hay rolls dot the valleys, and sentinel cypresses define the ridges or stand in lonely clusters around tall farm buildings. Fortified by thick soups in the walled city of Volterra—once a major Etruscan stronghold—we're off on the final sprint to our beloved Fonte Vecchia.

Historic Mysteries Beckon

Whizzing through our tiny village of Mercatale, we find the gravel turn-off rougher than we'd remembered. The cars must keep their distance or be in danger of careening off the road in the blinding west sun mixed with clouds of white dust. We nearly miss our obscure little driveway, with its infamous steep turn where you skid on gravel and hurriedly grind the gears down-shifting.

Fonte Vecchia looms with its imposing tower. We quickly investigate the spiffed-up kitchen and find our same bedrooms, with their dark beams and ceilings packed with bricks. In the gathering dusk, we check out the cherished pool and note a new olive grove sloping away from the house. We're thrilled to hear cuckoos calling to each other, one from the mountain above, the other in the valley below. Could they possibly be the same ones we heard in 1999?

Just before coming, Steve had received from Random House the manuscript of a book due out shortly. He had arranged an interview with the author, Linda Bird Francke, about her *On the Road With Francis of Assisi: A Timeless Journey Through Umbria and Tuscany, and Beyond.* Francke had spent a year retracing the steps of St. Francis and describing the important landmarks punctuating his life and work as he laboriously tramped on foot all over Italy. Planning to put together a radio show on the subject, Steve has rushed to finish the book before our arrival because he hopes to touch personally into several locales that were key in Francis' life and to find people to talk with there.

History, culture, and art come together as our focus this week, encompassing the wider interests that fascinate and repeatedly draw all of us to this region. It is not simply the path of a particular figure or story of a particular religious movement. Yet Francis' story is a phenomenon that ultimately influenced all three of these fields. It has become a cornerstone for everything that happened and was deemed of value, first in a little corner of Umbria and then throughout all of Italy—and now, of course, the Western world and probably beyond. In effect, the Franciscan movement is a reference point, an engine that has informed and driven many of the elements we love and cherish most about this part of Italy. It has established values that are still influencing the course of Christendom everywhere, but here they are sharper and ride closer to the surface.

We're a bit surprised that Steve is suddenly drawn to St. Francis. Until now he had seemed to show only a peripheral journalistic curiosity about matters of spirit, though they were common topics of interest among the rest of the family. He himself tiptoed cautiously around the edges. Always the questioner, he cocked a carefully objective eye.

The Francis phenomenon has been exciting to me for a long time. Back in 1952, I traveled to Assisi with my friend Annie, the two of us actually making a pilgrimage for another friend who at the time was completely caught up with the mystique of Francis—so much so that, like Francis, he had literally given away his possessions, including his car, and had embarked on a life of helping infirm or disadvantaged neighbors in our Vermont town.

With guidebook in hand, sixty years ago I hiked up and down Assisi, including to the top of Mt. Subasio to Francis' hermitage, visiting each church, each place that represented an important event or undertaking in the life of the saint. We stayed in the Convent of the Poor Clares. I was deeply affected by what I saw as I traversed the hot, dusty lanes. For eight hundred years these spiritual totems have stood to remind the world of the revolutionary lessons of simplicity and humility that Francis pressed his pope to recognize. I was continually suffused by the almost palpable "presence" of the saint wherever I went. It became very clear that I was on a holy walk, and I identified especially with Francis' young disciple Clare, who subsequently headed a parallel order for women. The prospect, then, of embarking on a repeat pilgrimage half a century later with our son lends an aura and frisson that clearly defined the week for me.

On the Francis Trail: Le Celle

Cortona, in eastern Tuscany, is a short drive over the mountain from Fonte Vecchia. Steve, Susie, Bel, and I circle the town outside the old wall and arrive at our first pilgrimage point, Le Celle (the cells). It's a Franciscan monastery tucked into a wooded gorge halfway up the side of Mt. Egidio; it straddles a rushing mountain stream. Three times Francis visited this imposing complex built on three levels. Once while here, he gave away his cloak to a poor, grieving man (to the chagrin of his friars, who despaired of getting him to wear anything but thin rags). It is also where he brought

Le Celle, a Franciscan monastery near Cortona

back to life a crushed construction worker—one of the continual miracles reported. When Francis was very ill and near death at age forty-five, he stopped at Le Celle. Though anxious to push on to die in Assisi, he was able to rally briefly and dictated his last testament here.

We climb down a path to the entrance to find a replica of the tiny cell where Francis stayed. His stone bed is fifteen inches wide with a flat rock for a pillow. Apparently his stigmata bled here, so the current resident brothers feel it is an especially holy place. In his time, other brothers were jealous of his legendary stigmata, so he would often cover his hands with his robe.

While waiting for a young priest to finish hearing a confession, the four of us stroll along the woodland paths, Steve dropping behind to record birdsong and the rushing stream that flows off the mountain under a huge stone arch, and to comment softly on the tranquil surroundings. I spot an elderly, bearded friar emerging to water and weed a little vegetable garden. Returning to the sanctuary, Steve rings a bell, nervously breaking the silence that posted signs request. The confessor priest comes out, promising to talk when he is done. Then, what we had thought might be a two-minute interview, goes on for twenty. The priest obviously enjoys sharing the history and lore of his monastery.

Assisi: A Spiritual Core

The next foray is to Assisi in Umbria, just Bel and I with Steve. As we leave Fonte Vecchia, the sky looks ominous. Thunder is growling, and black clouds are scudding in from the west. Our entire valley fills with white fog. The rain increases, and by the time we reach Santa Maria degli Angeli, down the hill from Assisi, it's definitely umbrella weather. We stop here to see the Porziuncola, the simple, tiny chapel, dwarfed now within this imposing church. It's the second one Francis restored. It also contains the little niche where supposedly he died (in 1226) with his brothers around him after they had transported him from Le Celle.

We then ascend the hill to the walled citadel of Assisi. Parking, we slosh up to the huge Catedrale di San Francesco, begun two years after his death. Francis' body, kept hidden for six hundred years (for fear it might be stolen), was discovered in 1818 and rests here now. Here is the room with Francis' relics: his patched grey habit (could it be the original after eight hundred years?) and a scrap of his supposedly authentic handwriting—the only one in existence—a blessing to his closest brother, Leo. We see no signs of the earthquake five years ago that heavily damaged the cathedral and killed a priest. With his microphone, Steve eavesdrops on a priest preaching in one of the chapels and also records impromptu singing by a passing choir from Colorado. We all admire the Giotto and Simone Martini wall frescoes in the lower church, and then Giotto's depictions of Francis' life all around the walls of the upper church. When we emerge, white mists are drifting down eerily to envelop the town.

An hour later the sun bursts out. We hike up the main street to Piazza del Vescovado, with the fountain where Katie played when she was tiny in 1999. This is where Francis' father squared off with his son in 1206 in a hearing before the bishop. Francis had stolen goods from his father's shop, and the bishop told him if he wished to serve God, he must first return the money. Quickly Francis did so and then also gave back the clothes he was wearing, stripping naked in the piazza. He announced to all gathered that henceforth his only father would be that in heaven. The bishop covered Francis with his mantle, and the crowd shifted its scorn to the father who had taken everything from his son.

The next landmark is San Damiano, where God told Francis, "Go, repair my house." This was his first restoration, financed by selling fabric from his father's store and his father's horse. It's a lovely church, outside the wall at the end of a peaceful avenue amid olive groves. We climb around several levels on worn stone steps, poking into little chapels and shrine nooks with wall paintings and primitive statues. Francis designated San Damiano for "the holy virgins of Christ." He installed Clare there in 1212, where she was cloistered for forty-one years.

Her Poor Clares was the second Franciscan order founded by Francis. They cared for the sick, did chores around San Damiano, and prayed and contemplated. They were also in a state of constant fast except on Christmas, when they were allowed two meals. Speech was mostly forbidden. Clare wore a hair shirt of pig bristles in penance to "mortify" her body. Outliving Francis by twenty-seven years, she fiercely held onto the law of her order that forbade owning anything. Apparently Francis had to work hard to keep the bounds of chastity and propriety between his friars and the Poor Clares, while also protecting the women.

Steve persuades a priest to find someone he can talk to later, and we get in the car to continue on, climbing Mt. Subasio to the Carceri, the hermitage Francis built for himself and his brothers for contemplation, far from other habitation. It could be here that he famously spoke to the birds and stilled the brook when it disturbed his prayers. We park outside this remote, severe stone structure in its leafy setting. The tiny rooms can be accessed only by four-foot-high doors that are so narrow (barely more than a foot wide) we squeeze through with difficulty. They were designed to keep the friars humble.

Into the Mists of Time

At the far side of the Carceri, Steve and I walk to a path dug out of the steep mountainside that rises in dense woods to our left and drops off sharply on the right. Ahead is a white wisp of fog that shimmers across our path and wafts up through the trees—many with thick, gnarled trunks growing out at a crazy angle over the drop and covered with lichen. It feels as though we're literally stepping into the mists of time, going back eight hundred years to walk in this forest with Francis. After about ten minutes, we reach a small stone shell of a chapel, open to several crude log benches set on the trail. Inside are tiny crosses of twigs where visitors have written prayers and weighted them down with pebbles.

It's an enchanted stroll, and we can imagine Francis preaching to his brothers in this wild place. Steve stops periodically to murmur into his recorder about where he is and what he sees, and to catch the sounds: doves chuckling on the hermitage roof, bells chiming the hour. As we're leaving, he hunts for someone to interview and approaches a taxi driver waiting at the entrance for a Japanese lady. Steve asks what has drawn him here. "What is it you like about Assisi?" The man waxes eloquent: "It's not necessarily Francis, but the air is pure, the life is simple and good. I don't need much money. There's something about the quality of life here that is very rich and satisfying." Everybody standing around applauds. He beams.

We wind back down the mountain to San Damiano, where Steve finds a Dutch priest to interview. The priest says, "I am here for the same reason Francis came: to discover my purpose in life—which seems to be to live in poverty and simplicity, to serve in any way I can. And, incidentally, I do believe all Francis' miracles really happened."

Roman landmarks before we fly to Sicily: the Colosseum and Forum

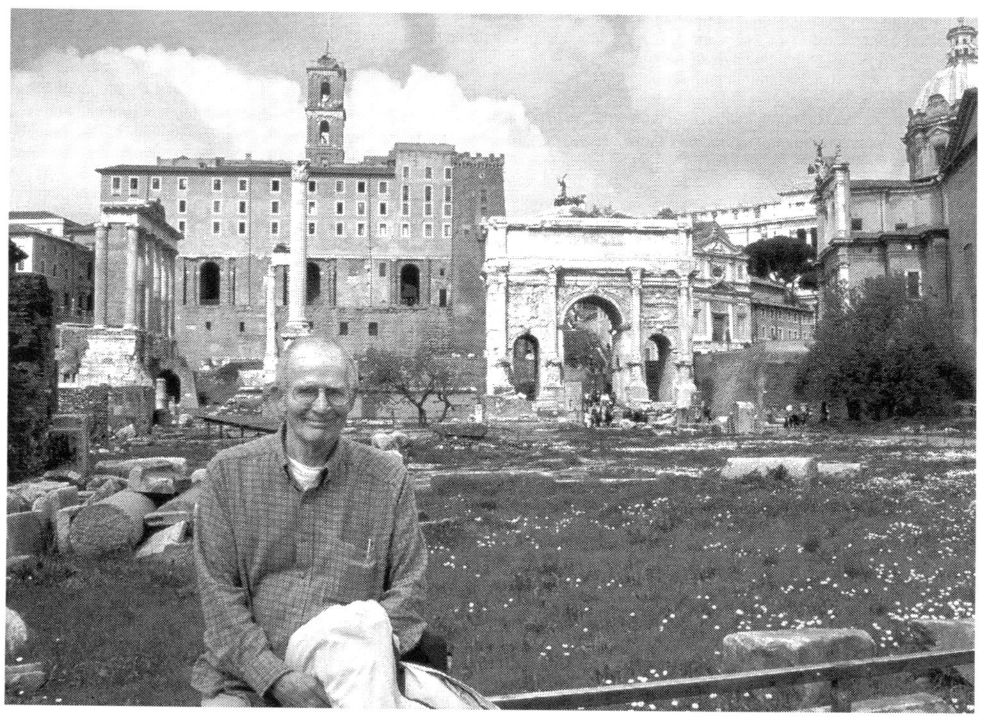

Sicily
Chasing Ancestral Ghosts

March-April 2006

Backstory

Bel and I quickly latched onto Angelynn and Eric's suggestion that we return to Italy within a year of our last trip. This time it would be the four of us going to Sicily, an area of Italy we'd never seen. Their idea was sparked by curiosity about the origins of Angelynn's mother's Sicilian family, especially since none in her clan has returned there. They hadn't kept up with relatives since her grandfather had immigrated to Milwaukee in the early twentieth century. The two of them boned up exhaustively—from early myths to the history and culture.

This would be another guided tour. Because Angelynn had not been to Rome, we signed up for a couple of initial days in the city where we had lived from 1960-62. So much has changed: there were far fewer cars then, and I used to zip around with great confidence in our little Hillman, parking easily everywhere. Now, as we've found in recent years, just crossing a street on foot can be heart stopping, and the general cacophony and crush of crowds are discouraging.

Rome: Calling Up Memories of a Life Here Forty-five Years Ago

From the airport, we whirl past new construction on the city periphery that is interspersed with majestic Roman aqueducts, wells, and arches—some relics incorporated directly into new structures. Congestion reigns, and many tiny Smart Cars drive up onto the sidewalks to park, almost like bicycles. Young folks in black leather weave suicidally around traffic on motorbikes. We're billeted in a quiet residential neighborhood in the far northeastern section of the city, within walking distance of our old digs.

Our group piles into two minibuses for a planned tour of Rome. This feels very odd when, years ago as residents, we sneered at or pitied the clueless tourists tramping glassy-eyed and sheep-like behind their guides. But it's also novel to be whisked effortlessly to the major sites, poking around the Colosseum, then past the Circus Maximus, and to the vast square of St. Peter.

A surprise bonus is finding a huge crowd in the square listening to a speech by Pope Benedict, who is seated under a red canopy on the steps of the Basilica. To enter the square, we must put all we carry through an X-ray machine, like airport security. Enormous television screens blow up the Pope's image all across the piazza, and his amplified voice intones loudly.

Later, on our own, we hunt for vestiges of the mysterious Illuminati (a shadowy, secret society, going back centuries, that supposedly is still ruthlessly grabbing and manipulating the power centers of the world—industry and government; its purpose to control). In Rome many of the symbols of the Illuminati are found in the Pantheon. We go on to revisit favorite spots such as the Trevi Fountain and Piazza Navona with its Bernini fountain. It's starting to drizzle, but we press on to find our old apartment on Via Ostriana. There's still the little sunken garden where Eric shimmied up the acacia tree at age three—to the envy of his Italian playmates, who always showed up in immaculate, dressy clothes and were never allowed to touch dirt or climb trees. It's where he taught himself to ride a two-wheeler, falling over and over on the steep concrete driveway. It's where Stevie, born on one of the seven hills of Rome, took his first tottering steps at the tennis court next door, where Bel played when not off at his U.N. job.

Sicily: Breaking New Ground

On our fourth day, we fly south to the island triangle off Italy's toe. We arrive at our base in the heart of Palermo and meet our Sicily guide. Getting our bearings, the four of us picnic on steps next to a "taxi" stand of odoriferous horses and carriages. Small buses careen past but must brake hard for the slower horses making elaborate U-turns. After exploring our environs, mostly on foot—noting that the churches and towers have a decidedly Byzantine or Arabic flavor—we bus out of the city to Monreale in the Conca d'Oro (Golden Valley). The roads are lined with chinaberry trees, whose hard berries are used to make rosaries. We labor up ninety-two steps to the bustling medieval village that grew up around Monreale's twelfth century Duomo and Benedictine monastery.

Probably the best-known landmark in the Palermo area, the Duomo was built by King William II in an unbelievable fifteen years, a feat accomplished by dozens of assembly-line artisan crews who worked simultaneously and then put the extensive complex together. It's a blending of East and West—Moorish and stolid Norman. Sixty-eight thousand meters of mosaics depicting Old and New Testament stories unfold around the high walls and merge in a gigantic Byzantine Christ in the apse.

The four of us are anxious to strike out on our own. The convenience of having travel details taken care of is always balanced against the strong need to break free frequently from the "herd." Arranging to rent a little Fiat Punto for a couple of days, we start out east along the top of the island, fearless Eric at the helm, Angelynn navigating. Bel and I bite our nails anxiously in the back seat. Traffic in the small towns snarls us up, so we look for the Autostrada, the toll road where we can zip along. After barreling through one tunnel after another—some over a mile long—(Eric calls it "the tunnel culture"), we find the exit to San Stefano.

Angelynn Checks Out Family Roots

San Stefano is where Angelynn's mother's family originated. Because her immigrant grandfather wanted passionately to become as American as possible, he passed down little of his Sicilian background. No connections were kept up, and recently Angelynn has become increasingly curious about exploring her roots.

San Stefano is the ceramic center of Sicily, its streets lined with factories and shops. We pop randomly into one store and are drawn especially to plates and mugs of a unique, saturated crimson, as well as to bizarre creations of whimsical creatures that support huge fountains and tables. Chatting with the owner, we find that Angelynn's family name, Gagliano, is well known in San Stefano. "There are still some Gaglianos living just down the hill near the sea. They were all fishermen," he tells us. A map is drawn for us and there are excited remarks about Angelynn obviously being "one of our own." We drive down to the shore, but she is reluctant to start knocking on doors of what look like mostly vacation houses. She says, "I think it's enough just to feel into the ancestral vibrations here, to see physically where my family history began, and to experience the wonderful landscape that shaped their lives."

We head inland to the Parco Naturale della Madonie, with the tallest mountain ranges in Sicily. A profusion of bright new greens and yellows and white flowering trees clearly say "spring." We coax our little car up steep curves to Castelbuono, one of several villages in these mountains, which provided refuge for bandits in times not so far in the past.

Winding up past the hamlet of Geraci Seculo, we notice that it's turning colder as we climb. Beyond the vertical rows of grapes and olives that fill up the valleys at our feet, splendid views open out to the higher peaks. Low-flying cumulus clouds cast moving shadows across the fields and the groves of cork oaks with their shaved trunks. Higher meadows are close-cropped by sheep and long-haired goats. Snow streaks down the upper slopes whose tops are hidden in cloud. We spot a long line of gigantic wind generators along the spine of one mountain range. Sixty percent of all energy in Sicily, we hear, is from wind and hydro power.

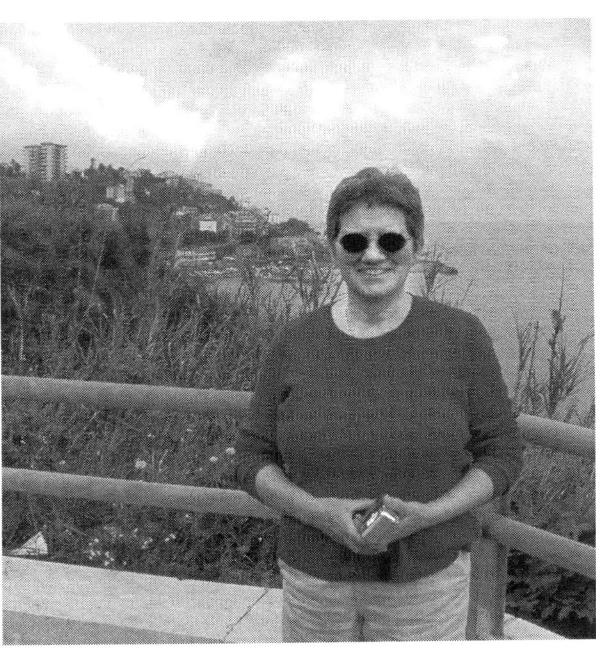

Angelynn finds her ancestral hometown, San. Stefano

Next is Petralia Soprano. At four thousand feet, the views from this village of grey stone houses circle 365 degrees. The peaks around it soar to six thousand feet. At one point, our pinched little street descends at a heart-stopping 35-degree angle.

To Mythic, Almost Inaccessible Erice

The following day we're off again for another independent adventure. Nosing our way out of Palermo is the most challenging part. We're amused to be held up at one intersection that requires *three* officious cops to make sure everyone stops for the red light. More often than not people just ignore the signals and dart through if they see an opening (as do we). This time we're driving west along the north coast. We simply have to stop at Lo Zingaro for a four-mile tramp on a trail that skirts a red cliff above the Tyrrhenian Sea. This was Sicily's first nature preserve, established in 1980, famous for small protected coves and pebble beaches, wild orchids, purple borage, yucca, *limoneum*, foxes, and eagles. As we hike in, Eric can't resist galloping down past the profusion of colorful wild plants to one of the tiny coves to wade joyously into the water.

Back on the road, we push on to fabled Erice. Built three thousand years ago on top of two sheer cliffs, Erice is veiled in myth. Originally it was a vast temple to Venus that served as a beacon for sailors at sea. In the Middle Ages, the temple was replaced by an equally huge Norman castle, Castello di Venere, that now stands as a majestic, crumbling ruin growing straight out of its rocky underpinnings. We wander at length, admiring the views and identifying the shining salt flats below in the coastal town of Trapani. The buildings in little Erice are all constructed of locally quarried white stone, adding to the town's storybook appearance. Intricately patterned cobbles on the steep streets are worn slick with time and make for challenging walking. It's considered too dangerous for tour groups.

Over the centuries, many groups tried to climb and conquer Erice, without success. Finally the Arabs managed to take it, but only when they found they could sneak up through the interior sewer system. The town is famous for its locally made rugs, ceramics, and pastries. Shop windows are filled just now with marzipan animals for Easter, along with exotic condiments—such as pesto with pistachios and vegetables, *bottarga* (dried tuna roe), lemon marmalade, and *caponata* with eggplant and garlic—and, of course, fine Sicilian wines.

On the way back to Palermo we hunt for Segesta, and are disappointed to find the gates have closed early. Segesta is a stunning, almost totally intact Greek temple isolated on a green plain. With binoculars we manage a distant glimpse, though—a luminous white specter rising out of nowhere.

Corleone and the "Godfather" Families

The next morning we're off early to Agrigento, our next group destination, on the south coast. The bus rolls beside fields with clumps of sheep and natural stone obelisks, with the saw-toothed pink and tan rocks defining the skyline. On the way, we stop in Corleone for a presentation about the Sicilian Mafia by a knowledgeable young historian. Constantly putting his own life in danger for speaking out against Mafia practices, he helped to create an information center here designed to educate people away from supporting the crime syndicate and to understand its history.

Sunning in the piazza in Corleone: old Mafia men?"

"The Mafia was born," Gino says, "when feudalism gave way to a free market economy, attracting primarily those professionally trained in violence, such as soldiers. Things turned around considerably in 1992 when Magistrate Falcone and Judge Borsolino—the courageous men who rounded up and imprisoned three hundred

Mafia in the 1980s—were brutally murdered near Palermo. At that point, the general populace rose up in disgust and said 'Enough!' New York Mayor Rudy Giuliani even offered to send over the FBI and CIA. The current *capo* (head) has been in hiding for forty-three years while his wife lives openly in town with their two young sons."

Our speaker tells us the Cosa Nostra is still around, and they wait to see how it will surface again. "Sicilians are strong on family," he emphasizes. "They work hard, and are sensitive about always being branded as Mafiosi. These days the Sicilian Mafia is marginalized by the more flourishing global game; members stick to extortion of local businesses and controlling public works such as road building."

Interestingly, just as I'm writing this, word comes over the wire services that Bernardo Provenzano, the above-mentioned notorious *capo dei capi*, boss of bosses, of the Sicilian Mafia, has just been apprehended. Living in an apparently deserted farmhouse outside Corleone, police grabbed him when he furtively reached a hand out a door to pick up clean laundry sent by his wife. Speculation is that though Provenzano's arrest is significant, some turmoil could result. The peace he had held in place could crumble, with renewed warfare breaking out between rival mobs. We find that *The Godfather* film was not actually shot in Corleone because the town wanted too much money, so we never do get to identify scenes from the movie.

After the lecture, we all amble around the main piazza, where gnarled old men sit on benches, leaning on their canes and blinking into the sun. We imagine that they were either important players in the far-reaching Mafia activities in its heyday or perhaps are even involved today in shadowy activities. They grin at us and offer to pose for pictures.

Patching up Ancient Greek Temples

In Agrigento, on a ridge between the Mediterranean Sea and the city of Agrigento, the Valley of the Temples holds the ochre-and-red stone remains of numerous Greek structures that were built between the fifth and sixth centuries BCE. Great blocks of rubble lie around flat stone platforms that were altars for sacrificing animals. We watch workers on scaffolding drilling holes in the Doric columns still standing and filling them with cement for stability. Symbolically the columns were seen as tree trunks that connected Earth to the gods.

We poke around Agrigento on our own. At one point, an old woman in slippers and woolen shawl in the Arab sector appears and beckons us to the Church of Santo Spirito. She unlocks the door for us with a battered key, and invites us in to sit and pray in the gloom while thin female voices sing in a distant balcony—nuns practicing responses to the priest's chant. Then we hike miles along the beach, watching kite surfers in wet suits lifted and tossed twenty feet above the water by fierce winds. At the end of the day, we find ourselves lobster red from too much tropical sun.

Communal Toilets Invite Sociability

Now comes the long haul: all across the island to Taormina in the northeast corner. En route, the bus stops at rural Piazza Armerina to see Villa Romana del Casale, the remarkable intact remains of a lavish hunting lodge that had belonged to an important Roman official, perhaps Maximiamus, Diocletians' co-emperor. Built over a period of fifty years in the third and fourth centuries AD, we find what are supposed to be the best-preserved Roman mosaics anywhere in the world. Delicate columns are Ionian and Corinthian. An aqueduct provided water for public and private thermal baths—heated by wood and shunted through clay pipes. Massage rooms, a gym, gardens and pools, tall-ceilinged chambers for family, concubines, guests and servants—all stretch over four terraces. We admire elaborate scenes of hunting, erotic love, and athletic games depicted in the mosaic floors. Initially the basilica was pagan, and then became Christian when Byzantines took it over. Most intriguing are the public toilets where a group of men and women sat sociably together over adjoining holes in a stone ledge to gossip, then would be wiped down by servants with sponges from a nearby fountain of running water.

Taormina, "Riviera of Sicily"

As the bus rumbles eastward, the landscape flattens, giving over to citrus groves. We bypass Catania, the world center for blood oranges, a business that has revived the region's failing economy. Mt. Etna, a distant cone, completely white with snow, soars in the far distance.

Sitting on a vertiginous hill, Taormina was founded in 304 BCE as a colony of Syracusa. Subsequently the city fell to the Romans, then to the Arabs, then the Normans and, finally, the Spanish. We zigzag up and up, past hotels that are fantasies of luxury, nestled in lush foliage and flowers. At our hotel, we continue climbing on foot, up several flights of steps to the reception desk because the elevator has broken down. A sliver of sea is visible from our room, and we glimpse the surprisingly close Italian mainland of Calabria. For several days, we explore exquisite architecture that reflects the various conquering cultures and a general atmosphere of medieval antiquity. Street entertainers on stilts and vibrant crowds come out each evening for the ritual *passeggiata* on the main Corso Umberto I that glitters with fabulous shops. We're constantly testing our knees and lung capacity on steps and steep inclines.

For several days, the four of us wander around on our own. A favorite hike is up to the Greek Amphitheater ruins—considered one of the most spectacular settings in the world, with snowy Mt. Etna dominating the skyline to the west (Eric notes a smudge of smoke blowing from the crater) and the blue sea spread out below. We climb above the stage area to the horseshoe of wood-and-stone bleacher seats for an even more spectacular vista. Later we reconnoiter for a tranquil picnic in the public gardens, where pigeons queue up at our feet for crumbs. Eric sketches the whimsical stone buildings in the park, and Angelynn finds a quiet meditation spot amid shady trees and bright flower beds.

One evening we hear a talk about World War II in Sicily. Our speaker, a local historian, says:

> Mussolini duped the people by promising a "new Roman Empire," but Italians never liked him, or the war, generally. The army went consistently without adequate clothes and supplies and had to fly obsolete planes. Most recruits were from South Italy because they had big families to support and needed the money. It was Churchill's plan for the Allies to invade Italy, first through Sicily (in the summer of 1943), and then move up onto the mainland. There was the historic rivalry between the American General Patton and the British Montgomery, each racing to get to Messina, the crossover point to Calabria. The most intense fighting took place on this eastern side of Sicily. Montgomery made it first to Catania and Taormina, but Patton dashed across the

north coast to beat him to Messina. The welcome Allied landing represented the end of the war for Sicilians, with two hundred thousand Germans escaping over the straits to the mainland. Apparently there was a secret agreement between the Italian American Mafia and American Intelligence; Lucky Luciano controlled the New York City docks from prison in order to deter saboteurs there.

To the Smoking Volcano

The fitting climax on our final day is Mt. Etna. It's almost two hours away, and our bus starts early, stopping at the village of Zaffarano to see an active bee culture operation. During a demonstration of the various products—honey, wax, and propolis (a medicinal resin from tree buds)—bees zoom around our heads. We sample the different honeys: eucalyptus, chestnut, cherry, wild strawberry, and lemon. The honey in this region is exceptional.

We ascend to the south slope of Etna, stopping at the tourist center where the snowfields begin. The elevation here is seven thousand feet. This center was wiped out in the eruption of 2002, along with hotels, but now they've all been rebuilt. At nearly eleven thousand feet, Etna is Europe's largest active volcano, one hundred miles in circumference. Recently it has blown almost every year; 2001 was the most "complex" event in three hundred years, creating six new openings. We understand that when a "flank eruption" occurs, a new cone-shaped mountain six hundred feet high may pop up in hours. We see a number of these poking up around the desolate landscape.

For miles along the way, the ground is entirely black, from gravel to enormous piles of boulders. One obvious lava trail snakes down to the edge of a town that was just barely spared. There has been no loss of life since nine German tourists were killed in 1979; the lava moves slowly enough that people can get out of the way, though a number of towns have been heavily damaged. We pass towns where all the buildings are constructed of black volcanic stone.

We join throngs of other sightseers, busily picking up lava rocks and hiking up over the black (and sometimes red) ridges of rubble, and up the sides of Etna, though no one is permitted to approach the actual crater. Cable cars are passing each other coming and going on the snow-covered slope that attracts skiers.

Reflections

Sicily turned out to be an adventure beyond what we had envisioned. Because of Angelynn's blood ties, the rest of us also felt an added pull to this richly colored island. Later she told us, "Besides satisfying my general curiosity, there was something about this whole trip that kindled a new attraction and sense of affection for my family's culture. I recognize some proclivities and patterns in my own life that clearly seemed to have trickled down from the ancestral interactions experienced here."

Bel and I also felt we had closed a circle now that we have embraced a last boundary of our beloved Italy.

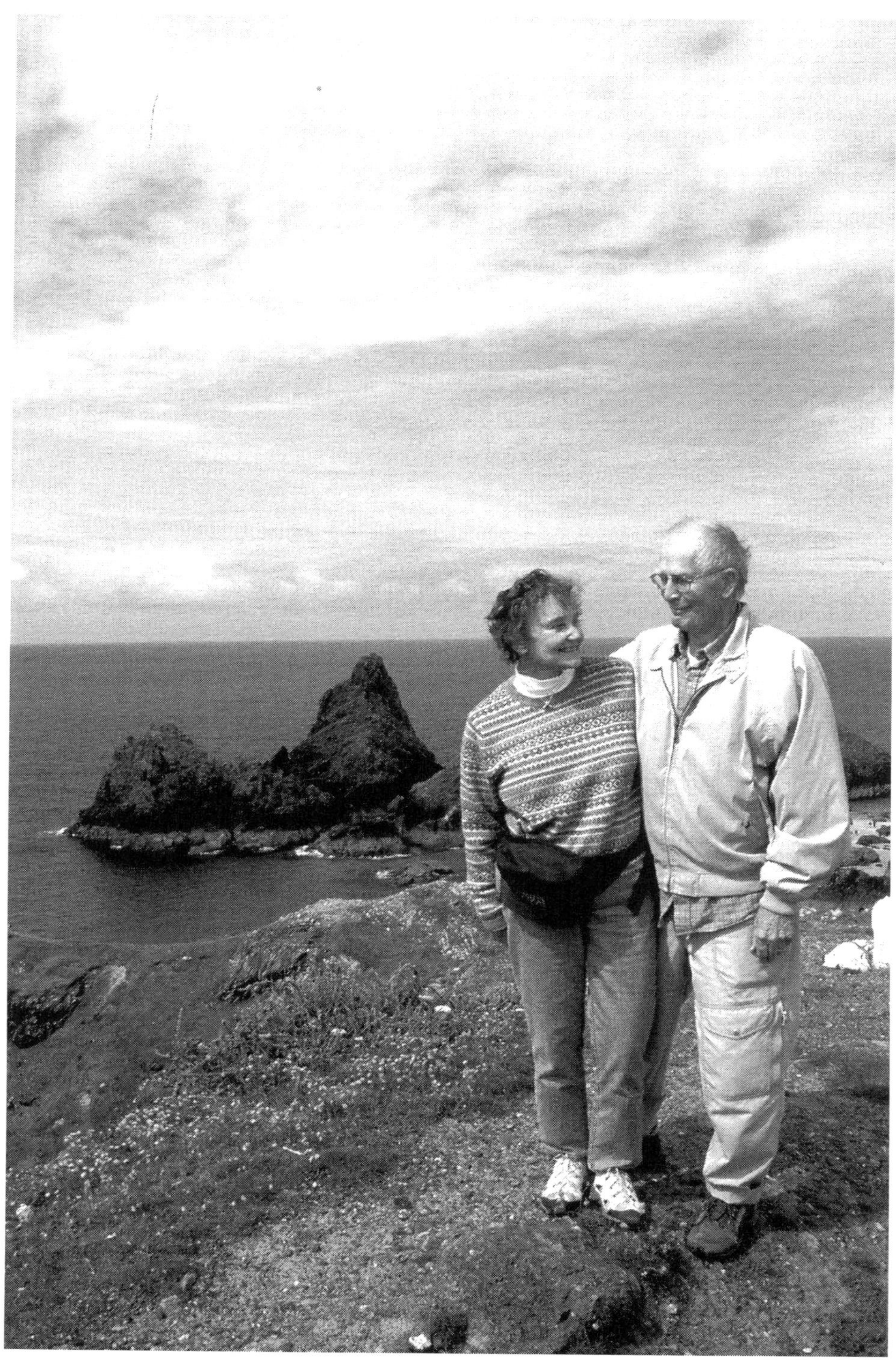

Headlands hike from Mousehole to Lamorna Cove

Devon and Cornwall, England

Digging for Cultural Roots

June-July 2007

Backstory

Ten of us—Steve's four, Susie and Ed, Doug and Marge, Bel and I—were drawn to England for another large-scale family journey. Our hats were off especially to Marge who, at the last minute, decided to join the group after all. The week before she had broken her ankle and backed out. At our urging, she soldiered on with a walking boot and cane. She surprised everybody with her ability to keep up on most of the rough stones and trails.

Aer Lingus Airbus dropped Bel and me in London, and we carried on by bus to Bath. The idea was for us all to get our sea legs for four nights in the city of Jane Austen before proceeding further west to Cornwall. Family roots tied most of us to Britain, and after so many years of being drawn to work or travel in Latin countries, we were curious about checking into how well our latent genes would sense an affinity to this island of our forebears.

Bath: Hitchcock's Birds, an Italian Garden, and Beethoven Amid Angels Climbing to Heaven

Anne has found us an amazing National Trust house next to the historic Bath Abbey. Bel and I bump our suitcases over uneven cobbles to Elton House, arriving shortly after Doug, Marge, Susie, and Ed. Then Steve's crew shows up, and we're set to explore our seventeenth century abode—four floors with no walls square. We're feeling a bit like crass upstarts; there's a venerable dignity reminding us that we're the somewhat rough, less cultured Americans who must change our pace, mind our manners to respect this museum piece. Ignoring decorum, though, nine-year-old Nicky happily discovers a key to secret upper floors, reached by rickety, spooky stairs. He and Katie, eleven, also invade the forbidden cellar with dank passages. "Look!" they shriek in delight, "there's even a cell with bars and wall shackles!"

We fan out in couples or families to explore the town on foot—most famous for the remains of its Roman baths with warm spring waters, probably also used by pre-Celtic tribes for healing. It's a delight to catch street musicians who offer constantly rotating concerts next door in the Abbey square, such as classical guitar or marimba. Seagulls join in noisily, swooping everywhere. We understand that they will fly into our house if windows are left open. Bel and I hear them screeching all night and see them flashing eerily white as they wheel past the lighted tower just beyond our little garden—a bit reminiscent of Hitchcock's film *The Birds.*

The buildings in Bath climb steep hills. They're mainly eighteenth century, of the characteristic yellow limestone cut into smooth blocks, with pitched tile roofs that bristle with chimney pots. One day Steve arranges with author Adam Sisman to drive to see Coleridge's cottage near Bristol. Sisman has recently written a book about the legendary collaboration between Coleridge and Wordsworth (*The Friendship: Wordsworth and Coleridge*). At the same time, the rest of us taxi out to Iford Manor and the famed Peto Garden. Harold Ainsworth Peto was an architect and garden designer who acquired the crumbling property in the early 1900s. He proceeded to transform a steep, awkward hillside into an Italian fantasy with a series of terraces, pools, fountains, and loggia. Opera productions take place in the cloister, with patrons exiting by the light of flares.

A few minutes of blissful repose for Anne and the kids at the Peto Garden near Bath

Now the sun plays on distant golden fields, while close up a symphony of organized color is punctuated by spiky cypresses and enormous spreading beeches. Cascades of field flowers tangle over stone walls. There are endless paths to explore, stairs to climb, little resting pergolas and benches with views. Peto made many trips to Italy to collect choice statuary, antique doors, and sculptures that make a great counterpoint to the richness of the plantings.

On our last day in Bath, by accident we stumble on a rehearsal in progress in the Abbey for a touted Beethoven concert. For an hour, we soak up the glorious *Emperor* Concerto. Soloist Peter Donahoe alternates conducting, playing the piano, and strolling to the back of this soaring space with its stone fan vaults to check the acoustics. The Abbey is fifteenth century Norman, with exterior flying buttresses and statues of angels climbing ladders to heaven—per a dream of the builder who thought he was being told by God to restore the original eighth century structure. Again, we Johnny-come-lately Americans feel eclipsed by the weight or authority of the buildings of our much more seasoned ancestors; we think of the few eighteenth century buildings still standing on our East Coast as really "old." We can't exactly compete with *fifth* century specimens found here and there in Britain.

After a final feast in our formal dining room with its scarred floorboards, we stroll once more to the Avon River, where the ubiquitous gulls are circling against sunlit clouds.

Devon: A Taste of Old England and Hunting the Hound on Dartmoor

We collect our three rental cars and are off to the West Country. Entering the county of Devon and mysterious Dartmoor, we half expect to see the great Hound (dreaded beast of the Baskervilles, hunted down by Sherlock Holmes) loping over dour, empty heath. Instead we find ourselves veering off onto really narrow, almost single-track roads, with twenty-foot-high hedgerows brushing the sides of the cars. At times, we fold in our side mirrors, and when we meet oncoming traffic, one car pulls into periodic passing places, a challenging British feature we're fairly used to by now. Doug, Marge, Bel, and I find our Sandy Park Inn, wedged into the corner of a country road, while the rest are booked into the Three Crowns in nearby Chagford. A tourist mecca, Chagford is filled with dazzling white houses lining twisting little streets—the epitome of English charm.

Anne and the kids are excited to find Alan Lee holding forth with a group of writers in the cozy Big Red Sofa bookshop. A local resident, Lee is the illustrator of *Lord of the Rings;* he won an Academy Award for his work on the film. Everybody then gravitates to St. Michael's church and graveyard filled with blackened Celtic crosses. Vistas of far hills are bathed intermittently with golden light as the sun dances in and out of boiling thunderheads. We march past exquisite gardens dripping and fresh-smelling from recent rain, then all rendezvous at the Bullard Arms for supper—enormous plates of steak and kidney pie cooked in Guinness beer.

Our contingent drives "home" and climbs the cramped winding staircase to bed in cozy, low-ceilinged rooms. Afterward, Anne says she's ready to move to Chagford, partly for the cultural ambience, but mostly just for the mesmerizing Dartmoor landscape. Steve also reports later that a highlight of the whole trip for him was taking a long, solo walk that night, up into the fields and hills. It's definitely an enchanted land.

The Moorland: Hound Tor

After "cooked" English breakfasts of eggs, bacon, blood sausage, grilled tomatoes and mushrooms, kippers, porridge, toast, and tea in our respective hostelries, the two groups join forces and we're off again. We thread through excruciatingly narrow roads, almost like paved footpaths, until finally emerging from the hedges to glimpse real moorland: open country with bracken ferns and prickly gorse. We pause at Hound Tor, one of several impressive outcroppings, and hike through a properly gloomy English drizzle to the foot of huge granite formations. Steve's family, with Conan Doyle gripping their imaginations, immediately scrambles to the top of the high rocks.

Past more desolate moors, where signs warn to look out for "wild animals." Sure enough, we soon come upon a pack of roving horses, which don't seem exactly wild; they shuffle over to our cars and poke nosey heads in our windows. Colts are suckling.

Marazion and Venton House

Pushing farther west, now in Cornwall, by suppertime we find our way to the village of Marazion. Following directions to our abode for the next week, we nearly miss the overgrown path leading to Venton House. The sun is glinting off the sea and bathing our tropical garden with purple, yellow, and red succulents. The house is stunning, situated directly on the brine-scented water. Off to the right, rising from the sea, we spot the castle of St. Michael's Mount. After picking our rooms, the cooking crew sallies forth to buy fish and chips and groceries. The rest of us investigate the path to the beach, climbing over a stile at the foot of the garden and down a ladder to black boulders and lapping tidal pools.

Warming up with tea before blustery ascent up St. Michael's Mount

Brittany, France, another island abbey inspired by a vision of Michael. During the Hundred Years War, it was appropriated by Henry V, became a fortress and castle, and was given to the St. Aubyn family—which still lives in parts of the castle. (St. Aubyn Estates owns and operates our rental house.) In 1588, the approaching Spanish Armada was spotted from here, launching the critical battle where the Spanish were defeated.

We set out on a steep path to "take" the castle. It's still raining, but mostly the wind is the challenge, blowing up a gale. The outlook becomes more panoramic as we ascend—the crashing sea, Marazion, and our white Venton House shining in solitary splendor up the coast a bit. The castle looms above us, and as we clamor over the last formidable rocks, we almost lose our balance and must crouch low against the wind. Steve hangs onto his glasses, fearing they'll blow away, and all of us, out of breath, finally stagger up through a great wooden door. We find the castle immaculate, gorgeously furnished with fine art, brocades, and superb rugs. Services are held regularly in a little chapel. Nicky's favorite discovery is a room just for the display of antique armaments.

The next day, Sunday, we're soaked in an unexpected downpour while hiking up the beach, then set off to explore the art galleries, pubs, and whitewashed buildings in Marazion. Steve's family gallops past us to whip off their shoes and wade in an icy low tide over the causeway to the Mount.

Storming St. Michael's

The following day we'd planned a long cliff hike, but glowering skies convince us that it's a better day for the castle. By the time we climb into a small motorboat and head out into the channel, rocking crazily in the waves, it starts to pour. In five minutes, we've landed at a small cluster of buildings at the foot of the Mount and warm up with Cornish pasties and pots of tea. A film put out by the National Trust that manages St. Michael's tells us this is the first "place" noted in Britain. In the fifth century, local fishermen saw a vision of the archangel Michael and built a church here. Over the next three centuries, it was a Celtic monastery.

Then in the eleventh century, it was handed over to Benedictine monks from Mont-Saint-Michel in

Over the Headlands from Mousehole

The skies have cleared, and while one contingent takes off for The Lizard Peninsula, the most southerly point of the British mainland. Doug, Bel, and I decide on "the big hike" from the coastal town of Mousehole (pronounced Mowzul). Trudging up a hill past stone cottages, we locate the coastal path.

We beat our way through high grasses and stinging nettles, slide around on stretches of muddy trail, traverse a brook, and pass through a dense forest that's a wildlife preserve. Finally we burst into the open and are rewarded with blue-green water sparkling below. Now it's up and down granite rocks, climbing along a precipice that overlooks the sea. Higher and higher, through towering rocks, layered and balanced—Brobdingnagian cairns.

As we round the headland, we glimpse a lighthouse and climb down to tiny Lamorna Cove. We've covered about three difficult miles in three hours and decide not to retrace our steps; we'll go back by bus. We grab lunch at the old Lamorna Wink pub ("wink" signifying formerly that contraband spirits were available). A friendly older couple from Surrey is anxious to have us know they are "strongly conservative." "We loved Reagan and Thatcher," they tell us, "but we hate that idiot Bush. And do you really think a colored candidate could be elected president?" (In June, the 2008 US campaign is well underway.) Then, "We presume that the Clintons are irrevocably tainted by the Whitewater scandal." With a startled shiver we begin to edge away from these otherwise pleasant, refined, old-school Brits. We recognize them as friendly, English-speaking "kin," but then find their "proper" class and race consciousness a strange throwback to a pre-civil rights time in our own South. They are of a benighted generation that America has mostly grown beyond. "No matter what happens in the future," they beam conspiratorially, "Britain and America must always stand together, as we did in World War II"—the war in which the husband had fought.

Starting out on rugged hike from Mousehole

St. Ives—Our City Fix

Another day we wake up to ominous clouds. The timing seems right for an expedition to St. Ives, the tourist magnet on the north coast. If it rains, we'll be able to duck frequently into one of the numerous shops. Warned of impossible parking and mobs, we opt to cross the peninsula in a brightly painted little train. We pile out, noting the curve of white sand and a stark hill at the far end topped by a lone sentinel church. We're swept into the milling throng, including prams, dogs, and children, that crowds the sidewalks and spills over into precipitous streets.

Our destination is the Tate St. Ives, an outlying branch of the eminent galleries in London.

The gleaming white Tate here is comprised of four floors, severely modern, with unexpected curves and ramps, a glass atrium and rotunda. Contemporary paintings are tucked into odd, dark corners, while the main attractions are works with moving parts: a foam-producing machine that spits out what looks like cotton candy on the floor; a contraption that throws its orange silhouette onto a wall; knife-like colored mirrors that shift subtly.

After sampling pricey watercress soup and crab salad on toast in the lofty museum café, we brave the streets again. Heavy showers send us inside for interludes of ice cream, coffee, or fudge and to chat with gallery proprietors. Nicky watches warily for the hovering, predatory seagulls, which yesterday snatched his entire just-acquired ice cream cone. At the end of the day it's a relief to turn into our grassy lane and bump down to the tranquility of our own isolated "estate."

Revived by dinner, Steve pushes us to join him in exploring Prussia Cove, a few miles to the east. Parking in a dirt lane, we continue on foot to the sea through rolling fields that stretch to the shore. A couple of isolated farmhouses poke up starkly against the dazzling pink and gold clouds of sunset. Smoke curls out of a chimney, and the smell of coal fire mingles with the salt of the channel. A pheasant rustles in tall grass. Katie and Nicky leap for handholds on a shale cliff, then wriggle through a fence to hop over flat rocks slanting into the churning water. Continuing down the path, we discover a little hamlet of exquisite, very ancient granite houses—mini castles. Back home, an almost full moon is rising, but the glow of sunset still lingers at 10 o'clock.

The Lizard and Kynance Cove

Because the others have said it's too spectacular to miss, Bel, Doug and I take off early for The Lizard peninsula. We veer onto a bumpy track of true moorland reminiscent of Scotland, with gorse and purple heather just coming into bloom. Parking, we hike down to the cove where jagged rocks soar up to frame a small sand beach. The tide is running out fast. After slipping over red and green serpentine stones to the bottom, we climb again to the coastal path that runs along the top of the headland. A horseback rider gallops past. We reach Lizard Point, marked by Britain's southernmost lighthouse beacon. The sea is breaking white below, and waves dash rhythmically against red cliffs. Lunch at the Point is an excellent fisherman's platter of fresh crab, shrimp, and mackerel while we scan for seals.

On our last day, Steve offers to drive Doug, Marge, Bel, and me to explore points west. We skirt Penzance, an ancient market center and the most westerly major town in Cornwall, and climb to the tiny village of Porthcurno, up a winding lane blocked in by hedgerows laced with wildflowers. At the very top of Porthcurno, we sneak in to park at the spectacular, open-air Minack Theatre. This is a stone amphitheatre carved out of the cliff, overlooking azure seas two hundred feet below—one of the most breathtaking sights in Cornwall. A play is in progress, but we can hike from a promontory down stone steps that lead to the bay. Then we drive on, through open country to find the Merry Maidens in a deserted meadow. These are a circle of nineteen granite standing stones. Legend has it that they were Bronze Age girls who danced on the Sabbath and were turned to stone for their sin. Some believe this is a ley line marker (where earth energies are believed to converge). Celtic celebrations are held here in the circle and among the huge cairns at the edge of the field.

Polyglot London

We're up at dawn the next morning, pack up reluctantly, and are off in caravan to Exeter—just making the deadline for turning in the cars. After an uneventful train ride to Paddington station in London, we say our goodbyes and split into three groups for separate hotels and agendas for the next couple of days. For Bel and me, it's déjà vu, retracing our steps from when we were here in 1953: the same museums, palaces, churches, Parliament, the venerable parks and pubs. We catch the pomp of riders galloping out of the Guard House at St. James Park, resplendent in red or black capes with gold crests on their helmets—horses wheeling and standing smartly at attention.

Sunday crowds are milling in the park. Drums lure us to a bandstand farther on, and we loll on the grass to enjoy a concert underway. Puffy clouds skittering overhead reflect in the little lake where at least twenty varieties of waterfowl splatter and honk. We chat in Italian to a couple on a nearby bench. It dawns on us that we are hearing almost no English spoken on London streets; on the buses it's more apt to be some Mideast language or Russian, German, French, or Spanish. We see veils and at least one burqa.

Leaving the "Mother Country"

Our 4 a.m. taxi whizzes easily through deserted streets to Heathrow. Because of a terrorist alert, we are stopped for random security checks at blocked-off roads—especially since there has just been a third incident; a jeep was driven into the Glasgow airport and exploded. Actually, during our time in London, we totally ignored the threats and were never aware of extra security measures or public concern. Steve reports that his family rode the tube all over the city without worry.

Reflections

So ended another memorable family journey. As we dug into and experienced our historical and spiritual origins in hundreds of small ways, I think all of us sensed our kinship with this part of the world—the Anglo-Saxon connection. Bel's family tree traces a direct line to the early kings and queens of England and to the signing of the Magna Carta in 1215. One ancestor, William Henry, whose parents migrated to America from Scotland, became George Washington's gunsmith and was a significant figure in our country's founding years—a "bridge" between the old and new cultures. My more plebeian forebears were mainly weavers in Huddersfield, a mill town in western Yorkshire. They landed on the Connecticut shore in 1629.

Unlike in the flamboyant Latin countries we've visited most recently, I feel an ancestral kinship with the English—and imagine that when they encounter brash young "adolescent" American interlopers, there is a reaction of almost parental bemusement. On our visit, I could see and feel the historical evolution from their stolid, restrained mores and habits to our looser, freer ones—but nevertheless the connection was there. For me, and for the others, I believe, there was a feeling of coming back to the mother "hearth," including encountering the many British place names we see transplanted in the New World. We recognize and admire the originals of the English cottage architecture we Americans have copied meticulously to decorate our New England village greens.

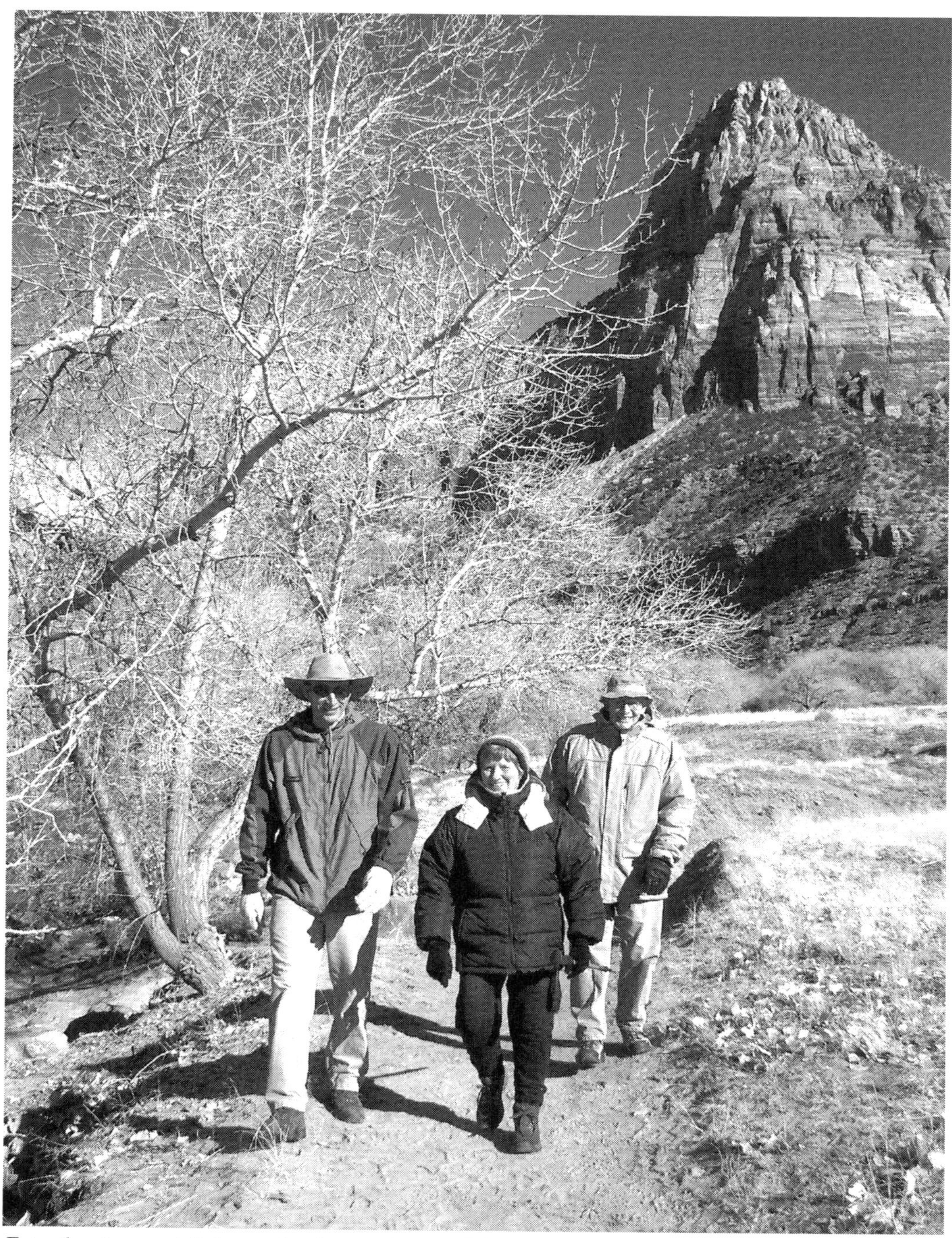

Eric, Angelynn and Bel emerging from a river trail, Zion

Into the American Southwest
Slowly, by Rail

December 2008 – January 2009

Backstory

After so many years turning eastward to explore Europe, we decided it was time to look at a part of our own country we'd never visited, the American Southwest. We found willing guides in Eric and Angelynn, who knew the region well. Another first: we decided to eschew the horrendous hassles in most airports now and try the train. All four of us made the enlightened decision to deliberately take ourselves out of the usual Christmas circus.

A Step Back into Another Century

Eric and Angelynn have driven ahead. Their plan is to stash their car and pick up a rented SUV, necessary for the rough going we anticipate. Bel and I board the Amtrak Southwest Chief in Chicago and are soon ensconced in a cozy roomette. It's evening in mid-December, and we're steaming south in a swirl of snow. The ubiquitous mournful whistle announces our passage as we hurtle through deepening gloom. Occasionally we pull into a small town with winking Christmas lights blurred by flying flakes.

Moses, our portly major domo with Rastafarian locks, comes by to sign us up for a gourmet dinner. All the meals are outstanding. We draw our curtains and snuggle into our tiny nest, built, it seems, for midgets or contortionists when it comes to undressing and climbing in and out of the upper bunk. Around Kansas, I peer out into the night at the immense expanse of snow fields as far as I can see and almost imagine Dr. Zhivago's troika sleigh hissing by on the Russian steppes.

The Great Plains Offer a Unique Majesty

At breakfast, a native Kansan tells us, "It's a special pleasure for me to be able to stand in one spot and see the sun both rise and set. In this state you can rest your eyes." The red ball flirts with the horizon and struggles up, turning the snowfields into a vast pink sea. There are no trees. Black Angus steers, alone or in clusters, root around in the stubble or gravitate to hay bales left out to save them from starving in fierce blizzards.

Occasional giant grain elevators thrust up from the flatness. A surprise wind farm looms, with some sixty stately turbines churning slowly. And then isolated, low oil rigs seesawing slowly, perpetually, hopefully. Portents of the new and remnants of an era passing.

After Dodge City, the terrain begins to undulate. Here and there in the treeless desolation, a thicket of evergreens indicates a lone farm—like a protective circling of wagons against hostile intrusions. Farms out here aren't measured in acres but in "sections" (square miles). A dozen horses stand motionless, their ankles in snow. Twenty antelope take long leaps away from our track.

Colorado. Irrigation ditches, mostly frozen blue, snake through tawny thickets of scrubby, gnarly trees, silvered branches gleaming in the sun. Way off—we're told a hundred miles by our talkative historian/conductor, Tom—looms Pikes Peak, with its impressive crown of snow. At fourteen thousand feet, I guess it would be clearly visible. Always there's our forlorn whistle, warning nobody in particular.

At Trinidad, we actually see a serious highway, with trucks rumbling past—human civilization! A sandstone mesa rings the horizon close in. Juniper bushes are dark dots against the ochre rock. We rattle through Raton Pass at 7,588 feet into New Mexico and pass the ruined ghost town of Morley. It's here that a posse caught up with one Cruz Torrez, a card cheat and bank robber, finished him off, and buried him next to the Santa Fe trail we're just glimpsing. Then in Las Vegas, New Mexico, the occasional upscale, modern house, a switch from the usual derelict little dwellings scattered throughout the cattle country.

The Art Scene in Santa Fe

Eric meets our train near Santa Fe with the rented SUV. Settling in to our motel, we rush out to the Plaza just in time to grab a lighted candle and join Las Posada, the Christmas ritual. Hundreds of people are already trailing behind a procession of Mary and Joseph with a small band of musicians. They end up at the crèche, but not before devils jump out on balconies to shout temptations in Spanish. The crowd boos and hisses back. Masses of *luminarias* (lighted candles in paper bags) line the streets and roofs of the buildings. We stumble over hard snow banks; it's crisp and increasingly frigid. A late service at a venerable Catholic church is in progress, and we pop in to soak up the atmosphere and to warm up.

Next day it's a real trick to find our tortuous way through unpaved back alleys to the house of my long-ago college roommate. Such rough streets seem to be the sign of a prestigious neighborhood—hard to find but crowded with the traditional (obligatory) sand-colored, low, flat-roofed adobe homes. The unassuming exteriors often hide luxurious, art-filled interiors, as is the case with Betsy and Bill's. It is a veritable museum, with fine art, carvings, Indian pottery, and lovely rugs.

A Glimpse into Prehistory

In galleries and shops we proceed to savor the abundant Southwest art and craftwork—American Indian and Mexican—that distinguishes Santa Fe, almost to the point of saturation. Then we're anxious to get out to see the historical remains of one culture whose influence lingers today. Our destination is Bandelier, the ruins of a ten-thousand-year-old Indian settlement, located in a canyon surrounded by cliffs of compressed, fused volcanic ash called "tuff." Grabbing a guidebook, we head down the trail, passing a couple of *kivas*, sunken round pits lined with stone where the young were educated. Soon we're climbing steep paths and then ladders to reach the many cave dwellings sculpted in the cliff face. In fourteen hundred, the height of this civilization, there were seven hundred inhabitants whose average age was thirty. We wonder if a good number may have fallen from their precarious perches.

On the ground are ruins of other dwellings—small rooms that originally rose to three stories. There were no doors at ground level; people entered the top floors by ladders that were pulled up for protection against enemies and animals. The Ancestral Pueblo People have been labeled "prehistoric," as they had no written language. In several cave dwellings, the *vigas* (ceiling beams) protrude to the exterior, a style carried through for present-day southwest adobe homes. The long-house is one huge cliff dwelling whose cave entrances extend deep inside and often up a floor, probably inter-connected. Petroglyphs adorn the cliff face.

On the Art Trail to Taos

Another day our friends join us for a day of back-country explorations. Bill is a sculptor and knows artists in all the little villages on the way to Taos. The snow cover increases as we climb (though Santa Fe is already over seven thousand feet). Hispanic Chimayo has its ancient *sanctuario,* with a healing chapel hung with crutches. Eric and Angelynn light candles to St. Joseph, patron saint for selling houses (theirs is on the faltering market).

In Taos, the snowy peaks are much closer, with ski runs on the backsides. The flavor of the town suggests old hippies and New Age types and themes. It's crowded with galleries and shops. The Taos Pueblo is a village of adobe dwellings, some four stories, where Pueblo Indians continue to live and ply the crafts that they sell. They try to preserve life as it was traditionally. There is no electricity in the homes. All have the typical round, corner fire-places. The tribe, with ninety-nine thousand acres, controls the town and the roads in the area.

The Desert Mesmerizes

Time to move on. We head south and west into Arizona. All day the deserted landscape keeps shifting. First it's sandy soil and low grasses with dense pinion pine or juniper. Next the terrain becomes absolutely flat, with just a sagebrush cover (we fill the car with its fragrance). Then it starts rolling, with ponderosa stands, then is flat again as far as we can see. The odd mesa and butte or volcanic cone pops

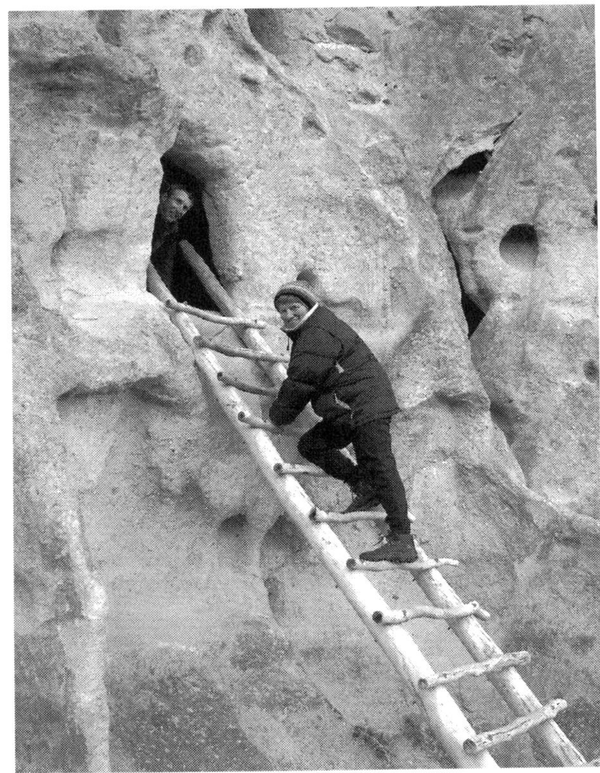

Exploring cliff dwellings at Bandelier

out of nowhere. Ochre sandstone boulders are big as houses.

We pass a Navajo reservation and then cross onto a Hopi reservation. There is no sign of human habitation. Wild horses wander across the road and approach our car. A coyote streaks by. I find all this wildness and desolation mesmerizing, especially as the sky fills with dark, churning clouds at dusk that touch down onto the far horizon. We roll into Flag-staff, where we'll base for a couple of nights.

The Grand Old Landmark

Up early, we're on the road to the Grand Canyon. It has snowed a couple of inches in the night, but as we progress north, the skies clear, and I spot three feral black pigs nosing in the brush. We admire the dis-tinctive, textured red bark of the ponderosas—new to us Midwesterners. Arriving at the south rim of the Canyon (the one part open in winter), we find we have this amazing monument almost to ourselves. This may be partly because of the cold and the fresh snow, but also because most Americans are home preparing for the holidays. The few other tourists are mainly Japanese, East Indians, and Chinese.

We drive a fair stretch on the rim road without passing a soul, then pull into our first lookout point. There it is—brilliant sun casting sharp shadows on the endless red, orange, and yellow layers of rock, ten miles across with a flat shelf all around that drops more than a mile to the Colorado River, a distant, winding thread. Water-sculpted towers swirl into cones and thrones. Stunted, twisted pines line the rim. It's a Christmas symphony, we realize, of red, green, and white. The civilization of the Grand Canyon goes back twelve thousand years, before the end of the ice age, which was ten thousand years ago. It was Anasazi, then Navajo, and is linked to the Pueblo Indians of Bandelier.

Leaving the better-known canyon, it's on to the Painted Desert and the Little Colorado River, brown and far below. The atmosphere as we drive is heightened by soft flute and drum music that Angelynn has purchased. We climb out and hike to the unsupervised, deserted edge of this canyon, which somehow feels even more spectacular and authentic because the layered rock pinnacles and towers are closer. Eric races around to lean happily over the rim of a thousand-foot drop.

Unguarded moment at the Grand Canyon

Arcosanti: A Futuristic Dream

Now we turn south to Arcosanti. Having followed (and researched and taught about) this colossal urban laboratory project for thirty years, it's exciting to finally see it—an experiment in architecture, ecology, and community that sprang up in the flush of the countercultural era. We bump down a dusty road in the Arizona desert and see what appear to be a few low, beehive-like buildings popping above the horizon.

When we get there, though, we find a complex web of sophisticated, breathtaking concrete structures: four-story towers, great half-domes open to the south, an amphitheater, silkscreen and bell-making equipment, kilns, farming, media rooms, a café and bakery, guest apartments and residents' rooms—on and on. We check out scale models of (Italian) Paolo Soleri's dream for a city of the future: five thousand people on twenty-five acres, living in structures to be built mainly vertically. His idea was to create a very small footprint so that everyone could enjoy but not damage the nature surrounding them.

Our bouncy guide, an Arcosanti resident, is a graphic designer who gave up $600 designer jeans for clothes from the common grab bag. Now he delights in sharing the technological wonders such as huge sun tubes and novel ways to collect heat, then store and circulate it in cooler weather. Architectural designs take advantage of the sun's angles.

There are photovoltaics and a wind generator. They're on the power grid—not trying to be the perfect society or an isolated Utopia—but are simply experimenting with better solutions to looming energy challenges.

The arts are strong here: residents hold frequent performances and costume parties. Income is generated by selling distinctive ceramic and bronze bells, bowls, tiles, and plaques, as well as offering hourly tours. They also collect tuition from the many who come to learn and apprentice in the various tasks. Ninety folks live in the community. Solari was still going strong until he died at ninety-three in April 2013. He lived in Phoenix, and would come up one day a week. Who knows if his dream will ever be fully realized, but it's a vision that invites serious study and has quickened the imaginations of countless young (and older) futurists.

New Age Central—Sedona

Our next destination is Sedona, but first we stop for lunch in quirky little Jerome, a hill town that had been a booming copper mining center in the 1880s. In 1953, the mine closed and Jerome suddenly became a ghost town. The population dropped from fifteen thousand to fifty. Then the counterculture moved in, and now Jerome's two steep streets are lined with rickety Victorian structures that are galleries and shops looking out over the desert. We poke around and watch some unique glass blowing.

Sedona is truly *the* New Age mecca, teeming with psychic readers and glittering New Age wares and themes. Prices are sky high, but we'll skip all this and head out to the flaming red cliffs and pinnacles surrounding the town. It's dramatic, especially with a full moon just rising behind the spiky skyline. Eric drives us around to catch many vantage points and also to see the warren of low but very luxurious adobe-colored homes hiding behind thickets of desert bushes.

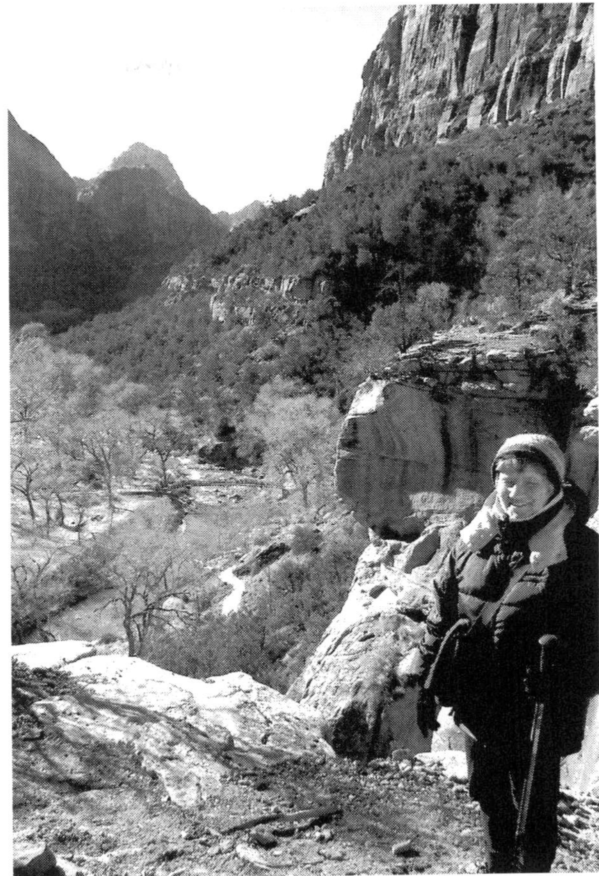

On the trail, Zion

We have a couple of high-energy days hiking into canyons with soaring coral rocks, often moving quietly, very aware that this remarkable natural display demands utter silence. Our boots scuff soundlessly through the soft red sand. We perch on boulders to soak up the sun and munch our sandwiches. Very few other hikers are about.

Grand finale: Bell Rock, a jagged pinnacle with Court House Rock on one side and Cathedral Rock on the other. Bel and I find a comfortable vantage point on smooth slabs near the base while Eric

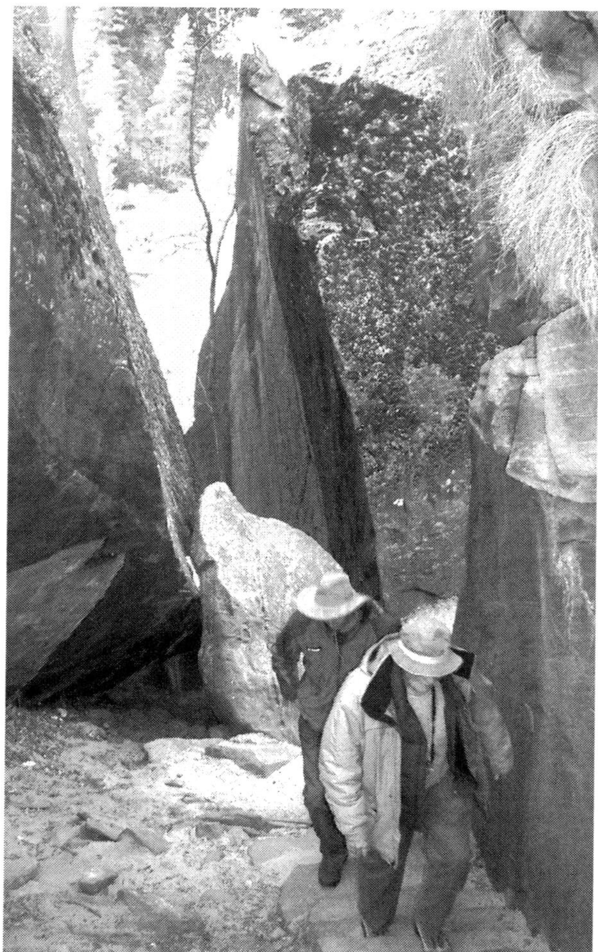

Two hats and a chimney at Zion

bounds off to scale the heights. In no time, he's on the top ledges, a dark, silhouetted speck. We spot a few other hearty climbers. A woman near us is explaining to rapt visitors that Bell Rock is an energy vortex, a revered "power point." Back to earth (our motel) for hot cookies and chocolate drinks.

A Perilous Christmas Climb

Now we point northeast for the long drive into Utah. The high, flat mesa follows us, and then the red cliffs disappear and canyon walls sprout green bushes. With more and more trees, we're entering the mountains, with ups and downs and hairpin turns. We barrel through a long, unlit, curvy tunnel into Zion National Park and burst out into the light. Suddenly there's a distinct alpine feel.

It's Christmas Eve, and snow is creating a checkerboard effect against north-facing cliffs. The ground is white. We press on to Springdale, a small village just outside the park, and check into our motel, tucked under the brow of an impressive rock. Eric inspects the hot tub outside; he has visions of floating under the full moon glinting on the peaks.

Christmas day now, and it's brilliant and cold. We're back in the park early and choose the Middle Emerald Pool Trail for a morning hike. It turns out to be a steep two-and-a-half miles, with a trail that's often only three feet wide and covered with ice and snow. After crossing the Virgin River by footbridge, we climb up one side of the canyon and circle around the back to visit a series of pools—some frozen—then around the other side and down. Signs at intervals warn to stay away from the edge, stating matter-of-factly: "There have been deaths from falling down the cliffs."

Keeping my eyes glued to the red rock or sand or ice under my boots, I adopt a sideways "crab walk," clinging to the inner cliff wall. I can't look at the sheer drop-offs inches away on the other side of the trail. Sometimes Eric guards the outer rim as we pass especially fearsome spots. I think it's this little caper that, ever since, has cemented Bel's trepidation about high places.

We all concur (after we're safely down!) that this has been the perfect way to celebrate Christmas, a delightful reprieve from scrambling to put together the usual holiday rituals. After the hike, we dress up a bit and adjourn to the elegant, rustic Zion Lodge for a gourmet feast. As we found at the Grand Canyon, most of the people we see on the trails and in the restaurants are not Americans. We're definitely an anomaly, and that feels refreshing.

A couple more hikes, along the Virgin River and up the Watchman Trail, and we're done.

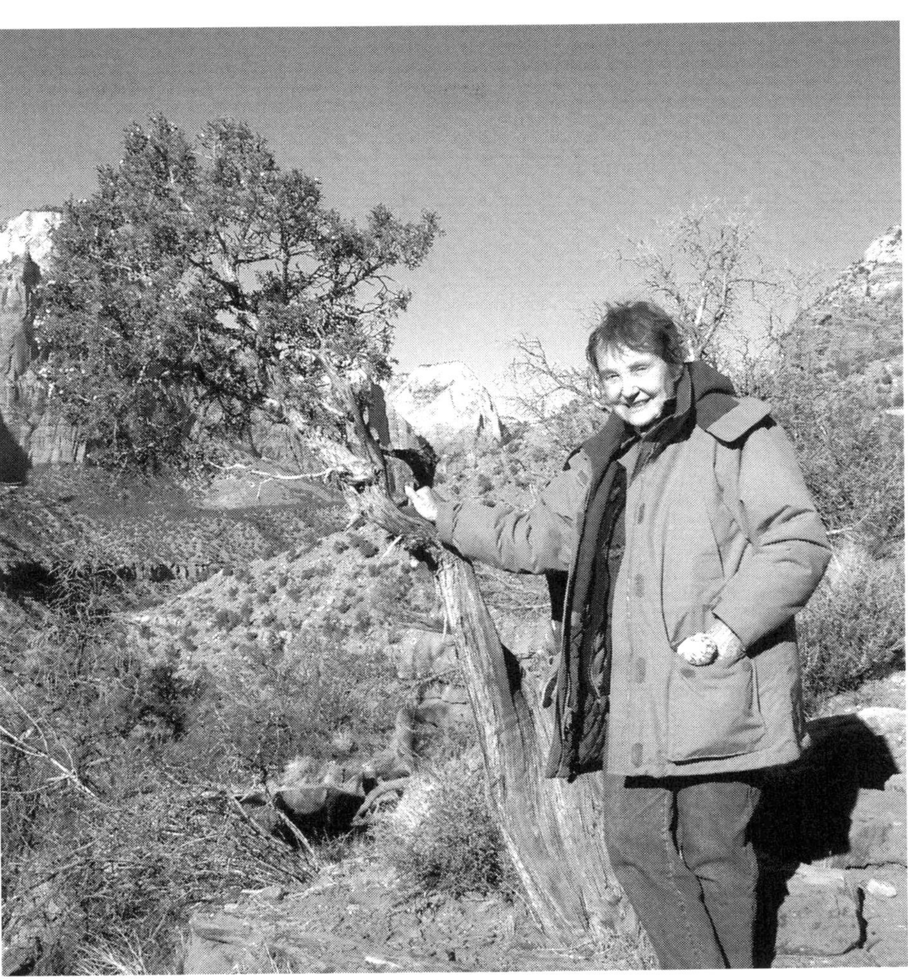

On the Watchman Trail: finale of Zion treks

Reflections

Bel and I were greatly indebted to Eric and Angelynn for retracing steps they have taken before—for sharing what have been cherished experiences for them in order to open up this new world for us. Their love of these lands was quietly communicated all along the way as they invited us to choice places to touch into a sacred quality and heighten awareness on many levels. The theme, the overwhelming impression, was of huge, soul-sized spaces and big rocks—soaring, colorful cliffs juxtaposed against the splendid emptiness and breadth of the desert country. Places where nature, not people, clearly dominate. Places foreign to those of us from father east. We returned expanded and rested.

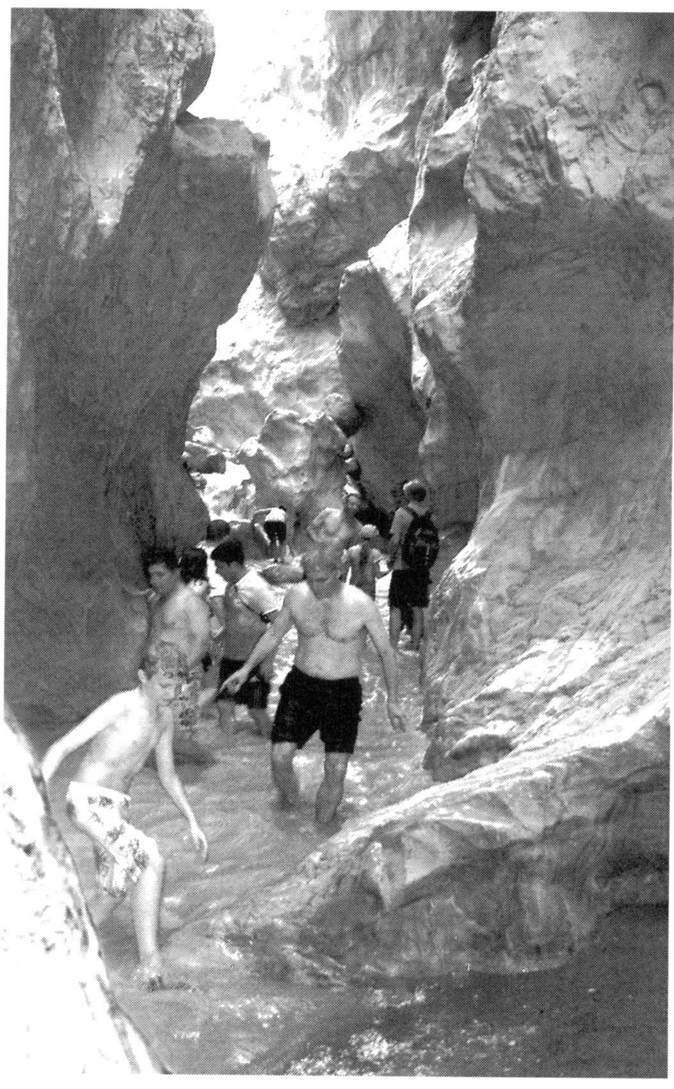

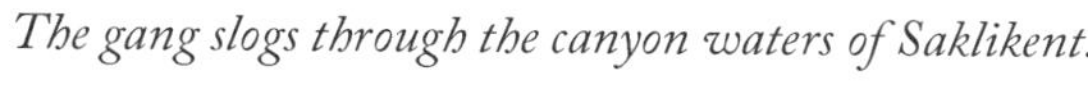

The gang slogs through the canyon waters of Saklikent.

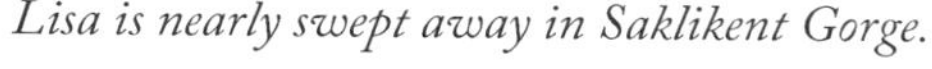

Lisa is nearly swept away in Saklikent Gorge.

Turkish Delights

June 2011

Backstory

The "Intrepid Nine"—Eric, Steve's four, Doug and Marge, Bel and I—managed to rendezvous in Istanbul, Turkey, but only after a series of dismal snafus. The Wisconsin contingent of seven was delivered two-and-a-half days late because of hideously stressful airline cancellations and three unexpected nights in Chicago and London hotels. After our aborted trip to Turkey in 2003, Steve, Doug, Bel, and I were doubly excited to try again. We had canceled reluctantly when it was rumored that the US invasion of Iraq would be launched from Turkey on the day we were due to fly there.

Soaking Up the Old City of Istanbul

We bleary Midwesterners can hardly believe we're finally sweeping in over the mighty Bosphorus Straits to set down at Atatürk Airport. Our frayed tempers melt away when we see the hotel that Anne has found for us—in the perfect location. As our cab pulls up at the Sari Konak in the famed old district of Sultanahmet, we're immediately dazzled by the vibrancy and exoticness just on our steep little cobbled street. Tiny boutiques are jammed together. Dashing, aggressive salesmen are selling stunning tiles, pottery, carpets, jewelry, and fabrics. Brilliant colors and intricate Islamic designs bombard us on all sides. We rapidly conclude that Turkey has to be one of the most dynamic, over-the-top cultures we've encountered.

Making up for lost time, we get out of the grimy clothes we've lived in for four days and everybody heads out to soak up the scene at hand. Directly on our left is the Blue Mosque, with its six graceful minarets. To the right, seen through a shimmer of shooting fountains is the magnificent Byzantine Aya Sofya (now a museum; see its history below). A bit farther on is Topkapi Palace. Families, dogs, and cats are out enjoying a festive afternoon in the park, which is sprinkled with manicured topiary trees. Everybody is super-friendly, chatting easily with us, including children selling roasted chestnuts and corn on the cob. Women glide by in various stages of veiling, from all-concealing, head-to-toe black *burqas* to headscarves (*hijabs*). While young women may not be able to show their hair, they highlight glamour and beauty with heavy, dramatic makeup.

Eric the artist dazzled by Islamic tiles in Topkapi Palace

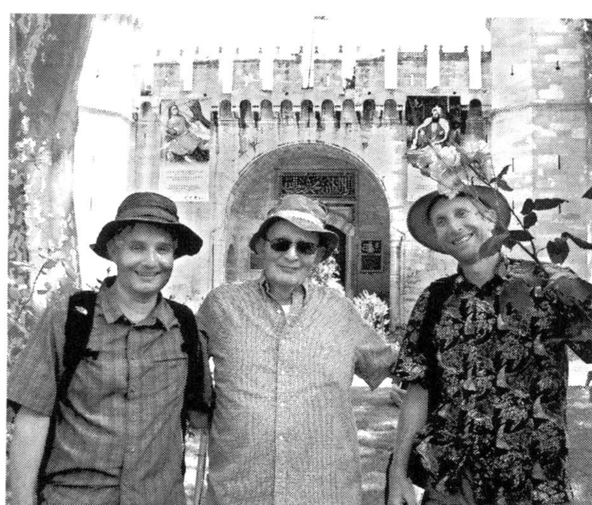

The three musketeers about to enter Topkapi

Suddenly the call to prayer booms out from the spires of the Blue Mosque, with answering calls from other nearby mosques—an antiphonal effect. An affable young man has been eavesdropping on our chatter and joins in, then invites us to his family's nearby rug store. It's the age-old ritual, and we're leery of getting in too deeply, but as soon as we're all seated in the shop basement, glasses of hot apple cider appear, and then they start flinging every carpet out on the floor, spinning the (questionable) histories of each.

When we escape, Steve (who came to Istanbul several years ago on a journalists' jaunt) steers us to see the Sunken or Basilica Cistern (Yerebatan Saraya). This is a sixth-century underground wonder of 336 eerily lighted limestone columns set in shallow water, supporting the roof of the cistern. The columns march off endlessly into acres of mysterious gloom. Huge, dark fish lurk lazily in this enormous storage tank, whose water was historically carried in by aqueducts from the Black Sea. We pass upside-down Medusa heads on pillars. The whole scene reminds me vaguely of the shadowy terracotta soldiers we saw in China, lined up in militant precision.

Doug and Marge, having already explored this part of the city before we arrived, take us to their favorite restaurant for a dinner of cold *mezes* (appetizers) with olives, garlic yogurt and cucumbers, pickled mushrooms, soft cheeses, hot sauces, and flatbread, followed by wonderful lamb *kebaps* sizzling on skewers.

Muslim Cultural Icons Up Close

The next morning we're revived and are off to Topkapi Palace. The palace is strategically located on a point of land where the great Istanbul waterways all converge—the Golden Horn, the Sea of Marmara, and the Bosphorus Straits. It was built by Mehmet the Conqueror in 1453 over the ruins of Constantine's palace. Place of legend, this was where sultans then reigned for four centuries. Just as we enter the park grounds, a noisy martial band bears down on us sporting gaudy red-and-black costumes and waving giant banners. We drift on—in full tourist mode—from one remarkable building to another, gaping at the Imperial Treasure, Throne Room, Armory—on and on until it all becomes a blur of exquisite tiles and glittering trophies.

Our favorite is the Harem. Suddenly, after pushing against crowds lining up at each attraction, the Harem is pleasantly quiet. Few people have decided to see this cloistered domain for the sultans' huge families of wives and concubines and their children. The only men allowed were the Black Eunuchs who guarded the women. There might have been eight hundred concubines at any one time—enough to keep the sultan fairly busy!

The group splits up, Eric, Bel and I opting for the Aya Sofya (Hagia Sophia in Greek). Eric haggles at a shop for baggy harem pants to pull on over his shorts so he can go into the holy places. For a thousand years, Aya Sofya ("Church of Holy Wisdom") was the largest Orthodox and Christian church in the world, designed to surpass in grandeur every other monument to God. Rebuilt by the Emperor Justinian in 537 AD, it had been damaged and rebuilt several times after earthquakes. Crusaders breached the walls of Constantinople in 1204, looted treasures from the church, and permanently divided the Greek Orthodox and Roman Catholic Church. In 1453 Mehmet II invaded and, in the name of Allah, declared the structure a mosque.

Then, in 1935, secular Atatürk converted the mosque to a museum. Over twenty thousand glittering gold mosaic tiles cover its 184-foot soaring dome. The dome is supported by forty massive ribs of hollow bricks that rest on pillars concealed in interior walls. The original icons and frescoes that had been covered up when the building became a mosque were eventually exposed again (Islam does not allow representations of people and animals). Aya Sofya is the main Byzantine structure still standing in Istanbul. We are enveloped in the magic of a hundred or so chandeliers with multiple lit bulbs hanging on two-hundred-foot chains from the high golden dome.

On our way to the Blue Mosque, we're momentarily intrigued by a woman totally sheathed in a

Marge and the Blue Mosque

black *burqa* sitting on a wall and energetically blowing soap bubbles into the sky.

Completed in 1617 by Sultan Ahmet I, the Blue Mosque showcases classic Ottoman architecture and is characterized by its elegant Isnik tiles of subtle blues and greens. At the tourist (not worshipper) entrance, we must remove our shoes that we carry around in plastic bags. I drape my veil over my head. An affable young man (not a guide, he insists) attaches himself to us and shepherds us around. We pause to watch family groups snapping pictures of two boys of about twelve who are decked out in ornate, sparkly white outfits and sequined pointed hats. They look a little shell-shocked.

Our "friend" explains, "They're posing for their circumcision party. This is a very big event in Turkey. They always plan an elaborate celebration before the operation, maybe to help the boys be less afraid of what is about to happen." Our guide is part of a family rug business (naturally), and we feel obliged to follow him up several streets to his store, where we're ushered up rickety steps to an attic to await other relatives/salesmen and the ubiquitous cups of tea.

Before anyone returns, we sneak uneasily away because we have an appointment to meet two missionaries. Bel wants to check on stories handed down in his family: about why his maternal grandparents—missionaries in Constantinople (Istanbul) in the late 1890s—undertook a grueling, two-month boat voyage when Ellen was eight months pregnant with twins, and to verify that William really translated the Bible into Bulgarian, as letters claim. And why did they leave after only three years? Betty and Ken Frank (a librarian and math teacher respectively who have founded several private schools over the past thirty years in Turkey) turn out to be a charming, knowledgeable, and sophisticated couple. Ken has a deep knowledge about how Islam works in this modern country (he gave us a book he wrote on the subject), but the couple has no information about Bel's forebearers, only speculation. The mysteries persist.

Starting South along the Aegean Sea

We fly south to Izmir on the west coast and pick up a nine-passenger van (needed for the luggage) and a smaller sedan. At the last minute, the rental agency persuades us to buy extra collision insurance because of what they admit are "insane Turkish drivers." Our drivers will be Steve and Eric. Riding shotgun with Steve is Anne, our navigator-in-chief. We proceed further south to Selçuk , our first stop on a trek that will take us to the bottom of Turkey on the Mediterranean Sea.

The terrain becomes decidedly Mediterranean—more hilly, with mountains jagging up in the distance. Terraced olives climb the slopes on one side of the fine, new highway, and pink oleanders dance down the median. The scrub and dusty soil remind us of Crete.

Selçuk for a Regimen of Superb Ruins

We follow instructions to St. John's House, which we are renting for three nights. It's directly across from the ruins of St. John's Basilica, where supposedly in 37-45 AD the disciple John brought the Virgin Mary and where he wrote his Gospel.

Our British landlady is on hand to welcome us. The house is magnificent—three stories beautifully designed and built by the same architect who helped to restore the basilica. The ceilings are wood, with more natural old wood for the cabinetry and doors. Tasteful oriental rugs cover brick floors. Arches are a major theme, gracefully defining the windows and doorways. Sitting on our balcony, we look out over a multitude of red-tiled roofs.

Trial and error (flooding) teaches us that we can't put anything down Turkish toilets; there is a metal bucket for paper. We also discover a splendid feature of most Turkish toilets that I wish we could import: the "douche." This is a tiny pipe ("butt washer," I called it) under the rim of the bowl that shoots out a stream of water that can be directed when you turn on a faucet next to the toilet. Even better than a bidet! Saves paper too.

Local history: Around 1200 BCE, Ionians fled from Greece to settle in the Selçuk area, establishing the important city of Ephesus, which became the capital of Asia Minor. Then, in the sixth century, the Emperor Justinian built the Basilica of St. John over John's tomb. After years of earthquake destruction and looting left the site a ruin, partial restoration of the basilica began a century ago and is ongoing.

On a food-shopping foray, Steve notices that the gas tank in his little car (supposedly delivered full) is nearly empty. At $9.00 a gallon, he fills it up for $100.

After supper, a quick, fierce thunderstorm clears the air, and the evening feels fresh and balmy. We set out on a walk to explore the ruins, first peeking into the fourteenth century Isabey mosque; it's empty except for an old imam hunched over his prayer book in a corner. At the top of our street, Nicky and Katie, now thirteen and fifteen, lead us in scrambling up the worn Roman wall to peer over into the ruins of St. John. We spot a huge stork nest atop one of the old columns and a mother winging in with a fish from the nearby sea for her four babies.

Steve steps into a little domed mosque where a young imam, alone, is singing along with the call to prayer booming over loud speakers across the city. When Steve expresses curiosity, they chat a bit about the rituals. In return for a donation toward restoration, the imam gives him an English copy of the call to prayer. We watch the shadows falling over the mountains, a thin strip of sea shining in the distance. Doves mutter around us as we hike down our street for bed.

A morning visit takes us to the House of Mary (the Meryemana) in a secluded forest. There are cave ruins where Mary, entrusted to St. John by the dying Jesus, was supposedly brought to live out her life. A board flutters with notes that pilgrims have left for Mary.

Ephesus, Ruins of a Roman City

Now we're ready for Ephesus (Efes). It's hot and cloudless, but tolerable with breezes. Ephesus is considered the best-preserved classical Roman city in the Eastern Mediterranean. From Ionian

A breather on the steps of the Celsus Library, Ephesus ruins

Main Street, Ephesus

beginnings and influences, it was built on the slopes of Mt. Pion, and then moved southwest of the mountain to the slopes of Mt. Koressos. By 600 BCE it had become a prosperous trading and banking center. Caravans came and went, ships sailed into its harbor. Most of the surviving and very extensive ruins belong to the Roman imperial period, just before and after AD. St. Paul showed up in 57 AD, but his zealous Christian teachings ruined the local market for effigies to a favorite pagan goddess, and he was chased out of town after three years.

Our hike begins at the south end of the ruins and follows the impressive, flagged Harbour Street that once covered a sophisticated sewer system. We flow with the mobs past the gymnasium, baths, theater, the agora (marketplace), and numerous temples. Terraced Roman houses with their public latrine—a social gathering place ("chat while you defecate")—are covered with a translucent roof for preservation. The outstanding monument is the enormous Celsus Library, where we rest on steep steps in the shadow of its two imposing tiers of columns. Then we push through clumps of wild poppies and hollyhocks to scuttle up the stone seats of the horseshoe-shaped stadium and dusty masonry remnants. At the end, on a lane lined with soughing pines, Eric, Steve and the kids volunteer to run the three kilometers back to Selçuk to get the van. The rest of us recover from the heat in a restaurant with ice cream and muddy Turkish coffee.

An Ancient Greek City Is Ours Alone

The next afternoon we set out for Priene, another notable ruin—this one a Greek city in Ionia. Everybody piles into the van with Eric at the helm, supposedly an hour's drive from Selçuk. After driving tediously through crowded new cities rebuilt after the terrible earthquake of the mid-1960s that killed some twenty thousand inhabitants, we realize we're royally lost. We find that Turkish drivers are indeed insane: at one point we come to a red light, and when it turns green we pull out, but cars in the other lane plow right through their red light as though it exists only to be ignored. We quickly learn that no one pays attention to lights or warning signs or rules of the roundabouts; all driving must be hyper-defensive.

The characteristic domes and minarets of local mosques—often painted in garish colors—appear frequently along our route. Most of the women we see in villages are veiled. Some towns are squashed between mountains laced with almost vertical dirt roads or goat paths. A typical scene in village after village is a little bunch of men lounging in front of a café playing cards or passively watching the world go by. The women are no doubt laboring at home.

Nobody speaks English, making it especially hard when we're continually lost and backtracking and trying to get directions. Anne is heroic and creative when she hops out repeatedly with the map to ask our way in gestures. Finally, we make it to Priene. We set out on a steep, rough hike under the brow of a gigantic peak—Mt. Mykale—and, as usual, it's blazing hot. At the top are the breathtaking ruins of a city built by the Ionians in 350 BCE, all the more special because we are the only visitors in this late afternoon. Most beautiful are five giant, intact, limestone columns—what is left of the Temple of Athena. The remains of this Hellenic metropolis go on and on. We find an amphitheater where Nicky and Katie try out the carved seats and slide down tilted pillars. We find mesmerizing the constant loud drone of cicadas and the sighing of pine trees all around, swelling like a symphony when the wind rises.

We revel in having the entire city to ourselves. Great chunks of fallen columns—hundreds—are lying everywhere. There is writing on some, as well as faded bits of frescoes and ornate carving on random stones. We scramble up and down the many levels, traversing the agora and climbing into the foundations of intimate rooms in the houses. At one point, the group splits up and we explore different return paths that circle the mountain, always crawling over rocks and relics. This is an especially meaningful adventure for me; I feel we really own this place for a bit. We've been permitted to steal quietly into its heart and breathe in concert with those long-ago inhabitants without the intrusion of their modern descendents. We've shared the satisfaction they must have felt perched in their lofty aerie/fortress from which to survey the entire region spread out below.

Coming back to contemporary reality in Selçuk is jarring. It's a busy Saturday evening, and when we try to get close to the supermarket, the total gridlock, along with wild drivers careening around us, makes this an almost impossible destination with our unwieldy vehicle. However, with aplomb and relish, Eric squeezes through spaces with millimeters to spare as his passengers duck under the seats praying just to stay alive. Incidentally, Bel paid $200 for gas to fill the van; from here it's clear that we can't moan about the rising prices in America, at least so far.

Detour to the Datça Peninsula—Paradise for a Moment

Eric has been dealing with a pinched nerve in his hip and leg; it's worse, but he's game to get started. We clean the house, pack up remaining food, and set off in the two vehicles. Our destination today is Datça. We'll have a one-night stopover there to break the long journey to the bottom of Turkey. Then it's on to a villa we've booked in the hills above the Mediterranean. As we ride, often in the distance, we spot rows of spires and can't tell whether they're cypress trees, minarets, or cell phone towers. Clumps of

The decadent life at Villa Asina on the Datça Peninsula

laborers are at work in farm fields. Marge has a theory: that the rug salesmen in the myriad stores in Turkey may be part of the drug trade, maybe acting as pass-through agents for merchandise coming in from Afghanistan. We discuss how a large part of the economy here must be underground. For instance, Steve had to wire money for some of our housing and actually must carry a great quantity of British pounds to pay cash for others.

Coming into fields of shale, our passengers note that it's starting to look like New Mexico or the Dakota Badlands. Then more change: past Marmoris, we're in fjord country, with serrated peaks plunging straight down to the sea. Masted schooners dot the water. We start out along the long, skinny Datça peninsula that curves, climbs, and dips. At the end, in the town of Datça, we're lost again. Anne snares a kind electrician who gets out his cell to call our hotel, Villa Asina, then offers to lead us there. It's a convoluted route we could never have found on our own.

Heaven in a Hammock

We draw rooms with ample balconies facing the Aegean Sea. It's deliciously silent. Guests lounge drowsily around the pool. Tea and sweets will be served soon, but Eric, Bel, and Steve's tribe all rush like lemmings to steps that lead down to the water. "The swimming is divine!" they report. Everybody takes turns swinging in the hanging thatched chairs on the lawn. Whimsical, colorful art—stylized animals and fruits in tiles and mosaics, and modernized adaptations of the Ottoman Iznik designs—is all around, embedded in the walls, steps and carved doors. The obligatory sapphire blue eye wards off evil.

I feel a bit shaky, so I slip into the pool to float and recover from our long ride. Eric's hip cramp isn't improving, and he thinks he is also running a low fever. As evening closes in, a warm breeze comes up to waft the mosquito netting draped inside thatched umbrellas. Swallows wheel and dip while Zorba's theme music issues quietly from the hedges.

We sit down to dinner in the garden at 8:00, which lasts until 10:30. The pièce de résistance, an enormous red snapper that's been steamed in a breaded crust, is presented dramatically and carved while we watch. In the middle of the ceremony, there's a sudden poof! A huge flash of fire leaps up from the kitchen (visible from our dining terrace), and all the lights blow out. The cooks race outside, terrified. When nothing explodes, candles are lit, an electrician is called, and dinner continues, shakily.

Regretting that we didn't book two nights in this paradise, we start off again. We pass at least a dozen huge wind generators perched on mountain ridges, a sign that Turkey is alert to the need for renewable energy. In the past couple of years, there has been massive infrastructure construction throughout the country, especially the modernizing and widening of roads. Turkey is booming economically and is clearly prosperous.

At one point, we find ourselves cutting through a cleft between a saw-toothed range of white rock on one side and layers of blue mountains on the other. We swoop down on Kinik, an entire city of greenhouses; apparently all produce is grown inside here rather than in fields. Tomatoes on poles press against the roofs.

Islamar: Our Mountain Aerie

Directions to our Villa Tranquillità are fuzzy. We descend into the nearest city, Kalkan, and then begin to climb a narrow road, hunting for our obscure dirt driveway. It's in the hamlet of Islamar, which, after a couple of runs for food, our drivers eventually figure out. Finally, success, and triumphantly we struggle to get the wide van through a cramped gate. A no-nonsense German-Swiss lady who lives across the road is on hand to greet us (grumpy that we're late) and recites instructions. The house is huge. It's crammed with ancient carved furniture, antique trunks, hookahs, and scimitars, along with modern sofas and chairs on every veranda, terrace, and balcony.

Eric's nerve pain keeps him awake much of our first night, and he badly needs to find a body worker. Our gardener offers to take him to a shack in the next village, where he is placed on the floor of the living room. The family crowds around to kibitz while two men work him over. He returns home with a heat pack taped to his back and finds he can now lie down without pain. He soon feels well enough to drive to town with Steve and Bel, where they investigate the possibility of hiring a boat.

Saklikent Gorge—Exhilaration Triumphs Pain

We're up for an early start to Saklikent Gorge, a major expedition. This is considered one of the wonders of Turkey. We opt for the back-roads route through primitive villages, where clumps of goats ignore and block our van. As we approach the gorge, we're swallowed in the shadow of looming, vertical cliffs—"Canyon of the Hidden Valley." Carved from the waters flowing from Akdag Mountain, the gorge walls are over fifteen hundred feet tall. They're so steep and narrow that the sun never penetrates, making this a welcome respite from the burning heat everywhere else. The air here is cool, and even cold, because of the frigid water frothing through the canyon.

From the parking lot, we're steered to the racks of rubber shoes that are obligatory for walking up the riverbed—which is why people come. We squeeze into shoes that immediately start to pinch and hurt, and then traverse a little bridge over the tumbling torrents. Following a catwalk along the cliff, we come to the moment of truth: to go for it or not. By this time, Bel's borrowed shoes have already raised a blister, and he's also wondering how his balance might be affected by the swift currents. He decides to sit this one out.

Maybe I should follow suit, but I'm just stubborn enough to refuse to admit my age and possible limitations. Have to keep up at all costs. So, after a moment's waver, I join the others, who are crowding down to the water's edge. A couple of guides will go along to steer us around underwater hazards, help us avoid sudden deep spots or drop-offs, and (in my case) grab my arm so I won't get knocked down in especially strong surges.

"Everybody, please hold hands!" the two guides shout to our group. We step down into what seem at

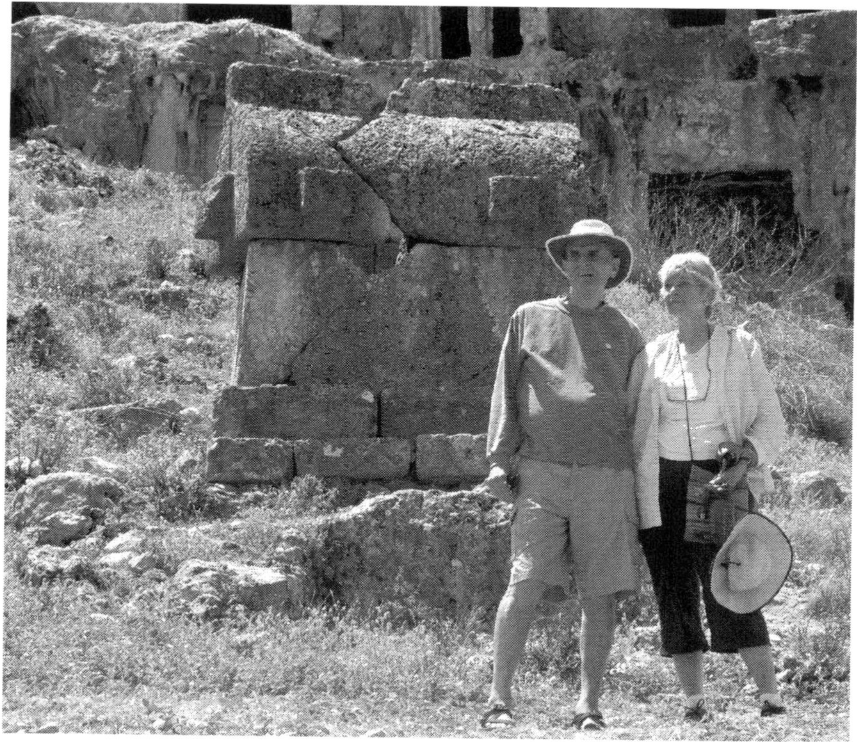

Doug and Marge brave 110 degree heat climbing to the house tombs of Tlos

first to be icy waters but that soon actually feel comfortable and refreshing. This initial dunking when the river boils up to waist level is probably the most difficult; it is indeed helpful to be steadied by many joined hands. Soon the currents are mostly less challenging, and it's primarily an endurance slog, where we're pushing uphill against the swirling waters. The toughest and most annoying part is when our rubber shoes keep filling with sharp pebbles, and we're able to empty them only infrequently on the fly.

Mired in the lovely cool gloom, busy becoming one with the river, we keep marveling at this spectacle of nature, the span between the two towering walls of the canyon not much more than twenty feet apart, with just a hint of daylight way above. Then there comes a point where the guides divide the sheep from the goats. The last lap involves trickier climbing, larger boulders to surmount, and swifter currents as the river floor grows steeper. Doug, Marge, Anne, and I hang out on a muddy little beach ("base camp") and nurse our poor feet while Eric, Steve, Nicky, and Katie forge on toward the "summit." A half hour later these four reappear triumphantly, and we all begin the return trek. "There were times," Eric reports, "when we were scrambling through the high water, we just slid and had to jump into pools over our heads."

It's a lot quicker moving downstream, and shortly we're back at the starting point, where again we form a human chain to brace ourselves through the powerful current.

Tlos: Attraction of the Long-Dead

Undoubtedly this has been enough exertion for one day, but no, because on the way home, we'll pass right by the famed Tlos ruins. Naturally we have to stop to look. Hittite artifacts show that Tlos goes back to 2000 BCE. Then it became one of the most important Lycian cities, and finally Roman. Most striking, at first, is its dramatic location—on a high promontory that dominates the surrounding Xanthos Valley. On an outcrop, we see rows of pillars defining a series of rock-cut "house" tombs so elaborate that they resemble little temples. One of the most imposing tombs was for Bellerophon, who purportedly slew the Chimaera from his winged horse Pegasus (depicted on a bas-relief on a rock face).

We pile out of the van, hit by midday sauna heat (around 110 degrees) and contemplate the daunting climb ahead. On the way, we pass a large sarcophagus standing alone in a field. On the plain below, a crew of archeologists is busily digging among the ancient banks of stone seats in the stadium and the gymnasium. They're trundling away rocks in wheelbarrows. We climb, stopping to peer into terraced tombs on the way and to find momentary shelter from the burning sun in the caves. The usual hardies leap effortlessly on up, past the necropolis, to explore the fortress/castle at the top. The rest of us are content to rest and paw through old stones and shards, hoping to uncover tiny treasures.

Everybody clamors back down to the parking lot, where a man is selling stone carvings. His veiled, long-skirted wife sits chipping the stone in her lap with a big knife. Their little boy, about seven, brags, "My English is better than your Turkish" in very good English. We can't argue.

On the way back, we get lost here and there on the dirt roads. Women in headscarves are selling produce at little market stands. At one point, we come to a river where a busload of tourists is gathered on the bank in two circles. One circle has just dunked in the mud and is totally black; the second one is holding hands and preparing to jump in. Some funky New Age ritual?

"Home" feels very good! Ice cold beer and bottled water, and then a leap into the pool—even better. After cooling down, I stretch out on one of at least a dozen chaises scattered around the four levels of our house. The bucolic scene: heavy clusters of grapes hanging from the pergola overhead and purple bougainvillea at my elbow. Down a few steps, a giant hammock, and under the pergola, a table for twelve with candelabras and a crystal chandelier suspended from a tree festooned with beads. The call to prayer is echoing through the canyon. Our gardener moves quietly through beds of yellow gazania and sets sprinklers among newly-planted palm trees. His wife plucks peaches for us from one of the fruit trees, and their two-year-old daughter skips by, waving and flirting. She responds to our "Merhaba!" ("Hi") with her own shy "Merhaba."

Down to the Sea in Ships

It's our big day on the Mediterranean. We've reserved a smallish motorboat (with optional sails) just for our gang. Two young sailors will take care of all our wants. Setting out from the Kalkan harbor, we skirt the peninsula and begin leisurely visits to several islands. Early on, two dolphins leap from the water in tandem, "a sign of luck for the day," our hosts say. Then a giant sea turtle surges to the surface and vanishes into the deep.

Five times we drop anchor and leap off to swim in the delicious, deep water, layered turquoise and teal blue. We're a considerable distance from shore, which turns out to be an unexpected challenge for some of us (me) to make it to land and then back again to the boat—it was farther away than I thought. But Steve's family, especially, is in its element; Anne beams like a Cheshire cat the entire day. Our crew turns into expert cooks, disappearing below deck in their tiny kitchen to prepare our food. Out come potato salad and fresh greens, a fish casserole, beans, yogurt, olives, rolled pastries filed with ricotta, fries, fruits, wine, beer, and sodas.

The islands we visit are mainly white limestone with wind-sculpted pines poking through cracks. There's a lovely moment when eerie, soft music emanates from a tall ship anchored near us; it turns out to be wind playing across the lines at the top of the mast. The kids and adults take turns with snorkels and masks and fins. At the last anchoring, one of our hosts swims ashore balancing a pink bucket above his head; he disappears into a cave and comes out with the bucket full of mud. After lining the guys up on shore, he pours the black muck over their heads. They proceed to smear it all over their bodies for photos from the boat. After washing off, they declare their skin to be soft as silk.

It's after 6:30 when we pull into the dock, and I realize that I've probably gotten too much sun. Suddenly I'm burning up and yet chilled, and so exhausted I can barely make it from the shower to my bed.

"The Conversation," a Little Sun Damage, and Final Rituals

Everybody else is pretty worn out too, and we're all happy to lie low the next day. We straggle out for a late breakfast on the terrace, and "The Conversation" begins. It seems that every time we're on a vacation, with whatever family configuration, there's at least one extended gabfest that turns into a sharing of serious life questions, choices, thoughts, and appreciations of each other. It is an important ingredient of our family dynamic—every time we get together, we "get down to it" and share our vulnerabilities and intimate feelings.

It's a treasured moment of closeness; nobody wants to leave. Nicky and Katie hang in on the periphery, listening avidly for a good part of the morning.

Anne diagnoses my nausea, headache, and general malaise as probable heat exhaustion. She whips up a concoction of salt, sugar, and lemon "to replace your electrolytes." Meanwhile others go off to swim at gorgeous Patara Beach, with its eleven-mile stretch of perfect white sand. Some explore our immediate environs. Doug, Marge, and Eric hike up to Islamar, our little village. Men are scything and goats are grazing on the side of the ravine directly across from our house. Marge reports checking in a cemetery: "We saw headstones where a birth date might be listed as 1202—that's according to the old Islamic calendar—and the date of death would be in the modern calendar, adopted later by Atatürk."

Steve takes a solitary walk and waves to a shepherd parked on a ridge above, with his four-legged charges. As Steve tries to figure out which path to take, the shepherd keeps signaling directions until they finally meet. Steve tells us later, "I suddenly found myself feeling envious. It could really be a very pleasant life, just lolling all day with my animals in the midst of breathtaking scenery, with plenty of time to contemplate the grand meanings of things." One wonders, though, is that really what shepherds do?

With a magic rehydration elixir procured at a Kalkan pharmacy, my symptoms rapidly fade and I'm ready to join the group for the next expedition, to Kaş. This is an almost excessively cute village up the coast, shops jammed together with stunning wares and endless cafés. Red and white banners flap smartly across the flagged streets; carved wooden balconies adorn all the buildings. Kaş has clearly become a magnet for the many young vagabond internationals we encounter—identified by trendy or hippie clothes and chattering in various languages. Dozens of boats crowd together in the tiny harbor. It's all very compact, colorful, and atmospheric compared to drab Kalkan.

Back at the villa, Eric fires up the charcoal grill for barbecued chicken and a lovely final dinner on the terrace. We note an island far below that seems to rise disembodied from the mists just as the *adhan*, the call to prayer, reverberates between the hills. We retire to our quarters to pack.

Past our villa on the way to pasture

Back in Istanbul, everybody scurries around to see what they may have missed earlier. Bel happily makes it to the Grand Bazaar, with its crush of glittering stalls, returning with a little bronze whirling dervish. We assemble at the rooftop restaurant of our hotel for a chilly farewell dinner, the Blue Mosque and Aya Sofya almost hanging over us. As it darkens, the six minarets of the mosque light up; illuminated white gulls sail among them. A last look out at the city: on one side, lights blink on, while boats chug up the Sea of Marmara on the other.

Reflections

On our last lap on the journey home, as I snoozed on the bus from Chicago, I had time to appreciate the astonishing blessing of each trip we take—that we are so considerate and caring of each other. For nine family members, including three generations, to make it through a grueling journey like this with only harmony and delight is an achievement I don't imagine many families could replicate! Each one of us seemed to have a talent or strength to contribute which, taken as a totality, created a resourceful, empathetic crew, extraordinarily attuned to each other.

When I jumped off the boat, Eric made it his job to swim companionably next to me, realizing that I might be getting tired. When I got up in the middle of the night feeling sick from too much sun, Anne was immediately on the job to research rehydration remedies on the Internet and to make up a concoction for me. The guys volunteered soon afterward to make the annoying trek down the mountain to comb Kalkan for pharmacies for medication. Marge and Doug were always alert to stresses or problems others in the group might be having and were ready with practical help. Even when Eric was in obvious pain from his pinched nerve and couldn't sleep, he didn't complain; it was only when everyone, greatly concerned, pushed him to find help that he approached the gardener to take him for therapy. And despite exhaustion and extreme discomfort, it never occurred to him to let the family down by not driving the larger vehicle, which only he could do.

And Katie and Nicky, along with the men, were always the first to suggest or lead the next outing or game, an enthusiasm that was infectious and pulled the whole group to exciting adventures we might otherwise have missed.

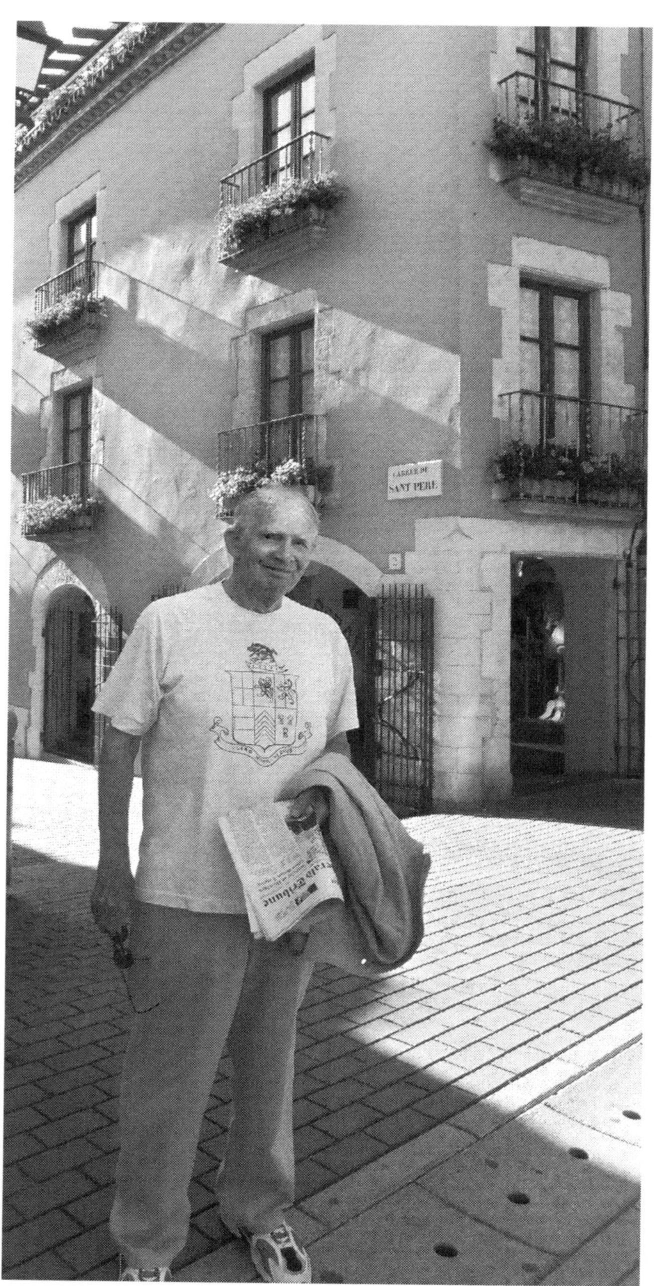

Colorful Begur, our base in Spain

The French Dordogne and Catalan Spain

Cultures in Stone

JUNE-JULY 2012

FRANCE

Backstory

It was at a Thanksgiving family gathering in Madison that, after the recent successful trip to Turkey, we started to think about another group affair. At first we talked about France, narrowing it down to the southwest of that country, when Steve became intrigued with the prehistoric cave drawings there. Then we thought that as long as we were near the Spanish border, why not push on to balance the inland French countryside experience with a taste of the sea on the Costa Brava in northwest Spain?

With the promise of a radio interview, Steve sealed visits to a couple of caves under the guidance of Christine Desdemaines-Hugon, perhaps the foremost expert on prehistoric cave drawings and artifacts in the Dordogne region.

This will be another family mob scene with three generations. For the flight to France, Steve's family, with Anne, Katie (sixteen), and Nicky (fourteen), will fly from Chicago with Bel and me. Doug, Marge, and Niko (twenty-nine), who all live in Virginia, will link up for a flight from D. C. Everyone will rendezvous in Paris for an overnight.

Paris in a Few Memorable Hours

Once in the air, the Wisconsin contingent breathes more freely, recalling the dismal airport snafu last year. That was when we went to Turkey (previous chapter), when two flight cancellations made us lose three of our four initial days in Istanbul. Miraculously, everybody shows up at the same time at the projected hour at our strategically located Hotel Muguet on tiny Rue Chevert. Our time in Paris is short, and those who have never been here want to cram in all they can. We hurry on foot past Les Invalides, the hospital and retirement home for old soldiers, commissioned by Louis XIV in 1670. Napoleon Bonaparte and many more recent military figures are buried under its impressive golden domed chapel. We're impressed with the embankment of copper-colored antique cannons, and then are on to the famous Alexandre III bridge. Wildly ornate, it has been featured in numerous films, most recently, *Midnight in Paris.*

We dance along the bridge, admiring its black Art Nouveau lamps with sculptures of nymphs and cherubs, and where, atop towering columns, the golden Fames restrain Pegasus. Little ferryboats steam by on the sparkling Seine below. Since Bel and I are wilting from jetlag (and have seen it all before), we wander back to the hotel. The others hike on—to see Notre Dame in the lovely, fading light, then to the Musée de l'Orangerie for Monet's water lilies. Located at the corner of the Tuileries Gardens, the Orangerie is a gallery housing important impressionist and post-impressionist paintings. For the grand finale, though exhausted, at Katie and Nicky's insistence, Steve's family presses on to catch the lighted Eiffel Tower.

Hurtling South on the Bullet Train

Next morning we're ready to leave for the Montparnasse railway station. Our two cabs arrive. Steve's speeds off first, and he shouts for the rest of us to meet them where we're dropped off. Big mistake: our cab pulls up at the station, but there's no family in sight. We frantically check out other possible entrances and note the clock ominously ticking toward our train's departure time. Thankfully Anne appears suddenly in the midst of the crowds. We round up the others and race with our bags down the tracks.

This is the TGV, the high-speed bullet train to Bordeaux that supposedly can travel up to 200 mph. Doug and I sit together for the three-hour ride—very smooth—and begin a leisurely review of childhood memories growing up together in Connecticut, a luxury we seldom have. Verdant fields with vineyards and huge wind generators whirl past.

At the Bordeaux station, we collect our rental cars for the rest of the trip: a little Clio for Steve's four, and for the other five of us, a seven-seat hybrid Alhambra van. Steve and Niko are the designated drivers. We're quickly out of the city and heading east. Niko proves immediately to be a superb driver—speedy, never rattled, and adept at turning around our large vehicle in impossibly tight spots. The slower route through small towns is more picturesque than the highways, but the continual roundabouts are hard on Nicky's carsick tendencies. At one point we have to stop while he hangs near a rosebush in misery.

Prehistoric Cave Country

As we proceed, the little stone villages become more interesting. Open fields give way to woodsy patches, then rolling hills, and then limestone cliffs—where the ancient caves are located. We've picked a villa in Les Eyzies de Tayac, the prime town in the heart of the cave country.

Anne locates our landlord, Roland, and he leads the way a couple of miles up a winding road above Les Eyzies. Abruptly we turn into a precipitous dirt drive opposite three grazing cows and shortly reach Le Secadou—our home for a week. Built into a wooded hillside, it's a charming, elegant house with a wide view that spreads out beyond the pool below. Our host is a former prize-winning chef, and he shows us around the amazing kitchen. There are both gas *and* electric stoves, with designated drawers with special pots for each one, two or three ovens, a Japanese hibachi, intricate machines for various kinds of coffee-grinding, and several esoteric machines and devices that even Anne hasn't a clue about.

Bel picks for us the one (very elegant) bedroom on the ground floor. Curiously, there's a freestanding bathtub in the middle of the large room surrounded by decadent stands of designer bath salts and scents, silk flowers, and erotic paintings on the walls. Most curious (and disconcerting) is the toilet, also standing in the center of the room. One would hesitate to enter the room without knocking.

The next day is Sunday, and beyond buying a few emergency groceries at the one open bakery, we make do and declare it a lazy day to recuperate from the long drive. Steve and Anne bring back several bottles of good wine, having been offered generous samples in the shop—how civilized! We take glasses onto our grandstand balcony overlooking the pool and gardens of cypress, tropical yuccas, hydrangeas, and giant lavender bushes. The view skims the tops of descending layers of trees to the limestone cliffs. At night, far below, Les Eyzies lights up like a distant Christmas display.

Now we're ready to explore our Perigord Noir region. Sarlat is the hub town for much of the history and architectural significance in the area. The dark, twelfth century buildings are photogenic, the cathedral impressive, and the ice cream selections wonderful (we seem to stop for *glace* "for stamina" at every opportunity). In subsequent days, we lose ourselves in the hanging gardens of Marqueyssac—a six-acre maze of trails that weave among bizarre, lumpy mounds of topiary hedges—and climb to the fortress town of Dome, with its thirteenth century ramparts overlooking the silver Dordogne River threading through squares of green and gold farm fields.

Canoes and Kayaks on the Dordogne

Then it's our day *on* the Dordogne River. Renting three canoes and two kayaks at Vitrac Port, we put into the river, paddling easily in a nice current. There are tiny patches of whitewater, but mostly it's peaceful and dreamy, and very quiet. Others are drifting placidly with us, and from time to time, a larger boat stirs up a wake. Tall bushes and willows dip gracefully into the water. Hawks soar, thrushes sing. In the four-and-a-half hours

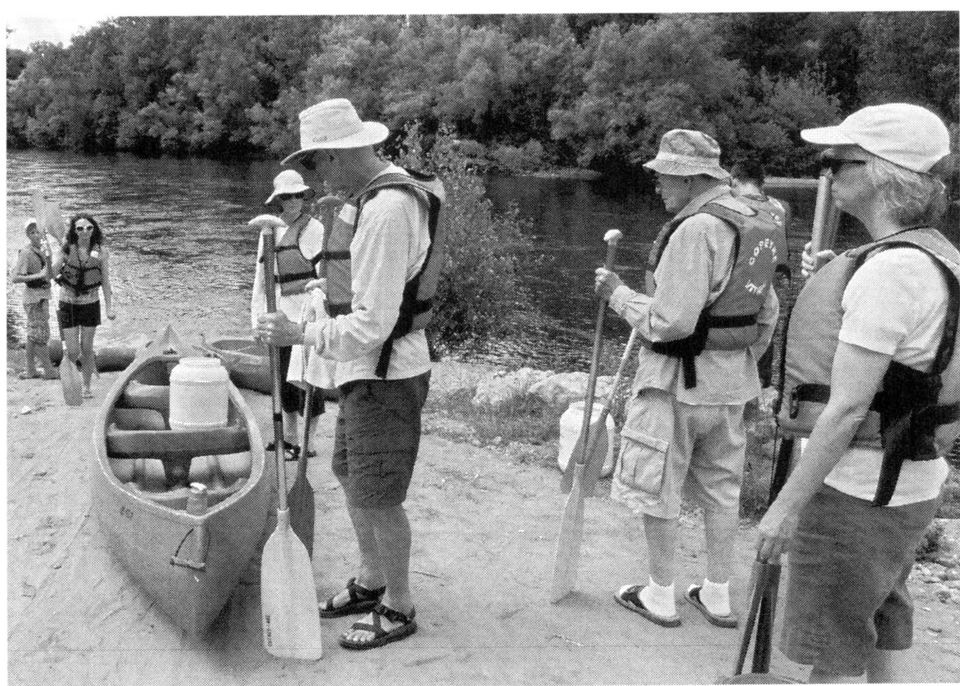

Preparing to canoe and kayak down the Dordogne River

Anne, our chef extraordinaire, opens yet another bottle of superb Bordeaux

we're on the water, we cover twelve kilometers and pass under three enormous, arched bridges. At La Roque-Gageac, we're ready for a break. We drag our five crafts up onto the rocks to take a look at this bustling town that climbs onto the cliffs behind. When suddenly we realize we're running behind schedule, we have to sprint to make our 4 p.m. rendezvous. We round up the troops and rapidly splash back through shallows to the boats. All the paddlers bend to their task and really begin to sweat. Anne is now piloting one of the kayaks alone, and when she pulls a muscle in her arm, is barely able to make it to the Beynac end point. Luckily, because we're late, the bus to drive us back to our cars has waited for us.

Can't wait to leap into our heavenly pool when we hit home. Over grilled pork with rosemary potatoes, we think up questions for Christine, our cave expert, tomorrow.

Stepping into Prehistory: Ruffignac Cave

It's the big cave expedition. In Les Eyzies, we pick up Christine. She rides in Steve's car the twelve kilometers to Ruffignac Cave. A prehistoric anthropologist, she is an attractive, blond woman in her early sixties. Born in England, she has, however, lived in France for many years. She leads Smithsonian tours of the caves and recently wrote a definitive book, *Stepping Stones: A Journey Through the Ice Age Caves of the Dordogne.* It describes the art and archaeology of several of the important caves, tracing the evolution of the Paleolithic/Cro-Magnon peoples (classified as the same species of present-day humans). Steve had been in touch with Christine for many months, arranging for her to guide us in two of the most interesting caves. Throughout the day, his microphone is turned on to record their conversation and her explanations of what we are seeing.

As we approach Ruffignac, a huge cave in the Vezere Valley, we find it situated beneath a high hill. Its dark, open maw is some twenty-five feet wide and maybe twelve feet high. It is presumed that Ruffignac, called "the cave of the hundred mammoths," was formed in the Pliocene Age, three to two million years ago, as water dissolved the limestone. Now it's mostly dry except for a small stream at the lowest level. Unlike some other caves, there are no stalactites or stalagmites because the limestone here is mostly waterproof clay. The cave's existence was known at least as long ago as the 1500s when papers were written about it. The Pissard family bought the property in 1915 and has maintained it privately ever since. Visits are strictly regulated to preserve the air/humidity balance.

The images have been dated to 13,000 years BP (before the present). Mammoth drawings indicate that the artists go back to Paleolithic times. Ruffignac was officially recognized as prehistoric because of the drawings of the woolly rhinoceros. For comparison, the Neanderthals went back to around 200,000 BP and were extinct by 30,000 BP. They were a different species than the Paleolithic (who were humans like us). The remains of animal bones, tools, and fireplaces at the cave entrance date to Mesolithic and Neolithic people (10,000 to 5,000 BCE, the Stone Age). "None of these people would have lived in the cave," Christine explains, "because it was too damp and cold. It's clear that they camped outside."

More recently Ruffignac served as a hiding place for the French Resistance during World War II.

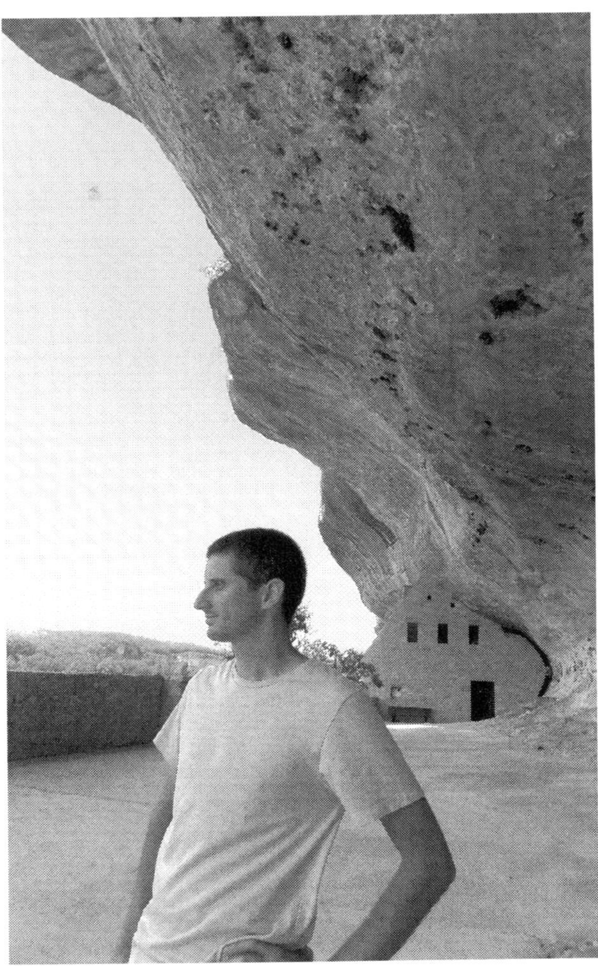

Niko at the Museum of Pre-history in Les Eyzies

We enter the cave to find a little shop tucked into the rock and crowds waiting to go in. The owners have built a battery-operated, narrow-gauge railway with open miniature trains to carry visitors into the cavernous interior. We pull on our sweaters (the temperature is fifty degrees), hop on, and rumble into the darkness. Steve struggles to record over the noise of the loud, French-speaking guide competing with Christine's spiel. The cave is ten kilometers long (we only go in about two), with three levels of galleries and myriad passageways. Natural shafts lead down to the deeper levels. As our train passes the drawings and engravings, a wall-mounted spotlight flashes on briefly to illuminate the art, then switches off, and all is dark. It's interesting that some drawings look very different when seen from different angles, and sometimes aren't even visible from the front. Details of the animals are anatomically correct (we see the flap to protect the anus of mammoths). Astonishingly, the artists painted the ceilings on their backs. These ceilings are now eight to thirteen meters high; they must have been lower then.

Unlike Lascaux cave (where visitors are no longer allowed), where the color of the paintings is filled in, the art here—250 images—is all black (manganese) line drawings. They are outlines of animals, not humans. The only hint of human presence: handprints. We see drawings of bison, mammoths, horses, woolly rhinoceroses, ibexes, oryxes, and goats, as well as sixteen mysterious tectiforms—symbols that are either house-like or snake-like. There is one image of a bear, and as we inspect the walls, we see scratch marks showing that bears hibernated here; there are large indentations in the stones indicating bear beds. These cave bears went extinct twenty-three thousand years ago.

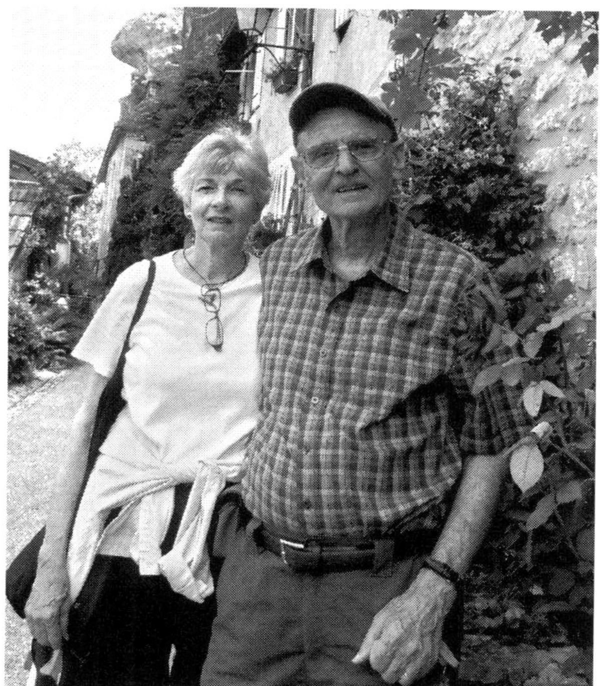

Marge and Doug stroll past houses built into cliffs in our 'hometown,' Les Eyzies

It is believed that some of the engravings were made by children. We're struck by the incredible grace and perfection of these line drawings, how they capture action and mood in a few spare strokes. A single outline depicts an animal clearly with its humps, horns, tusks, and often a "happy" expression. The artist indicated perspective by detaching a more distant leg from the body. Some drawings were made with a flint chisel, others with a finger. Like Christine, we're struck by the electrifying, near-spiritual experience of connecting intimately with the lives and ambience of these people who lived so many thousands of years ago. At the far end of the ride, we climb off the train to stumble around in the dark of a large "chapel" with many engravings. Animals are crowded all over the Great Ceiling.

We emerge into blinding daylight and heat, and proceed to Christine's favorite restaurant perched on the side of a sheltering cliff. It is charming and intimate; the staff knows her well and welcomes our group warmly. The lunch is outstanding—roast duck that falls succulently off the bones.

Fortified, we're ready to forge on to the next cave: Bernifal.

Bernifal Cave: Trusting Our Lives to a Wizened Old Farmer with a Big Key

Bernifal is just outside our own town, Les Eyzies, and proves to be a totally different experience from Ruffignac. Christine is closely connected to Gilbert Pemendrant, the seventy-eight-year-old farmer who owns the property and cultivates the fields. An older brother of the farmer, had been passionately protecting the cave, promoting it and taking visitors inside. When he died two years ago, Gilbert took over custodianship.

We park near the road and wait for the farmer to arrive. He bumps up in his ancient pickup truck. We shake hands all around, and then he drives slowly ahead, leading us on a half-mile hike through a hornbeam forest. This is an intimate, private tour, arranged by Christine just for our family. We climb the last rise and spot a large wooden door wedged between boulders on a steep hillside.

This is the entrance to a karst cave—limestone that is pitted from underground streams—discovered with its engravings in 1905. Apparently this entrance was originally open, but then collapsed and was obscured by debris for twelve thousand years (perhaps deliberately to protect the art?). The cave was entered at another point through the roof, necessitating climbing down a ladder. The natural entrance was reopened in 1935.

M. Pemendrant limps slowly up to the door of his cave and pulls out a large key. We squeeze inside and he locks the door behind us so that no one else approaching will come in. We're locked into the cave, and our only illumination is a flashlight powered by a heavy battery pack the farmer carries on his stooped back. We speculate a bit nervously what would happen if he dropped or lost the key or keeled over from a heart attack, or his light failed. If we're not standing right next to him, we're in total darkness. This cave is not nearly as extensive as Ruffignac, but big enough. We walk carefully, trying not to trip on the stalagmites, an obstacle course of spears sticking up all over the cave floor. Some of these almost meet stalactites hanging from the roof. The process of their formation is ongoing, and we're constantly splashed with dripping water.

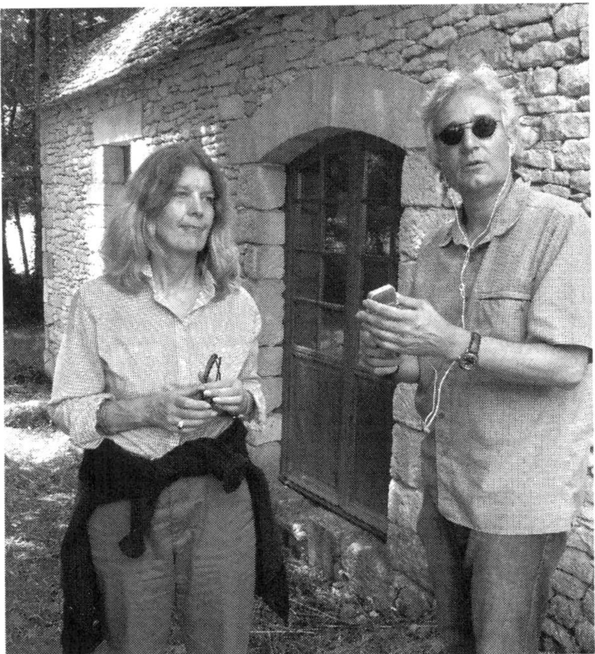

Steve records explanations of Christine Desdemaine-Hugon, our prehistoric cave guide before we explore Bernifal Cave

Conversation between Christine and cave owner Gilbert Pemendrante

Christine points out the drawings, some executed with a finger because the limestone is so soft, some with a crayon. Others are etched. Unlike the first cave, here there are also human as well as the usual animal depictions. Some of the animals are completely and ingeniously delineated by the natural contours of the rocks. The bulges and curves of the stone are used for suggesting creatures and build on this for a 3-D effect. The most startling feature is a haunting human face—*our ancestor!* The eyes (slightly Asian, as we imagine ET) look directly at us. From one angle the image looks male with a beard and topknot; from another, it is clearly feminine.

At one point, Doug has a request: "Could the light be turned off for a few minutes so that we may stand silently in the dark—to absorb or feel 'whatever'?" M. Pemendrant douses his flashlight. In the blackness, we hear only the drip of the stalactites in 100 percent humidity. Some later report sensing the presence or appreciation from those ancient artists as we were marveling at their amazing skill. Years ago Picasso visited the Dordogne caves and declared that those prehistoric forebears had mastered the secrets of great art that no one since has been able to equal. For example, they worked with cubism by showing animals front and sideways at the same time. "They could teach *us*," Picasso said.

Christine points out many tectiforms—the symbols created from patterns of dots that form roof shapes, sometimes superimposed on the animals, on the walls, and also on the ceiling. In all, there are some one hundred engravings and pictures. The most frequently depicted animal is the mammoth. We also spot human handprints.

At various points we must duck our heads and squeeze through narrow passages, being careful not to touch the rocks at any time. This could deposit bacteria that would eventually destroy the artwork.

Christine again emphasizes that these Paleolithic people never lived in the caves but entered them only to place their art. "Perhaps the pictures were not meant to be viewed, or by very few," she conjectures. She continues:

The indefatigable explorers atop Beynac Castle

> Maybe the caves were temples. They might have been spiritual places, with images that could be communed with from a distance—telepathically. It's possible that the people recognized the symbiosis between animals and the cave, and also among trees, rocks, creatures, and people—that they are all constituted from the same element. Maybe animals were

recognized as having perfected instincts that are superior to humans. I believe these people certainly recognized humans' interdependence with nature. This is reinforced by the contours of the cave that depict animal forms. Could this have been shamanism, animism? We can't know the spirituality of the Paleolithic societies. Clearly they appreciated beauty. The same things moved them as move us moderns. Beauty is definitely a spiritual quality.

Along with stone implements, needles have been found among the artifacts; the needles have fine eyes, indicating that the people used fine thread to make clothing. These were humans, fourteen thousand years ago, with brains and physiques similar to ours, not the stooped, ape-like Neanderthals who came earlier. Many of their artifacts are displayed now in the superb archaeological museum in Les Eyzies.

Christine points to a narrow, perilous, thirty-foot chimney that she once climbed with great difficulty to find a choice engraving at the top. She tells of wriggling into almost impossible spots over the forty years that she's been exploring and writing about caves.

Just as we're approaching the door, our elderly caretaker switches off his light, plunges us into blackness, and calls playfully, "Au revoir!" We're glad to step out into the heat (and glad the owner found his key to let us out). Other visitors are waiting and hoping for a tour. We retrace our steps through the woods, where both ground and trees are covered with moss. There's a faint whiff of jasmine. The farmer precedes us again in his rickety truck.

Beynac Castle: We Plunge into Twelfth Century Feudal Life

Another major expedition is to twelfth century, feudal Beynac castle. It's overcast and cool, perfect for hiking around the precipitous little village of Beynac. We snake up sharply from the Dordogne River to the castle, perched on the pinnacle of a sheer cliff, where from the watchtowers stretch grand panoramas. To protect the castle against assault, double crenellated walls and double moats were constructed. The Hundred Years War was going on, and because at that time, Dordogne was the boundary between France and England, the area saw a lot of combat. The castle was so well fortified and invincibly situated, however, that no faction could muster the power to take it. When it did fall, it was

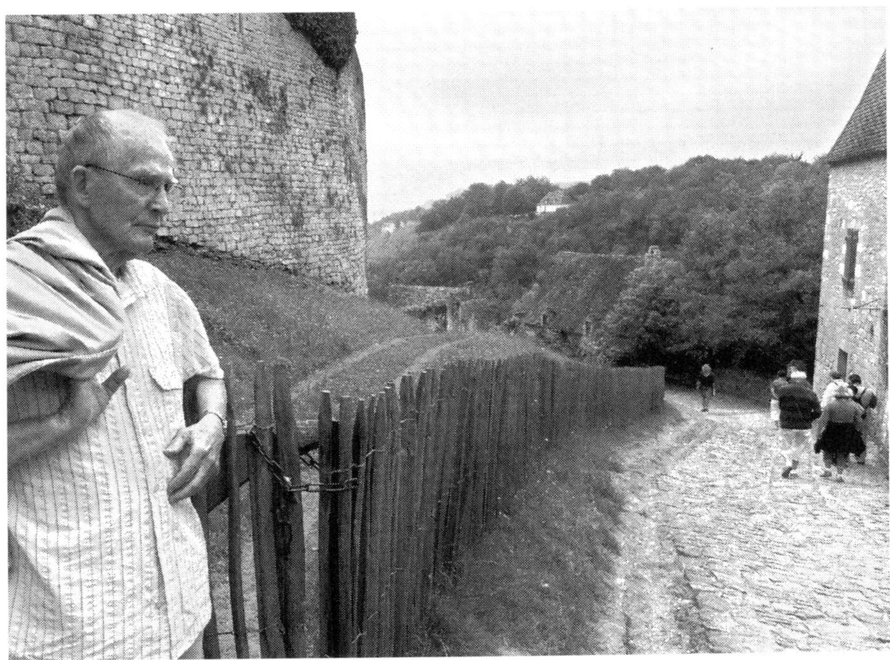

Road from Beynac Castle down through village

mainly through intrigue and shady doings. Richard the Lion Heart claimed the castle briefly during the holy wars, dying shortly thereafter in the vicinity.

Beynac Castle is an intricate maze of angled spaces and courtyards on many levels. Fanning out to explore at our own speed, we struggle up worn, stone steps, pulling ourselves by wrought-iron holders imbedded in the thick walls that once held torches. Some rooms open out grandly, with intricately carved chests that stand under faded standards and Gobelin tapestries. Javelins and spears are bunched or hung from the walls along with breastplates and facemasks and armored casques.

Descending to the kitchen, we find enormous cauldrons and large hooks suspended from the thirty-foot ceiling. Long tavern tables could seat a small battalion. Periodically we pop out from a stairway to a lookout with stout wooden pickets or a soaring wall. Turrets and peaked roofs abound in every direction. We get glimpses of canoeists—like our group two days before—dotting the river that cuts through the pastiche of agricultural fields.

Carcassonne, Cathars, and the Holy Wars

Our week in the Dordogne is over, and it's time to roll on to Spain. Our caravan heads east, winding through the gentle landscape and little, one-street stone villages. As we crest the taller hills, we're rewarded with sweeping views. Poppies and broom—scarlet and gold—adorn the roadsides. Acre upon acre, grapes and other fruit trees stretch in neat rows. The hazy foothills of the Pyrenees loom, along with vast stretches of sunflowers and then entire fields of purple lavender.

Still in France, we remember our history books and decide to stop in Carcassonne, the famed ancient walled city. Remnants of Neolithic settlements from 3500 BCE have been found here. Celts occupied the area in the sixth century BCE. Then a Roman colony was established. The city of Carcassonne was founded and officially recognized by the Visigoths in the fifth century. It was briefly conquered by Saracens when they swept across Gaul in 725, then fell into the hands of a succession of ruling counts.

At this time, Catharism was well accepted, and Catholics and Cathars lived together peacefully. Catharism was a Christian religious movement with dualistic and Gnostic elements that began appearing in the Languedoc region of France and other parts of Europe in the eleventh century, flourishing through the thirteenth. Cathars followed the Jesus of the apostles, rejected the Pope as corrupt, and declared that confession to priests was pointless. They attacked the Eucharist, saying it did not contain the body of Christ. Believing that Jesus was human, they didn't accept the Trinity concept.

In the early thirteenth century, Carcassonne was conquered by the Crusaders, and King Louis VIII of France incorporated it into the royal domain. At that point, the Pope went after the Cathars, who were persecuted and massacred. Finally they were attacked and wiped out by the Inquisition.

Now associated particularly with the Middle Ages, this period was mainly about heresy, holy war, conquest, and resisting invaders. Imposing Gallo-Roman walls still surround Carcassonne.

We park and hike up through the gates into the massive, soaring wall, complete with built-in turrets, a drawbridge and even a church. Cramped streets are flooded with tourists and kitschy shops filled with swords, shields, armor, and T-shirts with heraldic emblems. Katie and Nicky satisfy one of the itches caused by spending money in their pockets; both buy impressive daggers. The impression

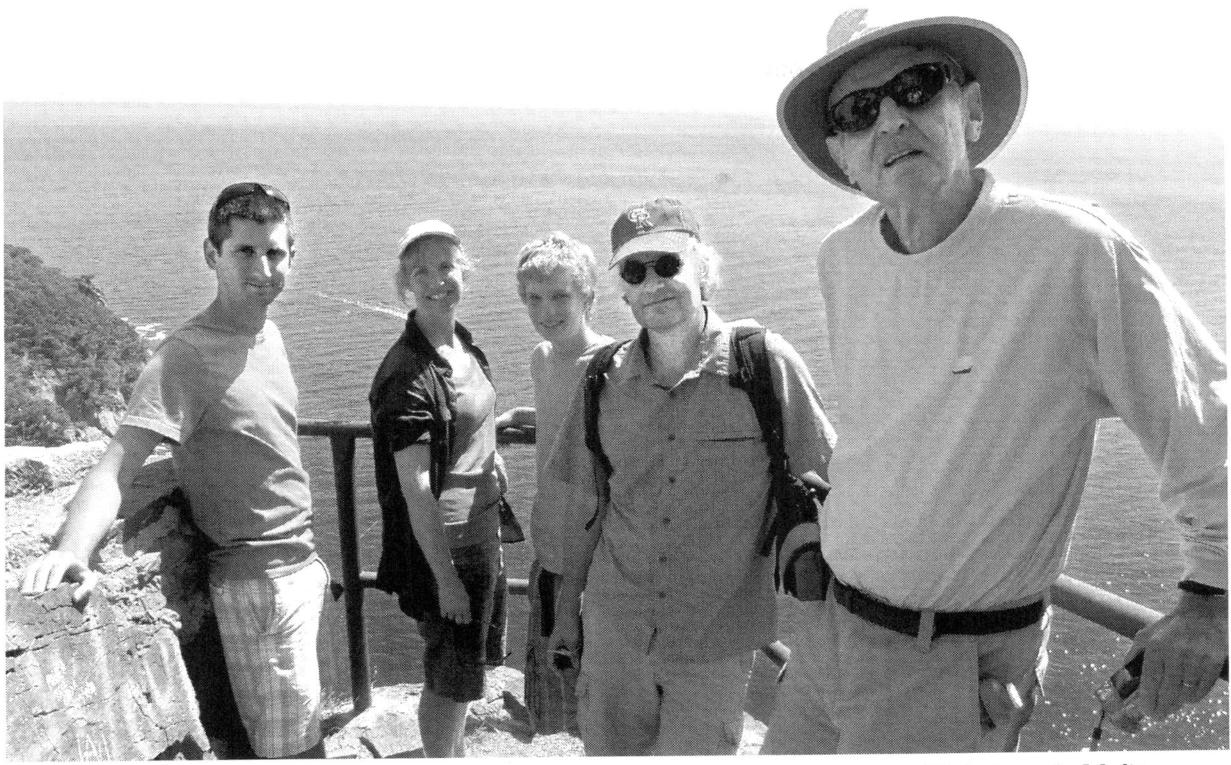
High above the Mediterranean

here is of sharp angles, massive proportions, much iron and stone. Originally the buildings were Roman and Romanesque, then medieval. We pass through the inner and outer walls, built for defense, and hike to the top to a fine lookout promenade. A peek into the cathedral, and by mid-afternoon, we're back on the road.

SPAIN

We're barely aware when we cross the border from France to Spain—such is the ease of being in the European Union; it's like moving from one state to another in the United States.

Acclimating to Our New Home

The vegetation turns drier, with desert-like scrub and sandy soil. Then, coming through pine forests, we begin to get glimpses of the Mediterranean Sea. Arriving at our town of Begur, the torturous, precipitous roads start to resemble the Riviera. Anne pores over instructions from the rental agency trying to find our street in an almost impossible maze. Miraculously she gets us there, but we must park the cars on the sidewalk to allow other traffic to pass.

Our house is built into a plunging hill. Climbing down steps to the front door, we fumble to find the keys, supposedly "under the second geranium pot." Bingo—but it takes a while to find the right key with a complex locking system. At this point, it's hard to assess our touted "view," since the area is totally enveloped in fog. After assigning rooms, suddenly the fog lifts and we can see the entire, stepped-down hillside that we're perched on, with an inviting wedge of sea a mile below.

Starved and exhausted, we need to brave the downtown to hunt food. Quickly our cars are trapped in barely passable streets. I find the traffic jams and impenetrable walls of pedestrians hard to take, but Katie is in heaven with the bustle, chic mobs, and dress shops. "My favorite city!" she crows, joining the seas of people surging up and down and grabbing little tables for aperitifs. At 9:30, the night is still young for Spain.

The Costa Brava

Our bedroom windows swing open wide in the night to let in the ocean air—cool, damp, salty. Morning light reveals the full sweep of the hillside. Our little beach, Sa Riera, lies at the bottom of a perfect V of treetops, where the Mediterranean glistens in the rising sun.

We are fed and rested, and Katie's agenda is suddenly crowded: run to the beach to swim, stroll through the town to shop, and soak up the buzz ("culture" she calls it).

Our week is filled with almost daily expeditions to discover the numerous beaches tucked into the undulating coastline. Even more important than swimming is taking in the long views by hiking on superbly maintained stone walkways that skirt the cliffs above the water. These paths connect the many intimate coves and periodically offer steep rock steps down to the dark blue sea. At Sa Tuna beach, we're lured up a cliff and onto an enticing peninsula, a long, rough jumble of boulders. Only the hardiest of the bunch make it triumphantly to a pinnacle at the end. Doug limps back, bloodied.

Another day we drive to San Sebastia, noted for its lighthouse. We climb up and inspect some sixth century BCE Iberian ruins of the Indiget tribes. Steve, Katie, Nicky, Niko, and Doug scramble through brush down an almost perpendicular path plunging to the sea. Katie horrifies her cohorts when she climbs out on a perilous limb (in bare feet for better grip) with a drop of hundreds of feet below.

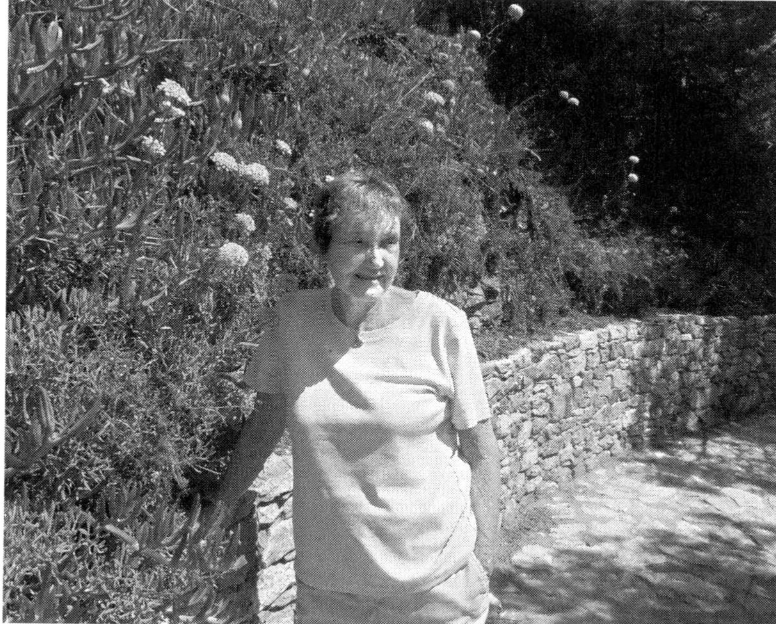

Scenic walkway above the Mediterranean on the Costa Brava

Begur and Peratallada

One evening we set out together to wander around Begur. It's another of those old towns with narrow streets and flowers spilling from window boxes and covering the sides of buildings. For me it's almost too precious, Begur strutting its most alluring aspects for the tourists. We rendezvous in the main square, and everybody plops down on the stone lip of the wall to watch the passing parade. Today there's only a modest crowd—nothing like the horrific Saturday night mob we encountered our first fraught evening—which made me want to rush back to the quiet country fields of the Dordogne!

Very fashionable women and girls promenade conspicuously. Steve notes that the shoes of the preening ladies are, in themselves, a show: vertiginous heels, in-your-face colors, straps that wind up legs. Trendy dress shops are full of gauzy shifts, fishnet tops, and the ubiquitous chiffon scarves knotted jauntily around the necks of both men and women, even though it's often insufferably warm.

The plaza, with its bell tower, reminds Bel and me of Oristano where we lived in Sardinia in the 1950s. We're very familiar with the Latin *passeggiata* when all the unmarried girls put on their finest and stroll up and down in the evening, arm-in-arm with other girls, hoping to be noticed by eligible swains. A fine Italian dinner follows—pasta puttanesca with olives, tuna, and red peppers over a black pasta (the spaghetti tossed with squid ink), and grilled scallops.

Niko has been feeling "unwell," as he puts it, almost since the beginning of the trip: achy and maybe feverish. Like Eric, who was ailing in Turkey with what turned out to be Lyme Disease, he quietly endures, but never passes up a chance to participate in the most strenuous outings. We're worried as to whether he'll be up for the challenging drive into Barcelona. Anne buzzes into town to bring back an antibiotic; no prescription required—a sympathetic pharmacist slips it under the table, so to speak

Taking a break from the beach days, we hunt down one of the loveliest of all medieval villages. Peratallada ("carved from stone" in Catalan) is a miniature walled town circled by a dry moat. Dating back to the eleventh century, artifacts have also been found here from the Bronze Age—5,000 years BCE. The cobbles we walk (and trip over) in the little streets are upended slates, tough to navigate. Walls, often just chiseled out of existing rock, are high and dripping with purple bougainvillea. It's eerily quiet. The few tourists speak almost in whispers. Everywhere we look, there's a more extraordinary scene with arches, a tower, or a little castle.

"The Conversation"

Back at our house, Anne produces a splendid eggplant-and-spaghetti dinner. Over pastries and ice cream, we linger at the table for another of our frank, in-depth family "conversations." This time it's about our personal work habits, compulsions, how we learn, how we use our leisure, whether we're disciplined or are procrastinators, whether or not we work best under the pressure of deadlines.

Bel admits, "I tend to put things off, and then get really energized when I'm under the gun." Marge and Anne say they probably fall into this camp. On the other hand, Steve says "I tend to plan, worry and anticipate, pacing my creative efforts." He must get this from me. Lucky Katie has a near-photographic memory. She says, "Why should I review for tests when I've already read the material?"

Then, who among us works best in the morning and who is sharpest at night? We find considerable variance here. When the person whose traits we're discussing doesn't volunteer information, their mate is only too ready to clarify. After all, who can be perfectly objective about oneself?

All of us reflect on our upbringing: our parents' influence and values—adopted or pushed against, sometimes according to the ethos or philosophy of the era we were born in. I seem to have been born rebellious: nearly everything my parents represented, I rejected noisily from early on. This is probably what sent me into countercultural circles and led me to revolt naturally against authority. Bel, though a rebellious hellion when he was small, snapped to awareness when his mother had a breakdown when he was fourteen and his father was away traveling on his job, and he suddenly had to take over responsibility for the family. In college, he was a leader, initiating good works on campus, while I was climbing naughtily through windows after hours.

Bel and I found it interesting that coming from such seemingly divergent character traits, we ended up pursuing philosophically alternative projects as a very compatible team. In sum, Bel tended to emulate his mother, a world-minded idealist, while I resisted the examples of my model citizen but conventional parents. It was years later before I could fully appreciate the depths of their wisdom and the strength of their values.

We looked at Eric and Steve. Eric has remained fiercely protective of his individualism, keeping a promise to himself that he would never work for anyone else (he's a highly original landscape designer and artist). He lives (sometimes precariously) in the moment, embracing with relish life as it comes, exploring the farthest reaches of reality. Steve, on the other hand, has chosen to move away from the nebulous alternative worlds that intrigue the rest of the family, and has carved a solid (but also unique) niche that depends on developing a following in the public eye (he and Anne together created one of the most prestigious public radio programs in the country, on which they explore cutting-edge thought and accomplishments).

Next we're off on revelations and observances about the convolutions of marriage—which for the comfort of all of us, I'll declare off limits here.

For our last Begur dinner, Anne outdoes herself with a frozen cake and ice cream dessert concocted out of all the sweet leftovers. We've done well at cleaning out the food supplies, always a creative challenge. Maps of Barcelona are studied. We pack for an early getaway for what will be the final day and a half of the trip.

To Barcelona, Heart of Catalonia

This is our last lap with the vehicles. Staying in close tandem, there's smooth sailing on the toll road, an easy fifty-mile sprint. It's not too congested, and we don't encounter the crazy drivers of Turkey. There are virtually no horns honking.

Niko's GPS works perfectly, getting us through tricky, one-way streets and tunnels in the city. After hearing reports that Barcelona is insanely crowded and trafficked, we're relieved to leave the cars behind. Three taxis ferry us to our Hotel Banys Orientals. It's perfectly located on Argenteria, a pedestrian-only street in the heart of the old city (this part is fifteenth century). We settle in and then flow with the crowds down our street, lined with colorful stalls of clothing, jewelry, pottery, and decorative fans (lots of these).

The group splits up to explore. Doug, Marge, Bel, and I dip into the lovely Santa Maria del Mar church, where an old gypsy lady in long skirt sprawls pitifully on the steps to accost visitors. Our destination is the Picasso museum on one of the tiny backstreets. We get lost several times in these little lanes that all look alike, with their dark buildings and archways pressing in on one another.

We know we're close to the popular museum when we bump into a long queue. Joining the line, we're entertained with some impressive Bach performed on an accordion—the musician sitting on the pavement, his case open at his side. Inaugurated in 1963, this is the only Picasso museum opened during the artist's lifetime. More than 3,500 works are housed in five conjoined former palaces. Picasso's close relationship to Málaga, his birthplace in the south, as well as to Barcelona, are depicted in fine, representational landscapes, along with striking portraits. Following his artistic journey from the early formative years, we see the influence of several earlier movements: impressionism, a bit of Lautrec. It's particularly fascinating to look at a progression of rough preliminary sketches and then see displayed the finished paintings that resulted. There is only a smattering of his cubist experiments.

We're all struck by the dynamism of Barcelona. Doug returns from a walk and notes: "Barcelona is clearly a vibrant, bustling city of actual natives, not geared artificially for tourists, but I noticed that it also seems to be a city of *love.* I kept seeing public smooching, young couples who obviously were delighting in each other. I didn't notice many 'old ones' on the streets except for the few ancient gypsies with bedraggled skirts and disheveled hair."

Anne has scouted out a promising restaurant on our street, and we all meet there. We wade past acrobats performing in the little square—somersaulting, whirling on their backs on the pavement. The small café specializes in tapas, so we decide (foolishly) to go with the "full assortment" item. Endless little dishes keep arriving: prawns, cod cakes, ham and potatoes, crispy chicken bits, strange green peppers, salmon dipped in soy, thin slices of parmesan, grilled tomatoes, and more. It's far more than anyone can manage. Oh, for doggy bags!

Steps to a swimming cove

The *Sardona* and Gaudí

Our final day. Again we split into two groups. While Steve's family and Niko see the Picasso museum and then take the metro to Antoni Gaudí's whimsical Park Güell (see more about Gaudí's work below). This park showcases Gaudí's unique architecture with a couple of houses and scatterings of structures that mimic natural forms with bizarre shapes and twists in vibrant colors. Doug, Marge, Bel, and I head for the main cathedral. We're surprised to find hundreds of people jamming the big square in front. A band is set up on the cathedral steps, and people are spontaneously jumping up to join hands and form large circles to perform the *sardona*, the Catalan national dance.

Traditionally the *sardona* band consists of eleven players: a special flute, drum, woodwinds, and brasses. The dancers toss their bags and packs into the center of each circle to move unencumbered. Probably most are local folks, but there may also be tour groups that have practiced the steps. Everybody seems concentrating well (and exuberantly) on the complex step-step-cross and skips and jumps. I count four or five circles of up to twenty folks in each.

Then we board a tour bus to get an overall sense of Barcelona—the port, World Trade Center, miles of sandy beach, the Olympic Village, daring "modernist" architecture everywhere. Upscale shops on tree-lined streets remind us of New York's Fifth Avenue. We hop off at the Sagrada Familia. This is Gaudí's art nouveau masterpiece ("Basilica and Expiatory Church of the Holy Family"). It was only a quarter finished by the time of his death in 1926; work is ongoing. We slowly approach the absolutely unique structure through a leafy park, getting a good look at the Passion Façade facing front. With sculptured stations of the cross, the entire building is incredibly complex and loaded with symbolism. Eight of the twelve slim spires are completed to date, representing the twelve apostles. It's a wild fantasy: gingerbread turrets and balconies jutting out everywhere, with tourists hanging out of them.

Strolling back to our hotel after our last dinner, and with toasts of appreciation to everybody, we stop to listen to a superb violinist in the next *placa*, and to buy our last ice creams. Farewell hugs all around, since our two groups are catching flights at different times in the morning.

Reflections

As we soared up and swiftly left Barcelona behind, I looked down on squares with neat rows of black dots on brown soil—like a pegboard. These were olive trees, the heart and lifeblood of Spain. The oil is often sent to Italy under Italian labels. We are hoping the country makes it through its financial crisis. Judging from the lively crowds and commerce we saw in Barcelona, it was looking quite viable, but the little slice of the country we saw may not be a particularly accurate gauge. With the majority of young people (men, especially) still forced to live at home into their thirties because of the dire job and housing shortage, the general economy is obviously in trouble. Currently this northeast corner of Spain—Catalonia, with its own distinct language and proud historical tradition—is agitating to break off to become an independent nation.

Why is this chapter's subtitle "Cultures in Stone"? I think it became apparent that in both France and Spain, it was indeed in the medium of stone that these civilizations were defined. It was the stonemasons and artists who left the imprint we see now: their stout walls, elegant solid buildings, and streets of cobble, haunting images scratched in caves. It is the work in stone that has endured. It has been the stuff of life and what has remained truly beautiful through the ages.

In Sum

The three parts of this book describe three distinct yet connected ways of seeing and experiencing the world. They also describe the evolving interests and prerogatives of the two people at the center of the saga—Bel and me.

In the beginning, both of us—who *had* to meet, I like to think—were quite separately compelled by the urgent sense of immense world need. We had each come out of college shortly after the end of a devastating world war and were exposed to preliminary glimpses of the destruction still evident in Europe: Bel while biking adventurously across several countries and then rubbing shoulders with delegates from many nations (some of whom—Germans and Americans—had fought each other in the war), together building an international youth center; and I, after shepherding college-age students to France for an immersion cultural experience by living with families who were struggling in the aftermath of the hostilities.

Bel landed in one of the most hellishly wasted parts of Naples, which had been bombed almost to oblivion by both the Germans and the Americans. He proceeded to create an oasis of help and hope for families there, Casa Mia.

I didn't know what was in store when I ran out of money after backpacking around Europe for several weeks. It was in the fall of 1952 that I happened to end up in Italy. I knew only that I wanted to hook up with one of the many assistance programs that had sprung up to begin to heal the region. Prince Engalicev at the World Council of Churches in Rome pointed me to Bel's project in Naples, and from then on, we were a team. That was over sixty years ago.

After working with homeless Neapolitans and then homeless Eastern European refugees, and Bel's stint with the United Nations High Commissioner for Refugees in Rome, in 1961, we came back to the United States. From our new base in Wisconsin, Bel plunged into addressing issues of poverty, race, sustainability, and cultural consciousness, first in our own backyard and then in countries in Latin America and Asia. I participated as a supporter, and always as an observer and recorder of our experiences.

At a certain point, first I, and then Bel, began to see that while physical conditions in the world continued to be critical—the challenges of survival and recovery—there were even more fundamental issues at stake, more subtle conundrums to explore. There was the vast, somewhat slippery subject of consciousness. The whole business of attitudes, beliefs, feelings, and values—of the intrinsic sacredness of everything and an awareness not only in humans but perhaps in all life—all of this was begging to be addressed. We would need to figure out how all of us living beings are connected and interdependent. This exploration began with my trip to Findhorn in 1976 and has colored all of our thinking and work since then. These were the "inner" trips described in Part II.

Finally, as we came into the latter phases of our lives, Bel and I recognized the need to step back periodically from the fast pace of *doing*, of initiating still more projects. We no longer felt driven. We still felt a strong hankering to travel, but now we saw the importance of going places to absorb a broader ethos, to observe, savor, and allow ourselves the luxury of immersion in many cultures for short periods of time. There was the double rationale of traveling out of sheer curiosity and also of wanting to have fun along the way. Including the growing family has made each such expedition that much richer. We explore together and we learn from each other as well as from each destination.

Thus all three modes of travel reflect how Bel and I—without a lot of effort or forethought on our part—have been moved from one life stage to the next. We haven't stopped yet.

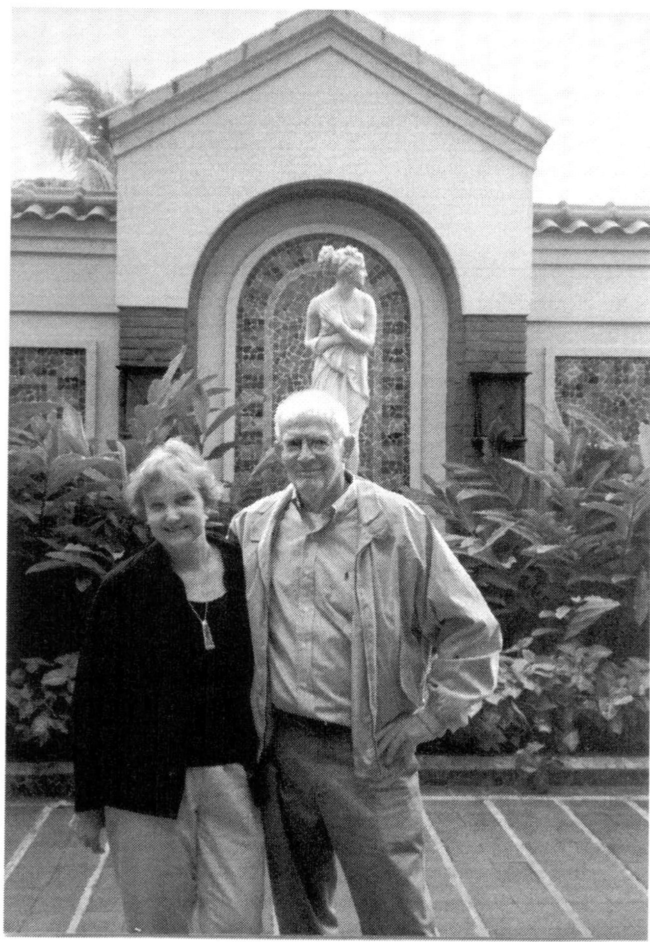

Cuba: Courtyard of Catalina Lasa Mansion

Appendix

Pronunciation of Scottish Words

Ceilidh: *kay*-lee

Erraid: *Air*-ed

Fionnphort: *Fin*-uh-fort

Glasgow: *glahz*-go

Lochaline: Lawch-*ah*-lin (gutteral ch)

Machair: *Mah*-ch-air (gutteral ch)

Moray Firth: *Murr*-ee Ferth

Stac Pollaidh: Stak *Pah*-lee (like Polly)

Glossary of Portuguese Words

cachaca: Brazilian rum

cruzeiro: Brazilian money unit

doce de leite: sweet spread made with sugar cane and milk

favela: slum or shantytown where the poor live

fazenda: large plantation, usually for cattle or coffee

festa: feast or festive celebration

jangada: fishing raft of logs lashed together (up to twenty-five feet long and seven feet wide), with a single mast; fishermen on the coast of Northeast Brazil go into the open ocean on these for a week at a time

Jornal do Brasil: the leading, prestigious, daily newspaper of Brazil, equivalent to *The New York Times,* published in Rio de Janeiro

luarada: full moon celebration

Macumba: version of voodoo rituals and dance practiced in Northeast Brazil, a mix of the Catholicism of Brazil's Portuguese settlers and worship of the deities of the African slaves they imported; the multiple African deities are often given the names of Catholic saints

mesa branca: the white table around which Spiritist mediums sit to transmit channeled messages

namorado: lover, sweetheart

reitor: university head or director

rua: street

Rural: Brazilian jeep-like truck; *Rurais* (plural)

seca: drought; every eight to ten years, Northeast Brazil experiences a seca when it doesn't rain at all, a dreaded natural occurrence when crops cannot be planted

sertão: back country, wilderness in the remote interior of Brazil

vaquero: Brazilian cowboy, herdsman

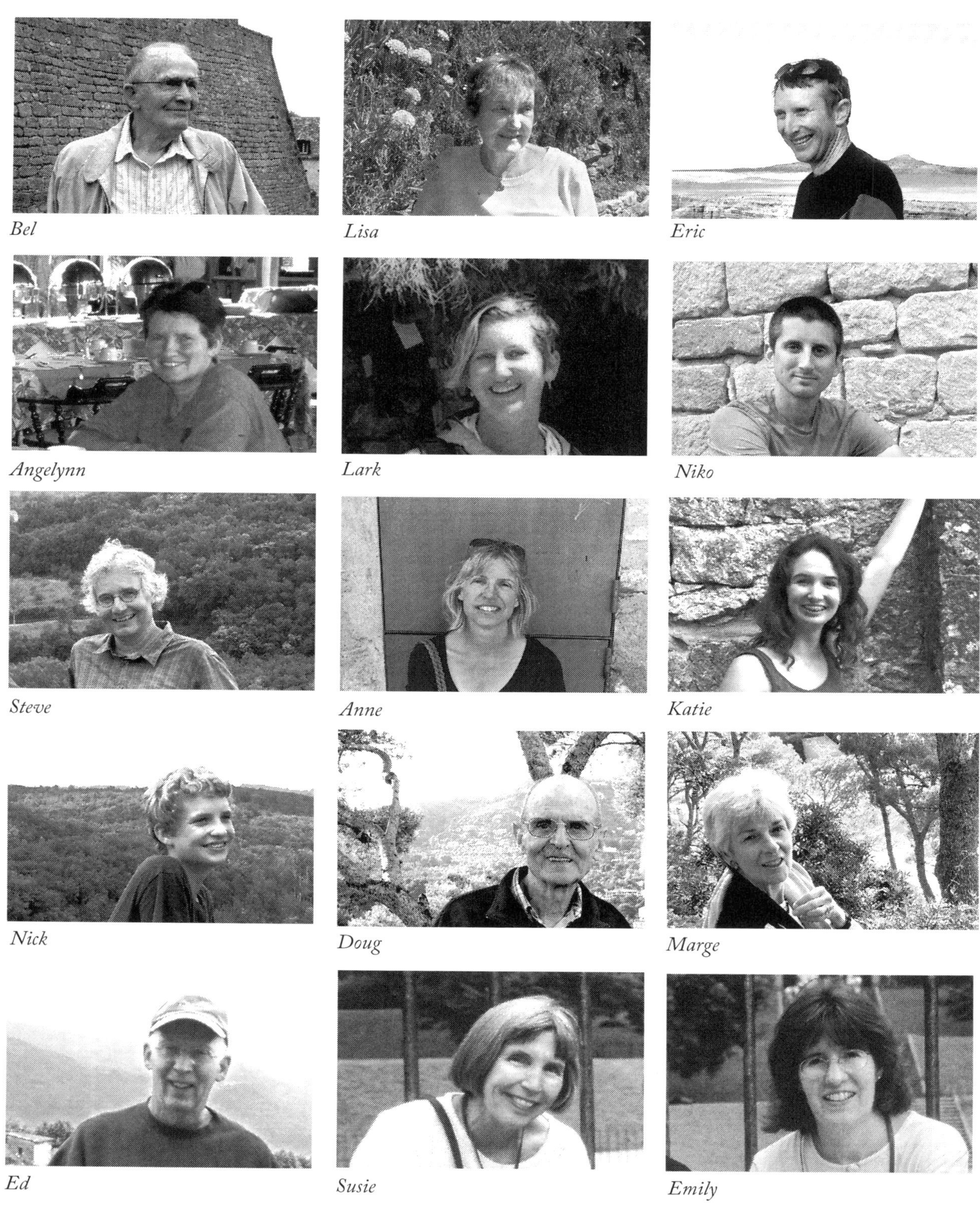

Bel *Lisa* *Eric*

Angelynn *Lark* *Niko*

Steve *Anne* *Katie*

Nick *Doug* *Marge*

Ed *Susie* *Emily*

THE TRAVELERS

Bel Paulson: Paterfamilias, "big picture," out-of-the-box thinker, ultimate risk-taker, able to coalesce enthusiasts to help tackle his far-out initiatives; professor emeritus

Lisa Paulson: Bel's partner in crime, compulsive observer and recorder of happenings in nature, on the road, in life—with pen, camera, and paintbrush

Eric Paulson: Number One son—philosopher, friend to all, artist, landscape designer, avid traveler and mountaineer

Angelynn Brown: Eric's wife—wise woman and artist who brings creative excellence and beauty to all she touches; indefatigable explorer of transpersonal mysteries

Lark Paulson: Eric and Angelynn's daughter—intrepid world traveler, yoga teacher; currently manages Wisconsin initiative to network local businesses around green, "slow" practices

Niko Paulson: Lark's younger brother—after years of bringing unusual philosophies about social systems to campuses and D.C. congressmen, now pursuing graduate degrees in economics

Steve Paulson: Number Two son—investigator of a spectrum of cultural thought and research (e.g. science and consciousness); co-founder/executive producer of trenchant NPR radio show

Anne Strainchamps: Steve's wife—co-founder of their prestigious radio show, plus hosting her own show focused on the arts. Balances both jobs and household with creative aplomb, and has organized most of the details for our recent trips.

Katie Paulson: Steve and Anne's daughter—finishing high school with an astonishing, eclectic academic record; has been a lifelong creative writer, badly bitten by the world travel bug

Nick Paulson: Katie's younger brother—high schooler with a strong math/science bent; serious photographer, fisherman/outdoor enthusiast

Doug Hill: Lisa's younger brother—former journalist and then gerontologist; poet, kayaker, and cross-country skier; known for his quirky sense of humor

Marge Bradley: Doug's wife—retired teacher; shares Doug's love of nature and travel, enjoys tennis, volunteering, and taking adult classes

Ed Strainchamps: Anne's father—musicologist, pursuer of culture and beauty; he and Susie are close friends and neighbors of Bel and Lisa in Vermont; they also lived in Italy, in the 1970s

Susie Strainchamps: Anne's mother—legendary cook and gardener; parlayed preschool teaching into being the exemplary grandmother; her acuity was key in planning some of our trip itineraries

Emily Strainchamps: Anne's younger sister—former social worker, political activist, now librarian in the Boston area, with young twins

ABOUT THE AUTHOR

Writer and artist Lisa Paulson grew up along the East Coast of the United States. In 1952, with backpack and idealism, she landed in South Italy, where she was to live off and on for the next nine years. In Naples, Lisa met and worked with Belden Paulson, who had created a unique social assistance center for homeless Neapolitans displaced by World War II. The couple married in 1954.

In 1957, Lisa, Bel, and their eleven-month-old son Eric returned to Italy to spearhead a project to resettle Iron Curtain refugees on the island of Sardinia. They remained in Sardinia for two years and then moved to Rome, where Bel worked with the United Nations to implement a plan to resettle the remaining refugees in Italian camps. While in Rome, their son Steve was born. The family moved to Wisconsin in 1962.

Between 1976 and 1998, Lisa made a number of extended visits to the Findhorn Foundation in northeast Scotland, the renowned community modeling more sustainable ways of living. These visits had a profound impact on Lisa and on the creation of High Wind, an intentional community she and Bel founded in the early 1980s. High Wind, a small, rural enclave abutting the Northern Kettle Moraine State Forest in Wisconsin, focused on matters of ecology, education, and spirit.

Over a lifetime together—both through traveling extensively and living abroad—Lisa and Bel have been drawn to places and experiences that reflect challenging cultural dilemmas. In more recent years, they have also sought out adventures with their children, grandchildren, and extended family that have taken them to some of the unusual spots around the world.

Currently Lisa and Bel divide their time between their solar home at High Wind in Wisconsin and the countryside of Vermont.

Lisa's previous books: *Voices From a Sacred Land: Images and Evocations* and *An Unconventional Journey: The Story of High Wind, From Vision to Community to Eco-Neighborhood.*

Made in the USA
Charleston, SC
31 January 2014